SUFFER QUIETLY

But I'm dying to be heard
A Memoir by
Sari Knock

Print book ISBN: 97817777653-0-9
Ebook ISBN: 97817777653-1-6

WHAT ARE YOU WAITING FOR

To my husband, Tracy, the love of my life.

Contents

Foreword

How often do we suffer alone in silence? How often do we put on our "I'm fine" facade when someone asks us how we are, even though our hearts are breaking? I can't tell you how many times I've held it together when I felt like I was falling apart, or witnessed someone I love put on that brave face even though I knew they were suffering. If this sounds familiar, or if you know someone who is working through circumstances in their lives that no one should have to go through alone, I am so glad you have picked up Sari's book.

I recently learned that sometimes, even the slightest negative comment we received as a child can become a deep rooted source of trauma that affects how we interact with the world. I carried some of those negative words with me, in the form of unconscious beliefs, my whole life. They took a huge toll on my self-esteem as a young teen. The bullying, feeling like I didn't fit in, and feeling that I was not loved, led to me wish I was not here on this planet, and at 13 years old, I contemplated suicide.

I was blessed to have two amazing parents who did their very best to provide a loving home for our family. There were moments of conflict, and some discussion, but most of the time, we overcame these issues by burying them and leaving them in the past. However, these issues were never really left behind, and that meant we had to carry these burdens alone and suffer in silence.

Many of my clients who have published their stories about overcoming adversity have also experienced this burial-method of getting over trauma, particularly when dealing with issues that affected mental health. But each of them knew that their unique life-experience, once unearthed, could become a source of strength to help others work through their own experiences. Each time one of my clients shared their story with me, it helped me see my own journey in a different light, and that brought about healing. One thing I know for sure is that sharing stories helps others know they are not alone, and provides hope and faith that there is life on the other side of trauma. These stories tend to have a positive impact on mental health, and we may never know how far reaching the ripple effect may be.

When Sari was referred to me and shared her story, I was in awe of her perseverance and resiliency. She submitted her raw and real manuscript and I was hooked immediately because she shares from her heart with wisdom and vulnerability. Through her story, I came to realize that suffering in silence, or feeling alone through trauma, big or small, has an impact on our wellness and mental health. It affects our relationship with self, with others, and the world.

Her journal entries captured a lifetime of pain, celebration, and the emotions of day to day life. Her unique way of capturing her growth, her perspective, and the evolution of herself in those entries was astonishing. Her book had a profound influence on me, and I found myself wanting to capture all of the moments in my life going forward so I can reflect on the patterns, the experiences, and the power of writing in a journal. I love this quote from Sari as it describes the desire to capture every moment:

> *"When your life is over, you take all your experiences with you unless you write them down" – Sari Knock*

As a publisher and a podcaster, I have heard many stories of overcoming obstacles. I have watched authors' lives transform as they publish their books and share them with the world. It takes bravery and courage to share your story. It also takes bravery and courage to do the work that comes with overcoming trauma. But in doing so, we can move to happier, freer, more authentic spaces in our lives. Sari transformed her life by realizing she could overcome her trauma and now she is using these experiences to serve others. Fourteen years in the making, her book reveals how we can move through adversity with love, boundaries, support and awareness. What a legacy she has left with us all.

We are very fortunate to live in a time where there is more acceptance, awareness and support to help individuals move through trauma. With various foundations and mental health associations, many of which weren't available for adults and youth only a few years ago, we are providing safe, judgement-free places to discuss trauma and its effects – hopefully, with more favorable outcomes for releasing the internal and mental anguish trauma causes.

Through Sari Knock's personal journey of childhood trauma, illness, love, and triumph, this book offers community, awareness and hope. I am very proud of Sari for having the courage to bring her story to the world and I am honored to have the privilege of publishing this book with her.

Heather Andrews
Get You Visible, Owner
10 x best selling author, Speaker, Story Coach
https://geyouvisible.com

The Expert's Opinion

Trauma. What is it?

Trauma is an emotional response to a terrible event like an accident, rape, or natural disaster. Immediately after the event, shock and denial are typical. Longer term reactions can include unpredictable emotions, flashbacks, strained relationships, and even physical symptoms like headaches or nausea.

As a psychologist, I have never fully understood why post-traumatic symptoms get classified as a mental health diagnosis. If the normal human being's response to trauma is anxiety, depression, avoidance, hyperarousal, insomnia, etc., why is the traumatic response considered a mental disorder or illness? Annoying? Interfering? Debilitating? Horrifying? Anxiety-provoking? Agitating? Limiting? Yes. But a disorder? A mental illness? It's an interesting thought exercise.

Nevertheless, the more I understand the brain and the neuroscience of what it means to be human, the more I appreciate the brain's attempt to protect us. The brain's job is to 1) gather data; 2) make meaning of it; and 3) use that data to predict the future and, in this context, help us avoid future trauma or risk. If someone is mobbed on a dark street at night, for example, the smartest thing their brain can do is tell them to never again go out at night, do not leave their house, and just stay home. Makes perfect sense. This conclusion and coping mechanism, however, has consequences and may significantly interfere with their ability to live a normal life, and a life with meaning, purpose, and joy. But it makes perfect sense. Brains do what brains do. In a sense, a brain's job is much like that of a police officer–to protect and serve.

Here's what we know about the trauma response. Shame, denial, anxiety, and depression all feed off of secrets, isolation, avoidance, self-harm, and guilt. All of those feed it, make it bigger, more robust, and keep it around longer. It's not the victim's fault that their brain wants to revert to coping skills that, on the surface, would appear to be helpful in preventing future trauma.

When people like Sari choose to give a voice to their trauma and their reactions to that trauma, it functions to decrease and often eliminate the trauma symptoms. Much like a water hose putting out a raging fire, *truth-telling* extinguishes the power of the trauma symptoms and true healing begins. Secrets cannot hide in the light. Secrets hate being spoken about. Secrets suffocate when shared because their oxygen supply of shame, guilt, anxiety, self-harm, and self-sabotage are cut off.

Books like the one you are about to read have the same effect. It is why they are so profoundly needed and helpful. Thank you, Sari, for bravely choosing to be a truth-teller. Your willingness to share will allow so many to look at themselves and their stories and say, "Oh how human of me." And your example of how you have moved through and beyond trauma will surely help others do the same.

Now, collectively, let's all give our brains some credit, thanks, and praise. Repeat after me: "Thank you brain for trying to protect me. Thank you brain for keeping me safe. However, I have a full life to live. I am learning how to be my own truth-teller. Because what I know for sure is--the truth will set me free."

Dr. Erin Oksol
Psychologist and Award-Winning Life Coach, 5X Best-Selling Author, Speaker

PREFACE

I began journaling when I was 13 years old; this memoir spans the next 40 years of my life, using my actual journal entries, presented in chronological order, and interspersed with a few mini-essays, such as "Shy" and "Our Family Home." Although some of these entries have been lightly edited for concision, they are MY experiences, in MY words, and often written right *in* the moment, raw and revealing. For many years, all I had was my journal to "open up to." It was my safe outlet to vent about deep secrets and heavy feelings, without the fear of being stifled, silenced, or judged. Journaling was a way of getting the swirling, twirling tornado of thoughts OUT OF MY HEAD. Writing down or keying in everything gave me the sanity that analyzing things to death in my head didn't. By expelling my thoughts onto a piece of paper or cardboard, even a napkin or into an iPhone, it allowed me to clear my head and calm the ol' noggin. It is a practice that has taken my life from chaos to clarity, in the stroke of a pen or keyboard. My thoughts are the buildup of pressure and my writing is its release.

Suffer quietly was an expression my grandmother often used fondly when anybody whined or complained; in *jest* she'd declare, *Oh, suffer quietly!* The *reality* of those words rang true for me my whole life. It IS the way I *have* lived it.

I am a *fiercely PRIVATE* person, so it might seem out of character to those who know me that I *am coming forward* with my story. This memoir took me 14 years to write; I did not impulsively jump into this undertaking without tirelessly dissecting *every* angle. I'm not a carefree or free-spirited person. *Everything* is meticulously thought out and carefully considered. The daunting task of telling my story kept coming up until one day I sat down and wrote for six months, and then I shelved it. Years later, I'd tinker with it and then shelve it yet again. A near-catastrophic experience in 2020, gave me the FINAL push I needed to complete it! I didn't *anticipate* it would take so long, but in hindsight, this is the *right* time in my life to release it. It needs to be set free, just like me.

Outwardly, in my everyday life, I'm a functioning, unassuming person with a job and responsibilities. By sharing my thoughts, it may reveal a neurotic person with a cynical and sarcastic attitude. Most people guard their private thoughts; I've just given people access to how a quiet person's mind can work. People have no clue who they are passing on the street, or work with, or live with...the person they think they have pegged is really someone they don't know at all. I deduced a long time ago that people really *don't* know me. They judge my exterior and they sense they have me figured out. I'm perceived in a *certain* way by others – snobby and unfriendly because I'm shy and quiet. I've never actually been able to fully be myself around people – I'm always guarded. Even the few who know me better have never seen ALL of me. I don't believe everyone shows 100% of themselves. It's not about keeping the "mystery" going either; perhaps inherently we *don't* want to reveal the vulnerable parts of ourselves. I'm showing people there IS more to me than what my *outward appearance* indicates. People make assumptions, but they have no idea what is *beneath* the surface. Looks ARE deceiving. They only see the superficial "cover," not the real substance *inside*. I've *never* cared what others thought of me. I'm not doing this to clarify their perceptions of me. People ultimately think what they want to and draw their own conclusions. My intention is to express the silent part of me that yearns to be heard REGARDLESSS of what people think. I'm simply giving my stifled existence a voice.

My intention for writing this memoir is to share my battles in the hopes *someone* can connect and resonate with them, and not feel so alone. To know it's *okay* to speak about horrible traumas and taboo subjects, and not stay silent. I led a life of no one knowing the extent of the emotional torment I lived with on a daily basis; I lived a quiet life of desperation. No one is exempt from what life launches at them. It doesn't come at us with perfect answers and instant solutions; it's usually messy and leaves you with *more* unanswered questions. Whenever *I* was thrown a curve ball, my instinct was to seek out *someone* I could identify with, so I wouldn't feel so isolated and lost. I was searching for a lifeline. It gave me comfort knowing I could relate to someone going through similar struggles. Sharing a private trauma *can* help others. It's helpful to let people in on your experiences. We ALL go through difficult times and can feel like we are alone, so my goal is to provide a lifeline to others.

I have purposely omitted a dozen or so friendships/relationships from the memoir because they weren't worth the keystrokes. They exist solely as a reminder of how my husband and I were taken advantage of and what type of people we DON'T want in our lives. While I do believe there *is* something to learn from *every* connection, some *are* a waste of time, effort, and energy and serve no purpose (except for my explanation here). Some people simply come into your life, wreak havoc, and leave. People we love *and* find objectionable *both* make their mark on our life. Having said that, I have *still* included some unfavorable relationships because life *is* both good *and* bad and *they are* pertinent in *my* journey. I *have* changed *some* names and places, to protect ME, *not* them. If those people wanted a glowing rendition written about them, they should have acted *better*. To those with *nothing* to hide – their names remain unchanged, with their consent.

Everyone's experiences can change who they are, but it's what we *do* with those experiences that determines a positive or negative outcome. We choose a path in the hopes of gaining some insight from it – either you grow or you get left behind. If we do *nothing* with the experience, then we remain *stuck*. Is it moving us forward, can we reflect on it with distance and detachment, or are we bombarded with the same amount of pain and trauma as the day it happened? Our lives are a continuous string of tests, with every breath we take, with every choice we make, and every obstacle we face. Are we making the *same* mistakes, unable to break old patterns? Are we capable of being more self-aware, and move into a healthier, more productive place? Well, in my 50-plus years, I have learned…not so much. As "enlightened" as I imagined I was becoming as I've gotten older, I also realized old patterns were still present. *Awareness of* and actually *changing* our behaviour are two dif-ferent things. Sure, I *aspire* to change the negative and be more positive, but ya know...it's easier said than done. We can *allow* our life experiences to immobilize us, to shape us into an inaccessible and unapproachable person, a walking/talking shell that's incapable of coping or being around others, OR they can shape us into pillars of strength and courage, beacons of light, allowing our truest selves to emerge from the cracks. Let your resilience shine through and make those cracks craters! A bad childhood doesn't define you. Every experience is an opportunity to learn *something*, to grow from, to heal a part of yourself. If we don't accept the learning, we remain trapped and debilitated. There is *no* healing in being a victim, nor is healing a *straight path*. It is an accumulation of bent and broken paths and trails leading us to one less bumpy road. Isn't the point then, to use our experiences in life to *better* ourselves? Life *is* a serious thing, until you have too many close calls and your perspective shifts and you suddenly think, Hey, wait a minute, I could drop dead tomorrow, maybe I need to do things *differently*, lighten up a little. Life gets *icky*, so acknowledge that life happens and move the heck on! No one ever said it would be easy; cry if you need to, yell, *but fight back*!

HAVE A VOICE!

Aren't we all striving for unconditional love and acceptance, a sense of belonging, of being appreciated and VALUED? I have spent my existence searching for those basic elements.
My ability to "be happy" has been clouded by all the tests I've endured. I'm a worrier and a perfectionist – well, I'm a Virgo – and often drown in my introspection, overthinking and "worst case scenarios," but my lifelong pursuit of "happiness," inner peace and contentment eludes me. I'm just *not* a happy person. I desire to change that.

My wish is for people to think of times in their lives when they faced seemingly insurmountable challenges and then came out the other side! I have been through experiences most people wouldn't survive, and yet here *I* am. So, deal with your shit, own it, and be proud of overcoming it, and *believe* in yourself! I believe my true self is *still* screaming to get out. The steps I've taken to *free* her is to no longer protect those individuals who have stifled me, and to find that muted voice within me – AND LET HER OUT! I'm done hiding the ugly parts of myself to spare others. I am who I am. I hope that together we can find our respective voices. It's never too late to show the world who we *really* are.

1981

<u>March</u>

*I'm 13. My friend Rikki slept over, as she often did. On this specific night, a recurring event in my life that I kept as a well-guarded secret came to light because of her. It would also be the last time **it** ever happened. I could never have predicted when I woke up **today** that my life would change **forever**.*

My older brother Kyle, 15, snuck into my bedroom this fateful night and tried to touch Rikki inappropriately. She flipped out!! Kyle ran out of the room and Rikki confronted *me*.

"Has he EVER done that to YOU?"
Being asked point-blank, I said, "Yes, *once or twice*."
"YOU HAVE TO TELL YOUR PARENTS!"
"Ya?"
"Yes, you should!"

I knew Rikki was *not* going to let this go. I went into my parents' room and told Mom: For a long time, starting when I was 10, up until tonight, Kyle has been coming into my room between 2:00 and 3:00 a.m., trying to touch *me*. He did it twice to Rikki tonight, and she woke up and told me. Other nights, if I woke up while he was standing there, he would make up some excuse, like, "I'm just borrowing or returning your comic book", or he was "just checking up on me" or, "Evan [Kyle's best friend whom I had a crush on] says he likes you - I just thought you'd want to know." I told Mom I wanted HER to talk to Kyle, not me. She said she would, and she wondered why I didn't tell her sooner.

I was scared of what you might say.
You can always trust me.

She went down to his room to talk to him. I deflected the severity of the situation so no more questions would be asked. I downplayed it, minimized it, and knew my parents would be satisfied with us "dealing" with him trying to "touch" Rikki and me. But they would never know the truth. They could never know what *really* happened. Never.

For Rikki to feel better and find a way to channel her anger toward Kyle, she suggested we start journaling. We wrote down all the things we wanted to say to his face so he would never try ANYTHING again. I had already lived with all this for so many years; I would do anything to make everyone else happy and "resolve" this incident *quickly*. We talked about what we should do, what we could say so he won't try this inappropriate behavior again.

Rikki began writing: "Threaten him, real bad. Make him feel really ashamed of himself." Then I wrote, "If he comes in one night, I will say, 'Rikki saw your shadow and she felt your hand on her stomach. I also recall you coming in at nights and asking me for things. Kyle, if you come back in here one more night, I am going to tell Mom and Dad and have them punish you severely. You are my *brother*. This just might be your last chance. Why can't you be like any other boy who is a brother? You are perverted and **SICK**. Rikki's brother isn't sick like you. Why can't you be more like him? Unperverted. Everything you do has something to do with sex, you "sicko"! It scares me when you come in at night because one day, I am going to mistake you for a "burglar" and try to kill you. More and more every night, I wake up with your hand on me, and I know you don't get your jollies just by putting your hand on me. There is more to it, and if you're gonna continue to do what you are doing, then you can just get the hell out of my life. We don't appreciate you coming in at night for you to so-called "checkup on us." I am your sister and you are my brother. If I catch you again, I am going to involve Mom and Dad. I think you are so perverted you need help. Don't do it to me, do it to your girlfriend, if you have one.'"

My oldest brother, Levi, 19, ignored me for five years **straight***, when I was between the ages of 8 and 13. Not one word. Those are years when a pre-teen/teenage girl is looking for guidance, peers, and older siblings to look out for them. I didn't quite fumble enough through that period of life; I didn't need* **more** *turmoil and hatred directed at me. He loved to send death looks my way, but no words. It was a game to him. He loved to make me suffer. Levi was forced to move out – after he hit me one time. If that is all it took, I wish he'd have done it sooner! That lasted about six months, and then he was allowed to move back in – on the condition he speaks to me. I thought,* The damage was already done, why bother making him talk to me now?

1982

After "coming clean," it was business as usual at home. Kyle never abused me again, but It was never mentioned again either. From that time on, we pretended to be a happy family, sharing our feelings over Sunday dinners. I dreaded having to share because they never knew how I was REALLY feeling. So, I stuffed it down and pretended. It was always easier to just pretend.

I was fired from my first job, at McDonald's, because I was too shy. Yes, that is the reason they gave me. They also told me I didn't smile enough. I guess it's difficult for me to smile when I'm hardly a joyful teenager.

SHY

I was a debilitatingly, painfully shy child. At five years old, I remember being at Nursery School in Montreal and it was snack time. Tables were separated into what *fruit* you brought. My *mistake* one day was to take my *orange*...and sit at the *apple* table. The class bully, a girl, taller and *way* bigger than me, was more than happy to point out my dreadful mistake to *everyone,* and the teacher made me move. I was so ashamed and embarrassed that I cried the rest of the day. It physically hurt me to have attention drawn to me, right from an early age. All my life, I was never anything other than an outcast, trying to fit in but never achieving that lofty goal.

On another occasion, at six years old, I was walking home from school. I was about four houses away from home when a nine-year-old boy – the neighborhood bully – yelled over to me from across the street.

"Hey, you, stop!"
So, I did, Dead in my tracks.
"Get down on the sidewalk and lie face down!"
I did.
"Now kiss the sidewalk!"
I did.

I kissed the dirty ground, then scrambled to my feet and bolted the rest of the way home. I could hear him laughing, all the way. The power he must have felt. The shame and fear I felt.

My grandparents, who lived downstairs from us, had a male border, Hymie, for many years. He would eventually become a nanny for my mother, helping her out with anything that needed doing around the house.

One day, alone with him in the kitchen, he pulled his erection out of his pants and told me, a-six-year-old, to touch it. I ran away screaming. I told my mother *right away*. He was kicked out of the house *immediately*. I was confused by what he had done, but I also *knew* it was wrong. I *knew* my parents would protect me. My grandparents were *never* told the *real* reason Hymie was asked to leave, and he and my grandmother remained friends until the day he died – 40 years later.

None of these incidents helped me come into my own, blossom, or grow into a fun, carefree child. At home, I was despised by one of my siblings and bullied out in the world – an easy target and afraid of everything. I was a wallflower and tried to blend into the scenery.

And then *the* abuse began…

OUR RELATIONSHIP

It's important to understand my relationship with my older brother Kyle – what was *portrayed* to everyone and what *actually* was.

<u>**Before**</u> the abuse, we were best friends, two years apart in age. We had most of the same friends; always hanging out, we went to the same school and just enjoyed each other's company.

<u>**During**</u> the abuse – we were STILL what *appeared* to be close. He was the most likable guy around. He was everyone's buddy; the dependable, reliable guy, the one you could call up and go to the movies with, the confidant, the *nice* guy.

Kyle and I NEVER spoke of the abuse, *ever*. He NEVER knew…that <u>**I**</u> knew. I know that sounds odd. For all those years, he believed I had *no idea* what he had done, late at night, EVERY night, often three times a night – for three years. He believed he was invincible – he could do his dirty deeds, slither back to his room unnoticed, and keep up the facade of being this swell guy. At the breakfast table, he was right as rain, like nothing ever happened. And I had to pretend and do same. But I knew differently. I DID know. I likened him to Dr. Jekyll and Mr. Hyde – I knew the REAL Kyle, while others knew what they *saw* of him, what he wanted them to see. But what you see is *not* what you get.

Since I never came forward, because I never told a soul, because I decided I needed to protect this disgraceful secret so no one would know him to be anything other than this decent person, so my parents wouldn't think they created a monster, so Levi wouldn't have a reason to gloat – I suffered.

Boy, did I suffer.
I suffered *quietly*.

Even **_after_** the abuse stopped, I played the role. Though my hate for him grew, I was my brother's closest friend – my offender, the person who murdered my soul, my spirit, my childhood, my adulthood, my relationships, my body, my body image, and my self-esteem – was, for outward appearances, my buddy. The world knew us to be inseparable. No one ever suspected, and no one was the wiser. I became a master at pretending and wearing my social mask. I was the best at keeping up appearances.

This was my life.

1983

All year I pined away for a boy at school. He told my friend Myriam he thought I was nice and pretty– but boring. I was CRUSHED.

I spent a lot of time sick at home from excruciating periods, going to doctors, and having tests done. I was finally put on the birth-control pill to help with the pain.

I graduated Grade 9, and then my family drove to California for the summer. We met my father's side of the family for the first time. I saw my first palm tree and it was my first time seeing the Pacific Ocean. And, of course, we went to Disneyland!

1984

I was 15, turning 16 when I spent three weeks in Montreal for the summer. It was a significant time for me because I had my first boyfriend, Aaron. He's my Montreal best friend Toby's cousin. It was a long-distance relationship that ended before the end of the year.

It was challenging for me to be close to him or open up. I figured that all boys want is sex. That terrified me. Men in general feel like a threat to me. Getting close to me means learning the truth about me, and that was not going to happen.

Kyle moved to Edmonton to go to university.

*Levi went to "find himself"; he traveled around Asia for two years in search of answers he couldn't find here at home. He began writing to me from every country he visited. I think it was easier for him to **write** to me rather than talk. We maintained a pen-pal relationship for those traveling years. We were trying to connect on **some** level. He was a self-proclaimed atheist, rebelled against Judaism, but eventually found himself gravitating toward Israel. His intent was to find some rabbis and ask them ludicrous questions, and throw Judaism in their faces. Instead, to his surprise, they ANSWERED his burning questions, and he found the niche he'd been searching for his entire life. Israel would become his permanent residence.*

1985

<u>May 2</u>
I'm 17. Kyle moved back home. Mom and I came up with the idea that I try hypnosis as a form of therapy, so I can be more confident and not be so shy and awkward. Today was my first session. I *did* feel more confident after and was able to go on a group outing from synagogue.

<u>Nov 18</u>
My best friend Janis moved in with us. Things aren't good at her home (obviously).

My parents sat Kyle and me down in the living room: We have something to tell you. Your father and I have decided to separate…

I heard nothing else. My mind raced, and I tried to stay as still as I could so I could just absorb the bomb that just went off. I wanted to throw up. After a while I felt a burning sensation on my right ankle. I hadn't realized I was using my thumbnail to gouge a deep gash across it. As my mind raced, I had been sitting there mutilating my leg. My mother noticed and asked me if I was okay.

No, I don't think so. I was in shock. Shocked MY parents were splitting up after almost 30 years of marriage. It made *no* sense. None.

My father moved out first, then they swapped residences: my mother moved into his apartment and he came home. I remained in the home with my father.

OUR FAMILY HOME

We epitomized a "close-knit, happy family." By all appearances, we seemed to be the picture-perfect unit. My parents counselled other couples looking for marital advice on how to repair *their* relationships; we were the standard people aspired to be like. For a time, we even ran a dating service. The four of us, not Levi (he had no interest in spending time with the family), would *dialogue* every Sunday – someone would choose a topic and we'd take 15 minutes to write down our feelings, and then share. We ate dinner every night as a family, more often than not with extra people at our meal tables. We opened our "ideal" home to others to live in so *they* could find refuge, have a safe, soft place to land, and find *protection*. It was always a busy home, with laughter, food and entertaining-- a functioning, dysfunctional place.

It was all a facade; it's how it *appeared* from the outside. The *truth* was *far* from what we portrayed; it was chaos, secrets, and disarray. This way of life was "normal" for me, second nature. We simply helped others; it's who we were, what we did, what we were best known for, and what was expected of us. No one *ever* suspected this generous, open and giving family was far from a model one. We had no business being anyone else's sanctuary.

1986

I'm 18. Dad's best friend died of a heart attack – he was 42 years old. It was my **first** *funeral – seeing the casket, and then the open grave…it knocked me for a loop. His 20-year-old daughter was so distraught, she jumped* **into** *the grave, screaming and crying. It was horrifying.*

A few days before graduation, Leslie, my buddy since Grade 7, her dad passed away from leukemia. I couldn't even begin to imagine what that was like for her.

Mom began her master's degree program in family therapy in Seattle in June. She would be going there for the following three summers.

Aug 27
Josh and I have been dating for a bit. I really like him. He's a little rough around the edges, but he makes me laugh. He's coming to my birthday party! I thought we'd get closer today, and just have a fun time. Instead, he left with another "friend", and I know they will wind up sleeping together. I'm heartbroken. Why would he do that to me? Happy 18th birthday to me.

Dec 12
My parents got back together. I *finally* understand the separation was NOT just my mother's fault. It took me a long time to realize there *are* two sides. I blamed her. *Everyone* blamed her. But I get it now, and I understand her decision to leave.

1987

Apr 4

Janis and I went to a club, Malarkey's, and there *he* was, so handsome and rugged. He had dirty blond, longish hair, and piercing blue eyes with the longest eyelashes. Funny, I don't go for blonds. But he was so darn cute! I was struck by this undeniable energy when I first saw him – BOOM! It was love at first sight. He was unlike *any* guy I had *ever* met. I never imagined <u>we</u> could be together, me being such an awkward, shy, inexperienced girl. He'd never pick a girl like *me*. I was SO out of HIS league. He asked me what my name was. I told him, I even spelt it out for him. He gave me a hard time with checking my coat, saying it costs $3. I'd been there before, they *never* charged for that, so I threw my coat on the counter and told Janis to "deal with it." I was feeling bold. I looked back at him and made another mental note of how *modelesque* he looked, and continued on with my evening. I was dancing away, the bar was packed, and *he* was standing at the DJ booth, pointing his finger at me and waving me over. It took a while for me to realize he meant ME. I made my way to the booth and he handed me this note:

"Sari:
I think you are a real sweetie and I would like to get to know you better. If you think that it's possible to do so, please leave me with your number.
Tracy
Thanks"

My reaction? I laughed at him. I'd NEVER heard of a *guy* named *Tracy* before.
I know, I get that a lot.

He bought me a rose. I was flattered and honored. There were so many girls fawning over him, and he picked ME. It was getting near to closing time and a slow song came on – "Lady in Red." He asked *me* to dance. He's a good dancer. He's SO handsome! He'd asked me to wait around for him until he closed up the bar, so we could finally talk a bit. We made plans to go out the following evening. I gave him my number. He was "older" and I liked that; me being 18, he 22. He's in his 20s, working as a bouncer/doorman; he's so hot! I really like this guy!

Apr 5

Tracy and I spoke on the phone for hours and I made him guess what my middle name was. He got it on the **_first_** try. Who guesses TANIA on their first try?! Spooky. He says he plays a lot of volleyball – played all the way through junior high and high school and throughout college. We went on our first date, along with his two best friends, Norman and Dennis, and I brought Janis. We went for ice-cream. I hate eating ice-cream in front of a boy; there's no dainty way of eating it. He gave me one of his plastic bracelets that he wore. He kissed me. Wowzer.

As excited as I am to be with Tracy, I'm anxious and nervous. My experience with "nice guys" has led me down an ugly path. It scares me beyond belief to get close to a man. I'm tainted goods. I wonder if he'll be able to *tell* what I've been through.

June 28

I received a letter from Levi today. The first sentence was: *"Please forgive me. I am sorry."* He went on tell me how long overdue this apology was, and how he deeply regrets not speaking to me all those years when I was a child.

*"I was old enough to know better. It seems so long ago but the effects are still being felt. I damaged you, and I caused such a break in such an important family bond. So much time has passed; you are already a grown woman. I have been too cruel. When I visited you, you asked me 'why?' I did not know. I **still**_*

*do not know. It was causeless hatred. There were things you did that irritated me. In hindsight, they were nothing near worth the years of separation. I made bad choices. I was punishing you for **my** problems. Despite a deep regret, it is impossible to take back, to make it not happen. I remember sometimes you had made a reconciliatory gesture, and I had ignored it. So many years lost. It is a tremendous loss. The damage to the relationship is **my** responsibility. I need you. You are my only sister and yet I terribly wronged you with malice. Let me know what I should do to make amends. Out of rage came the senseless hatred. I ask you for compassion. I don't want to be exiled from you."*

Huh. How do you react to something you've waited *years* to hear? I never imagined he'd have *ever* reflected on those terrible years. So, I sat down and wrote him back. I acknowledged the courage it took for him to write and send me that letter.

"I NEVER understood why you hadn't spoken to me all those years. We are like strangers, but I'm willing to build on it. It's hard for me to forget what happened; it affected me deeply. If it took you going to Israel to come to this realization, then I'm glad you went. It's never too late."

July 19

I spend every spare second with Tracy. I can't *not* be with him. Dad and I got into a rip-roaring fight about Tracy. I don't think I ever screamed so loud, so hard, and for so long in my life! Dad didn't like that I asked Tracy to come over after he was done work. Tracy came over and had to turn around and leave. I was so embarrassed. Dad threatened to kick me out. I agreed I *should* leave. I provoked Dad to hit me so I'd have a real GOOD reason to get out of there. He wouldn't, and didn't.

Oct 23

I hadn't heard from Tracy *all week*. He never came to the house when he said he would. Disappeared. Pretty crushing actually. I don't know what I did wrong? I've been an absolute *wreck* all week. Mom and Dad thought they were going to have to commit me. I was beside myself. I couldn't stop crying, I was hysterical, a basket case. Today I open the front door to go to work, and there's a note stuck in the door from Tracy. He wants to meet and talk. Apparently, he misses and loves me.

1988

<u>July 28</u>

Levi wrote me another letter:

"I was ashamed and sad all over again to find out how much you had been hurt by me. I will keep trying to repair the damage and to prevent such a sin from occurring again. Let's work together to never again be strangers I will not break off with you again. It ain't over! We are going to have a new relationship. You may want to pay me back, and separate from me. But I won't accept that. Until we are both very old, I will keep trying."

<u>Aug 27</u>

It's my 20th birthday today! We are planning a party at Tracy's house. We went to the grocery and bought steaks, pop, and chips. In the car, as we are planning the evening's festivities, we are blocks away from his home, when suddenly something so unexpected happened.

There's like a flash of something. A distant sound, objects crashing and crumpling, glass shattering, screaming voices, everything spinning, banging – then everything stopped cold. Excruciating pain. I instinctively flip down the visor in the car and gaze at myself in the mirror. Blood trickling down the right side of my face. My head had gone through my side window. Tracy had jumped out of the car to scream at the other driver. Since my head was bleeding on the side he couldn't see, he didn't know I was hurt. A little kid was on the hood of our car staring in at me, yelling to the bystanders that I'm bleeding.

I'm rushed to the hospital. All I could think of was the guests will be waiting at the house. What'll happen to the party? Unlucky for me, the doctor who treated me – I was his <u>*first*</u> patient. He was stitching the side of my face, and with each stitch, he'd make a *tsk* sound, like he wasn't doing it right. When he finally finished massacring my face, I went to the bathroom. He had not even removed the shards of glass from my face or hair. Nor had he cleaned up any of the blood. Great. Straight out of a horror movie, only this *wasn't* makeup.

After I cleaned *myself* up, I went out into the waiting area, where everyone we had invited to my party, including both of our parents, were waiting. What an amazing sight, such concern. It turns out the man who hit us – him in his tank of a Lincoln and us in our trunk-in-front/engine-in-back MR2 – was drunk. He was three sheets to the wind at 4:30 p.m. He ran a Stop sign. Tracy saw he was not stopping and braced himself on the steering wheel. He jarred his arms pretty bad, but luckily that was all. I needed stitches all the way along the right side of my hairline, I had major seatbelt burn along my chest, and my knees smashed together upon impact, so there was some bruising. They discharged me and we went to Tracy's house – and I had my birthday party! Mind you, I lay down for *most* of it, but damn it – IT'S MY BIRTHDAY!

<u>Aug 29</u>
I'm starting college today, taking university transfer courses. At least my doctor has me off work from Chi Chi's for a week. Tracy came with me to make sure I didn't fall asleep or go unconscious from the concussion. Kyle leaves for Israel. He's going to live there. I guess he had to follow Levi? He *promised* me he'd NEVER become like him: religious.

<u>Nov 10</u>
Mom worries about me cutting off from family, sleeping at Tracy's house…Tracy makes my parents VERY nervous. He is not Jewish; he keeps me out late and works in a bar. At one point they even staged an intervention for me, thinking I was a raging alcoholic. Tracy bartends

and I talk a lot about the drinks he makes. I guess that translates into me drinking a lot.

Nov 18

When I was at work, I saw Josh there. He asked if we could talk after work. He told me I affected him in a way no other girl has or had. He liked me so much, he was afraid of his feelings, so he did what he did that night of my birthday party; yes, they slept together. He said that was *the* worst thing he's *ever* done in his life, and always hoped he'd get the chance to talk to me about it. He said, to this day, he's never gotten over me. I was in love with you, I loved you. He likes/ed me because I always listened with interest and I *got* him. I *wasn't* aggressive like the other girls, and he couldn't deal with that. He asked me what I'd do if he asked to kiss me, *now*. I said I wouldn't do that because of Tracy.

What if I did it without asking?
I'd push you away.

He said all he wanted to do was kiss me the way I *should have* been kissed back then at the party.

Well, that's your fault you missed the opportunity then.
I've done everything short of telling you I love you tonight, and I do love you. I believe I loved you then, but I was too afraid to admit it.
So, you fixed that by sleeping with *Pam* so you didn't have to deal with your feelings for *me*? I would've given my eyetooth for you to have paid attention to me THEN as you are NOW. I have no plans of leaving Tracy for you.

Nov 19

Tracy and I went out for dinner and I told him all about last night. He said he feels distressed; twice his girlfriends left him for their exes. I assured him I'd never leave him for Josh. I kissed Tracy, told him I loved him, and told him to never forget it! We went and hung out with John (Tracy's friend). He makes his own wine!

<u>Nov 22</u>

Josh has called me *every* night so far (Mom told me because I haven't been home). I do believe he's living in the past and Tracy's getting pissed.

Mom went to Montreal – Zaida (Grandfather) is not doing well. He fell down their steep stairs.

1989

Our neighbor committed suicide on New Year's Eve, in their garage. That really affected me – I don't think I've known anyone who's taken their life before. He must have felt so desperate.

Feb 20
Mom and Dad are trying to send me to Israel – again. It's on the pretence that it's a "family" trip, planned for the summer. I love Tracy so much; I couldn't stand to leave him for a *day*. They will pay for the trip too. I'm so confused and starting to feel obligated to go. I need to talk to Tracy.

Mar 24
Dad turns 50! He also got laid off from work. After 25 years with the company, he gets canned. Man. What a shitty birthday.

Bubby (Grandmother) called – Zaida has taken a turn for the worse from the fall – he's peeing blood and is on oxygen.

May 10
Dad was saying to me how a future with Tracy *couldn't* work because of the conflict of religion. A Jew and a Catholic could never work. I disagreed. If we love each other, and we do, we'll *make* it work.

Mom asked me again about going to Israel – for six months! She would even help me pay my living expenses. They are *desperate* to get me away from Tracy. Ain't happening, folks!

I got Tracy a job where I work; he's going to bartend. We get to spend *more* time together. Sorry, Mom and Dad.

May 25

Mom asked me *again* about moving to Israel. I won't go to Israel, but California IS a place I COULD live. She said she'd help me with my living expenses there too. I think *anywhere* Tracy ISN'T, they'll be okay with.

I got a second job, enumerating.

June 14

Our beloved cat Snuggles died today. I had just gone outside to call for her and a lady asked me if I knew whose cat this was...lying dead in the street. I freaked out! I slept at Tracy's. We spent all night reminiscing about what a sweet cat she was. She was only six months old.

Tracy said he wants to move out with me.

June 16

Mom completed her thesis and *is graduating with a master's degree*! Mom, Dad, and I drove to Seattle for the ceremony. I'm so proud of her. How did this professional woman wind up having a kid who hates school and doesn't know what she wants to do with her life?

June 21

Mom and Dad are having a "talk" so I made a quick exit to Tracy's. Later, when I came home, Dad's bags were packed and waiting at the front door. I only had a few tears. They said they both deserve to be happy. He said *this* time, he's *not* coming back.

June 23

Dad came into my room to tell me he's **_not_** moving out and he's going for counselling, so at this point, there will be *no* separation. They are trying to fuck me up in a major way. I *didn't* feel any less relieved.

July 8

Leslie's wedding! She married a real kind, quiet man, Dave. I think he balances her out. Tracy and I caught the bouquet and garter. Myriam and her boyfriend slept over. I told Mom that Tracy and I are getting married *since* we caught the stuff.

So, what does that mean? You're thinking about marriage now? Maybe.

Gonzo (my dog) got into a bad fight in the alley with another dog. That dog, half pit bull, half Siberian Husky, had Gonzo by the shoulder and ripped it open. I was screaming. Some guy who lived across our alley intervened and was bashing the other dog with a baseball bat to get him off mine; the dog didn't even budge. The owner just stood there and did *nothing*. Gonzo had to stay overnight at the vet.

July 29

I got my driver's license – on Mom' birthday! Tracy traded his new MR2 for a Stingray Corvette.

I quit my job at Chi Chi's (I'd been there a year and a half). At my enumeration job, my boss offered me an office job. Yes, please!

A friend of Tracy's and mine was in an accident on Deerfoot Trail. Some kids threw something over the bridge into traffic, hit HIS car – he's paralyzed now.

Lesson of the day: In one second, a life can change *forever*.

Aug 6

Tracy, Janis, her boyfriend and I went to Bragg Creek and had a bonfire in a field. I drank eight beers, one right after the other. I *don't* even drink beer, but that's all we had. Privately I talked to her boyfriend about my past with Kyle, *without* mentioning *who* I was talking about. It's so much easier talking to a stranger – and having a couple of cans of courage in me. It's the first time I'd talked to anyone about Kyle. Her boyfriend shared that his mother and ex-girlfriend were both raped by their respective fathers.

Yup, I was floor-licking drunk. (I threw up for the next three days – partly from talking about my past, partly from alcohol poisoning).

Aug 12
Tracy's cousin got married in Lloydminster. We both caught the bouquet and garter – again. Hmmm. Is there a third wedding in our future?

Aug 20
I left for Toronto for three days to visit Rikki, then to Montreal to see Zaida in the hospital, he fell *again*; Mom and Dad were already there. He's not doing well at all. The doctor says he has Alzheimer's too. He looked so skinny and weak. He doesn't remember people. He doesn't know Mom or Bubby. It's so sad to live your whole life, and then forget your loved ones, yourself. On a bright note, I got to see Toby! The good with the bad, right?

(Toby is my best friend from Montreal. I've known her since I was a year old and she six months – my family moved to Calgary when I was nine because my mom's sister, Ruth, and her husband, Ruben, lived there).

Aug 23
This was the best I had seen Zaida since I'm here. He was awake and I fed him. I said I love you to him and when I turned to leave, he said, I love you too. I almost fell over. *He knew me*! He knew who I was! He knew *who* he was talking to. He hadn't said it to Mom, or Bubby or anyone else. I feel SO honored. My sweet Zaida. I will treasure that always.

Aug 25

Tracy and I talked about our wedding. It was the first serious talk we've had about it. Tracy suggested we go ring shopping, *that's* how serious he was. He announced we'll be married *in a year*. I like that I get to pick ANY ring *I* want. It's funny; the guy would've married me right after we met. I was pro marriage *until* my parents split. My view on marriage has shifted drastically. I see no point anymore. You PRETEND you're all happy, but really, you're not? I can't take any more pretending! We've been dating for two years now…I'm warming up to the idea. I *do* love him.

Aug 27

My 21st birthday! I had brunch with Mom and Dad, and then Tracy and I went ring shopping even though we almost broke up yesterday. I was prepared to walk away, but I *was* hoping we could work through it. And we did. Every relationship has bumps in the road. We decided we had something worth fighting for.

Sept 6

Mom and Dad are *telling* me I have a major conflict with Judaism (since being with Tracy). I assured them I'm no more or less Jewish since meeting him – I'm at the same level I *ever* was. Tracy came over and I told him what they said. He was disappointed, and said he felt he *had* really made progress with my parents. He said it *doesn't* look like a future *is* possible for us. I talked to Mom later, and she felt badly and said to me she wants to call Tracy and tell him nothing she said was against *him*, and could they keep being friends because they had come such a long way. Whoa. Maybe a future IS possible.

Sept 20

Mom, Dad, and I went to a Personal Growth Workshop with John Bradshaw. For years they've talked about the brilliance of this man. He has insights, depth, and understanding into human nature that others don't. At the workshop, we got into groups and each member of the group affirms you – telling you that you are special, you are a wonderful person...I cried. I talked for the first time...*about Kyle*...publicly. It seemed like a safe place to do so, with strangers. I felt like I HAD to talk about it already before I burst; 11 years is a long time to hold something in. I said they were *the first* to hear me tell the story. They told me they see a lot of pain in me, and encouraged me to tell Tracy; I had not yet. When IS the "right" time to do that? Do what's right for YOU. I felt...uplifted, relieved, raw...to finally share my deep dark secret. They commended me for being so young and confronting this.

Sept 21
We finished the workshop this afternoon. I was still emotionally drained from the past few days when Tracy picked me up; I was still very deep in thought. We drove back to my house and parked – that's when I told him. I finally found the courage to tell him. I don't know how.

He thanked me for finally opening up to him. I had tried so many times before to tell him – having a little too much to drink, and thinking *then* I'd have the guts to tell him. He'd always try to pry it out of me, but in the end, I couldn't tell him. The vault was sealed. He always knew there was "something", and he'd wait until I decided the timing was right to tell him. I'm so lucky.

I asked Mom if she could recommend a good therapist. She seemed surprised. I was surprised that she was surprised.

Oct 19
Gonzo, my amazing dog, died. The vet said either he would throw up or starve to death from throwing up. He was skin and bones. I told Tracy that everything feels like it's coming to a head. I think I opened a huge can of worms, and I don't think I'll be able to close it again. I threw things around today and cried all day. He said, You've always got me.

<u>Nov 6</u>

The throat doctor told me I could have my tonsils out if I want. My family doctor had told me I needed to get strep *eight* more times – *and I did*. Yes, he actually said that. I made the appointment – January **8** (my favorite number). That's a long wait, sigh.

I can't stop thinking about Gonzo – it still doesn't seem real. Our cat Snuggie would've turned one two days ago.

My job is over – the enumeration is complete and updated. Time to look for work!

I had another discussion with Mom about me going to Israel. This time, it was discussed as *a two-week period*, not six months. I might be able to live with that. All I want to do is cry.

1990

Feb 5

Tracy gave me a kitten as a get-well present for getting my tonsils out! He's long-haired, black and white, and we named him Slinky.

Mom and Dad asked me if I was engaged. Can you imagine? They thought I wouldn't tell them if I *was*. I was very thrown by that question. Dad left the room and Mom started talking to me about how she never knew the gravity of what Kyle did to me. *I* was talking to Mom as if she *knew* the WHOLE truth while *she* was talking to me about the *few times* he "tried" something. We were having *two separate conversations*, each thinking the other had a clue what the other was saying.

I'm like, *What*?! Mom, how could you think it was NOT a big deal?!
Well, he tried to look at your chest.
Mom, he did things to me for three years, EVERY night!!

She looked so confused and was grappling with trying to form a sentence. In reality, she was hearing this for the FIRST time, in its entirety. I think my defence mechanism all these years made me *think* I told them the *whole* story. I wanted to believe I told them ALL of it. Of course, at the same time I thought all these years, why did my parents make it seem like no biggie? The confusion of all these years came to a head.

What did he do to you?
What *didn't* he do to me?!

Mom ran out of the room to bring my father into the conversation. They were flabbergasted, distraught, and horrified. Once the confusion lifted, they apologized over and over and over again for not being there for me. They never protected me nor detected anything was happening. Mom said, We *won't* go to Israel; instead, we'll have the boys come *here* (so I could confront them). Mom and Dad said I needed to get on the road to healing, and there won't be any more secrets. Levi WILL know what Kyle did and they will both face up to the consequences of what they did to me. They said I don't need to protect Kyle anymore; I have to start thinking about myself.

Feb 7
I totally talked myself into breaking up with Tracy – I have a completely independent feeling, and it feels so right. It feels like I don't need him for the first time since we've been going out, like I'll be okay *without* him. It's a very weird but good feeling. It's like this new exposure of my past is *freeing* me.

Feb 12
I'm still feeling different, like I'm becoming a *new* person. Under the weight of protecting everyone else, at my expense, it's unveiling a layer of lightness. Mom, Dad and I talked some more about the "family secret" today. I decided I need to start talking to my friends about it. Mom made a good point – a secret has power and control, it can rule you, take over. If you don't allow it, it can't have that power over you. There is no "right" time to tell someone. It is what it is and you need to get it out. I've held it in for *12* years now. It's going to take a while to get it all out.

Feb 13
I'm having trouble finding a therapist; *no one* wants to help me. I'm too "normal functioning." That really upsets me. I obviously need the help, but what, I'm not suicidal or doing drugs? I just need some support! Everything happens at once with me. Not one thing at a time, but a million different parts that need tending to. Mom tried calling abuse

clinics as an option; we may have to go the private practice route. This will cost them money, but they are willing to put it out for me. I called Tracy and kind of let it all out on him and said I'm going through a rough time; I just need some support.

Feb 15
Word was *put out* to the boys to come into town. They hemmed and hawed and weren't sure. Of course, this request is without telling them WHY they are being summoned. So, Mom and Dad put it to them like this – it's a family crisis, we need you here, *now*!

We'll have to get back to you on it.

Dad said, Treat it like one of us *died*! They complained we were ruining their lives, and disrupting them by doing this to them. UNBELIEVA-BLE!! It never occurred to me they would NOT come in if we said, Pretend someone has died, it's THAT important. They've become so selfish – the world revolves around them. I guess reality doesn't fit into their Torah (the Old Testament) learning schedule.

Feb 16
Levi and Kyle called at 1:00 a.m. They said they can come *in three weeks*, after *Purim*. Jewish holidays take precedence after all – God first, *anything* Jewish second, third…tenth, THEN family. Good to know.

I got an appointment with a therapist; Dad drove me down this morning. The therapist, Madeleine, is strikingly beautiful, elegant, and has this calming quality. I think I will be able to talk to her. I learned a lot of new things, like I have the option to press charges. I kept thinking, if KYLE doesn't get help, he *could* do this again, if he hasn't *already*. I never cried once in therapy, not once. Not even watery eyes. After all the crying I have been doing lately, it seemed odd to me. Tracy called and I cried to *him*. I cried more when I got off the phone. I think I realize Tracy doesn't have to be my number-one source for support. Mom suggested I use one of *her* friends. I chose Olivia; she's a guard in a male prison, but is so pretty, and dainty, but tough. I can take the pressure off Tracy because I know this must all be overwhelming for him. It seems to be the only thing I'm talking about lately.

Feb 19

Olivia came over this evening. She came to talk to Mom and Dad too, to help *them* cope. The question was raised if I'd feel comfortable being in the same house as the boys when they come. I said I wasn't sure how I'll react until they are here. I may or may not even want to sleep at home. Mom suggested I stay at Tracy's.

Olivia remarked how calm I am about all of it, and that maybe I haven't felt it in my gut yet, only my head. Mom told her how much I'm crying. Olivia said, you're feeling the sorrow of it, but not the anger and that it might come out at a later date. Dad says he might resort to violence, and I said I may have to step in and protect them. Olivia said my dad will have to control himself because I will fall back into protection mode, and everyone will assume their old roles, and the healing process will be delayed. I said, If ANYONE *should* be hitting them, it would be ME! She said, That is the first *real* statement you've made.

If either of them try to leave, and go back to Israel, for Kyle, we can say we'll press charges if you don't go into therapy and you'll go to jail for six months, or take their passports away and say when they get back to the *Yeshiva* (Seminary), all the rabbis will know what they've done. For them, that would be an incredible shame. Mom said she would *not* go along with charging Kyle. I felt let down by that.

Feb 24

I had therapy. She said when she is done with me, I'll trust again.

I went to the mall with Olivia. We talked about Tracy and me. We talked about problems I foresee for us regarding religion. She said to simply ask Tracy what his priorities *are*. I came to the conclusion I'm overwhelming myself with scenarios of what *could* be. I want ALL the answers *before* we enter into a marriage! That's ludicrous! She said to take one day at a time. The answers I have now may change when the actual situation arises.

Mar 5
The boys come in at 9:00 p.m. Dad put a lock on my door, but I slept at Tracy's.

Mar 6
Today is Doomsday, THE day.

After procrastinating as long as I could, Tracy finally drove me home. I felt sick to my stomach as I got out of the car. Kyle and Levi both came to greet me at the door. I didn't stick around to chat. I went *straight* to my room. Mom came in to get me – we were going to get started right away. I was shaking. It was physically painful trying to get those first words out. I had planned and planned and figured this out – how would I start? What would I say?

So, I began...12 years ago, Kyle started to sexually abuse me...

They both cried, and Levi was shaking his head in utter disbelief. Kyle sobbed. Throughout the whole discussion, they listened, took full responsibility, and didn't deny ANY of it! NONE! I told them quite clearly the impact it's all had on my adult life. They were blown away. They both said they have every intention of sticking through this with the family. They will help in any way so as to help me heal.

Kyle said he'd figured out *logical* reasons for why he did what he did. Part of the problem was how sex magazines and videos were so available to him, and how it only added fuel to the fire. He started explaining how he felt cheated out of dates with girls. I said, I hear you making excuses, and no excuse in the world could justify what you did, and if you want to talk about feeling cheated, I've never been able to have a normal relationship with other people, much less a guy. I can't even say 'I love you' to my own parents! Every man I see I view as a potential rapist or threat.

The boys are *against* seeing a family therapist. I told Kyle I don't care how much he thinks he has changed and "grown," living a spiritual life in Israel, he WILL pass this down to his children if he doesn't do something about his problems *now*. I wouldn't be the least bit surprised if you have a kid who becomes an offender in some way. I know the power of a good therapist, and you need one!

Levi asked what I suggest they do. I said, I have made provisions to be at a friend's house until I can feel comfortable in my own home with all five of us here. Until then, I will be away and only come home for the meetings. I won't be here for idle chitchat and small talk. I won't put myself in that position. I think they were shocked I was prepared to do all that. I'm making decisions now that are best for *me*. I am becoming a person they are not familiar with – I'm not meek anymore. I'm not protecting anyone anymore. Mom and Dad said, We will have a series of meetings, for as long as Sari needs to get said what she needs to.

I slept at home tonight – and I locked my door.

Mar 7
I woke up and came out of my room only to see Mom and Dad patting them both on the back, supporting and encouraging them, making it okay for *them*. I had no problems confronting Mom and Dad about it and privately I stated, It will appear to them that you are *minimizing* the situation if you are comforting THEM. They NEED to feel alone in this. I see them as getting off easy because the parents are coddling them. They NEED to feel how it feels to be alone, alone with no one to turn to, like I did for years.

They understood. Mom asked me if I will be staying for Shabbat (the Sabbath).

NO. Shabbat is a *family* thing, *family* time, and we are *not* a family!! We are broken.

My therapist told me I am having trouble seeing Kyle as a good *and* bad person. I could only see him as this good person, hence my protection of him. She said, A *good* person *wouldn't* have done what he did. She said when I talk to him, I need to remember him as he was when he was doing what he did to me. I have to realize Kyle, as the good person he portrays to everybody else, is *also* Kyle the creep. I need to let go of pretending he was good. I spent too many years pretending; it would take a while longer to *unlearn* how to do that. To be the destroyer of this person's reputation; people will shoot the messenger when **I** am the one to dispel the way people thought of this person, all his "goodness," all his "sweetness."

In our meeting today, Levi said he has to keep reminding himself that we are at different levels of healing. He feels he's *well into* the healing process, while I'm just at the beginning. I said *if* any new relationship is to come out of this, MY needs will come first. What I need from them will be the basis.

Levi told me he heard what I said yesterday. He said a lot clicked into place for him after listening to the impact it all had on my life. Levi spoke of WHY he ignored me for five years. I said, Quite frankly, I will *never* understand why, no matter what explanation is given. Levi said that whenever he sees an eight-year-old he's reminded of what HE did to me. He looks at one and can't even imagine them going through what I did -- so young. He felt I disapproved of him, and I'd make those *tsk*ing sounds, as if being impatient with him. I told him that's why I stole his crisp paper-money collection – and spent it! Revenge! I took *something* of his that was dear to *him*. He cared more for the money collection than he did of any member of this family.

Levi said I have such a strong character to come out of something like this all alone. Mom said it is such a rare thing that the offender and victim are ever in the same room together, never mind confronting them. She also said how rare that a 21-year-old goes through a healing like this at this point in time. Dad said, I don't want to invalidate the changes you guys have made in your lives, but the main priority here is Sari. We do not want to minimize what happened to her, or condone it. Kyle admitted to what I said yesterday, that he must get rid of whatever it is in him that made him do it in the first place. The potential will always be there. If he was capable of doing it in the first place, what's to stop him from doing it again?

After our session, Levi said, Let's end this on a positive note. I said, As far as I'm concerned, there is nothing positive about any of this so we WILL leave this on a negative note. I got up and left and went to my room. They both came knocking on my door.

Why can't you come out and explore other aspects of our relationship, instead of just coming out of your room for meetings?
I will not sit there and chat about the weather; I will not pretend all is okay.
Why would you have to pretend?
I simply do not feel comfortable. This is all pretty raw for me, and just sitting there afterward is impossible. YOU guys feel comfortable, but *I don't* in the least. I prefer to keep it this way.

Levi said he still did not understand the depth of my pain. They both thanked me for the gathering.

Mar 8

Tonight, I sat at the table for dinner. Perhaps I don't feel as threatened. Mom wanted me to stay for Shabbat. I said that was pushing it. Dad was apologizing to both of them for not being there at puberty to talk to, that he was an awful father. I could hardly stand it. Levi kept going on and on about how much Kyle has changed.

I interjected, I need to say something. Levi, you need to stop rescuing Kyle all the time. The two of you have gotten off pretty easy. If Kyle is going to feel pain, *let him* because it's still *nothing* compared to what *I* went through, and all alone. I didn't have anyone like the two of you have each other. I don't care who tells me how swell Kyle is, and all his positive changes; it means squat to me. Maybe I'm not ready to hear about all these wonderful changes you've gone through because to me, you're STILL that same person who came into my room every night. I remember how you'd bring your friends in too, to do whatever they wanted. He said he didn't remember that part. Well, *I* sure do!!

Levi asks, Why couldn't we just do this by *mail* if you can't hear the good Kyle has done and become? Dad intervened and said, This is a slow process and Sari is just beginning with it, and she has to say what she needs to. Mom reminded Levi he was never silenced when, during his childhood, he'd rail on about Mom and her unfairness as a parent. I told Kyle that I still have fear he'll have a reoccurrence in Israel – with no girls around (with being at an all-boys school); he has limited to no contact with women, which will only "frustrate" him. How will he re-channel his sexual frustrations? This worries me. I had brought up our dialoguing days as a family, every Sunday. I said, Dialoguing never did any good because we only shared what we knew others wanted to hear. Look at where we are now. If we were so *open* and *honest* – why do we have a huge family secret? Behind all the "honesty," there were lies and secrets, with everyone *pretending*. We showed everyone what a perfect family we were, when in fact we were putting on a facade. The 10-year-old in me is determined to be heard now, and she WILL be heard.

<u>Mar 9</u>
I saw Madeleine. She made me think back to the times Kyle came into my room – how I felt and what he did. I felt like an object, a slab of meat with no thoughts or feelings. I don't think he actually cared if I woke up or not. My body was not my own. I felt like a blow-up doll; it won't talk back. I felt frozen with fear. I wanted to cry or scream but

couldn't. Then I'd want to hurt him so bad, but that would wake Mom and Dad up and then they'd ask questions. They had enough problems with Levi, they didn't need this too. How could I burden them? I sensed they *wouldn't* know how to handle it. After all, they couldn't handle Levi. Kyle ruined relationships for me. I simply avoided them, until Tracy. I could never take the chance of them *knowing*. I could never take the chance of *Kyle* knowing I *knew*. And nothing has changed – back then, he was showing everyone what a great guy he was, and now, he's **<u>STILL</u>** telling everyone what a great guy he is. Same old, same old. Same pattern. He *hasn't* changed.

Mom, Dad and I discussed whether Levi KNEW about what Kyle did. We figured the only way to know for sure is to ask.

<u>Mar 10</u>

Maybe I never said "I love you" to Mom and Dad because they'd tell me they loved me, but they couldn't keep me safe. So, if that's what love is – who needs it! My therapist told me to write Kyle a letter *as a 10-year-old. Not* to give him this letter, just for my own sake, and getting out my thoughts and feelings.

Kyle,

For ten years I have loved you. You've been there for me. I've counted on you because you were my big brother. But you let me down, Kyle, real bad. I can't trust you anymore. I don't know what you're doing, but I sense it's wrong. Do all brothers do this? I'm frightened. I'm afraid you might ignore me the way Levi does. Every night I anticipate your visit. I tuck the covers in so tight around me, hoping it might change your mind. It doesn't. I feel like a body with no face or brains. I feel so powerless. I dream about hurting you, but that would only wake Mom and Dad up. They have enough to handle with Levi. I cry every night after you leave. I run to the bathroom to clean up. Some nights are worse because you visit two or three times. With all the fear inside me, did you really think I *could **ever** fall asleep? Then I have to face you at the breakfast table. I suppose you hoped I wouldn't remember any of it. You're wrong. There wasn't an incident I **didn't** remember. So, we go on, business as usual, after all, Mom and Dad can't suspect a thing. You scare me. I trusted you and you betrayed me. It's ugly. I think that is all I'm good for – being a piece of meat. No one will love me now.*

Dad asked <u>THE million-dollar question,</u> Levi…*Did* you know what Kyle was doing to Sari? Is this a surprise to you, or are you not surprised?

He diverted his eyes and looked down; he paused while carefully choosing his words.
I knew. I knew what he was doing. I knew he went to Sari's bedroom at night.

My heart skipped a beat. He knew? I don't understand.

Dad asked, How could you *know* and say *nothing* to us, or *stop* Kyle?

I wanted to punish Sari. I knew what Kyle was doing would be bad for her. I didn't care. I never considered asking Kyle to stop, or telling you guys. I let him do his thing. I just didn't care.

He hated me more than I *ever* even realized. How sick. How cruel. How unforgiveable. To allow the abuse to keep happening? It's *incomprehensible* how an individual makes the decision to **NOT** help out their little sister. My well-being was of no consequence to him. He was a monster without remorse.

Its Shabbat now and we're *"not allowed"* to discuss anything until Monday. I slept at Tracy's for the weekend. I don't think he's handling my emotional state very well. I feel like I need to watch what I say around him. I'm trying to release everything and not keep it bottled up. I feel like I'm being stifled every way I turn. My friend Colleen said,

39

Oh, don't worry about it for now, you'll survive. I don't need someone telling me when to and not to think about it. Let me just be! Don't make me wish I *didn't* tell people. I just don't want others to let me down. I feel like this is my problem and it's like pulling teeth to get my friends to help me. It's always been my fear – needing things from others.

Mar 12
We had our "family" meeting. After, Mom and Dad came into my room to see how I was doing. I said I had a whole list of things I was *going* to say – then I didn't say *any* of it. I felt no urgency in saying anything. Mom freaked at first – Why didn't you say what you needed to? They need to hear these things! Then she realized this was a HUGE *breakthrough*.

I don't need them anymore! I don't need to confront them anymore! I SIMPLY DON'T NEED THEM!! I'M DONE!! They can go back to Israel. I won't feel like there is unfinished business. Mom said she sensed something was different with me, a look on my face – I was smiling. They both said this is a miracle! It's the beginning; I'm finally on my way to healing.

They brought the boys upstairs, and I told them exactly that – I'M NOT A VICTIM ANYMORE!! It's like a huge burden has been lifted. I DON'T NEED THEM FOR MY RECOVERY! I just can't stop smiling. I feel relief. I slept at home and kept my door *open.*

Mar 13
Olivia called. I told her about my breakthrough. She said she is so proud of me. She told me how strong I am, and she can hear the confidence in my voice. I had dinner with everyone; I *even* made small talk. Levi came to my room after and said he noticed me putting in an effort by coming to dinner. He said he realizes it must have been difficult, but I joined them anyway.

<u>Mar 15</u>

Mom and Dad came to therapy with me. Madeleine said she's worrying we may be slipping back into old patterns, playing the same tapes. Here you guys just faced this huge issue, and to not revert back to pretending all is okay, like you would at the breakfast table the next day. You did that in the past, all the while bad things were happening. Mom said she's afraid I'll cling to home base more so now. I said I think quite the opposite will happen. I am getting to know myself now; I'm becoming more independent. I don't even know what ME is all about. I've just been trying to survive with all the garbage I've accumulated since I'm 10. I'm in here somewhere. I just need to start chipping away at this protective shell. I don't want to just survive – I WANT TO LIVE!!

We get home and we are told that while we were away, Levi and Kyle had consulted their Rabbi in Israel and going forward, they will be asking HIM if it's okay to talk to the family about this issue. Otherwise, the subject is now *closed* for them. So, now the option to ever discuss this again has been taken away from me; we are no longer "allowed" to talk about it. They only got in touch with *one* Rabbi, and are waiting for a *second opinion* from another. So, we must now wait to get word from a Rabbi as to whether or not they are *permitted* to help me further? They can't decide for themselves? They'll tell us what framework we're now ALLOWED to speak in. A *Rabbi* is going to tell them what *I* need? Huh? If I need to talk to them, they will need to consult with a Rabbi first? AND what subject matters we are *allowed* to talk about. I knew this was too good to be true. The Rabbi called Mom and told her that only *I* need therapy, and there will be no more family meetings.

<u>Mar 20</u>

I went to therapy. She said this is the same stuff as before – Levi and Kyle pretending that I don't exist as a person, by not allowing me to speak. We can exist in the same house, but the rule is – we don't talk. So, what's changed? She suggested I keep a reminder at the house of me *for them* when I am *not* there, so even though I may not be there, *I will NOT be forgotten.* She suggested a doll with a knife through it to symbolize my pain they choose not to see. My pain is *inside,* therefore it can *easily* be forgotten; it's invisible. I dressed very weird for dinner – lots of heavy makeup, shorts on top of my pants, and skeleton earrings. They both noticed. Levi kept telling me I don't need to talk about it, that all the answers lie in the Torah (the Old Testament).

I yelled, FUCK THE TORAH!! You both did this to me. The Torah had **nothing** to do with it and now you hide behind it?! Cowards. Levi told me the answer for my "getting over" this is to go to a *Yeshiva* for three months. I said, What the hell is *that* going to do?? My faith in Judaism is *this* little right now (I indicated with my fingers). Why would I want to go live the lives **you two** are? He said, Well, how is rehashing constructive? Who's rehashing?! This is all coming out FOR THE FIRST TIME! How the hell do YOU know what I need? How dare you. He says, Well, YOU can't seem to tell me what you need. Kyle said, God WAS there; he just didn't know what He wanted from him. Cop out.

Mom said I was prepared to be let down by both of them and that is what's happening now. I said, There is no way I will start a relationship with you two when you disqualify my feelings. Levi burst out crying. What the hell was HE crying for? What a joke. I just sat there twiddling my pen. Did a Rabbi "allow" him to cry?

Mar 25
Mom said Levi and Kyle want to speak to me. It's against my religion. Kyle said he's waiting for me to feel comfortable; he wants to take an interest in my life. They want to lay some sort of foundation *before* they leave. I said, *I'm* going at the pace *I* need to. Nothing will be solved and be "okay" *before* you go. It takes time. Kyle said he wants to let me know he wants to start creating a *new* relationship with me. I told them they have both closed the doors on any further discussion, so where would we even go from here? Levi said, A baby walks, then falls, walks, then falls. That's how we'll be, make a *start*. Kyle said he re-

members we used to do things and go places together all the time. He would like that back. Riiiight.

Mar 29

I did Guided Imagery at therapy. "Little Sari" told Levi and Kyle off so badly. I made it so they *couldn't* talk back, they *had to* listen. They felt shame and guilt. I gave them necklaces -- Kyle with my bed on his, Levi with an eight-year-old me. I'll picture them with it around their necks when they go back to Israel on Sunday. The "Little Me" got angry. I realized that the point is there isn't anything they can do or say that'll help. I find fault in any "good intention" they have toward me. I don't need *anything* from them. They have eviscerated my needs to make it easier on themselves.

Mar 31

Levi came over to talk to me. He begged me not to put so much pressure on Mom with my problems. To not say things to her that will upset her. He could see we have a close bond; therefore, it would be easy for Mom to get "wrapped up" in my problems, and I should protect her by not being a burden to her. Kyle chimed in, saying that what wasn't said here can be said in letters. I said that if I ever write them a letter, it'll be about "my issues," *nothing else.* Kyle said he hopes he can respond to my letters the way I want.

Unbelievable. They are outta here tomorrow!!

Apr 1

They left – HALLELUYAH!! YIPPEE!! YEAH!! Dad said he hopes they get their kosher meals on the plane, and if they don't, they should complain. Well, that just made my day – thanks for talking about them, Dad. Whatever made him say any of that to *me*? Angry, angry, angry! I need more of Tracy now, more attention. I need him around more. I'm feeling very alone, abandoned, scared. Nobody seems to have the time for me now. I feel empty.

Apr 2

Mom called from work to see how I was doing. I cried a lot. People don't know what I'm going through, so how could I expect them to know what I need? Mom said when she was little, Bubby used to take her and Aunty Ruth to the country each summer to rejuvenate themselves because they were always so sick. She'd like to take me somewhere for *three to four months* so I could heal without the hustle and bustle of the city, somewhere hot. I said, That's a long time. She said it's something to think about. I tried to think of all these things to keep busy and stay out of the house, and then I realized I don't need to escape from my *own home* anymore. I can relax now.

My horoscope said, '*You may be searching for security in a relationship but have doubts about where your true happiness lies.*'

Apr 3

Tracy called and told me to make reservations somewhere for tomorrow, our anniversary. I was surprised because I knew he had volleyball. Mom called a lady about a support group for me. I feel isolated. I feel cursed for having to deal with this. No one REALLY understands. I feel Tracy distancing from me. He admitted it's all overwhelming because he can't do anything about it. He feels like he's letting me down, and admitted to distancing from me. I said, I won't *always* be talking about my situation. Sometimes I need to cry, be emotional, and him just being there is comforting. Maybe I *should* go away with Mom.

Apr 4

It's our third anniversary. It was a good evening. We went out to the Bragg Creek Steak Pit for our celebration. Tracy bought me flowers and we had a wonderful night in spite of the distancing. Things are starting to feel right again. It's been an emotional rollercoaster for both of us.

<u>Apr 10</u>

I went to therapy. Bubby is visiting and I can't stand listening to her go on about the boys. Of course, she doesn't know and never will, but I need to listen to this? Madeleine said it must feel like an old place again – pretending. Listening to people sing Kyle's praises, but now I'm not willing to go along with it. To get Bubby to stop talking about them, Mom and I tried explaining THEY were the reason I'm in therapy, but not tell her ALL of it. All she said was, she is shocked to hear Kyle and I aren't as close as we appeared.

I'm not sure where I fit into Tracy's life. He's definitely distancing himself from me and picking up any volleyball game he can. All this emotional turmoil – Tracy didn't sign on for this. I don't know how to rectify this.

<u>Apr 11</u>

I'm really feeling empty. Not a friend to turn to. I pondered what it would be like if I killed myself. All this pain would go away. I've been crying all morning. I just wish I could be *normal*. I wish I *hadn't* told anyone about what happened. It seemed so much easier keeping it to myself. Have I really done the right thing? This is such a lonely place to be. Maybe Levi is right, I'm just being a burden to everyone. I needed to talk to Tracy. I told him I don't know what to do anymore. I need to get past this crappiness. I need to feel close to him again.

<u>Apr 18</u>

I ran the idea of breaking up with Tracy past Colleen. She was shocked. I just don't know what to do anymore. The distance is growing and growing. The healing process is taking up all the space right now. After three years together, maybe *this* is what happens. I talked about it in therapy. Am I really prepared to call it quits? I cried. Later, I talked to Tracy about it. He disagreed with my conclusions. Is it all in my head? I doubt it.

During the next few weeks, I went to Radium Hot Springs with Mom, Dad, and Bubby, applied for a few jobs, barely ate, and did lots of exercise. I had more thoughts about breaking up with Tracy. We'd reconnect then drift apart again. I didn't feel like being around people. Then I started a new job at the makeup counter in Superstore, and I also felt like Tracy and I were falling in love again, but it was fleeting.

May 5

My parents bought me a new bedroom set – a bed, dresser, and headboard – a clean slate. No old reminders. I'm reclaiming my power!

I'm being told I look too thin. I'm losing weight fast. People are worrying about me, but I'm fine.

May 22

Bubby called – Zaida died at 6:20 a.m. I hopped the first flight to Montreal with Mom, Dad, and Aunty Ruth. I called Tracy to let him know; I was sobbing hysterically. He said he loved me. Toby came by in the evening; my faithful, dear friend. Boy, did I need to see her! She said, How do you feel about being an aunt? How do you feel about coming in for a wedding?

Happy news. Happy, happy news! I told her about *them* coming out. I finally told *her* about Kyle. She was in total disbelief. What a day. I'm drained. The funeral is tomorrow.

May 30

The lady from the support group called – they have an opening for me.

Later, I get a call from Josh to go for coffee. He looked way more distinguished. We reminisced. He said he used to get girls and didn't want them, now he wants girls he can't have (me).

It's the challenge for you. Once the chase is over, you lose interest. If I didn't have a boyfriend and was available, you *wouldn't* be here.

Back then, I liked you more than you'll ever know. Then he joked, Let's get married! Do you think you and Tracy will ever get married?
Why, would you want an invitation?
No! But I could give you everything you want.

He talked about having a very good job and that our timing always seems to be off. He recalled the time at Malarkey's when he asked me if he could kiss me and I turned him down flat. He said *that* has been the only time he's *ever* been turned down. He told me he regrets not pursuing me more back then. He apologized again for doing what he did at my birthday. Then he left. Perhaps he was looking for closure? Tracy has some competition (joke)!

June 1

Mom and Dad are trying to cut down on expenses, so I suggested selling the house. Maybe I'll finally move out on my own. I told Tracy my priority is moving out now. He thinks I should get a car first. I was left wondering how he feels about me. I want to be loved, desperately.

June 6

I keep wondering if things would be different between Tracy and I if I had *never* told him about Kyle? We are deteriorating at a rapid rate. I miss the old us. It's too painful and exhausting to continue on the way we are. I have Josh calling me and telling me the flattering things I wish Tracy was telling me. I want Tracy, no one else. I spent the night at Tracy's.

June 7

We woke up happy enough, joking around. Tracy said he has to get a move on so he'd have enough time to bike to work. I said, We have to settle something *first*.

Where do we stand with each other? How do YOU see things now?
Pretty shitty.
Is it that you don't want to see me anymore?

Not exactly. I don't have the intense feelings I used to have.

My heart sank.

He said, I have nothing to offer you, and I know I'm hurting you, and I don't want to, anymore. This may not be forever, just now; I need to sort out how I feel.
I said, I've never loved anyone the way I love you. I sure won't make *that* mistake again.

He was crying. He said he loves me and always will. For now, I think it's best this way. He was staring out the window. I guess I don't want the commitment.
Is this where I give you back the key? Give you your ring back? Do you want the cat?

He looked at me with great sadness in his eyes. No, I don't want anything *back*. I know I've been stringing you along and I don't want to, anymore. Then he asked me if I wanted breakfast.
We sat down and had a BLT that he prepared. I took one bite and ran from the room crying. He was crying too. We calmed down, finished our breakfast and I said, Well, no use prolonging the inevitable.

He grabbed my coat, held it open for me and handed me a few Kleenex for the road. I turned snidely to him and said, Have a good life!
He said, Come here, and he hugged me. He started sobbing and holding me tight. Then he kissed me on the cheek.
I looked up at him and I said, I'm going to miss you.
I'm going to miss you too. He kissed my forehead, I turned and left.

I told Mom and Dad – they were shocked, but supportive. I wish the hurt would go away. I wish time would fast-forward a couple of months so the pain would lessen. I'm just so confused. I love him, yet I *should* believe this is for the best. I feel like crawling into a hole and dying.

Josh called. I told him Tracy and I broke up today and he wanted to see if I wanted to go out.

No, I'm not up to it.

I looked at Tracy's horoscope: *Welcome a fresh start, added independence. New love could be on the horizon. Obligation is lifted.*

Wow. If that doesn't say it all right there.

Tracy called. He said he still doesn't understand it all. He told me we could talk about it some more.

I suppose things can only get better from here. I'm going to get stronger from this and move on. If we were meant to be together, we will, if we are meant to be apart, we will. I feel stronger than the last breakup. I believe it all is for the best.

June 8

I didn't cry a single time today. I think deep down inside I'm still hoping we'll get back together though. I really need to do what's best for *me,* and realize things weren't good for a long time. I was very unhappy. Maybe now I can get some self-respect back. I'm going to get stronger from this and move on. No more compromising. I learned a lot from him.

Josh called again. He asked me if I'm still upset. Uh, ya!

June 11

I didn't cry today, but I have a tremendous need to see Tracy, to see his face.

I had that support group; there were only five of us. I shared about me confronting Levi and Kyle. I didn't think about Tracy much today; I'm getting used to it. Last time we broke up, I was devastated and incon-solable. Now, I feel stronger. I'm not keeping my hopes up of Tracy coming around. It'll all turn out for the best. I deserve someone who'll be there for me, and maybe Tracy isn't the guy. I am going on with my life. No sense dwelling on it, or getting depressed – it's out of my control. I think he'd be surprised to see me now. I haven't cried once since the actual breakup. I'm in control of my choices now. I am a lot stronger than I'm sure he thinks I am. There IS life after Tracy!

June 12

I'm getting ready for work and Dad knocks on my door. He hands me a rose that was left in our front hall with a note that read, *To Sari, Love always, ME*. It was from Tracy. Was I shocked? You bet! I could take it a million different ways, but I'll go with the simplest – it was a nice gesture. Nothing more. At least he was thinking about me. Don't read into it. I *do* feel sometimes he gave up too easily.

June 18

I went to the support group. I talked about how I seem to have a handle on the abuse, my grandfather dying, and breaking up with Tracy. Then I broke down. A lady said, Not only are you grieving for your grandfather but over the abuse and the death of your relationship. Feel it and grieve it. I've been suppressing my feelings because I just want to get on with things. I allowed Tracy to get close to me – I just hope I can let someone *else* in. I need to remember the reasons we broke up. I was unhappy; he was unhappy; it WAS for the best.

June 26

I decide to ignore Tracy's birthday two days ago. He'd have expected me to acknowledge it, but I didn't. I'm at work and I get a call; it's Tracy. He sounded sad. I'm just calling to see how you are. I'm good, keeping busy and going out. Well, call me sometime. I'm thinking, Why? He *wants* his space, he's got it! Why is he calling me? I don't get it. This is what *he* wanted!

In the next week, I was let go from my job at Superstore for being too shy, again! My manager said two customers complained about me being rude and unhelpful. She didn't believe that to be true, but thought my shyness is what gets in the way. Screw them. I am who I am.

I was feeling like I need to move on from the support group, I felt stuck – I was helping others more than myself.

July 4

Tracy just called. I told him I didn't recognize his voice. He sounded sad, which only made me feel stronger. I told him how great I was feeling. Well, I better let you go, you have things to do. Yup!

July 5

I get another call from Tracy. He's locked his keys in his car and asked if I still have the other set? Yes. Could I please bring them to him at his house? Okay. I went home to get the keys, all the while thinking I'm crazy for leaping to his aid like that. It felt weird not kissing him hello. We walked out to his car, and then he gave me the keys back.

You want me to keep them?
Ya, who'll bail me out the next time it happens? He said he went home last night, got to his room and was looking around for me. I really expected to see you there. He grabs me toward him and gives me a big hug and kisses my cheek. He said, See you later.

I am feeling soooo good. I love it!

July 25

I called Tracy. I said that there are so many rumors circulating with our friends over *why* he wanted to break up with me – religion, other girls...I told him I'd rather talk in person about all this. I went to his house.

He said, You are right; we DO need to talk. I'm just not ready to. Do you think I've forgotten about you?
Yes. Maybe you WANT to forget me.

It's not that easy.
I figured you kept calling because you "want to keep in touch," "be friends." He kept shaking his head. Why do you think I have all your things around the room still?
Why do you keep all that stuff?

Saved by the bell, his mom came upstairs.
I said, I better be going. He walked me outside to my car. He grabbed me and gave me a hug and kissed my cheek again. As I looked back to him in my mirror, he had a big smile on his face. It had kinda felt like old times. He made it clear he still loves me, misses me, and thinks about me – without spelling it out. I've been thinking he'd forgotten about me and gotten on with his life. I feel…hopeful. We will talk when he's ready.

July 27

My brakes failed on my car yesterday. I'm lucky to be alive! Man! I needed to have some fun, so I went to Colleen's party. She tells me Tracy is there. He came up to me and asked me if I wanted to go over to his house later.

You could stay over if you like. I'll leave the key in the mailbox.

I kissed him on the lips, bye. I stayed at the party for a while. When I saw Norman leaving, I asked if I could get a ride over to Tracy's. Tracy was surprised I showed up. I slept over.

July 28

Mom asked if Tracy was at the party. Yes.
Was it awkward? A bit.
She asked me if I still feel a "zing" when I see Tracy. Yes.
She smiled. She reminded me I wouldn't get back together with him if things were the *same*. True. IF it were to happen, things *would have to be* different.

Aug 10
I found out today Tracy has a girlfriend. She can have him. I feel I had hope – and now that's gone. I don't have to wonder anymore where we stand. It's time to move on with my life!

Aug 11
I went down to Tracy's work to get some of my stuff back. I was feeling good. I looked good. I was toned and tanned.

He called me when I got home – asking why I came down to his work, and admitted his feelings for me *haven't* changed one bit. He still loves me.

So, what are we doing? When two people love each other, they're usually together, not apart.
I *do* love you.
I love you too, but it doesn't matter now.

Aug 12
Mom had me listen to part of a tape that was sent from Kyle. "Hopefully you can look at me someday in the future without pain or a reminder of what took place years ago." Ya.

Tracy is finally ready to "talk." I went to his house. His mom told him about a job opportunity at The Kananaskis Hotel. He'd bartend and has an interview on Friday. Okay, well good luck with that.

I'm going to Montreal with Mom and Dad on the 17th. Good timing.

Aug 19
Toby's getting married and wants me to be her maid of honor! She also told me she miscarried her baby. I didn't know what to say.

Zaida's unveiling is today. It was very freaky to see his headstone. I saw other family members' graves. Everyone went back to Bubby's house, to eat and socialize. They had a cake and everyone sang "Happy Birthday" to me.

Aug 21

I call Tracy and he tells me he IS moving to Kananaskis. My heart sank. I tried to cover. I cried. I didn't expect to cry. I feel dumped all over again. Nothing more I can do. One needs to face things and not run away. I feel *he's* running away. I need to let go of Tracy. I've washed my hands of him. Josh called. How does he manage to call *every time* Tracy and I "break up"? Hmm...

Aug 28

My 22nd birthday was yesterday. Colleen took me to Banff for the day, and then out for dinner. Tracy will fit right in, in those surroundings, in the mountains, and lots of young people around to make new friends with.

I was hanging out in our backyard with Mom and Dad. Suddenly *Tracy* comes into the yard. WHAT THE HELL? He hands me flowers and a card. We went to have some privacy in the house, but not before I motioned to Mom and Dad that I was throwing the flowers over the hedge in disgust.

I ask, What's this for?
Well, it was your birthday yesterday, wasn't it?
Ya, but you could've ignored it.
Did you want me to?
It doesn't matter now.
Why do you say that?
You're going to Kananaskis; you're starting a new life.
You can visit me anytime.
That's a strange invitation. You're fucking with my head; you know that, don't you?
I don't mean to.

Sept 10

I started bawling about how my life is going nowhere. Mom said, What you've been doing now is more important than money, school, job…You've done more work on yourself than 95% of the people out there. She said not to put pressure on myself, to figure things out, allow myself the time to heal first. Better to get the learning and growing done *now*, rather than 50 years from now, *or never*. She said, You, yourself know all the emotional turmoil you've been through. You know all the work you've done. Forget the rest. Allow yourself to be depressed or angry – it's all part of getting over and past it. The longer you keep it back, the longer the healing takes.

Sept 14

I get a call from Tracy. He said he left something in my mailbox for me. There's an envelope. It's a card. The card was telling me how sorry he is and saying how he needs to be by himself for a while, he loves me, and he'll keep in touch. I didn't know what to think.

Sept 22

Mom told me that after Yom Kippur (Jewish High holiday), she's leaving Dad again; this time for good. I wasn't shocked at all. I was expecting it. She said she's not sorry for having been married to him all these years. No regrets. She told me I need to decide *who* I'll live with. She'd love to have me live with her. I don't know. She said, Bubby at 80 is finding her freedom, me at 50 and you at 22. Mom said she was worried I'd react to her the same way I did with the *last* separation. I said no way. The shock was enormous last time, cutting up my leg to dull the emotional pain; but it's different this time. I'm not angry toward her the way I was. I want them both to be happy, and it's very apparent the only way they can be *is* to be *apart*, for good.

It feels clearer and clearer to me that it's really over between Tracy and me. It just simply is.

Sept 24

I get home and there's a letter from Tracy. I can't believe he wrote to me his *first* day at work. I cried reading it. It was painful to hear him say he loves it out there. I *don't* want to be friends with him. Either we are together, or we are not. I won't write back. I need to disappear. Crawl into a hole. I just want to get on with my life already! Why won't he let me do that?

Sept 25

I went to see a psychic. I *need* to know I *will* be okay. I need to know I *will* survive *without* Tracy in my life. I need hope. I need to know something *positive* will come out of the breakup. She told me THE guy and I will have a strong, enduring relationship. I'll be married in 1992. Crazy! I just broke up with a guy, that seems awfully *soon*! Then out of the blue she says, Your parents will be better off apart. They'll be happy. You need to let go of the past. You are tougher than you look. Your guy will genuinely care about you and your life.

The life that lies ahead of me sounds so wonderful and exciting. I don't want to miss any of it!

Oct 6

I really feel like I'm getting over Tracy. Figures, I get a call this evening, "Will you accept a collect call from Tracy?" Holy shit! Sure. He's been sick all week. Me too. He asked me when I'm coming down to see him. I felt like laughing. He asked me if I got his letter. Ya. He says I'll be getting another, with directions on how to get out there. He sounded lonely. I'm confused by the phone call. I *wasn't* upset by the call, I just thought, I'm okay, he's not.

Oct 7

This evening, Mom and Dad sat me down to say they're officially separating. I actually started laughing. Nervousness? Mom's moving into Kyle's room, then, in the New Year, we'll be selling the house and we will find our own places to live. They were both very frank and calm. Dad said there is no room for reconciliation; the next step will be divorce. They want to do this as quickly as possible. The awkwardness of living under the same roof while separated could be too much. So much change!

Oct 10

I called our lawyer regarding the accident on my birthday in 1988. The bid has been made now, so Tracy and I need to go down *together* to discuss a settlement. I tried calling Tracy; it's very difficult to reach him. Residential housing doesn't have phones. The person who answered at the front desk said she could put a note under his door. I'll just call him tomorrow.

Oct 11

I finally got in touch with Tracy. He was surprised to hear from me. I told him we have to meet with our lawyer to finalize the case. I thought that there'll be no more ties to Tracy after this settlement. And yet, I'm not feeling strongly about that. I'm not feeling I need to move on from him. This isn't good.

Oct 17

As I was getting ready this morning, Tracy called and said he'll pick me up to go to the lawyers. When he arrived, he handed me a handwritten letter on a place mat. He said he misses me. Why?

He doesn't respond. We reach the bottom of the stairs to where we were headed at the lawyers and he says, You asked me *why* I miss you, and that deserves an answer – things aren't the same without you. I think about you every minute. I keep expecting you to come see me. He asked me what I'm doing on Sunday. Nothing. Do you want to come out for the day? Just then the receptionist said the lawyer is ready for us. Phew.

After our meeting, in the elevator, Tracy says, so you haven't answered my question. He asked me again.

I'm being hesitant because you made it *clear* before you left that we have nothing to talk about.

All I've done since I'm out here is *think*. There is nothing else to do out here BUT think.

What would I go out there for?

Dinner, a nice *romantic* dinner.

ROMANTIC?! I won't be jerked around! I gave "us" my all. I put my heart and soul into "us." I did everything I could to save it.

I just want to be with you. I have never, not for one minute, stopped loving you.

He drove me home and said, Maybe you're hoping I'll forget the question. Well...?

What would happen if I *were* to go?

We'll just see how things go.

He let me out, kissed my forehead and said, I'll see you Sunday.

I'M SO CONFUSED! What should I do? I guess I'll go and listen to what he has to say? It sounds like he's put a lot of thought into this. I suppose all that psychic stuff goes down the toilet. All that time out there, the solitude...he came to the realization he missed me.

Oct 21

I'm heading to Kananaskis. I told Mom and Dad I was going to Banff with Colleen.

I went to one of the lounges to meet Tracy.

He said, Doesn't this feel like a *first* date? So, do you still feel I'm going to screw you around?

I don't know yet, why don't you tell me *why* things have changed for you.

Well, what I think happened between us was that you were the most serious girl I've ever gone out with. Three years is a long time, and I felt I had to be *sure* you were THE one.

So, we had to *break up* for you to see?

Not break up, just be *apart*. I had to be sure.

What made you *sure*?

I've had all this time to think, that's why I came out here. Everything I do reminds me of you. I kept thinking of everything we've done and everything we can do…together.

We went for dinner. I said, I fear this is a passing thing and you could change your mind *again* tomorrow, or next week.

He shook his head and said that wouldn't happen. He asked me if I'd met anyone.

No. I saw someone for about a week, but he wasn't *you*. If we *were* to be together, we'd have to do things *differently*. It's very strange we are talking like this here, now.

You could come out *here* to live and work. Are things going too fast?

I just can't believe we are talking like this.

I spent the night.

Oct 22

I was in a pensive mood; I was still absorbing everything from yesterday. Tracy asked me if I was glad I came out.

"Ya, I guess. Are *you* glad?"

"I was asking you – you seem to have a few questions at the back of your mind."

"I was trying my hardest to move on."

"Did you? Do you want to move on with your own life, or do you want to move on together, with me?"

"I want to be with *you*. I *want* to make this work. Does this mean we're not broken up anymore?"

"Yes, I love you."

We said goodbye and I went back home. Mom and Dad *believed* I had been in Banff with Colleen. Phew. I'm not sure how they'll react to this news. I hope Tracy meant everything he said. I really hope.

Oct 28

Mom, Dad, and I went through the house and split everything three ways. Not your *usual* divorce. I suppose being the only child around, I get dibs. I haven't talked to Tracy much. I'm not sure how this is going to work.

Tracy called at 2:30 a.m. I thought something was wrong. No, he misses me and thinks about me ALL the time. Then he started singing, "I just called, to say, I love you..."

Nov 9

I figured it was time to tell Mom and Dad about Tracy and me; I can't put it off any longer. At dinner I started, I have to tell you guys something, but once I tell you, it's the *end* of the conversation.
Dad asked if I was pregnant.
No! I'm going to Kananaskis this weekend to be with *Tracy*.
Mom said, I can't help you make wise choices, *you* have to decide.
I decided I don't care if I get their blessing or not.

Nov 12

I had a great weekend with Tracy. He told me he had a girlfriend for a bit but broke it off with her.

"Was *that* part of figuring out if you wanted to be with *me*?"
"Yes, part of it."
"Why did you stop seeing her?"
"She wasn't *you*."

I told him he could've been honest with me, and I will not put all of myself into this relationship again if he's only going to hurt me again.

"I won't ever be hurting you again, no more."
"Do you even *know* what you want?"
"Yes, I want *you*."

He asked me to move out there, to come work out there.

You'd tire of me; you won't have time for me.

He said he'll never forget the day I walked out his front door. I'm *glad* it affected him.

Mom came into my room and talked about her plans to have us *both* go to Israel next summer. I protested and said *she's* the one who wants to go to Israel so desperately, *not me*. She said she needs to know where I'm headed *before* she moves out. She thinks by being with Tracy, I *won't* fulfill my dreams. I told her he and I will achieve our dreams *together*!

Dec 1
Tracy keeps asking me when I'm getting a job out there, because then it'll feel like *home*. Mom finally asked me if Tracy and I are going out again.

I guess you could say that. We're talking in a healthier manner but there are no guarantees; we'll see what happens.

There was no trace of anger in Mom – nothing. She said it all with a smile. I was relieved. It's the first time she has been "okay" with Tracy and me.

Dad asked me if I'll be moving in with Tracy. He'd be happy about it, Mom   concerned. Dad's done with the whole situation with Mom; he's ready to pack and move. Mom signed papers on an apartment; she moves on the 15th.

Dec 7
I went to visit Tracy and I brought Slinky with me. On the ride up, I thought the cat was peeing on my coat that was on the car floor, so I took my attention off the road for a *second* and it landed us in the ditch.

I was so freaked out! I flagged a car down, and they drove us up to the residences. I could see afterward, had I gone in the ditch another *few feet* up, I'd have driven right *off* the cliff! I'm REAL lucky! I got a tow truck and hauled the car out. Tracy's so thankful I was okay.

In the end, the cat never peed on my coat. AND who cares if he HAD? It's not worth driving off a cliff for!

Dec 17
I went to visit Tracy. He asked me if I'm happy with the way things are going with us. Yes. He is too. He wants me to move out there and move in with him. He was dead serious. He said it's something we both need. He wants there to be no doubts and, to be sure, **I** want to eventually get married and have children. I'll think about it.

Dec 21
I received my cash settlement from the accident. It's finally over!

This is the last Friday-night dinner Mom, Dad, and I will have together. The movers come on Sunday. The end of an era.

Dec 31
New Year's in Kananaskis. I looked hot! I felt so good and had so much fun, until I got sick – throwing up blood. A woman in the bathroom who happened to be a nurse told me I probably have an ulcer. Colleen and I sang karaoke, my *first* time – "That's What Friends Are For." At midnight I kissed the entertainment guy! Tracy was not impressed. It was all in good fun.

1991

Jan 4

I'm making travel plans to go to Montreal for Toby's wedding. I picked up the tickets, and went to Mom's apartment for dinner – Dad was there too.

I found out from Leslie that she's pregnant and due in July!

Jan 13

Tracy and I were talking about marriage and kids, and is he okay with stepping on a glass at our Jewish ceremony? Of course. We talked about who'll stand up for us, Friday-night Shabbat rituals, and will he have a problem with any of it? No. We agreed we *won't* marry in a church *or* a synagogue. We decided to marry on our anniversary date: April 4.

Jan 14

There was a scud missile attack on Israel a day or two ago. Mom and Dad are trying frantically to get in touch with Levi and Kyle. If something DID happen to them, I'd have to leave the house because people would be flocking to give condolences and I'd say something I'd regret. I wouldn't want to hurt Mom and Dad that way.

Jan 15

Well, the dickheads *finally* called and I had to listen to Dad say "I love you" to them about ten times. The tension with the situation in Israel may go on for a while. Mom asked if I'd move to Toronto with her, to get away from people who know that Levi and Kyle are my brothers. People know me *there*, too. I won't run away from it. Mom said she'd quit her job and move out there with me. Nice gesture, but there's no point. She said she doesn't want to see me go through any more pain. I'm thinking it's another attempt to get me away from Tracy.

Jan 17

Ten scud missiles hit Tel Aviv and Haifa. Mom was crying and Dad left the house. So many calls came in asking if *they* were okay. People kept thinking I should be all broken up about it. I wasn't. I told Mom I'll give her my TV so she can watch the news at her place. She appreciated that.

Tracy told me to apply for a job in Kananaskis. He's trying to talk me into moving out there again. I think he may have convinced me this time.

Jan 31

A friend of Mom and Dad's was asking me how my brothers are. I answered flatly, I don't keep in touch with them – you'll have to ask my father. I'm SO tired of answering questions about them. I think it will be a good idea to move to the mountains. I need a break. No one out there knows about *them*. It'll be a relief. I don't want to talk about them anymore.

Feb 5

I started making a list of things I'd take with me, and I started crying. This is really it! I keep thinking, Oh, poor Dad, but he seems to be getting on with his life. He has a new girlfriend, Nina. He's going to sell the house anyway. Ya, it's scary, but I want to be with Tracy. In time we'll all adjust to all the changes that keep happening. Time heals all.

Feb 7

Dad drove me out to Kananaskis yesterday, and today I applied for a Room Services position. Spontaneously, Tracy and I checked into the Banff Springs Hotel, just with what we were wearing! As a job perk, Tracy gets 50% off food and beverages and 70% off accommodations.

We had champagne and strawberries. People treated us like they thought we had money. It was pretty cool. Tracy said, I go nuts when you're not with me. I need you with me all the time. That's why I want you to move out here.

Feb 12
I got a call from Room Services – I got the job! They asked me to start on *Friday* (today is Tuesday). Tracy is so happy. Slinky will be coming out with me to live. I said to Tracy, We'll *officially* be **living together**. I told Dad first – he was immediately happy for me. When I told Mom she said, I hope you enjoy your new life.

Feb 14
I took Mom to therapy with me. She's having a hard time letting go. Madeleine gently told her to let me make my own decisions, let me get on with my life. Tracy picked me up from Mom's. Mom and I said goodbye. Tracy and I thought how appropriate it is that we're moving in together on Valentine's Day!

Feb 28
Dad called. He told me that Nina, his girlfriend, moved into our house yesterday. Then Mom called – they are going to start divorce proceedings. She said this is reality now; no sense in prolonging it anymore.

Tracy and I went to Montreal for Toby's wedding.

Mar 9
Toby's wedding day! All us girls went for breakfast, then had our hair done; mine was in a beehive do. We had our makeup done too (then I redid mine the *proper* way). Toby looked *spectacular*. I helped her with her veil and train. I had a six-rose hand corsage.

Finally, the wedding. It was a very moving ceremony. Toby kept holding my hand before and after the ceremony. I felt very close to her. Interestingly enough, Toby sat her cousin Aaron and his girlfriend at our table. It was *incredibly* awkward – I hadn't seen the guy in seven years. I remember how he got so serious, very fast. He wanted to marry me. Look at us now.

Toby threw her bouquet – it hit the ceiling and *I* caught it. Everyone thought it was so unfair, like she was aiming for me, so they called for a re-toss. I caught it *again*. Tracy caught the garter. We are getting pretty good at this since it's happened a few times before. Lots of people asked when WE were getting married.

We got back to the hotel and there was a bottle of champagne waiting for us (Tracy set that up). Tracy poured us some.

He said, I have a strange toast. I realize I don't have a ring, but I want to propose anyway. *Will you marry me?*
I almost shit. I said, Did you *just* say what I *think* you said? Yes.
I think I'm going to cry.
Me too.
We both had tears in our eyes. Is this what you *really* want; you've thought about this?
Yes, very much.
Then YES!

He had made me a "diamond" ring out of a paper napkin and slipped it on my finger. He told me, in Calgary, he had taken my father out for breakfast and asked him for my hand.

May 9

Tracy and I moved back to Calgary today; it's way easier to plan a wedding from here. We moved into his parents' place until we can find one of our own. I don't question things about our relationship now that we are engaged. We are on the same page and it feels pretty solid.

I got together at Mom's with Dad. They wanted to talk about our wedding plans. They said they *won't* attend the ceremony if a minister's marrying us. Tracy agreed he'd get married by a Rabbi. Mom is afraid I'm assimilating more and more into the Christian world, although she said *she'd* be the first person to *discourage* Tracy from converting – if he doesn't do it for *himself*. Support is even better than converting. Huh.

I called Toby to ask her to be *my* maid of honor.
Sari, yes, I'd be honored to stand up for you!

June 2
Mom and Dad sold the house last week. I cried. It hit me – I no longer have a family home, but I'm excited to create a new one with Tracy.

We were going over the guest list for the wedding with Mom and Dad. I really think Mom sees Tracy in a whole new light – a good light. It seems like everything is happening at once – wedding, divorce, needing a better job, trying to get a loan, and moving out. It's taking its toll on me. I cried all night. What am I doing with my life? I feel like I'm blipping through life not contributing anything worthwhile. I feel unworthy.

The divorce papers were signed.

June 22
I quit my job at Ultimate Fashions; Dad came down with me. Mom coached me on how to handle it best. They were racist. They asked me if I was Jewish when they hired me – and never treated me the same when I said I was. I don't need to work for a place that lowers my self-esteem. I don't need to feel untrusted, unaccepted, different, and unworthy. I deserve better.

June 27
Tracy wants to move out of his parents' house. Mom won't let the two of us stay at her place while she's in Israel. We don't know where to go. Things have gone from worse to worser. Tracy and I hit a rough patch

while he was away in Baltimore, on business. It's okay now. We saw Mom off today. I went to try on some wedding dresses.

July 2
Mom and Dad both called separately to say Tracy and I CAN stay at her apartment. It would be alright for us to move in for the summer.

What changed your mind?
Bubby.
What'd she say?
They're *already* living together – why hinder them now? But no pets. No cat, no birds.
Way to go, Bub! We moved in – and brought the cat.

July 11
I went to try on more wedding dresses. Mom called – she has laryngitis. She's sorting blankets and laundry for the army on a Kibbutz (a collective community).

July 17
I saw my doctor about my nose. I've been living with this deviated septum for about 10 years and a friend suggested I look into it. I was having trouble breathing, but it was just normal for me. The doc confirmed there *is* an infraction. He was surprised my nasal passage was allowing me to breathe okay *until* now. If I leave my nose and do nothing, as I get older it will double in size. HOLY SHIT! Like I need a *bigger* one! So, the good news is I'll finally be able to breathe properly AND get a smaller nose. Bonus.

July 28
I went bungee jumping; Tracy volunteered me. He works at the site and thought it was a great idea for me to try it. I gave in to major peer pressure. I was shaking so bad I thought I'd die. They weighed me and tied a bungee cord to my feet. My head was saying no, my body was saying yes – and I jumped. 3,2,1 – BUNGEE!! I couldn't look. I could

hear myself yelling out, *Holy shit,* on the way down. I kept my eyes closed for the first bit, and then I opened them. I was free-falling. It was intense. Nothing like it. I couldn't speak for about a half-hour after – my body was in shock. It finally wore off. I got a video tape of my jump. Proof!

Aug 23

I met with the nose doctor again. My operation is scheduled for September.

We moved everything out of the apartment yesterday, back to Tracy's parents' house. I hate not having a home. I picked Mom up from the airport. I didn't recognize her – she was wearing a wig. She told me stories of the army, bomb scares and being sick. She said the boys miss me. Big whoop.

Sept 10

Mom told me with all the life experience I've had, it has enhanced my beauty. Other people would have laid down and died – I dealt with it and am a better person for it. She shared that Kyle has become a quiet person. He's going through hell. Good. Let him suffer. If *I* have to live with it for the rest of my life – he should too.

Sept 14

Rikki came to town to visit. I told her the full extent of Levi and Kyle. She was blown away. It was quite different from the few instances she knew of at 13. She touched my arm and thanked me for telling her. I asked her not to tell anyone else. She agreed that it's private. I feel like I've come full circle in telling **_her_** the *entire* story.
She also told me that I looked great, and I'll never need to diet. While I didn't actually believe her, it was nice to hear.

Tracy told me we have to come up with $1280 in two days or else they will take away his truck and my $5000 GIC. They'll be sending collectors if it's not received by Monday.

We need a big break.

Sept 23
My nose job is today. I got to the operating room, and they couldn't get the IV line in right. I don't remember anything after that. When I first woke up in recovery, I had a sense of claustrophobia, wanting to get the cast off my nose. I couldn't breathe. I think they put something in my eyes – Vaseline. Blurry and burning! The first thing I saw when I got back to my room was Mom. I slept most of the day. I went to the bathroom – my eyes were beginning to get bruised already. They say it will take six weeks for the bruising to go away. There was this white tape with a bridge splint on my nose. Mom stayed until 7:00 p.m. – Dad came after that; Tracy came back shortly after. He bought me a pink rose and a sweet card. I bled a lot. They had to keep changing the gauze at the tip of my nose. By the end of the day, my eyes were puffy and black and purple. I had a rough night. The nurse wouldn't give me more painkillers.

Sept 25
I'm staying at Mom's to recuperate. I think she's enjoying having me there to fuss over. She's been great. They took the packing out yesterday. It hurt like hell! My swelling is at its peak. My cheeks are huge! My nose burns. It's itchy under the cast. I'm still wobbly on my feet. Where the IV was on my left wrist is bleeding. I'm a mess. It's hard to get used to this new nose; it looks so *perky*, but I can't tell yet. It's easily *half* the size it was.

Sept 27
The swelling is almost gone. The bruising is turning less purple and more yellow. They say the third day is always the worst. I'm mostly eating soda crackers and drinking ginger ale. Pondering my nose – my face will be more "cheeky" because I don't have the *long* nose anymore. And that huge bump I had on the bridge, it's gone, they tell me! Everything will be different. It's kind of exciting! A new me!

Tracy and I move into his friend John's brother's basement suite in three days. Tracy said he got the money he needed on Sunday. He's paid everyone back. He said, It's all back to normal.

Oct 1
I'm going "home" today. Tracy picked me up and said to my mom, I'll drive carefully, I have precious cargo. It has a huge kitchen. Huge! I got a $100 check from Bub – "to cheer me up." Grocery money – we can eat!

I got my cast off. My nose IS perky! It'll be a relief when people look at me – my nose *won't* be the *first* thing they notice.

Oct 4
We made our first grocery order – a real order, like a real couple, in a real house. We have a home. This wasn't a summer residence or house-sitting. This is HOME. KD and Chef Boyardee were the *first* things I bought!

Oct 7
My first day back at work at the hotel. By the end of my shift, I was asked to go into the manager's office. I'm so sorry, Sari, didn't anybody tell you? The girl you were hired to replace is coming back.

I almost cried.

Oct 10
I got a call last night from a guy at Star Auto. He heard through the grapevine I was looking for a position as a receptionist – they happen to be looking for someone. Could I come down tomorrow at 9:30 a.m.?

I went down, was shown around, and he told me what the duties would be. He went off to talk to the receptionist – Ruby. He came back and said I have the job. I was so excited. Looks like a great group of people to work with.

Nov 2

I went wedding dress shopping again. The *first* dress I tried on was IT! Unreal. I found a great headpiece too. We decided FOR SURE we're getting married April 4. The wedding will be at 8:00 p.m. because it lands on a Saturday, Shabbat. Tracy was very okay with that. I was surprised but glad. Tracy and I went to the jeweller and I tried my ring on again. It's stunning. Tracy said as soon as he gets a job, I'll get my ring.

I'm in no rush.

Nov 10

Mom picked me up to go dress shopping for her. Only a few blocks away from home, she asks me to pull over to talk. She tells me she *never* forgets what happened to me. It affects every aspect of her life. She can't believe she allowed any of that to happen. Mom said I *should* separate the two situations – Levi and Kyle – because they're *different*. I didn't think so. At a time when I tried to get Levi to like me, or explain things to me, he *never* gave me a chance. I'm not ready to separate them. Kyle, **not once,** has apologized or asked for my forgiveness. When you have to *ask* for an apology, it's not a *real* apology anyway. They are so despicable; I just want them *out* of my life.

Nov 14

Tracy had champagne for us and announced, We're celebrating. I caught myself suddenly looking in my champagne glass for a ring. You are looking at the new assistant manager of Boston Pizza (BP)! I couldn't believe it! I was so happy for him, for us!

Dec 3

I ordered my dress and veil! Tracy told me that the owner of BP told him if he needs help with the wedding, financially, he'd be glad to help. Wow! There *are* still kind people in this world.

Dec 13

I went out with some friends; Tracy was working. Tracy's former best friend, Dennis, sees me and comes over. His first sentence is to congratulate me on the upcoming wedding and the very next thing he says is how much he hates Tracy. I'm only happy for YOU, Sari, NOT Tracy. If you're happy and you think this marriage could work, then hey, go for it. He starts bringing up all the *old* crap. Tracy would be nothing if not for Wyatt (his brother) and me. He wouldn't have got his job at the bar downtown and he would know *nothing* about volleyball. I got him his job at the golf course too.

It's mind-boggling how he distorts the FACTS. The fact is everything he just said is the other way around! Another sad attempt to sway me – he was trying to tell me Tracy was with this girl at the dance festival, when I KNOW Tracy was with ME.

There *was* a time I'd buy into Dennis's bullshit stories – I'd hung on *every* word BECAUSE he *was* Tracy's *best friend*. I know better *now*. This was his sad, last-ditch effort to break us up. He told me how miserable I was whenever Tracy was around. He'd tell me what a good friend he was to Tracy – lying for him to me. He was always undermining Tracy. I just couldn't listen to it anymore – he's just a wretched, little person trying to trash Tracy, with one last attempt to attack his character.

I said, This is water under the bridge, ancient history. Why do you have to bring it up?
Hey, I just wanted to congratulate you. If you're happy and you can hang onto him and you want to marry him, go ahead.
I said, You had a HUGE part in the breakdown of the relationship. Does any of it even matter anymore?

He kept insisting *he and I* were such good friends and that Tracy kept accusing him of trying to steal me away from him.
That's because you WERE! You STILL are!

I KNOW Tracy never accused him of doing that, but he always knew how Dennis tried to.

He said, I wanted you *so* much, but I figured, hey, you're my friend's girlfriend.
Bullshit! He was NEVER that noble. He tried things on me at every opportunity.

All I ever wanted was to *talk* to you.
Bullshit again! That's why you'd throw rocks at my bedroom window at 3:00 a.m. – on several occasions!? To *talk*?

He accused Tracy of trying to steal his girlfriend from him.
Huh? Funny, your girlfriend says nothing of the sort EVER happened. *I asked her!* She says you're a lying piece of shit.

He asked me what I'm doing with a guy like Tracy. You should be with someone like *me*.
Ya, such a good friend you are. Such a great guy. Yes, we are happy, and yes, we *are* getting married.

I looked at him with pity. It's been almost five years since he and Tracy were friends. Just a deplorable person. I stood there shaking my head when he spoke – pathetic. This time I considered the source. Dude, grow the fuck up.

Dec 24
Tracy kept asking me if I love him.
Are you testing me?
Ya, and I will be for a while. I want to make sure you won't regret marrying me.
Why would I?
Don't you have any doubts?
I *did*, but not anymore.

Tracy and I went to the Carriage House to see their facilities. It's looking good! We went to the jeweller and picked out Tracy's wedding band. I looked at my ring again.

Dec 31
New Year's at BP; Dad came too. Tracy sang "Unchained Melody" and said, This is for my fiancée – we're getting married April 4. I was tickled pink. I was so proud of him. Dad was even getting choked up.

1992

Jan 14

We started our Jewish conversion classes. Tracy's not converting but has to take the classes so we can be married by a Rabbi. We picked out our invitations. They're grey and burgundy with a frayed bottom and it opens upward. Mom got her dress; it's very elegant and flattering. Tracy's mom got us a DJ. Mom and Dad are going shopping for our engagement party. I *really* need to lose weight and get this body into shape for the honeymoon. I've *got* to do something.

Tracy and I talked about our honeymoon and I asked, How we are going to pay for it? He said, Relax. Ten times out of ten we find the money and everything works out. I know.

Jan 17

Bubby booked her ticket to come out for the engagement party. Mom told me to find an engagement dress and she'll pay for it. Very generous. We were discussing the meal for the wedding: it has to be kosher. We booked a hall for our Social – to raise some money for the wedding!

Jan 27

I had my *second* nose surgery; I'm still not breathing right. I'm doing it *now* so I can heal long before the wedding. This time feels better than the first – easier.

Jan 30

I got a letter from a collection agency – if they don't get their money by *tomorrow noon*, they will sue our parents, and *their* credit will be bad for

10 years. I couldn't believe it. In the middle of trying to make ends meet for the wedding, we need to come up with $2400. Shit. Tracy said he's getting a part-time job to help pay for my wedding ring and loan.

Can we use your GIC?
Yes, that's what we'll have to do. I'm scared for us. I was crying the whole time. Once our wedding is over – we'll have *nothing*!
That's not true. We'll still have the money from the Social.
But that'll be used for paying FOR the wedding. Someone up there doesn't want us to get ahead.
Do you trust me? Yes.
Everything will be alright.

Feb 2
Mom, Dad, Tracy, and I got together for more wedding discussions. We decided on a "kosher style" dinner. Tracy and I would buy eight to ten place settings so the kosher people wouldn't be eating off of tinfoil plates and using plastic cutlery. Mom was very pleased and relieved with that decision. We'd do anything to make her comfortable.

Feb 15
Tracy *didn't* get the loan. He said he feels so badly he's letting everyone down financially – me, my dad, and his parents. Tracy and I went to buy my engagement dress. Tracy picked it out. He has good taste. I received a letter from Rikki – she can't make it to the wedding or be my bridesmaid.

Feb 18
I asked Ruby from work to be my bridesmaid. She said she'd be honored. We sent out our invitations! I had the "implants" taken out of my nose. I can breathe!

Feb 22
Our engagement party! Aside from my flu and fever, I had a really good time! Dad was bursting with pride over Tracy and me. Mom

really went all out. She even hired a cateress to help. Mom really bothered with all the food and little touches. It was an amazing, unforgettable night. And it was so nice to have Bubby there. Mom and Dad have completely come around since Tracy and I got engaged – realizing this IS happening; so they embraced it, rather than keep fighting it.

Feb 26
Tracy and I seem to be switching roles. I used to be the one who *had* to resolve things on the spot and make myself sick with every argument. Now I'M the one who feels a need to walk away from it, cool off, get distance – and he's the one who needs to talk about things. Interesting. People tell me he seems more settled, happy, and content. We have class tonight. I gave the Rabbi his invitation.

Mar 1
My bridal shower was at Mom's friend Kerry's house! It was a very nice turnout. Beautiful, thoughtful gifts. They made me wear plates with bows taped to them on my boobs and a bow on my head. After I got home, I kept crying – that I will never get into shape for the wedding. I get fitted in *three* days. That'll be swell. Moo, moo. Tracy kept <u>insisting</u> I *wasn't* fat!

Mar 2
Tracy said, I love you, honey. I really love you. We're so lucky, we have each other. You're my soul mate. Out of the blue again he'd say I love you.
Are you going to be this great, saying all these wonderful things, ten years from now?
Of course.

Mar 4
Our monthly anniversary – four years and eleven months since we met! One month until the wedding! I had my dress fitting. It was really overwhelming. I put everything on – the dress, blusher, veil, shoes…

Mom paid for *all* of it. We went to pick up the bridesmaid dresses – they're still not in! The saleswoman said, You're getting married April 4. You'll get them by *then*. No, I want them BEFORE then. I have a matron of honor coming in from out of town. She didn't care. She said they'll be in March 31. Unreal!

Mar 8

My second bridal shower – at another friend of Mom's. A nice intimate gathering. My mom's friend said, You're *still* a skinny-minnie; I see you haven't gained *any* weight. That felt pretty great.

Mar 9

One year we've been engaged, and Toby's 1st wedding anniversary! I'm worried and crying a bit about money for the wedding. Tracy said I can still get the interest from the GIC until the GIC comes though – that's $500.

He asked this morning if I'd be upset if we *postponed* our honeymoon.

Of course, I would be! Very much! Why would we do *that*?

Financial-wise.

I don't care; we ARE going on a honeymoon! We get ONE chance to go on one.

Okay.

I got in touch with our award-winning baker friend from The Kananaskis Hotel. He said his wedding present to us will be to make our wedding cake; ANYTHING I want – he'll make. I gave him carte blanche. I trust his abilities. I gave him our wedding colors and said, Go for it!

Mar 10

Dad called. Levi is getting married. Major shock. He said he doesn't know if he can afford to go to Israel. I almost shit. I started to cry. I thought, He's upset for LEVI! His beloved son. Then he said, I will in no way jilt you guys out of the money *you* need for *your* wedding because of this. I'll pay for everything I said I would. I asked him how much he wanted to spend. I'll spend whatever is needed for the wedding. No cap or limit. Okay. I was really upset by Dad's reaction. I felt cheated. Yes, cheated. All this happiness and love that'll be poured in Levi's direction – from Mom and Dad, and others. I certainly WON'T wish him well, or acknowledge HIS impending marriage. Fuck him!

Mar 13

I went with Mom to Edmonton for the weekend for a conference on Judaism. The Rabbi heading up the conference was talking about intermarriage – what a *tragedy* it is. That it's better to be a good Jew – observant and close to God – than be happy. What a crock! He also said that if a person intermarries, they're not identifying with what it is to be Jewish. Well, that was a nice positive experience BEFORE my mixed-marriage wedding.

Mar 20

I went to the doctor for some antibiotics. I felt so awful. I was rocking myself and crying, I hurt so badly. I threw up. I didn't know what to do for myself. I took a bite of toast – and threw it up. Tracy took me to work. I didn't know how I'd function – but I was afraid for my job, so I went. They sent me home. At least they saw I tried. I've had a fever for two days.

Mar 21

Our Social is tonight! I stayed in bed most of the day. After I showered, I felt a bit better, and ate a little. What a relief it stayed down. I hadn't eaten in three days. I felt real itchy too, but it's my party so I'll give it my best shot. Around 100 people came. We made about $1150! I now have full-blown laryngitis.

Mar 26

I GOT MY RING! Tracy and I were just casually standing around, talking, and he slips it on.

What the…? I look down. Just like that, you slip it on? No fanfare? Funny.

And the bridesmaid dresses are in!

Apr 3
Toby came in on Wednesday. We had the rehearsal and then dinner at Aunty Ruth and Uncle Ruben's. I went shopping alone today. I had my hair dyed and I bought two pieces of lingerie. I had no idea what I was doing; I've NEVER bought lingerie before. Dad then drove me to get my dress. Tracy and I were like zombies all day. Exhausted. All the girls went to stay at the hotel tonight. I joined them later. We made the guest gift candies all night. Bubby gave us a check to pay for the reception.

Apr 4
MY WEDDING DAY!! I ordered room service and had a HUGE breakfast. As all us girls were leaving the hotel to get our hair done – Tracy was driving up. I hid in the gift shop until the coast was clear. He was coming to do *all* the decorating. He's so talented. I had my hair done down, but all loosely curled and pinned up at the sides. She put my headpiece in with the veil. We decorated Colleen's car with pom-poms and went for lunch. We got back to the hotel and Toby checked Tracy and me in for the honeymoon suite for tonight. I got the Rabbi to come up to the room so I could sign the *Ketubah* (marriage certificate). We had our makeup done in the room. I was not nervous **at all,** all day!! I was very calm and very content. We had *every* season today – wind, snow, rain, sun…that's April in Calgary for you.

I was half an hour late getting down to the ceremony; it was 9:00 p.m. Everyone gasped and ooh-ed and ah-ed when I walked in. Tracy instantly cried when he saw me. He cried through most of it. I didn't. I shocked myself. I thought I'D be the blubbery one – not Tracy. I was very touched by that. When we kissed under the *Chuppah* (canopy), Tracy cupped my face and said, I love you very much.

After the ceremony, everyone went to a different floor for a cocktail party while we had pictures taken. We couldn't afford a photographer, so there was no plan for pictures, but Tracy got us one at the last minute. Nice surprise. We went back downstairs and were announced into the banquet room as Mr. and Mrs. Knock.

Dinner was good – prime rib, French beans, carrots and roasted potatoes. Well, it *looked* good – I barely touched my dinner. At the table Tracy said, You'll never know how much I love you. He did a stellar job of decorating, most impressive. He had made a triple-layered and twisted burgundy-and-white heart-balloon arch for the head table, placed all the centerpieces on each table, and picked up and set all the flowers around the room.

It was sprung on me to make the toast to the groomsmen. It was a horrible speech. I was mortified. I fumbled my words; I had nothing interesting to say. I was awful. Everyone else's speeches were very touching. I didn't cry the whole time, until Dad spoke – about Tracy. He said, Tracy is a real *Mensch* (decent human being). He's like a son to me. It just felt like Tracy had *finally* been accepted into our family. Toby helped me plan our evening getaway to the bridal suite. Tracy and I danced to "Lady in Red."

Nobody believed me that my parents *were* divorced. Dad's girlfriend was at the wedding but still, it didn't seem like some huge effort between my parents; they seemed at ease. They *even* danced together. Ruby caught my wrist corsage – I'm keeping my bouquet. John caught the garter. Since it was a late start to the wedding, there was barely any time left for dancing. They gave us an extra hour. Wow, how gracious. By 3:00 a.m., Toby helped me get up to my room and change. When the time was right, Toby's husband told Tracy, You're *not* going out with the rest of us (back to our house), then stuffed him in the elevator, threw a room key at him and walked off. I was waiting for him – with champagne and wearing burgundy lingerie.

Apr 5

We went for our complimentary breakfast, then went home and
packed. We still had *no* idea WHERE we were going to go for our
honeymoon. It felt wild and spontaneous and a little nerve-racking. We
opened our wedding checks. Tracy said, We're piss poor, but we're
living off love. Aw. Dad drove us to a travel agent. We said to the
agent, *This* is how much money we have – *you* tell *us* where the seat
sales are going to. So, we went to Vegas, baby!

Apr 28

Tracy got another full-time job, so he has *two* full-time jobs now. He
will work at the bungee site from 12:00 p.m. to 7:00 p.m., and then BP
until 3:30 a.m. He'll sleep in between. I've been scoping out part-time
work too. We'll make it work.

Apr 30

I was fired today from Star Auto. They gave me a whole load of crap
about me not being able to handle the workload and other bullshit. I
KNOW the *real* reason they let me go. Let's just say the girl who replaced me DOESN'T know how to type, and *she's* the new receptionist.
I bought a newspaper and have an interview tomorrow.

May 26

Our phone has been disconnected. I had to go to a phone booth to call
one of the interviewers. Do you want the job? YES! Come in tomorrow
at 8:00 a.m. YEEHAW! Tracy told me he had borrowed the money from
his BP boss to pay for my ring. I never knew.

MARRIED LIFE

You hear stories about when the ring gets put on that finger, *everything* changes. Yet life feels the same as it did *before* we were married. In a good way. And everyone wants to see *the* ring. I'm loving having a new last name; I get a kick out of it. I keep recalling how well the wedding went. All the planning it took, and it turned out so well. The two weeks we took off for our honeymoon in Vegas were sublime.

Tracy is very attentive, thoughtful, and loving. He calls me to tell me he loves me, takes me for date lunches and date nights (the drive-in is our favorite), he leaves me flowers in the kitchen to find when I wake up in the morning, and leaves me love notes all the time. I'm feeling very loved by Tracy, with the way he talks to me and shows his love for me. We enjoy long talks about everything and nothing, just taking pleasure in each other's company. It's those quiet moments where we don't have to say a word and we know how the other feels.

One night at the end of July, Tracy came home late from work and said, I love you. I waited all night to tell you that. I thought about you every minute of the night. Things are just getting better and better between us. We had a great discussion about having kids. Tracy said he'll stay home and take care of them while I go to school. Suits me! But we also agreed neither of us are ready for them yet.

I started a new job as a customer service manager at a car dealership. I'm happy there and they are happy with my work, continually giving me new projects and responsibilities. Tracy and I worked through the summer, but found many opportunities to take advantage of the beautiful hot weather with BBQs and patio dates. Tracy sent two dozen roses to my work for me on my birthday. I'm spoiled.

Sept 12

I went bungee jumping for the second time. I screamed only *twice*. I'm fatter than I've ever been. I'm madly trying to exercise and get rid of it. I've never weighed this much in my whole entire life (120 lb. almost). I weighed myself on Tracy's bungee scale – 125 lb.! AS IF!! On our home scale – 120 lb. I THINK NOT!! There is no reason why I would've gained 10 to 15 lb. in a few months. At the wedding time, I was between 110 and 115 lb. This is ludicrous. Starvation tactics seem to be in order. I've been between 108 and 110 lb. all my life. This can't be happening. Tracy told me the bungee scale is 10 lb. *over* the normal. Thank God!

Sept 18

I had a wonderful long talk with Mom after dinner; I was there until 1:30 a.m. She was telling me how much she admires and respects me, how proud she is of me, of what I've made of my life since disclosing, and how I've coped and moved on, and am *not* depressed. I'm married, happy; I have a *husband* who loves me and whom I love. How mature I am. The reason why I've felt so *old* since I'm 18 is that I lost my youth. I had to grow up *fast*. *No wonder* I feel old. It had to affect me in *some* way. It took its toll. We talked about how offenders (who've been abused themselves) don't have the capacity to put themselves into the shoes of their victims and remember what it felt like for them when *they* were a victim. We don't know if Kyle was or not. Mom believes he *wasn't*.

She said, Do you think you could've handled this job you're in two years ago? You couldn't focus. You've gotten better jobs as you've felt ready for them. She was amazed how I settled right into marriage with such ease. She said, Thank God you have Tracy. We talked about how everything from these past few years was *necessary* for the healing. Mom separating from Dad was necessary for me to go through – the pain, to deal with that, so I COULD deal with something *bigger*. Them getting back together was important too because I needed them *both* there for me, to parent me. It wouldn't have worked as well for me had they been apart. Everything happens for a reason. Mom said she has enjoyed watching me grow up and become the person I am. I told Mom, Sometimes I get a kick out people trying to figure me out – and some think they *have*. That makes me laugh. What if I HAD talked about all this back then – while *they* were still living at home? I would've been forced to see them every day. Mom said she would've been so busy punishing Kyle that they would've forgotten about MY needs. I would've felt responsible for the breakup of the family. Levi would've hated me *more* than he already did. I needed to know Mom and Dad didn't split BECAUSE of me. But I *know* they divorced for *other* reasons. Everything happened in its right time.

Sept 19

Owen (a groomsman) had suggested to Tracy that he and I consider moving out to Kelowna – where *he* just moved. The possibility of moving there would be amazing. I tried those Dexatrim pills this morning – I took six and worked out twice. At Mom's for dinner, there were questions from the guests: Do you miss your brothers? Do you keep in touch with them? Will you ever see them? I'm aware that people *not in the know* will always inquire about them. I just hate it. It gets awkward. I *try* to hide my contempt for them.

Oct 7

We met with Owen and his girlfriend, Penny. She said we HAVE TO move out there. They have a handyman business and will get Tracy in there. They make good money. She said she and I will become good friends and we'll all get a house together. It sounds like an adventure.

Oct 15

I took two Dexatrim yesterday morning. I got a call from a collection agency – we owe almost $1000 *immediately.* SHIT! No amount of pouting or feeling sorry for myself will get the bills paid faster. Better things are out there for us – I know it. I went out for dinner with friends. The guy asked me if I was being polite at dinner by eating like a bird or do I have an appetite? My friend said, Look at her! That felt nice. I haven't heard a "thin" remark in a while.

Oct 23

Tracy and I are going to visit Kelowna and see what's up there. We took Slinky with us; he's an amazing traveler, so calm and content.

Oct 30

I went to Mom's for dinner. All day I was very anxious about telling her and what her reaction would be. After dinner I finally say, There's something I have to tell you. I've been trying to find a way to tell you.
She looked concerned. I know you've wanted to tell me *something*.
It's nothing bad...Tracy and I are moving to Kelowna.
She momentarily looked stunned. How did this come about? I told her the story.

When do you leave?
Tracy's probably giving his notice *today*, so he'll be out there in two weeks. I won't be going out for another month. So, what do you think?
I couldn't bear not living in the same city as you. But now that you've told me, I feel *relieved*. I always knew YOU'D have to be the one to leave *first*. The two people in the world I've always felt responsible for is you and Bub. Bub now has Ralph and now you tell me you're moving. It's such a huge relief.
I hesitated and wondered how I was going to tell you. Now that I have – this isn't the reaction I was expecting.
Me either; I really surprised myself. She was so calm. She said, Now I can pursue the things I've wanted to but didn't because I couldn't leave you.

By me leaving, it basically gave her "permission" to leave too and carry on with *her* dreams for *her* future. She said she feels this is the best thing that could've happened – for both of us. A fresh start for Tracy and me. I feel good about it. I *know* we can do well there.

Tracy told his bosses; they were going to promote him to general manager in November.

Do you *regret* giving notice?
No, we're *still* leaving.

He could've made real good money; I have a solid job...but we're going away to do even *better*!

Nov 5
A good friend Tracy grew up with killed himself, with a gun, out in a field. He had a lot of problems, but no one realized until it was too late. He must have felt so desperate and alone. Tracy was devastated. They were super close in school. I've never experienced a friend committing suicide, and I could tell this was hitting Tracy hard. He let me be there for him as I listened to him tell me stories about his dear friend.

I told Dad we were moving. He was sad, but he said he'll be spending a lot of time out there with us and that he'll help us move out there too, since he owns a large truck.

Nov 16
Tracy left for Kelowna. He said, If I can get you out there earlier, I will. He has to find us a place to live first. He called at 2:00 a.m. to say he got there safe and sound.

Nov 20
Mom called. Levi's wife, Maria, is pregnant. I'm going to be an aunt. I thought of writing him a letter. Then, I remembered all the reasons why I shouldn't. According to him, Tracy does not exist. He is a non-person. I cried. Mom said Maria asks tons of questions about me and *does* hope to meet me. She thinks I'm beautiful. Mom said *they* will

NEVER accept Tracy. They'll accept my *children* because they'll be Jewish. I'm *not* looking for their blessing. Mom said, Tracy's good for you and to you, I'll never deny that. I'm your mother; therefore, I can accept and acknowledge Tracy. I said, They're hypocrites. Kyle and Tracy were *friends* when we were dating, now he's religious so Tracy is unacceptable? Screw that.

I remember when Levi came to visit once, when Tracy and I were first dating, he was trying to seemingly be a "protective older brother" and decided to grill Tracy regarding his intentions toward me. So, he asked him, What's your definition of *love*?
Tracy said, It means caring, sharing, and being with the one you love. All Levi responded with was, that sounds like a dog. He was so confrontational, arrogant, had a holier-than-thou attitude, and basically was being an asshole.
Mom came in to see how we were doing after our chat. Tracy said, Can I ask you a question? What's your definition of love?
She answered verbatim what Tracy had just expressed.
Tracy said matter-of-factly, That sounds like a dog. That's what your son just said to me when I answered exactly how *you* did.
She wasn't impressed (with her son).

Nov 24
Tracy found a house, so I gave notice at work. We get the house December 1. No pets are allowed. Why did you agree to this house then – that's pretty major! Besides our cat Slinky, we have a cockatiel named Babe.

Everything will work out – isn't that what I always tell you? Ya. I called the courier company to see where our boxes were – our boxes went to Montreal. I had a fit. I hope this is *not* a sign of what's to come.

Dec 1

Tracy finally received the boxes. Owen and Penny moved into the house today. Penny told me that Tracy is lost without me. He's lonely and unsettled. He misses YOU.

1993

Jan 3

Well, I'm moved out to Kelowna. There's lots of tension between us and Owen and Penny. We're off to a good start. Owen keeps making fat jokes about me, then· says he's kidding. I said, It's a very touchy subject with me. Slinky and Babe are staying with my friend Janis for now; she's living in Penticton. I sent a bunch of résumés out – I have two possibilities. The handyman biz is slow, so within two days Tracy got a job at a pub, and went from bartender to general manager! Owen will work there too. We celebrated.

Jan 6

I have a cold. Janis can no longer look after Slinky. She and her boyfriend, Deacon, came over to bring him back and we went to Tracy's pub to eat and hang out. We were talking about the sauce on the wings and the hockey game that was on TV when suddenly, without notice, Deacon yells at Janis, You're really fucking pissing me off so you better shut your fucking mouth! I was speechless. Stunned. He'd just managed to belittle and humiliate Janis for NO reason! I sat there wanting to say something but couldn't. Janis looked like she was going to cry. She started talking about anything – and I thought that was the end of it. I was still in shock from the outburst. It was a totally unprovoked attack. Some time passed, then Deacon grabbed his coat and said, I'm leaving. Janis pleaded, Can you please tell me what's wrong? I'll tell you what's wrong – your friend here (me) is a complete asshole, she's boring as all hell, her friends are boring – your boyfriend (Tracy) is okay though. I said, Ya, and you're a real gem. He got right in my face, calling me every name in the book. I said, You have no right to talk to me that way! He ranted on. I felt sick.

I was trying so hard to grasp what had just happened. What did ANYONE do? What the hell just happened here?! Janis asked him if she could get a ride with him. He stated, This bus is leaving NOW! Come now or don't come at all. They left. I was stunned.

Tracy had missed it *all*. He was in his office when this took place. He asked me what happened. I told him. I was crying now. It really shook me up. There is something terribly wrong with this guy. He's very sick. I was racking my brain trying to figure out what I'd done wrong, actually *believing* I provoked him somehow. Tracy said, It's not you. I said, it's just that I've never had anyone in my entire life talk to me that way. Tracy put his arms around me and we went home.

Penny called Janis for me, to make sure she got home okay. She said she was fine. She was crying and apologizing. You have nothing to apologize for. Did he give you any reasons for the way he behaved tonight? Ya, but not very good ones. This is what he does. I think he came into the room, so she said goodbye in a very small voice. Everyone thinks she'll for sure leave him. We had all been saying how it's great Janis finally met someone *decent*. Looks sure can be deceiving.

Jan 10
Mom and Dad called. They are thinking about bringing Levi, Kyle, Levi's wife, and the baby out for the summer to Calgary. What do you think? I cried. I need time to think.

Jan 12
I'm tired of hiding Slinky every time the landlord comes over. Owen and Penny said we should get rid of the cat – bring him to the SPCA. Apparently, we are putting their living there in jeopardy with having Slinky there. I said to Tracy, Time to go house-hunting, eh? He agreed. We'd sooner move than give away our child! Later, Penny asked if we'd found a place for the cat yet, telling me how they feel betrayed, disrespected…I said I'd just as soon pack and move to keep my cat with me. I'm not going to get rid of Slinky to make YOU happy. Penny

called Tracy stupid for signing a contract on a house that doesn't allow pets. She said, We're friends, I'm not trying to come down on you, *but* if the cat isn't gone by the end of the month, we're giving our notice. Then you'll live in your house and we'll live in ours. FINE. I asked Tracy if we can write up a new contract so we can leave and they can stay. Of course. Unreal. All they do is fight, and bang doors, and yell at each other.

Jan 22

I looked in the paper for another place. Apparently, Owen is going to propose to Penny on Valentine's Day. A match made in hell. We NEED to move. I called a therapist. I'm on a waiting list. I feel the need VERY much to seek more therapy.

Janis said Deacon has actually felt bad for the way he treated me, but he still dislikes me. News flash: we don't want to be friends with you either!

Owen pretty much ignores me. He used to be a real nice guy – then he met HER. I don't trust him anymore. Penny makes up stories and lies…fuck 'em both!

Jan 28

I don't have anyone to talk to who understands what it's like to go through what I did. I told Tracy I need more therapy. My heart wants to be intimate, but my head blocks it out. I want to overcome my problems – for both of us. I'm tired of feeling this way. He said, If you need me to be there in therapy with you, I'll definitely be there. I was touched by that offer. Tracy said, You're my best friend; we're in this together.

Jan 31

The pipes in the house froze. According to the landlord, it's OUR fault and it's *not* his problem. Huh? Owen thinks we're going to get an eviction notice tomorrow. We hashed everything out over the cat again, how we've put them in a bind, and how WE'VE ruined a wonderful friendship. Tracy said to them, If you had YOUR way, we'd be putting our cat to sleep. No, just give him *away*. Penny said, I *could've* told the landlord you have a cat, but I didn't. Clap. Clap. Clap. Well, bravo for you. Here's a fucking medal. Tracy and I are looking at a house tomorrow. I said to Tracy, We're taking it, *regardless* of what it looks like! I can't live this way – Penny is still not talking to me.

Tracy has been bringing the cat to work – the landlord is supposed to be by to fix the pipes.

Feb 3
Owen and I talked. I asked him what his problem is. You've been ignoring me. Everyone has their problems, but you *don't* ignore people. He eventually apologized for treating me that way. That's all I wanted to hear.

I don't take well to being ignored. Ignoring me pushes *every* button I have. Being ignored from eight years old on changes your psyche. When it happens again, even as an adult, there is an immediate physical and mental reaction. You go from zero to livid in milliseconds. And the mind goes a mile a minute trying to figure it out.

He told me he proposed to Penny on Feb 1. I was the *first* person he told; not even Tracy knows. I got a job working at The Grand Hotel. The therapy place called – I have an appointment next Thursday!

Feb 15
Penny was telling me about her friend who was sexually abused: I can't believe how NORMAL she is. She has a job and a husband, but I don't know *how* she copes. How can you *ever* deal with that?
I turned out okay.
What do you mean?
It happened to ME, and I'M a functioning person.
Are you serious? Oh my God! She was stunned.

Never judge a book by its cover.

Ya, I guess sometimes I *can* say it for the shock value. Sometimes you just need to shut people up.

Deacon told Janis that he doesn't want to live together anymore. She asked if she and Babe could move in with *us*. Sure, anytime is fine. I started therapy. Yippee!

Mar 8
I found a house. Our douchebag landlord gave us a shitty reference. He told the guy we *never* pay rent on time. BULLSHIT! We can prove we do! We've been on time, *every* time, for our rent. Other bills, no; but our rent, yes. Nope, the house fell through – he won't even give us a *chance* to prove we *are* trustworthy tenants. They can suck my ass!

Mar 16
I talked to Tracy about my therapy. What exactly did Kyle do to you? I guess I'd never really spelled it out for anyone. I couldn't look at Tracy while I told him. Tracy pulled me close and snuggled me. I bawled like a little baby. Deep sobs. It all came gushing out. I'm mad at Kyle! I can't believe he could do this to me! I thought I was past the anger. Guess not. I asked, What do you think of me now that I've told you? I don't think any less of you, if that's what you mean? I needed to hear that.

I got laid off from The Grand Hotel. It's been way too slow.

Mar 22
I have therapy at 9:00 a.m. We talked about forgiveness and how all this is affecting Mom and Dad. I said, I feel uncomfortable around children. My therapist said I probably resent them. You look at them and think, I want that innocence. I lost my childhood. I look at them at the age I was when it all began. I shocked Mom by telling her things *began* while we lived in Montreal – not Calgary, like everyone believed. It became full blown in Calgary. In Montreal, it was more curiosity,

pushing the envelope and being inappropriate. It was bad enough. Then in Calgary ... My therapist suggested I get *The Courage to Heal Workbook*.

Apr 2

The landlord popped in with an eviction notice. We have ten days to get out. We have nowhere to go. At least Owen's being evicted too! And it has *zero* to do with our cat! I think I'm feeling a bit overwhelmed. In the span of a few weeks: two friends are pregnant, one is suicidal, Tracy lost his job, I got laid off, I disclosed everything about Kyle to Tracy, and an eviction notice. Janis told me I *deserved* what I got from Deacon. UNFUCKING BELIEVABLE! She says that I make people unwelcome in my home. I suppose letting people – herself included – crash at our house when they have nowhere else to go is *unwelcoming*? When we have even *less* than others, and STILL give? I'm angry. I feel like punching things all the time. I don't. I'm spread way too thin. I don't judge people, but I get crapped on all the time. Janis's changing before my eyes. She *agreed* Deacon was unstable – *now* she believes his demented outburst was *justified*? This person, who's been my best friend since I was 13, pretends she doesn't know the person I am. I've given her a home, found her a job, I drive her *everywhere*, buy her food…fucking ingrate! She can't think these things of me and expect to *stay* under *my* roof. I feel so used and backstabbed.

Apr 20

I had to write an analysis of myself in group therapy.

She seems meekish. Very aware of what's going on around her. Very serious facial expressions. Big eyes. Ears open. Wide-eyed. Rigid. Stiff body. Aware of what others think, perceive her body.

It's always dark. Hearing noises. EVERY single sound in the house is heard by her. Blanket up to her face. Feels vulnerable. Blanket way up high. Knuckles. Tight grip. Feisty. Fear. Fear. Light beam downstairs. Waiting.

Very awake. Trying not to sleep. CAN'T sleep. Dark, but can see clearly. Very clear. Shadow. Always a shadow. Kicking, pulling, fear, vulnerable. It's time. Lying. Needs a book. Returning a book. Crouching behind the bed. She has to keep her eyes closed, but she sees it all.

Stench. That smell that always accompanies it. ALWAYS! Want to kick him across the room into the closet. Doesn't. Wants to scream out to Mom and Dad. Wants someone to wake up, to know what's going on once and for all. Save me! Save her. Protect us.

She struggles to keep the blankets tight. He's too strong. He wins every time. She tries, she really does. Every muscle, tense. Trying to fight it all the way.

Uncleanliness. She must wash off the evidence. Get rid of the smell. Get rid of the fact it ever happened. Dirty. Shameful. Disgust. Anger.

Nothing ever happened. Best pals. Friends. No one will ever know. Forget. The past. Finished until next time. Done – until tomorrow night.

Apr 25

No wonder I hate sex. I hate everything about it. I've never had control over my own body. Kyle subjected me to more than I care to remember. I was bombarded in a zillion ways with sex. No escape. So young. Even when he'd *babysit* me. It was year after year of abuse. I often thought he was a kid himself – he didn't know what he was doing. Tracy assured me, Oh, he knew.

Apr 30

My old boss from The Grand was in a car accident. He lost his arm, has 66 stitches in his face, a crushed lip, and is on life support. He was driving drunk. Another girl I work with was killed a few days ago – by a 74-year-old drunk driver. She was 18. Shitty things sure happen to people in this town.

May 2

Tracy and I got a puppy – we named her Ebony! She's a Spaniel Lab, six and a half weeks old. We moved into our new house and *didn't* give Owen and Penny our forwarding address. The house is a dream; it's in a cul-de-sac, on a hill and overlooks the Okanagan lake. We have 10 fruit trees on our football-field-size backyard. We have grape vines growing along the patio railing. There is a massive garden that grows potatoes and cucumbers. Every *color* rose grows there. It's peaceful. THIS is how I imagined living in Kelowna. The Quails' Gate winery is two blocks from our house.

I started a new job at a car dealership. There's so much to know – it's overwhelming. Tracy has been scoping out sights for our new boat rental business. Roger, a friend from Calgary, moved in with us temporarily. He's *supposed to be* a "silent" partner, but it's not looking that way.

May 27

We finalized a location for the business. Janis mentioned to me how funny it is *I'm* gaining weight and *she's* losing. Ya, pretty funny. She's *back* with Deacon. I accept people without judging – but I'm only human. Where is anyone when *I* need them? I get screwed every time! You'd think I'd learn. I think I give too much of myself. My friends from Calgary don't write or call. NO MORE. I need to take a stand and quit being such a doormat! I spoke to Mom – she suggested Levi and the gang come out HERE, **_to Kelowna_**, during the summer for a few days. Um, I don't think so! NOT EVER! *I* will *leave* if they come here!

The bank repossessed our truck. The paychecks Tracy was getting from the pub were bouncing – our loan came out of those payments. Tracy said, this place is going to bury us.

Tracy and I were out on the lake yesterday and we got stuck in our boat; the fan belt blew. A storm was coming in and we were in the middle of Okanagan Lake. It was scary. We had *one* oar – Tracy paddled once or twice with it, to no avail. So, he threw it *into* the lake. We just sat there. Then off in the distance we see a large boat. It gets closer. We're being saved by a YACHT! We boarded them, they tied our boat to theirs and we were brought to shore. They were very hospitable. Now THAT'S the way to be rescued!

June 2

I am fucking invisible. Is anyone out there? I feel so alone. Deserted. When is enough, enough?! I can't take much more of Janis living with us. Tracy believes she'll be out real soon. Not soon enough. I need a break. I keep going for drives. That's not like me. She has tainted our sanctuary. I feel like punching things, hitting something. My mental health is on the line. I've been doing an awful lot of crying. I doubt the progress I *know* I've made. This depression doesn't feel like its lifting. I have this constant need to run away. I am fading away.

June 6

We opened our Sunvalley Boat Rentals business! We have wave-runners, ski boats, canoes, wetsuits, and skis. This is going to be so great!

June 15

Group therapy ends today. My inner child is coming out in *full* force. I now have the resources I didn't as a child. When I wanted to run, hide, or escape – I couldn't. Now I can do something about it when I feel that way. I'm very needy now. I'm doing the best I can to help myself. This has been so hard. Some people don't deal with it at all. I have to relive all the pain, shame, fear, and anger I experienced as a child. I have to go through it all over again so I can get better.
Janis broke up with Deacon. I don't think I give a shit anymore.

June 21

I wasn't feeling well at work. My stomach hurt; it was achy and painful. I told them I *had* to leave. They told me to go to the clinic. I did. They examined me and said I have to go to Emergency ASAP. They took me by ambulance to the hospital and I went for tests. When I was coming back from X-rays, Tracy was at my bedside. He thought I was dead. I hadn't called him to tell him I'd left work, and on a hunch, he called the hospital to see if I was there. Yes, she is here. He said, *Never do that again; I was so scared.* They wanted to operate – they think I had appendicitis. They gave me some liquid Gravol and let me be for a while. The tests came back showing I did NOT have appendicitis. Unreal. They didn't know what the problem was; maybe it was just a virus. They are sending me for an ultrasound next week.

July 10

I lost my voice. Literally, not figuratively. All clear on the ultrasound. Owen seems to have set up a Jet Ski rental business just down the beach from us. Jackass!

Our hydro got disconnected a couple of days ago. I paid them. I wanted to buy a car from my dealership – a New Yorker. I was talking to Tracy about it – they won't let us do a monthly payment plan. I can't get the car then. Roger whips out his personal check book and writes a check for the full amount. I couldn't believe it.

July 18

There was an accident at the boat site. Two girls Tracy works with crashed their wave-runners. Pieces of the wave-runner were imbedded in one girl's leg. The police and ambulance were there. Two wave-runners are out of commission now. One girl needed surgery, but will fully recover. We couldn't have felt more terrible about the accident. We never wanted anyone to ever get hurt by our business.

July 25

I went tubing on a friend's boat; he is a paramedic. It flipped. Everyone thought I had snapped my neck. I hit my knee to my head. Everyone said I flipped two to three times, then snapped my neck back. I was lifted onto the boat, where I rested for a bit. I was okay. I was very lucky it wasn't worse.

Aug 10

Mom called. Levi's wife gets on the phone. They are in Calgary. She said she would have really liked to have met me. Then who should get on the phone? LEVI! It freaked me out! We did the one thing I never wanted to do, and that was make small talk. There were big lulls in the conversation. The whole while I'm going, Fuck, shit, this isn't happening! Maria stayed on the phone the whole time. He said, I was hoping you'd come in for a visit so we could have a heart-to-heart and really sit down and talk. I said I didn't think that was possible. Maybe you'll come to Israel? I doubt it. Mom got on the phone. I told her I was NOT prepared for that! I tried to absorb the conversation afterward. I didn't feel much except that I didn't want to talk to him, and I had a huge knot in my stomach. I wonder what he's told his wife about all this – me. I hadn't spoken to him in three years, and before that another few.

Aug 12

Our phone was disconnected – I had it reconnected today. Roger is accusing Tracy of stealing *all* the money from the long weekend. Un-fucking-real! ROGER spends ALL the money. He drinks and smokes ALL the profits away. Then, in a moment of sobriety, he believes *Tracy* spent the money. Unbelievable. Tracy doesn't even get a salary from it. He works his ass off all day at the lake, and then works his night job.

I started a part-time hostessing job at a pub.

Sept 29

In therapy, we talked about children. I said, I look at a friend's daughter, who is eight, the age I was, but she seems more like a baby – so innocent; I seemed much older. My therapist said, No wonder your trust is shot! You trusted a brother who couldn't be trusted. How does an eight-year-old analyze that!? At a point in your life when you're beginning to develop your sense of the world, it all screws up on you. I said, I felt I never had a childhood, that's why I have a low tolerance for people who do childish things. I can't get into the headspace of a child. When kids do silly things, it's like f——g grow up, use your common sense! I want them to grow up *fast* – like I did, to not be a kid anymore. I can relate to them as an adult. My therapist said, at eight, nine, ten…you were forever analyzing. You were always figuring out ways you'll survive the night…instead of thinking about what children think about. You developed an adult mind. She asked me why I thought I didn't "tell" sooner. My mom and I have discussed it, and we feel that many years ago, I knew my parents didn't have the tools to help me cope with something of that magnitude. On some level I knew they wouldn't know what to do. Timing is everything. They were better prepared to handle it when I DID tell them. They suggested therapy right away. They supported me 110%. They sold the family trailer and used that money to send me to therapy.

Sept 30
I told Tracy I need to quit the hostessing job. I'm not cut out for that scene. I can't handle the come-ons, and defending that I AM a *happily* married woman. We need the extra money, but I'll do something *else*. He doesn't feel I was in the right environment either. Being *there* while working on the abuse – the two just don't mix.

Oct 4
They shut our gas off – $400 to reconnect. Tracy went down and got it all reconnected – we have heat and hot water again! Janis announced that she was moving out because she needs to be on her own. She thought we'd be mad. We're not mad – we want you to be happy, do what you gotta do for you.

Roger picked up the wave-runners to winterize them.

Oct 21
Roger broke into our house and stole *everything* from the business. He stole the wet suits, cash box, checkbook, files, life jackets, gas cans, oil, signs, and skis – GONE. I was horrified. Tracy put a freeze on the business bank account. Roger tried to unfreeze it. When Tracy saw him, he admitted to stealing everything.

Tracy called his lawyer. His advice: call the cops. We changed our phone number and the locks. Roger came by the house later in the evening to intimidate *me*. Make sure Tracy calls me, or there will be hell! He shows up AGAIN. Tracy was home this time. He demanded Tracy go down to the bank with him tomorrow so he can get HIS money. He said he came for the checkbook and receipt book. I'll pick you up in the morning and we'll go to the bank and it'll be over. We'll call it even. *He* did something wrong, no wonder he wants it over – and he *will* get nailed for it. I thought he was going to hit Tracy. He was fuming. He said he'll file a case against Tracy. Tracy told him to stick around because the cops were on their way. Roger was drunk and had drugs on him – as if he'd stick around.

The police called a half-hour later – they said they were going to get in touch with Roger. Tracy gave them his address and number in Calgary, his girlfriend's number, and said he could be found *now* at the bar. The officer said he'll catch up with him *tomorrow* because he'd rather not confront someone who's inebriated.

Oct 22

Roger called me *four times* at work. I said, Breaking and entering, threatening, harassing – they aren't very becoming of you. Stick to what you know – getting drunk. Tracy knows where to get in touch with you – at the bar. Don't call me here again.

He *shows up*. He had *just* come from seeing Tracy. He's frantic. He says he can't find Tracy. I better get him to call him, OR ELSE! Has his drunken mind deluded him AGAIN? He JUST <u>saw</u> Tracy and tells me he can't reach him. UN-REAL! Pathetic.

Oct 23

Roger called Tracy's *dad* to say he's suing Tracy. Tracy's not worried – as he shouldn't be. Tracy's done nothing wrong. Roger's the one who broke the law. And the money in the account that he wants so badly – it's a GST rebate. It's Tracy's money too. He's such a coward. He always saw the business as a way for Tracy to work his ass off, and for him to reap the rewards. He'd always make Tracy *hand over* the day's earnings – then head straight for the bar. *Every* day. He won't get away with this.

Oct 27
Roger showed up at my work again. He asked my boss for the bill of sale for my car. He was waiting outside for me, smirking. He said he's putting a lien on the car and asked me where the car is.

I went to do work banking and I called Tracy. I called work first before going back. They tell me Roger's *still* there, he's not leaving. He says he won't leave until he talks to the owner. Nowhere on the bill of sale does it have Roger or the business' name. *It's in Tracy's name.* It's OUR car. I went back to the main building and crept around the corner to see if he was still there. He was in the owner's office with the door shut. He comes out.

Where's the car?
I'm not telling you.

My boss wouldn't give him the info. He even told him he *can't* put a lien on the car. Tracy shows up. I hate that Roger has involved all the people I work with. I was told to get a restraining order – he's basically stalking me. I broke down in front of everyone at work. I can't take this anymore. He can't keep getting away with this.

Oct 28
We transferred the car into MY name. There is absolutely no way he can touch the car now. I don't think we'll make rent this month. Roger was always *supposed* to pay rent – he *never* did. People always said they'd never leave us in a bind; but when it comes down to it, people look out for themselves, which is what WE should be doing. Kelowna was supposed to be a fresh start for us. It has been nothing but shit. We have to sell the New Yorker. We need the money. We'll use the money

to pay the rest of the loan from Calgary and be done with it. Tracy said he's going to get a 9-to-5 job. The waitering job isn't cutting it. He'll keep it for the *extra* hours, though.

Nov 3

I was called into my boss's office. We're going to have to let you go. We hired a senior accountant and have to make room for her. You being the low man on the totem pole, I'm afraid you have to leave. They gave me a two-week check and my separation slip. You don't have to come in again; this'll be your last day. I told Tracy – good news, we have rent money! Tracy and I are able to laugh about it. It's really not surprising anymore. These things are happening for a reason.

Nov 12

Tracy got a letter from his mom – court papers have been served to his dad. We have until the end of the month to pay up. Tracy called our bank for help. It turns out they've *already* sued Tracy's dad for the remainder of our loan. Tracy's dad paid it out this afternoon. Mom deposited $500 in our account. She can't afford that! So, because his old boss bounced his paychecks, we are in this horrible situation with the loan. Man.

Nov 23

I'm told I have posttraumatic stress disorder (PTSD). I feel like I have it in me to become an alcoholic and druggie. If I didn't have Tracy, I'm afraid I could drink myself into oblivion. But something stops me each time I want to go there. I'm afraid of what I might do. I *could be* the addictive type. I *want* to feel out of control and reckless. I just want to stop dealing with everything.

We sold our car in the auction and moved into our new place – the main floor of a house. This is our third move in Kelowna.

*December included going to Calgary to visit, and to have my **third** nose surgery, on December 31. We went back to Kelowna two days later. Bubby moved from Montreal to Calgary, to live with Mom.*

1994

Jan 17

My therapist recommended I see this sexual abuse specialist. The treatment will desensitize me. It's described as a rapid eye movement therapy (EMDR). You follow the therapist's fingers as she moves them quickly from right to left, activating part of the brain that releases traumatic experiences on a neurological level. All I've wanted was to not have all this be *right there* – all the time. I know no other way. This has been my life. I will be relieved to not have to carry the burden, the memories and the *freshness* of it. Please let this work.

Jan 24

I started a new support group. I talked about being so negative – how hard it is to be positive. I was comparing my abuse to others. I minimize and deny mine ever happened. If I keep myself busy with *other* people's problems, I don't have to deal with *mine*. I feel alone and raw. One lady said she'd rather her daughter had been raped by a *stranger* than have been molested by *someone she trusts*.

Jan 26

It's my first visit with the specialist. She needed background on my childhood, of course. I never really realized the impact Levi had on my life. How his everyday putdowns, accusations, resentment, bullying … most definitely DID affect me! She said he was acting out *his* aggressions on me – the littlest one of the family, the youngest and a girl.

I researched sexual abuse. Things that can result from the abuse: sexual disorders, withdrawal, poor body image, suicide, low self-esteem, eating disorders, unwanted or intrusive thoughts, body memories, and triggers.

Check.

Jan 28

I had my *regular* therapy. I'm not comfortable sharing in group. A wall goes up when I try to talk about myself. I get a kick out of people thinking they know me but really *don't*. I need to be approached *first* – *then* I'll talk your ear off.

Tracy and I had lunch with some people who have a possible restaurant business offer for us (our partner would be Damian if this goes through). They will put in the money, but would like Tracy's people skills and business know-how to help run the place – it would be a 50/50 partnership. But Tracy *doesn't* have to put any money in. Okay! Let's try *this*.

Feb 2

I met with the specialist again. Pretty deep stuff. She said I will need two more sessions with her. She told me my parents weren't parenting. She finds it hard to believe they *didn't* know what was going on. I assured her they had no clue. In a *visualizing* exercise, she said, now take the little girl *out* of the bedroom. I thought, That's *all* I ever wanted, for someone to take me *out* of that godforsaken bedroom. I have control over my life now. When she told me to go to a safe place, I thought of Bubby and Zaida's house. Interesting. I have the skills to get out of the frightened state, into the coping one. No one will EVER do that to me EVER again. The physical stuff heals, but it's the years of manipulation that leave the scars.

Feb 7

I want to sue my nose doctor. Three operations and I *still* can't breathe, *and* it's crooked! I went to see another ear, nose, and throat doctor for his opinion, in Calgary. I brought him pictures of my three operations.

He said it may be a problem with convincing the jury or judge to see there IS a problem. They'll say she's attractive; her nose looks straight to me; I wish I had *her* nose. That's unfair. He said we need a plastic surgeon to say, Yes, the doctor was negligent and shouldn't have done that or he'll say, any doctor would've done the same thing: our case hangs on that. He had three chances to get it right – and he didn't. I mentioned he was the same doctor who took my tonsils out and that it took a long time to heal from that. He never saw me or looked at the progress of my nose between operations.

Feb 9

I saw the specialist. I had come to the realization that at *every* moment we were EVER left alone, Kyle took advantage of me! When he babysat me when our parents were out for the evening, showing me porno mags or movies – basically exhibiting inappropriate behavior at every turn. I NEVER had a moment's peace, even when the family went camping. My therapist called him a sexual predator. I talked about how we were best friends, I trusted him. In spite of everything, we were *still* best friends. Seems odd, but in the life others saw, the public life, we were. He was my ally. However, the closed-off, private, behind-closed-doors life was another story. The loss of that friendship saddens me. At the time when Tracy came into my life, Kyle moved to Israel. All my attention was going to Tracy, and Kyle needed someone else to latch onto – Levi. I made him promise before he left that he *wouldn't* become like Levi, religious. He *promised*. He hated the person Levi had become. Sure enough – he's like Levi! We talked about how Levi treated me like I was invisible. I was feeling abandoned and rejected by *both* brothers.

I feel the EMDR has helped me relieve some of the distress and disturbing images of what happened.

I went to regular therapy. She said, If you took an eight-year-old girl and stood her in this room and you know that she'd been abused for a couple of years by her brother, whose fault would you think it was? The brother's, of course!

How come you can't do the same for your *own* eight-year-old self? I want you to go to a toy store. Check out the games designed for eight-year-olds. Get into the frame of mind of an eight-year-old. Stop thinking intellectually as an adult about what you should've done, and realize the way an eight-year-old thinks.

Two therapy sessions in one day – emotional overload. I suggested to Mom that *Kyle* pay for my therapy.

He can't afford it.
Well, neither can I!

Feb 16

In therapy, it occurred to me that the guy who lives downstairs from us reminds me of Kyle. He has his excuses for *popping in* all the time. I feel dread, unsafe, and always on my toes. When I am home, I'm so quiet so he doesn't know I'm there. He uses our phone three times a day – Tracy lets him use it because they don't have one. I don't feel secure in my own home. He's creepy. We've got to get out of that house. As an adult, only I can do what I need to keep myself feeling safe. We *must* move out for my sense of safety and sanity. I never knew how to keep myself safe before.

Feb 18

THEY HAVE THE RESTAURANT! It's theirs! Tracy has a restaurant! We're trying to come up with a name for it. We're calling it *Britches*.
I think Janis and Damian are getting closer. They hang out, eat lunch together, and see each other outside of the restaurant.

Mar 10

We were supposed to have opened a few days ago, but the refrigerator crapped out. We lost ALL the food, and we had to re-buy, re-prepare, and re-do EVERYTHING - an expense we couldn't have foreseen. So today is the Grand Opening! We had painted, put the paintings up, hired a cook from Earls, bought all the food, tested menu items; we put together a menu – all made fresh. I made a sandwich board sign to put out on the sidewalk. Here we go!

Apr 4

We moved into our new house. Just the two of us. It's our second wedding anniversary. We're too busy with the restaurant to actually do anything together. Damian is frustrating; he comes in late, leaves early, and spends all his time in the back office playing games on the computer, or he's out with Janis. Gee, I'm so glad we introduced them. Ya, I own a restaurant, look at me! Why he evens bothers showing up is beyond me. He's just an extra body floating around; he doesn't actually *do* anything. *We* do all the work around here, and Janis comes in only to talk to *him;* she ignores everyone else. It's very frustrating. He's very moody. He also decided to take *all* weekends off, without even discussing it with us. So, Tracy removed the games from his computer today.

I have one year to make my claim on my nose. I still can't breathe, and it's getting more crooked.

Apr 26

Mom's going to take a year off and go to Israel; she'll sell her condo, and all her furniture. She asked if I'm upset with her. NO! I'm *happy* you're doing what you want to. She said she'll take a risk and change her life. Good for you! Bubby will move in with Aunty Ruth and Uncle Ruben.

May 1

We did a big catering function – Damian showed up an hour late. At the height of the busyness, he leaves – for two hours. Tracy said he wants to buy him out. Good idea. He said, It's Roger all over again. Damian *lets* Tracy do all the work and expects all the benefits. It was suggested to me to get a job before Tracy and I get further into a hole. Too late – we're already there. I told Tracy I don't want to get a job *now* because the liquor license will be in soon and we'll be hopping. Then we'll have to hire someone to help out.

I got a call from my lawyer – they have a doctor for me to see regarding my nose. He has testified before, and has no problem giving his opinion. I have an appointment at the end of the month.

May 8
Tracy finally spoke to Damian, telling him that Damian hasn't been giving 100%. Damian agreed and apologized. Tracy said, You're not into this restaurant at all. Do you even *want* to do this anymore?
Yes. I just get bored and frustrated – so I leave.

An investor in the restaurant, Gary, suggested we take over Damian's parents' loan. Another friend is trying to help us get a loan for the restaurant. Too much money is going out and not enough coming in. We need that liquor license! Gary told Tracy that from the first day he met Damian, Gary could see that Damian didn't want to be there. He *told* Damian to get out and let Tracy do his thing.

May 26
We got our liquor license yesterday. We are going to Calgary on the weekend for Mom's Bon Voyage party. I got ALL my hair cut off. It's REALLY short. I like it! It's all part of my transformation.

July 16
The fridge in the restaurant went out during the night. We have to restock *again*. Later in the day, Tracy and Damian go to the restaurant and the cook has quit and cleaned out the restaurant – he took EVERYTHING. He took all the paintings, every ounce of booze, ALL the food in the fridges and freezers and all the cash in the till, and then he left the front door wide open. Someone said they saw him *celebrating* at Earls. He's pretty proud of himself. We always took care of him – paid him *first* before we paid our own bills. Tracy said he'll just go work with John and his brother and make more money painting than

what the restaurant brought in. I used my UI cheques to keep the restaurant afloat. It was our savings that supported everything and everyone. We heard that the cook did what he did because he thought *we* had all this money and we weren't sharing. He thought we were hoarding all the profits and he was the only one going without. He was delusional to think that he had a bigger stake in the restaurant than we did. We paid him upfront each week.

July 18

It turns out the cook *went back* last night and took all the *quarters* out of the till. He was going to take the phone too but decided not to, bending the antenna instead. Tracy said, No more money is going into this place. We're done. We have no money to replace *anything*. Damian got the keys back from the cook. He may have made copies though. Tracy said he wants to press charges. Everyone else is saying we have to forget about all this and move on. So, the cook puts us out of business and we're supposed to – forget about it?! I should write a book about our first year in Kelowna – no one would believe all the shit we've been through.

July 30

The restaurant is supposed to be shut down tomorrow. The bailiff came in and seized what was left. I called Uncle Ruben for help. He's flying in today. He looked over the contracts and documents that were signed. The seizure was done *illegally*. They had to give us *written notice* before having a bailiff come in. That bought us about two weeks. We have no money for rent. We are just waiting for an eviction notice.

Aug 12

Tracy's Uncle Al died. He had a heart attack a block away from his home. He was a larger-than-life man. He'll be dearly missed. It was a blow for Tracy, as they were quite close.

We have an appointment with a lawyer regarding a letter we need to give to Roger.

Mom left for Israel.

Sept 5

I'm tired of these one-sided friendships – I need to clean house. I need to have people around me that are *good* for me. Mom called. She said Levi's wife wants to talk to me. We chatted for a bit. Mom then says, Someone else wants to talk to you, and puts Levi on. He basically quizzed me about the synagogue out here and on how big the Jewish population is. Then he said, Either we'll see you in Kelowna or in Israel. Ya, right! I told Mom how awkward and uncomfortable the conversation was.

Later on, I wrote Mom a letter:

*"In my own time, **I** will decide IF I make contact with Levi – I will not have it forced on me. Nobody seems to remember or care that I need to be the one to decide if contact will be made. I felt tricked. You can't keep doing this the whole year you are there. I'd appreciate some courtesy and respect of my wishes. I find it necessary to state this loud and clear so it does not happen again. If this is going to be a problem, then maybe consider NOT calling me from their house so you're not put in this position again."*

Sept 10

Tracy's stereo was repossessed this evening. Damian called and said he gave his parents the insurance money that came in. Sure, you did. $1000 isn't going to put a dent in $50,000. How's he paying back the other $40,000? You're not the almighty restaurant owner now, are you?! He probably has to do some *actual* work, like in a real job. For some reason, I feel by the end of this year that it's going to be a turning point for me. I hope in a *good* way.

Sept 27

I called our lawyer; we had received a letter from Roger's lawyer. It states Tracy owes him *$5000*. Absurd! They plan on outlining what Tracy owes him in the *next* letter. I can't wait; this should be good.

Janis calls (we haven't spoken in months) regarding Damian needing to arrange paying for his parents' loan. Apparently by being his girlfriend, her loyalty toward us goes out the window, again. Tracy already told him he's paying the loans from his dad, my uncle, and three *other* investors … **_before_** paying any part of *that* loan. *We* can't pay *EVERYONE* back and Damian pays *nothing*. He hasn't paid anyone anything yet!

The nerve. He has Janis doing his dirty work for him. And SHE'S okay with it! Tracy and I talked about moving away – living on a boat somewhere. I said, It seems someone who lives on a boat should be a writer. We talked about what kind of book we'd write. It needs to be something people could *relate* to. Who'd even read my book? What's so interesting about *my* life?

Oct 1
Damian calls from Calgary; he wants more money from Tracy. He's clearly *not* paying *his* part. He has no job. He wants Tracy to send money so HE can use it for *himself* – not to give to his parents. I have a bad feeling about this.
Our basement flooded and we lost a lot of stuff.

Oct 12
We went to Calgary for a visit. I mentioned to Dad the prospect of us moving back, and of us all living together. He was very happy. Tracy got an application for CP Rail.

Oct 18
I went to get some sinus X-rays done. Tracy talked to our lawyer. John tells Tracy that Janis called *him* to ask if Tracy's working, and what kind of income we have. Basically, Damian sicced Janis on John to see if Tracy has any money. She knows me *15 years, we were* best friends; she knows Damian *six months* – and does this? Wow. Karma's going to be a bitch, ya bitch!

Oct 23

Damian called to tell Tracy that he and Janis are moving to Calgary, and wanted to know if Tracy has any money for him? Nope. Tracy believes that Damian has papers he wants Tracy to sign, asking him to be responsible for half the debt. Tracy never signed anything at the beginning; surely, he's not going to NOW. Tracy explained, Uncle Ruben and Tracy's dad get paid *first*, and then the *other* restaurant bills…Damian is the LAST on a *long* list of people being owed. Does he actually expect Tracy to pay ALL the bills, 100% of the debt? I wanted so much to have a clean break when we moved – now we won't. I just want them *out* of our lives. I told Tracy to discuss this on the *phone* with him – he is *not* welcome in our home.

Oct 27

I almost punched the fridge, then the wall. I'm glad I didn't. I cried instead. I'm feeling very depressed about everything. I'll cry at the drop of a hat. I miss Mom. I feel very lost.

In November, we went to Calgary to find a place to live. We put a damage deposit down on a place. Dad gave notice at his place. We moved into our new house in December and Dad moved in with us.

Dec 14

Damian showed up at our door – at our new house. Dad answered the door. He said we owe him money, where can he find us? They're my family – you'll have to get your information from someone else. So much for our fresh start.

Tracy got a job at CP Rail! He'll be a third-generation CP Railway man!

We applied for welfare since Tracy won't start his new job for a few weeks.

1995

Jan 16

Tracy and I received our welfare check.

Lesson of the day: You can't have any pride when you need help.

I got a job at the university through the welfare program. It's a six-month contract even though they told me I was overqualified. I'll be a relief receptionist and working in the file room to revamp their system. I have no friends to really tell about this. Everyone was so supportive when we *left*, but it seems so hard to let me re-enter their lives now that we're *back*. I need to make NEW friends. I had a skinny day. I looked thin in my black leggies. I tried to throw up – I ate too many sweets. It didn't work.

Quite the contrast with Kelowna, such a beautiful town, and our home overlooking the lake was phenomenal – but our life there was so ugly.

Jan 22

I was invisible in Kelowna, and I still am here, even in my own home. Dad is so in tune with what Tracy needs, which is nice, but I feel swept under the carpet. This preferential treatment is starting to take its toll. Weeks of celebrations for Tracy's job – I get nothing. Not one toast. Not one word about MY job. Nothing. I told Dad how I felt about the inequality; he said, Oh well, it's done. We argued for a while. Tracy's childhood friend, Connor, moved in with us.

Jan 31

I was in a car accident today. The lady in front of me braked abruptly. All of a sudden, I'm hit from behind. My head went forward, and then snapped back, hitting the headrest. I was dazed. A guy helped me out of the car. I only left a mud mark on the bumper of the car in front of me. The Cadillac that hit me had major front-end damage. We all traded insurance info. I just stood there. An ambulance came. They put me on a stretcher, and I went to the hospital. My head was in this contraption to keep it in place. They called Tracy and work for me. All I could think of was how mad they'll be at work. I went for an X-ray; Tracy arrived soon thereafter. They said, No work for three to four days, no driving, and you start physio tomorrow. I got a neck collar. I couldn't sleep. My ribs started hurting, my back and tailbone hurt. I thought all the bad shit was supposed to *stay* in Kelowna!

Feb 1

I started physio. Levi called. Maria's expecting again.
Ignoring his "big" news, I said, Can you tell Mom I was in a car accident yesterday? I'm okay, but a letter will take too long to get there. I *never* intended for him to know my business, but I needed him to tell Mom.

Feb 2

Levi called again. He said he gave Mom the message. Dad spoke to him. I could hear Dad say, *I love you too* at the end of their conversation. Did I hear correctly? Tracy concurred. Dad had said he wanted nothing more to do with them…*I love you too?!* Unreal!

Mom told me to contact a lawyer regarding the accident and not to settle for anything right away. They want to get me while I'm still dazed and will agree to anything. I don't know the extent of my injuries yet, so I'm not jumping into anything. My neck is so swollen. I love my job – I really hope they realize this *wasn't* my fault and still want me when I get back on Monday. Work called – I still have my job. Relief!

Mar 6

Aunty Essie, Zaida's sister, passed away. Aunty Ruth said she'd have a ticket for me if I want to go to the funeral in Montreal. I doubt I can get the time off. No job is that important to miss this, especially since your mother will be there. Okay, I'm willing to lose my job to go. Work gave me a week off. I feel like Zaida is dying all over again through Aunty Essie. Well, they were siblings.

Mar 14

It was a nice celebration of Aunty Essie. Even though it was for a funeral, it was great seeing Mom.

Back in Calgary, I got some antibiotics for my ear infections. My left eardrum is suctioned shut. There's lots of scarring from childhood. Very painful. I thought my ears just needed popping from the plane – I guess not. There's no relief from my whiplash. I keep wondering what all this means. All this bad luck. It's big life changes, not just piddly shit.

Mar 23

I went to get my ears checked. The doctor said the left ear is getting worse. Not only is the eardrum infected, but also the canal leading to the outer ear. Great. He gave me stronger antibiotics. My lawyer called. Do you want to settle? No, I'm still in treatment – it's too soon. Okay, we'll wait.

Apr 3

I bought a little blue '84 Honda Civic from one of the Kelowna restaurant investors. We paid him cash for the car and paid the rest of the money we owed him too. All done! No more payments there. Thank you, Aunty Essie, for the inheritance.

Dad's new girlfriend, Marsha, moved in.

Apr 4

Our third wedding anniversary. Tracy had three dozen roses and chocolates in a velvet heart-shaped box delivered to me at work. I had always wanted to get flowers at work.

Tracy built *me* a fish tank as a gift. I laughed. HE'S always wanted one.

Apr 11

We had dinner at Aunty Ruth's. She asked me, Do you remember your childhood very well, or have you blocked a lot out? Was it a happy childhood?

I kind of froze. I had no idea what she was getting at. *Nothing* came out of my mouth.

She said, I hardly have any memories of my childhood; most is blocked out. I sighed a sigh of relief, realizing it was an innocent question. Her daughter's pregnant. We talked about my *unreadiness* to have children. Bub said how Levi used to continuously hit and beat Kyle and me. He didn't like us because Kyle hung out with *me and* resented me. I came along and Kyle would have nothing to do with Levi. I hadn't realized Bubby understood and saw all that. I got a speech from Bub about hurrying up and having children. How old are you? Twenty-six. Don't be one of those people who wait until they're in their 30s or 40s.

May 3

Tracy starts his electrical apprenticeship today for CP! Up until now he was a laborer. The bills are piling up and we're not getting any help. *We* are supporting five people. This *wasn't* the plan. I started acupuncture to help my neck and back.

May 5

I went to see my lawyer. She told me to keep an injury diary and to keep up with the physio. There is no rush to settle. If it takes two years or longer, it's not a problem. Just concentrate on getting better. Only when you reach a point where you're better or things aren't changing, and you've done everything – *then* do you file.

May 16

I told my doctor I *don't* want to continue with the acupuncture – it's making it *worse*. The needles made me bruise and bleed. I felt stiffer and there's no relief from the pain. My headaches are *explosive*. She said the treatments are supposed to make me feel more *relaxed*. Well, I'm all tight and in pain. She kept twisting the needles in farther, trying to loosen up the muscles. She said she'd like to see me one more time before I quit. I just want to get better NOW!

This whole living with five people isn't working. Tracy and I are the only two cleaning up, the only two cooking, buying food…

May 29

John was talking to Owen: Penny split, taking *everything* – the Jet Skis, the truck, the van, the tools, ladders and equipment, ALL of it! She told him, You mess with me and I'll take it all! I guess he messed with her. What goes around DOES come around. Hee, hee. Now it's Roger's, Janis's and Damian's turn.

June 8

I'm ready to snap. Nothing is going right at work, then I go home and there's more crap to deal with. And my neck – the pain is tremendous, throbbing, and it spasms *all* the time. The muscles feel rock hard. I stopped going to acupuncture; I'm going to physio now. Still no relief. It's so horrible. Mid-back pain. Explosive headaches. I'm taking the strongest back pain medication – and it *doesn't* work. Four months of this non-stop pain. AAH!

June 11

I was talking with Tracy at breakfast. Why don't I just leave this place? I just want to be alone. I deal with shit all day long here, at work; is it a wonder I snap at everything? Nothing gets dealt with anywhere. It's taking its toll on me. I gotta get away or something's gonna give, because I can't take this anymore. Tracy said, Do me a favor and go talk to your dad. So, I did. I told him that his stupid jokes are very insensitive to me.

I'm just trying to be one of the boys.
No excuse! He apologized.

I spoke to my lawyer. I'm going to more appointments and I need to start with a massage therapist now, too. I can't afford all this. She said my insurance will pay for it.

June 29
Tracy and I really need to be on our own, we've had enough living with other people. I've been in a car accident. I'm trying to manage the basics of living, then coming home to *healthy* people who don't clean up after themselves. I really figured Dad would work out. Unfortunately, we can't afford it on our own. I need peace and quiet. Peace in my life. There's too much turmoil. I need no hassles. HELP!

July 15
I started massage therapy. I'm officially a *severe case.* She's very concerned about my nausea and light-headedness; it's not a good sign. I'll need to see her three times a week.

It all started with Dad saying, Do you want me to move out? You seem to always have a problem with me. I told him how much pain I'm in *all* the time. I found out yesterday it may not be muscle damage but nerve damage. You never show *any* interest in my healing. You haven't asked me in *six months*, how I'm doing. I'm so tired of cleaning up after all of you. I'm putting myself first now. I'm so tired – I'm totally and completely drained and exhausted. I'm not handling life very well at the moment.

I was sitting outside on the step crying when Tracy came out. I said, It's clear to me *I'm* the cause of all the friction in this house. You and I don't seem to be getting along, and Dad and I sure aren't. Why am I here? I need to go away for a while. I'm slowly dying here. My sanity is on the line.

I think I'll take three sleeping pills tonight (as opposed to one). There's no way I want all this swimming around in my head. I need a break from it. Sleep…

Colleen called. I told her about tonight's events.

You're shocking me. I can't believe this. Are you and Tracy okay?
I don't know. Do you want to hear another shocker? I almost threw myself out of a window today.

Dead silence.

July 16
I go downstairs to do some laundry. Dad says, I've been thinking a lot about what you said yesterday and I want you to know how concerned I *am* about your healing. Do you want me to move out to relieve some of the tension?
No, I don't want you to move out, but we must find a *better* way to communicate. We're five people living in a house. The whole point was for it to be cheaper on everyone and easier all round – a *good* situation. It's not. If we *all* pull our weight, it'll work out. I'm not handling my life very well. I used to do much better. I need to get away and regroup, get a better handle on things.
We were both crying.

I really wanted to die yesterday. The emotional pain hurt so badly. I really didn't feel like there was any reason to stick around. I'm glad the feeling has passed.

July 17

My lawyer received a letter from MY insurance company saying they want an independent medical exam (IME) of me before they dish out any more money. Apparently, they don't believe I was injured in the accident. Bring it on! I've been examined by NINE doctors and isn't it fascinating they *all* report I have tissue damage and muscles that aren't healing. And yet, I *must* be the epitome of health! Never mind that two cars were totalled in the accident. Please. Go find the people that ARE abusing the system! I've been in physio since the day after the accident and have continuously been seeing doctors, hoping ONE of them can recommend some sort of relief for all this pain. Believe me – I'd love nothing better than to be perfectly healthy. No one CHOOSES *not* to be.

July 18

I asked Mom for a therapist's number. I've been depressed and I can't stop crying. Mom was so supportive. I need someone to care about me. I think this was the break I needed. I got an appointment with the therapist for *September*. Mom suggested I go to sleep and ask a *specific* question – I'll get the answer in the morning. It's worth a shot.

I finally talked with Tracy. We need to reconnect. I won't apologize for being depressed. I'm doing the best I can. I need your support. A person can only handle so much and it all came to a head on Saturday. We deal with things in our own way. I'm straightening out my life. I'm at the bottom, but I'm working my way back up.

At physio, she told me, We've plateaued. She's not sure what else to do for me. Great.

July 24

A guy I worked with at Star Auto, who was also a friend of Tracy's family – him, his in-laws, and a nephew died today while vacationing. A freak accident. Kirk's wife and their two small children were driving behind their RV in a car, and watched the whole thing happen. I can't even imagine. Her parents and husband dead in one shot. He was only 27. The funeral will be on Saturday.

In contrast, I became an aunt again today; Maria had a girl.

Lesson of the day: A death and a birth – they go hand in hand.

Aug 3

It's my last day at my job. Six months has come and gone. I've been on several interviews. I have sent out tons of résumés. Now we wait. I cried all morning. What is my purpose on this earth? I have no direction. I have ugly thoughts of suicide and Tracy leaving me. I have no job, no friends…why the hell am I here? I had a whole suicide letter in my head – who I'd say what to … everything. I should just turn to drugs – numb myself, fill a void. Sure, Mom loves me, but really no one is HERE for me. I NEED TO SNAP OUT OF IT! How would I even be remembered? The girl who couldn't hold down a job? The girl who married a *Goy* (non-Jewish person)? The girl who was repeatedly raped by her brother? Ya, let's put THAT on my tombstone.

Aug 14

I got a job as an executive assistant at a real estate company. The boss wants to mold me. They want someone *without* real estate experience so there are no preconceived ideas about the business. They will fully train me. They want *my* opinion. I get to learn the Internet. Sweet.

Aug 16

I have the IME today. He denounced physio, massage, chiro, *and* acupuncture – you'll heal *on your own*; those are just *temporary* solutions. Go swimming, walk, and don't sit at the computer for long periods of time. It's definitely a muscle issue, nothing's broken.

Well, that was helpful.

My doctor said the guy works for the *other* side, so naturally he'll tell them what they want to hear. At least the massage and physio give you *some* relief.

Ya, who is *he* to say I don't deserve *any* kind of relief, even if *it is temporary*? Assmunch.

Aug 25

Tracy comes home and asks if I'd like my birthday present *early* and hands me his knapsack, I open it and there is a *kitten* inside! He's five weeks old, short-haired, and black and white with HUGE eyes. Now we have a short-haired *and* a long-haired black and white cat. We came up with the name Gizmo because, well, he looks like Gizmo from *Gremlins* – big ears. I'm so happy. Slinky and Ebony were very welcoming of him. They're all going to be great pals. I'm not sure how great Babe, our cockatiel, is feeling about another cat in the house though, but he's safe in his cage.

Sept 1

Dad got a call from Kyle this morning: he's engaged. I cried a bit because I thought, *Everyone is so happy and I'M the one who deals with it all, everyone else talks to him.* I feel resentful and I told Dad how I felt. He says he feels torn. I *knew* he'd say that.

Bubby seems well enough to go back to her place in Montreal, and take care of herself.

Sept 7

Since Marsha moved out, and it's just me as the lone female in the house, being in this house with *four* men is getting to me: Connor's buddy moved in as well. All the sexual innuendos and jokes, the language … because everyone is so busy being "one of the boys". It's like I'm living with Kyle again! I can't stand it! So, I said something. I said, I will NOT "lighten up" or "mellow out!" It's very insensitive for you all to constantly be making sexual remarks. Do it when I'm NOT around. Nobody has a gun to your head making you talk derogatorily.

I hope I gave them *something* to think about.

Sept 30
Tracy and I were sitting at the football game. There was a family in front of us with kids close in age, two boys, and they were treating each other so *nicely*. I said to Tracy, It would be nice if OUR kids were like that.

Ya, but you don't want kids.
But YOU do.
By the time YOU'RE ready to have them, it'll be too late for me, and I'll be too old.
But you love kids; I couldn't do that to you.
I'll go with whatever you want. If you choose not to have any, that'll be fine by me. We have our animals.

Oct 10
Dad gives me a card from Levi and Kyle.
No, I *don't* want it.
He has a picture of his grandson. Do you want to see the boy?
I've seen him.
He just looks at me like he couldn't figure out WHY I could care less. When I get news from them, do you want me to tell you about it? No. Like we're all going to share in the *joy* of Kyle's engagement? Screw that. I read the card. I wish I hadn't. Both of them want me to go to the wedding, December 20. Later, Dad asked me if I read the card.
Yes, then I tore it into a million pieces.

Oct 19
I feel I have a wall up where having kids is concerned. I want to *want* them. I want to feel the same way as when someone else tells me, I want this so bad I can taste it and nothing in the world is more im-

portant than having a baby. I'd make a bad mother. I'd be overprotec-
tive. I wouldn't want bad things to happen to them. I hope my therapist can help me out with this.

Oct 24

I was talking to Mom about the time *they* came in from Israel and *I* was
the one to leave to Tracy's house. *They* should've gone to a motel or
something. Why should *I* have been the one to leave? Oh ya, because *I*
didn't feel safe!
You're the innocent party here and you seem to get the short end of the
stick all the time.
Yup, odd man out. *I* keep paying.
My therapist asked if it's still a family secret.
Ya, I guess it is. My aunt and all of them don't know. I *don't* feel a need
to tell them.

Oct 26

I went to see my doctor. I wound up crying out of sheer frustration. I'm
in pain ALL the time, nothing is working, and no meds help. She read
the IME report to me. The doctor said there is NO spasming in my
neck. WHAT?! I was SO relieved when he DID feel it spasm, validating
how I felt – so he LIED in the report! She said, These are people
insurance companies look for.

I'm supposed to go to massage three times a week, but I missed a few
because I lost my job. I go once a week now. And it doesn't cut it.

Oct 27

Dad was telling me he and Mom are chipping in for Kyle's wedding.

I don't want to hear any of it!
They'll be sending you an invitation to the wedding; I hope you'll
respond to it.

I will respond to it IF **_I_** feel like it. I will not respond for *anyone* else's benefit! I'LL decide.

I talked to Tracy about it.

I'm glad I can talk to you about this and that you don't mind.
I'm the guy you're spending the rest of your life with.
What if I told Aunty Ruth and Uncle Ruben?
Maybe they NEED to know because of their grandchild. How would you feel if something happened and you *didn't* tell them?
I thought of that. It's something to think about, and then they can do what they will with the info.
Maybe if others in Israel knew, they'd get him the help he needs.
I believe he's never dealt with it.

<u>Nov 6</u>
I asked my therapist if I have the *right* to only tell my aunt and uncle and have them keep it to themselves.
Of course, you do. You need to say, Look, I haven't been able to get past these issues. I feel I can possibly do that by sending up red flags over there so Levi and Kyle can start taking some responsibility.
I told her *they* say I *don't* need therapy, that my "cure" is I need to go to a *Yeshiva* for six months. What I need is for my family to rally around ME and support ME.
You *don't* need to *forgive* them. It's not necessary to move on in the healing process. Never mind forgiving *them*, could you forgive *yourself* if he ever did it again to someone?
I tend to minimize it – to think it's *not* a big deal.
It's a VERY BIG DEAL! You have abandonment issues, from your parents and others. You needed to leave your *own home…*

Later, I said to Tracy, I'm losing my nerve. It just feels so huge.

Nov 17

Tracy and I went to Aunty Ruth and Uncle Ruben's for dinner and to have "the talk". After choking down dinner because I was losing my nerve, I said, I'd like to talk to you guys, can we move into the living room? I want to let you know the REAL reason why I don't talk to Levi and Kyle. I was quiet, trying to choose my words carefully.

This is really hard. Kyle sexually abused me for many years, from 10 to 13 years old.

They both got up and immediately came over to hug me. Aunty Ruth sat on the floor in front of me and kept her hand on my arm, comforting me. They said they were very shocked. Aunty Ruth said she always knew there was more to it than only the religion. Mom never breathed a word about it. They told me I had so much courage and bravery by telling them and that they respect me so much.

I said, It's out of my concern for the kids who are to come that I'm saying something.

Uncle Ruben said, None of this is your fault; you're not to blame for *any* of it.

Aunty Ruth asked what I need to do to feel better, and get on with my life.

Just to continue with my therapy, and writing helps.

They said how wonderful it is that I have such a supportive husband.

Nov 18

I told Dad about last night. He was crying. He wrote a letter to Mom and showed it to me. It said he can't go on giving things to his sons, who would do such atrocities to their own sister.

I said to Dad, They keep getting rewarded. *He's* getting married and *I'm* in therapy.

He told me he had put money aside for Kyle's wedding but never had the heart to send it. I'd like to take you and Tracy out to dinner and celebrate; we'll celebrate reclaiming our lives!

Nov 20

My therapist said I should be so proud of myself – that took a lot of courage.

I said, Dad is finally *off* the fence.

Do you feel as though you've lost your mom (with her staying in Israel after her leave of absence)?

No, not really, but I need to speak to her *before* she gets Dad's letter.

She said, Your mom will have to respect your dad's decision to cut off from them. We all have to make decisions we can live with.

They will all chalk this up to religion – me being the non-religious sister and all.

Let them. With Kyle, society accepts that sexual abuse is wrong and therefore you are justified in slamming the door shut on him, but there's no label for what Levi did. The devastation of the emotional abuse all those years is probably *worse* than what Kyle did. Kyle did the physical, but Levi *knew* about it. He *had* the power to stop it. You probably wouldn't be sitting her right now if Levi *had* intervened. He had *all* the power, and he knew it. He was 16, 17 and 18 years old, and he did *nothing*. What he did was far more devastating, and is NOT forgivable.

He was NEVER a brother to me – I owe him nothing! They are dead to me! I just wish everyone would stop asking me to try to have a relationship with them.

Dad said he'll wait until AFTER the wedding for anything to be said by him.

Right, we don't want poor Kyle to *not* have his perfect little wedding! ARGH!!

Dad said to me, In the summer when they came out, he told Levi that he loves his children *equally*. Levi was shocked. Dad asked, You figure because you're *religious* I should love you *more*? Yes.

Huh, so being the prick he was to me my entire childhood, he STILL figured he DESERVED more of Dad's love? How much more deluded can he get?!

Dad asked me if there was anything they could do for me to open the door I've shut on them?

Nothing. Through their words and actions, they've *shown* me how unworthy they are of having a sister in their lives.

Nov 28

I've just been feeling so drained. All this emotional stuff. My head is swimming. I was thinking, What if *they* had turned to *Buddhism*? Would everyone *still* be so quick to say, Look, they are staying out of trouble, they've found peace … why don't you open that door a little? Or is it *because* they've turned to *Judaism* that it's so much easier for people to say, My, look what they've done with their troubled lives! Give 'em a chance!

Fuck that shit. They have given themselves *new* identities, names, clothes, careers, languages, homes … it's all just a cover. One big, fat cover to hide from what they've done to me. If they were brave enough to stay in Canada, to face me, and deal with what they've done instead of the continual denial and lack of responsibility for their actions, **perhaps** there'd have been room for a chance of communication. Instead, they've taken the cowardly way out, and people are helping them do it. Let's go on trips when they visit Calgary, let's not bring up the past because that'll just upset THEM! Let's all pretend and it'll go away. They are cowards in the biggest way. You see, this wonderful religion they've found won't "allow" them to get off their high horses long enough to do the right thing. It's all about them; nobody rock *their* boat, and nobody say anything to make them face up to their dastardly deeds. The big question when they came out was whether Levi knew or not? He *admitted* to knowing.

Punishment? HA! Poor, poor troubled Levi. Let's give him a break. He really *tried* with that apology letter six years ago and nothing since but, boy, did he try! What's the matter with you Sari, why aren't you giving them a chance? Because that would make things easier FOR EVERYONE ELSE!

Since the day I was born, Levi's hatred of me grew. He never had one ounce of love or compassion for me. He proved that by keeping vital info about Kyle *all to himself,* and allowing YEARS of abuse to continue. He probably felt Kyle was doing him a *favor* by ruining my life FOR him. He always believed I was dirt, unworthy of life, an obstacle to getting love from Mom and Dad. What better way to punish me than to allow the abuse to continue?! My *only* crime was stealing his precious dollar bill collection, and, boy, was *I* punished for that! He destroys my life and what does he get? Trips to Calgary, a paid wedding and a wife, gifts, praise, kids, and a Rabbi to make all his decisions *for* him.

And Kyle, what does HE get for his crimes? Trips, a wedding, no one EVER questioning him about his past. What do *I* get? Six years of therapy, support groups, broken relationships, blame, shame, loss of identity, no self-esteem, a shattered life that I have the privilege of picking up the pieces from, constantly being told I need to open the door to them, no childhood, no protection, no real siblings, listening to people praising them for the admirable life they've chosen…

I'm trying to survive a cruel, heartless brother while fending off the sexual frustrations of the other, with no one to turn to. And I'VE got to crack the door open to THEM? Not in this or *any* other lifetime. Anyone who can't accept that, I don't need or want in my life. If people ACTUALLY cared about MY feelings, they'd stop pushing me to make peace with them and let me do what I feel is best for me! I'm sorry if my *selfishness* offends anyone. Why, all these years later, am I still being asked to let them in? I don't owe them a goddamn thing! How about **I** murder **THEIR** souls, and then express my sorrow in a heartfelt letter, and we can all go out for coffee, visit some friends, and maybe go to the mountains? Then of course I'd become religious so it could never be discussed again, and then I could tell THEM how THEY should deal with THEIR grief. And people can send ME gifts and praise ME for the path *I'd* taken, and we can ALL pretend nothing ever happened!!!

Dec 7

I have been super busy unpacking since Tracy and I and Dad and Connor moved into our new house.

My doctor is going to be injecting my neck with steroids. It should relieve the muscles and loosen them up. I felt nervous. It was over before I knew it! Acupuncture made things worse; so I hope this works. Later on, I could feel the PAIN. Wowzer! No relief.

Mom asked me if I feel betrayed by her being in Israel. I expressed again I know it's *her* dream to be there, unfortunately *they* are there too. She said she needs to let her work know if she's coming back or not.

Do you want me to come back to Canada? I was the only one Mom was asking that question of.
I've *never* believed you'd come *back* to Calgary or Canada. You have found your niche there; I wouldn't take that away from you.
You've been so supportive since day one.

She must've got Dad's letter because she said that even with all they've done, she'd *never* cut them off, unlike Dad. She said that Maria says she feels like she's *betraying* Levi by having a connection with me. I simply don't care. I said, They don't really care they lost a sister – big whoop. And they never so much as got a slap on the wrist. She agreed.

I was telling Dad and Tracy, I *don't* have brothers. They are strangers and people I'd NEVER want in my life.
Tracy said, As far as I'm concerned, they'll never acknowledge me as your husband.
No, they won't, and you are *one million* times a *better* man than they could ever hope to be.

Dec 11
I went to therapy. She said that when Mom and Dad speak to *them*, THEY can put the responsibility back on them. They could say, Given your behavior toward Sari, can't you understand why she feels the way she does? Have you ever shown her that she should behave *differently* toward you?

I said, Levi CHOSE to be cruel to me. I saw him being nice to his friends. It was apparent he COULD be a nice person. I don't think Kyle set out to destroy my life, not the way Levi did. Levi revelled in it. They have never empathized with what they put me through. They need to understand how much they fucked up my life!

Dec 20
I told the doctor there is *more* pain after the injections. It's been almost a year since the accident. I'm so frustrated. If these injections are making it worse, we need to stop. There's nothing more he can do for me.

I got to my car and cried. I'm doomed to be in pain. I called my lawyer. Somebody put me out of my misery already! It would be the humane thing to do.

1996

Jan 8

I went to therapy. She said that my role in the family is changing. I was the one keeping the family together, not rocking the boat, the protector. Now, I speak my mind if I'm dissatisfied with how I'm being treated. I need to break the old patterns. I'm not going to be the little girl who keeps her mouth shut anymore. It then dawned on me *why* I yell when I get angry. I think that after being shut up all my life, now I feel that I *won't* be shut up anymore, and I yell because I still don't feel I'm being heard.

Jan 12

Toby called. The worst possible thing happened: her baby died this afternoon. This time tomorrow they will have to induce Toby to get *her* out.

I wish you weren't 60,000 miles away, Sari.
Me too. I don't know what to say. I'm not going to pretend I know what you're going through. I'm here for you.
I know, I wouldn't have called if I didn't find *some* comfort in that.
It might be the first time I *ever* heard her cry.

Jan 30

I called Toby. Her stepdad, Jimmy, died. Her sister's father-in-law died *two hours later* – in the same hospital, two floors down from Jimmy. Everything happens in threes. She said people are still wishing her Mazel Tov (congratulations) on the impending baby. They obviously don't know the baby died, and that Toby still has a pregnancy belly. Someone else told her the baby's death was "for the best"; I'm surprised Toby didn't strike her where she stood. Wow, *my problems* seem so small in comparison.

Feb 1

I have a job interview at a home-builders' company as a receptionist. I'm feeling very lonely and depressed. All those wonderful friends who sent me off to Kelowna and wished I wasn't going are now gone. I try to reach out, I get nothing back. There is zero interest since I'm back. Tracy is very busy with his work and volleyball. Apparently, I'm what they call a "volleyball widow." And his friends invite HIM out for a beer, never including me. If I dropped off the face of the earth, no one would notice. Maybe it's best we never had kids. I think that's why I journal – I can say my true feelings and not get shut down. Paper doesn't judge.

Feb 20

I got the job and start Monday! Tracy and I went out for dinner and discussed *me* being a surrogate for *Toby*, my idea.
Tracy said, Giving a couple a child they so desperately want is so important.
They may not take me up on it, but at least it's an option. Then I asked Tracy straight up, Do you *want* kids?
Yes, of course I do.
Who knows, maybe by doing this for Toby, I'll want one of our own.

Mar 12

I got a cold. I can't remember a time my back hurt more. I couldn't even find the tears to cry. All I could do was whimper. I have a fever.

Aunty Ruth called to say they got served with papers from Damian. NO WAY he knew my aunt's address, *Janis* told him. BITCH! Damian needs to get a life and stop spending money on lawyers, and pay his parents back! I feel sick about this. ASSHOLES! We need this? He never worked; he schemed. Tracy said he's not worried about it.

I called my lawyer, Samuel. He suggested Tracy declare bankruptcy; Damian can't get a cent, EVER! Tracy has no assets and nothing to lose. This won't affect me. With bankruptcy, Tracy will be able to establish good credit. He gave me names of several trustees.

I went to see my accident lawyer since she's in the same office as Samuel. She suggested I see this chiropractor, Dr. Bell. There are only two doctors in Calgary who do this particular type of treatment. It's about $200, but she'll try to get him to waive the cost, and get paid out of the settlement.

Damian called Tracy's parents. His mom said she told him if he *ever* calls again, there will be hell to pay! Way to go! What an asswipe, involving people who have *nothing* to do with this.

Mar 16

I suggested to Toby about using *me* as a surrogate. She laughed at me. I was not happy with that reaction. She said she won't quit trying to have her *own* baby, but will keep it in mind.

Dr. Bell called me about my trying his treatments. He said he could really help me. Once he aligns me, the healing can *finally* begin. I'm all in!

Apr 3

My first appointment with Dr. Bell. My body is trying to compensate for being misaligned.

That's why your muscles feel tight and spasming all the time. Once the head is on straight, the body doesn't need to compensate anymore. The nerves will be free to be normal, and breathing, your ears, digestion, energy level...all will be better. You have no energy because you're using up all your energy in the muscles.

He wants me back in tomorrow for an alignment.

Apr 4

Dr. Bell showed me my X-rays – I'm three degrees rotating every which way. I'm VERY unbalanced – physically. Everything has shifted. I said, I feel like I've been hit by a truck; I just ache all over. I lay on the table, and with very little pressure below my right ear, he pressed down. He said the subtle pressure he'll be using is pressure like a pencil tip concentrated in one area, so it feels like nothing, but he uses his whole bodyweight to apply pressure to that nerve spot. He said I may feel better, worse, or nothing at all. He instructed: For the next six weeks, no exercise, just light walking, no sports, no lifting, and no reaching. You need to keep your neck safe and as straight as possible, so the treatment can work. He did more pressure on my neck. He did about three spurts of that and took more X-rays. He said he can tell the muscles are *already* relaxing. Not to be alarmed, but if you hurt in places you haven't before, it'll be because your muscles will be pulling in the opposite direction, evening everything out the way it's *supposed* to be. You may notice in an hour, two hours, two days...a normal spine has an *arc*, mine is perfectly *straight*. He wants to see me twice next week, then once a week.

It's not the best wedding anniversary – I was so exhausted from the day. Tracy and I watched a movie and went to bed.

Apr 8

I have been on about six interviews in the past few weeks, with it always coming down to me and someone else. UI ran out after six months, so I have a few weeks work at Samuel's office helping out; he has me transcribing. We are filling out papers tomorrow for Damian's lawyer. I found out today I lost out on *another* job; it was down to two of us again. Man.

Apr 11

I was reading about bulimia, so I tried it *and* took a laxative. I just want to flush out all the toxins in my body, exercise more, drink more water, eat less junk food, feel better about my body and myself – I'm feeling so fat. I tried throwing up again, but I couldn't. I exercise, but I'm not seeing results fast enough. I need to do something that'll speed things up – summer is around the corner. I don't ever remember *not* hating my body. I looked at younger pictures of myself and what a rail I was, bony. And I HATED how I looked. I'd kill to look that way now. I'll *never* be satisfied with how I look. It's time to take charge, time to look the way I *want* to. Ya, maybe by the time I'm 100.

Apr 12
I weighed myself for the first time in years – 123 lb. I FREAKED! I need to lose 10 lb. FAST! I took a diet pill, then had a good workout, didn't eat, went to the bathroom, took all my clothes off to shower. I weighed myself again – 118 lb. I've heard people with bulimia feel that's one part of their life they HAVE control over. I feel it's just one more part I DON'T have control over. I kind of feel *out* of control with my body. I don't feel I have *any* power over it. I feel shame and guilt and out of control. Maybe one day I'll look back on this part of my life and just understand it's what I was going through at the time. I dunno.

Apr 26
I was in the bathroom all morning. Flat tummy! Later I had pizza and all I could think of was getting it out of me. I'm so depressed. I'm crying. I've been trying for the past 40 minutes or so to throw up. I'm a fucking failure at being bulimic! I can't do *anything* right! My throat is so raw. I'm taking *two* laxatives tonight. I weigh 113 lb.

May 4
I weigh 115 lb.! GODDAMMIT! I took five laxatives and ate six prunes and went to the bathroom seven times. My therapist hasn't returned my calls. I took six more laxatives.

May 8
Success! It's the first time throwing up with barely trying. I was so pleased.

The situation with living with Dad is *so* not working out. It's coming to a head. Tracy and I are fighting. I'm trying so hard, and just missing the mark with each interview. Tracy does believe I'm trying; it's just getting worrisome at this point.

I'm there for a friend, and when *I* need her, she's too busy. Same old story. Take and take. But she just called me up crying. I give so much of myself, then I'm dumbfounded when there's no one around for ME! I should be used to it already. I have no one to turn to. Maybe I'll get hit by a truck and everyone will be relieved.

Tracy made me go with him to volleyball. After, when we went out for a beer with some of his teammates. The topic of dinner came up, so I shared what I ate. Tracy says to everyone, Can you believe my wife thinks she's fat?!

That felt nice.

May 12
I weighed in at 111 lb.! I'm SO happy! THRILLED!

It's Tracy's dad's birthday so we went to his parents for dinner. When I hugged him, he made a comment: Sari, where are you? My arms are way around you; there's nothing there! I was very pleased.

May 17
I thought I was only going to see a dental specialist for a *consultation* – he did root canal! It was so hard to keep my mouth open from the TMJ.

Samuel's office called about Tracy and his lawyer getting together for a question period with Damian and his lawyer.

After dinner I'd gone to the bathroom and laid a towel across the bottom of the door so no one would hear me. I noticed that the towel was drawn back in one spot. I looked through the bottom and realized

Tracy had looked in. BUSTED! I opened the door and Tracy asked, What were you doing? His arms were crossed.

Going to the bathroom.

People don't go to the bathroom *standing up. What* were you doing?

I don't know what you want me to say.

Fine. He didn't press it.

I thought, *Oh shit, why did I allow myself to get caught? Did I WANT to get caught? He's probably going to be watching me like a hawk now.* So, I came up with this lame thing to see what Tracy would say.

I think I must be lactose-intolerant – my stomach hurt right after eating ice-cream.

No, that's not it.

Well, what do YOU think, Dr. Knock?

You skip meals, you go without eating then eat, you don't eat dinner…

I argued with him, professing I DO eat dinner.

You asked but clearly you don't want to listen.

May 22

The throwing-up is effortless, automatic now. Dani (a friend from Tracy's volleyball) asked me how much I weighed. I wouldn't answer. She pressed so I told her – 111 lb.

You're a bone rack! Her husband told me I'm TOO skinny. Thanks, I thought.

May 27

I started massage therapy. She opened the space between the vertebrae and my skull, allowing a freer flow of blood and oxygen. I saw Dr. Bell right after the hour-long session. I'm feeling light-headed, dizzy and nauseous. I got home and I couldn't stop throwing up. And it had *nothing* to do with food.

Toby called – she's pregnant. She said she *wasn't* going to tell me.

If you can't tell ME, who CAN you tell? True.

I'm still trying to get an appointment with my therapist. I *need* to see her before this throwing-up thing gets the better of me. My massage therapist called me at home. I told her I got sick from her treatment. She said there was a lot of pressure in my head and neck. We'll go easy on the cranial stuff.

May 29

My root canal is finally finished. I went on an interview. I got word from another job that they went with someone else. I tried calling my therapist *again*. I NEED to see her! Good thing I'm not suicidal. Geez. I finally heard back from her office – she's booked until *July*. Well, shit. I'll take the next cancelation!

May 31

Dani came over. She told me that Tracy called her Thursday, saying he thinks I'm throwing up my dinner. Well, I believe Sari *may* have an eating disorder, but *she* doesn't know it yet; she's not throwing up though.

I had to put a lid on this – I'm not eating regularly because I *don't* feel hungry. Once I get a job, I'll eat like a cow again. I've been through a lot; it's not too hard to figure out why I have a loss of appetite.

June 3

At massage, she told me not to worry about paying for a month or so. I need to take my mind off the money and concentrate on getting better.

My therapist called – there's an opening *at 11:00 a.m. tomorrow*! I'll take it!

They are already garnisheeing Tracy's wages because of Damian.

June 4

I *finally* saw my therapist. I *never* mentioned the throwing-up. Maybe I didn't think it was something that NEEDED being mentioned. I have it under control. We talked about the stressful living situation (living with four men) and the Levi and Kyle stuff.

June 14

I brought Gizmo in to get neutered, and then I went to Kimberley with Dani. After watching the movie, she announces, We have to deal with your eating disorder.

What eating disorder?

Oh, come off it! You know exactly what I mean.

What do you mean?

Sari, you think I don't know?

Know what?

You're skin and bones! I *know*, Sari! I know what you're doing. You don't have a body image problem?

Of course, I do. For as long as I can remember I've *hated* my body.

Tracy told me you throw up your dinner. You asked me *how* to throw up once.

Ya, that never worked.

If it *had*, would you have kept on doing it?

No way! I hate throwing up more than anything in the world. I'd never do that.

She seemed relieved. She said she'd tell Tracy if it ever came up again that I'm not and would not do that.

I continued pleading my case, Its genetics. My grandfather, my grandmother and my dad never gained weight. I don't see myself as skinny.

She was quite satisfied there was nothing to worry about. So, you having diarrhea and an upset stomach all the time is just stress?

Of course! My chiro even said so. Okay.

Phew, I got through that one.

June 26

Mom called; she's in Montreal; Bub fell again. She's in bad shape and has given up. Dad gets on the phone with Mom. She must have said something to him about him disowning Levi and Kyle. I only heard *his* side of the conversation. He said, Oh no, I *never* meant to say that. I must've been insane when I wrote that. I would *never* give up my two sons and all the grandchildren. What I wrote was *obviously* not what I meant; I just wanted to light a fire under them. I was mad at the time. I didn't intend for it to come out in that way. Do they want me to write to them first?

What the fuck is going on? He MADE me read that letter. We mulled it over and discussed it at *great* length! He knew **<u>EXACTLY</u>** what he was doing and writing. I'm shaking. I'm bawling my eyes out. He finally does something right, then yanks it away and denies it all. FUCK!

Mom called back to speak to me. I told her the way it REALLY was. Maybe you need to talk to your father.

I went to Dad, armed with the letter info I'd made notes on. I've got to talk to you. I know when you wrote that letter you meant *every* word of it. I heard what you said to Mom. I feel sick. You dangle your support in front of me, then snatch it away. No one wants to rock the boat. I wanted to go to Israel just to blab to the wives the kind of people they're married to.
You can do whatever you want; no one's stopping you.
Actually, my therapist stopped me.
Why?
She said they wouldn't believe me, and I'd be hurting the kids. The point here is you *denied everything* you wrote in that letter. I think you're trying to reconnect with them because you, Tracy, and I aren't getting along. You *disowned* them and they could care less! You'd think there'd be SOME reaction to it on their part - scared, angry, hurt...SOMETHING!
They were probably just adhering to my wishes.
COP-OUT! A NORMAL person would *react*!
I'm almost 60; I'm tired of the fight. I've stood by you for 10 to 12 years.
I muttered, More like 6 to 7.

It's been years and they've *changed*. They have done lots of work on themselves.

Don't even go there. Ten years may have gone by but they're the *same*.

I'm sure they stopped doing what they did back then.

You don't know that! *No one* knew when it was happening to ME.

Aunty Ruth called; Bubby was hospitalized today in Montreal. She was partially paralyzed on her left side; she had a mini stroke. She has bad bruising on the back of her head and knee. It sounds bad. I sure hope she'll be okay.

July 4

I received my 100th *"sorry, we went with someone else"* speech. I punched a wall.

Mom called. She wants me to come out to Montreal.

Tracy's nieces and Dani and her kids were over for a BBQ. I got a little drunk and apparently spent hours on the bathroom floor crying about Levi and Kyle. Dani stayed with me the whole time. Man, this emotional shit rears its ugly head when I least expect it. Dang.

July 9

At my chiro appointment we talked about the stresses in my life that are preventing me from healing. He suggested meditation and some relaxation techniques.

Later in the afternoon, I stood up maybe a bit too quickly and I couldn't see for about 10 to 15 seconds. My eyes were wide open and I saw *nothing*! It scared the hell out of me! I had a few hot flashes and felt like passing out several times.

Dani said my vision loss and dizziness was because I'm not eating.

I made a deal with Tracy that when I get back from Montreal, I WILL find a job. I'll be in a better headspace when I get back. I think getting away will do me good. I'm 106 ½ lb.! This is going so great!

July 13

I've been in Montreal for three days now, seeing lots of Toby, Mom, and Bub. I weigh 101 lb. I took three laxatives this morning, four more at 2:00 p.m., three more this evening and six before bed. Mom and I are having our usual disagreements. She is talking to me about Tracy converting, and me learning more about her "world."

I said, I think I've been VERY clear I don't need you pushing *your* world on me. I don't push *mine* on you!

She needed reassurance she's not alone in this. I believe I've SHOWN you -- you *aren't* alone – I'm HERE!

I think you need to TELL people what you NEED and not make people guess, then get upset when they don't read your mind.

July 19

I took eight diet pills in the morning, then eight more before dinner. I'm cleaning up the house for Bubby coming home on Sunday.

On Toby's scale, I weigh 100 lb.
I joked to Toby that maybe I'll stay another month: Don't worry, I don't mean *here*, at your place.
It doesn't matter; you don't eat or sleep anyway. She kept feeling my body and making skinny comments.

July 22

I've been up from 2:30 a.m. to 6:11 a.m. having a panic attack. I haven't been able to reach Tracy. My mind is racing. I'm crying. I miss him so much. I just need to talk to him. I miss home – Tracy, Eb, Giz, and Slinky. I called Tracy at 8:00 a.m., he answered! RELIEF! He misses me.

Mom and I had a discussion about my employment situation.
I said, All I've ever wanted is to find a vocation and do it! I've yet to have a pull toward *something*.
She said if I find something I'm interested in school-wise, she'll pay for it but *only* if I complete it. If I don't, I owe her the money back. Deal!

July 24

Bubby's not having a good day – she's very weak and having palpitations. We played Rummy Q to take her mind off things. Mom and I went to the Jewish cemetery. I saw the *whole* family. It was nice to "see" Zaida.

We were visiting Mom's friends, Aunty Paula and Uncle Harry. He has lung cancer and pneumonia, and their son has AIDS. Oh man, SO sad. They are such a wonderful family. They don't deserve this.

We went to the Employment Centre to get info on training programs paid by the government.

I weigh 102 lb. It's good food here, it's hard to NOT eat it!

I spoke to Tracy – he's filing for bankruptcy at 8:00 a.m. tomorrow.

July 26

I received $478 from the insurance company for chiro and massage.

I don't get why I'm 10 lbs *lighter* in Montreal? I weigh 111 lb. here! What the...?
Tracy said, You're a bone rack.
I gained five pounds while I was out there.
GOOD!
I took seven laxatives.

July 30

I *finally* agree to go to school, and no one at the Employment Centre would help me because I'm NOT on UI. I just need some info! I'm such a loser – no direction, no job, no money. I found out today I *didn't* get two jobs.

Aug 3

A friend tried to kill herself tonight. Tracy and I stayed with her, watching her all night. It brought Tracy and I closer. We couldn't stop holding hands and telling each other we loved one another. I said, When we broke up that *first* time, I felt that desperation she's feeling right now. I'm not certain this won't happen again. I certainly hope not.

Aug 5

Tracy asked me, Why do you lie to me about not dieting? Why didn't you tell me you were taking pills?
What pills?
The one's you're hiding from me. He went behind the headboard on the floor and picked up the bottle of diet pills.
I was relieved they weren't the *laxatives*. The lady at the vitamin store said they'd help with energy.
THEY ARE DIET PILLS!
They don't even work, so I chucked them in the garbage and, obviously, I missed.

Aug 6

I went to my car and saw that the key holes on both sides were bent and scratched. Then I noticed the car bra had been ripped off. PANIC! I realize someone tried to steal my car. They did some major vandalism. I called the police. I called my insurance. We're NOT covered under Comprehensive. It's now all my own expense! I cried my eyes out. My first thought was Damian and Janis – retaliation for Tracy filing for bankruptcy.

At chiro, he took X-rays of my hand. Your hand is not broken, just bruised. He said he's only been able to get my body to 60%. He would like to refer me to Dr. Hasick in their office. He can get you to 100%. He has more experience, so I feel I need to pass you along to him at this point. Of course, if he can help me, sure!

We went to look at a house to buy with Connor. We found out today WE GOT IT! We are home OWNERS! We move at the end of the month. Tracy and Connor got a mortgage together from the bank. Apparently, bankruptcy people tell you that you are allowed to have a home to live in.

Aug 16
My first appointment with Dr. Hasick. We talked about *other* factors that may be hindering my recovery – stress, emotional issues...What stresses are in your life?
Job change, house change, my grandmother had a stroke, my husband's aunt died, and the threat of Tracy being laid off *all* the time…

Mom, Aunty Ruth, and Bubby are in Calgary today from Montreal. Bub can't be on her own, so she'll stay with Aunty Ruth for awhile to recuperate.
Mom was telling us how at home *she* feels in Israel.

Do you feel abandoned and betrayed by me?
Again, no, not all. If you're happy, we're happy.

We talked about my father. He's cutting right off. There is NO relationship. He doesn't even know about the house. I've seen him *once* since I've been back from Montreal.
Mom said to keep the door open. She brought up feeling distance from Tracy in the past few years.
Tracy said, I never knew how to approach you. I was afraid you'd treat me like the boys do.

Of course, why would you think any differently? Why *would* you trust I'd be different? Suddenly it all made sense.

I'm not a bad person. I don't understand why just because I'm not Jewish that I don't count, I don't exist to them? Quite honestly, if that's what religion does to people, I want no part of it. I work with every race, color and religion at CP. I wouldn't not acknowledge or speak to someone on *that* basis.

Mom coyly asked, So the subject is closed on religion?

Yes. I don't believe in it. I'm happy being who I am; religion only hurts people.

Mom said she feels closer to Tracy than she ever has.

Aug 17

I was afraid to weigh myself with all the food I've eaten, but I did – 109 lb. Okay, not too shabby.

Dr. Hasick said the adjustment held. I went from 22 degrees to four. I *didn't* need a treatment. It feels like I've been hit by a Mac truck, but at least I'm straight!

Aug 21

I cried my head off about Dad – done. He's hurt me for the last time. Never again.

Mom said to me, You know, you got the *best* of him. He was never closer to anyone than you. Just like Zaida (I was closest to him).

I said, No more open door. This is IT. He's alienated himself from everyone, one by one.

I talked about upgrading my English, math, chemistry and biology so in Sept '97 I can get into something good! She was pleased.

My father had to give me money for the house cleaning. We'd all agreed we'd split the cost.

Does it even bother you that you have no idea what's going on in my life?

No, at this time it *doesn't*. And he walked away.

I'm just baffled. He was so callous. You *can't* take that back. That door just slammed WAY shut! I want him out of the house NOW! I could've said I have cancer and he'd probably say he didn't care.

Aug 27
Yes, it's my 28th birthday today. Toby sent me a huge white teddy bear! Tracy and I went to Dani's for dinner. I go outside and everyone yells, SURPRISE! Mom, Bubby, Aunty Ruth, and Uncle Ruben were *all* there! I couldn't believe it! What a lovely surprise. Bubby almost didn't make it to the party; she wasn't feeling well. What a great day! 31 degrees out, 106 lb.!

Aug 31
Dad moved out.
There were nine of us helping for *our* big moving day. Uncle Ruben came to the new house and said Bubby may have had another stroke. She's in the hospital.

Sept 1
Mom told me Bub fractured her arm and had a CT scan. She'll be in the hospital for a week.
Dani told me my scale is 7 lb. HIGHER than the normal. So, if my scale says 110 lb., it's *really* 103 lb.? I don't know if I buy that, because I can't be *98 lb.*!
Mom told me I have a lot to be grateful for – a new house, a good man, going to school…
It's surprising to hear Mom talk about Tracy like that. I think this visit made all the difference.
Dad called Mom. He has NO IDEA *why* I'm mad at him. I can't deal with this.

Sept 8
Dani said she and her husband have noticed that I'm *not* myself. Maybe I need to consider taking something like Prozac.

Maybe, I just have a lot on my plate – the move, stuff with Dad, Bubby sick, starting school, Tracy's bankruptcy, in pain everyday ... I can't remember things and I have a concentration problem.

AND you're underweight and you still feel fat.

I've been punching walls. I never did that before. I dropped my Chapstick behind the nightstand and I almost burst into tears over that.

Sept 10

I went to see my doctor. I explained my concern about loss of memory and concentration and what's on my plate. He prescribed an anti-depressant. It'll improve your overall mood too.

Sept 25

I'm so frustrated over math. I felt like crying. I punched a wall yesterday and sort of again today. Why am I doing this course again?!

Tracy had a creditors meeting. Damian was there – he was very smug. He knows where we live now. We kind of have a restraining order against him. Tracy's trustee said to let her know if he tries to make contact.

Sept 29

Dad asked where we moved to and if we bought.

I told him.

So where do we go from here? I don't want to lose a daughter.

That's funny because our last conversation you told me you *didn't* care about me.

Ya, well, what I said **_at that time_** I wasn't interested.

Oh, I see, so a father tells his daughter to her face he doesn't care, and I'm supposed to, what, be okay with this? How do I know in a few months you won't *not* care again, then when it suits you *to be* interested, I've got to be okay with that? I can't let you do that to me again. You have no idea how much pain you caused me, how *deeply* you hurt me. I need to know you actually feel remorseful for saying what you said. I was yelling now – you REALLY need to hear this. We are talking about how deeply YOU hurt ME, with your words. What if I'D said them to YOU? Just how forgiving would YOU be?

I feel badly I said those words to you.

There's no need to rehash this. I've said my piece.

I heard you.

We exchanged numbers and addresses.

He said, Just because we've had words doesn't mean I don't love you.

Well, I don't want to lose a father either.

In talking to Mom later, she asked, Why are you mad at *Levi*? It's only my wish we become a family.

I'd LOVE to have an unfragmented family; however, it's THEIR doing that we are the way we are!

She leaves the day after tomorrow to go back to Israel.

I feel like a huge cow. I've got to get back to my 98 lb. I felt better then. I'm 108.

Oct 28

Here I've been feeling so immensely fat and hard on myself for eating so much junk food and not working out, but I just weighed myself and I'm 97 lb! Go figure. And I totally binged last night. But most of it came up. I'm working out lots. I took eight laxatives.

Nov 9

I weigh 96 lb. Myriam moves back to Calgary next Sunday. I'm so glad.

I'm really fucked up. I really fucked with my head when I figured out *roughly* how many times my bro abused me. I came up with high triple-digit numbers. Would that not fuck a person up? I'm so glad my therapist can fit me in this month.

I'm on a new anti-depressant. I'm looking after Bubby tonight; we call it *Bubbysitting*.

Nov 25

I saw my therapist. I don't want kids because I'd just project my paranoia about bad things happening to people onto my kids. I can see myself being an obsessive parent.

She said she feels I'm very perceptive and sensitive to issues, so I'd see the signs. I'd do things differently than what my parents did. I'd make it okay for them to talk to us. Most people become parents *without* thinking about it; here you've done nothing BUT think about it. She believes I'd make a wonderful mother.

Toby's been trying to reach me – she's been in the hospital for three days with contractions. She's okay now. They have a name picked out. I'll bet she names it after her grandmother.

I called Myriam. She was thrilled I called. She couldn't figure out how to reach me and was going to call my dad for my number, but Leslie advised her strongly against it. We spoke for two hours and I shared about Dad.

You're not the same person you were before I left. How so?
You're stronger. You're very wise. To be able to say to a parent, I don't care who you are, you can't treat me this way!

We talked about my fear of having kids. I think the problem is I grew up fast, I could never relate to children. I'm not comfortable around them. Tracy knows what to do and say. HE has patience.
She said she *didn't* feel maternal during eight months of pregnancy! Lots and lots of fears.
I found that helpful to hear. I just don't want any regrets when we're 50. I see Tracy and me as *regretful* if we DON'T have children.

Aunty Ruth and Uncle Ruben made the difficult decision this morning to pack up Bubby's apartment in Montreal. She'll remain here permanently.

155

I took eight laxatives, threw up three of them, so I took three more. I need to weigh a good weight for my physical next Wednesday.

Dec 4

I weighed in at 107 lb. Last year, I was 118 lb. She's not concerned as long as I'm comfortable with my weight. She said I *should be* between 120 and 133 lb. Interesting. She gave me yet *another* anti-depressant. She said she gives up if this one *doesn't* work.

Dec 11

While driving home from school, I almost needed to pull over because it felt like my head was going to explode. The headache was SO intense, it scared me. The intensity subsided a little after a while.

Dec 17

Apparently, Dad can't get over things that were done and said – seven MONTHS AGO!

Huh? YOU can't get over things WE did? You said to my face you didn't care about me and *I* GOT PAST IT! You should try getting past things, it's very freeing! You CHOOSE to be stuck.

Are you and your therapist having a good laugh at my expense?

Ya, I can see you picturing us having a good ol' knee-slapping, rolling-on-the-floor laugh at *you*.

Well, were you?

O. M. G.

Apologies were already made *seven months ago,* but apparently that's not good enough for you. It was thrown back in our face. We were past it, so why are you bringing this up all over AGAIN?! You seem to need to go over it again and again, rehash and rehash! You've just crapped on every bit of progress we've made since deciding to re-establish our relationship. In a week or two, you'll forget we had this conversation, and you'll bring it all up AGAIN! I can't go through this anymore.

This is too much. This can't continue. I want nothing to do with him. He wants to live in the past. So be it. I won't be a part of that world. He just undid *all* of our progress.

Dec 20

Dr. Hasick asked, What's going on in your life? Obviously, you're expending all your energy on *other* things, other than healing and yourself. You can only heal yourself. So, what's going on with you? Are you in school now?

Yes.

What do you WANT to do?

Good question. I told him about the career test I took at the university. It says I should be a writer. I just thought of it as a hobby...

He cuts in, I can see your energy level surge as soon as you talk about it. From one second to the next, the energy's there when you talk about *writing*. So, what's stopping you from pursuing writing?

Nothing.

1997

Jan 2

Toby had a baby girl, 6 lb., 8oz. That's what _I_ weighed at birth. She's named after _both_ Toby's and her husband's grandmothers. The baby shot out after four hours of hard labor, the doctor almost dropped her. You've waited so long for this. I'm SO happy for you guys.

I got antibiotics for my two ear infections. Connor's girlfriend moved in. I call her the roomie. Ya, this is going to work out swell.

I weigh 108 lb. Not bad. I figured with the holidays and no exercise I'd be around 115 lb.

Jan 8

I'm so done with this roommate thing already. Sharing our home with people who have no regard for others, are disrespectful, and take advantage. We are just done with it. I punched a wall again today. Tracy made me promise I'll never punch a wall again. I just get so angry that I don't know what _else_ to do. I broke the skin and my knuckle was bleeding for quite a while.

Tracy said, I can't live like this (with those two), are you ready to move out?
YES! This isn't _our_ house anymore. This WAS our sanctuary.
I sent away for some info on writing and I talked to Tracy about pursuing it.
I weigh 105 lb.

Jan 17

The roomie TELLS us to get our cat declawed, lock him downstairs, *or* get rid of him! And the bird has to go too. OR maybe we'll get rid of YOU! Yes, let's get rid of our pets for *your* convenience. NOT! It's Penny from Kelowna all over again! The bitch goes to the bathroom and all I hear is, *Get the fuck out of here, you stupid cat.* She gets out of the bathroom and tells Connor she's going to *kill* the cat. You BETTER go say something! Then she yells at the dog – *Get the hell out of here!*

HE needs to say something to US? Are you fucking kidding me? If she touches a HAIR on my pets…

Then she yells, *Fucking animals. Always in the way!*

Ebony comes running down the stairs. I kept saying over and over, Good girl, good dog. Pat. Pat.

Jan 19

So, all four of us had a talk. They suggested divvying up the house, each couple getting certain *designated* rooms. Tracy and I looked at each other like we KNEW they were going to suggest this.

Tracy said, Uh no.

Connor said, *Or*, we can *sell* the house.

Ya, THAT'S what WE want. You and Tracy have a 32-year friendship; THIS is not worth losing it over. This WAS our safe place, and now I *dread* coming home.

Tracy said to her, You *obviously* have a problem with our animals. You spray them with you water gun.

No, I *don't* have a problem with them. But you let your animals do whatever they want – they're so undisciplined.

I said, THEY were here *first* and getting RID of them for YOU is *not* an option.

Gizmo jumped on her lap. The roomie just sat there with her arms folded, scowling.

Tracy stated flatly, He always goes to people who *don't* like him.

Jan 23

The roomie called me. We had a long conversation about needing to get along and finding a way to live together for however long we *all* live there. She said, I haven't forgotten whose house this is. Later in the evening it became *abundantly* clear her peace and harmony speech was bullshit. I SHOULD have been more skeptical of her "good intentions." Later that night they were drunk and high, and rang the bell 100 times, banged on our door and cranked the music. Real mature.

Jan 28

I'm done exams!

Tracy said, THEY are leaving, they've been pre-approved for a mortgage; we*'ll* get the house. We just need to be on our own *so bad*.

Myriam calls every day. She's so considerate; she asks how my exams went, how the house is...I'm truly *not* used to that.

Damian is after Tracy *again*. They think they have Tracy on *fraud*. Damian is such a stupid idiot. The truth will come out.

We had MAJOR "discussions" about the house. Uncle Ruben's mediating, but those two just won't listen. Even though we are actually all on the *same side*, they only know how to *react* and think the worst of us. Tracy finally said, You can have it ALL. The house is YOURS! I'm fed up. I'd rather live in a *shoebox* than live *here*!
The roomie gets in MY face. You want a cat fight? I'll give you one! Don't get me started 'cause I'll beat you hands down. And she walked away continuing to threaten me.
I yelled out to her, Why don't you just shut up!
Uncle Ruben explains to Connor *again* how the house thing *will* work to *everyone's* benefit. Then suddenly, as if a light bulb went off, Connor has a *revelation* and *gets it*. Well, why didn't you *tell* me all this in the *beginning*?

WE DID! We've been trying to tell you for DAYS; you weren't listening! Your girlfriend there keeps yapping this *can't* be done. How does she even *get* a say? She DOES NOT own *any* part of the house!

I heard her say to Connor, Okay, maybe it *can* be done. ARGH! Later she knocks on my door: I just want to apologize. I've been stressed and my temper rears its ugly head. It won't happen again. Maybe now we can all try to get along.

Good grief.

Feb 7

Tracy comes over to kiss me goodbye and says, Start packing! I just found a note by her water gun that said, *Touch this and pay the price.* I don't need to be threatened in *my own home*. She does not realize SHE is the cause of <u>ALL</u> this upheaval. So, I smashed the water gun into 15 million pieces.

We'll be staying with Tracy's grandfather.

Feb 16

Moving day! There is so much snow out there; the U-Haul truck got stuck *six* times. We put everything in storage except our bed and a few other items. Giz settled in SO quickly; he's very happy there. He can finally relax, and not feel threatened and intimidated. It goes without saying Ebony and Slinky are pretty relaxed there too. Babe is happy anywhere. And the fishies are fine. This new living arrangement is going to be so great – Tracy's grandfather is so quiet; he doesn't yell and is *always* happy and positive.

I went to the grocery store and I thought I was having a heart attack; I was clutching my chest. I couldn't breathe. It took about five minutes before the pain started to subside. I don't have time for this!

Dani suggested I had that pain because of my low weight.

No, I eat like a cow. It's from all the sore muscles from the move and everything else catching up to me – it just came to a head.

Feb 24

We are signing the house papers at Connor's. We'll get our money from him on Wednesday. He and Tracy shook hands. I didn't say one word while we were there. Later, I told Tracy we need a plan, something to work toward. We weren't meant to have *that* house. We're excited about saving some money and finding a *new* home. I *yearn* to be settled in one place. We just lost our home, but I feel hopeful.

Feb 26

Connor gave us $700 instead of the agreed-upon amount of $1000. He decided to take $300 for February's mortgage. *That* was the last straw. The friendship is OVER. He never mentioned anything before; suddenly, he decides this is what it is. ASSHOLE! Screwed right until the end.

I got my marks – 50% in math, 81% in English. I passed math! Yippeeee!

Apr 4

Our five-year wedding anniversary! We went to Lake Louise for the weekend and had dinner at the Chateau. Aaaah, peace and quiet.

May 6

I finally got a car, a used white Grand AM. I love it! I'm going to apply at Mount Royal College (MRC). We went house-hunting. I haven't had an adjustment since February – three months! But now I'm definitely out of alignment.

May 19

We went to see a few houses – the second one was PERFECT! We walked in the front door and just *knew*; it felt like we were *finally* HOME. WE MADE AN OFFER! Nothing needs to be done or fixed on the house; it's great just the way it is. They countered and we accepted!

The possession date is July 21. Tracy and I went for a walk in the rain. We are pretty pumped!

June 17

Tracy is in court for his bankruptcy hearing. Damian's lawyer started talking all fancy and I thought we were *done for*. Then Tracy's lawyer blew them away with MAJOR cleverness. They tried to drag ME into it by saying since 1995 I haven't bothered to look for work, how I'm able-bodied...How the hell would THEY know? Tracy's lawyer mentioned I AM in school. There's no way I'm going to shelve my education for Damian. In the end, the judge ordered a conditional discharge, with Tracy owing Damian $5000 within two years. The $5000 goes to the estate, meaning *the creditors* get their money FIRST! *Then* Damian's lawyer gets *his* money – so Damian gets NOTHING! Tracy can earn ANY amount; there's no cap on the household income, CASE CLOSED. Damian left the courtroom muttering, *Fucking low-life worm* (about Tracy). Tracy and I practically *skipped* out of the courtroom with such relief and satisfaction.

June 23

I was referred by my doctor to the Sleep Clinic. He took down a lot of info about me. I prayed we would never discuss the abuse, but he asked – anything in your *childhood* that would be making you have a hard time sleeping?
Dammit. Yes.
Anything you want to discuss? No.
He set me up with a program to begin changing my sleeping habits. He also prescribed medication. I saw my therapist right after.

June 24

It's Tracy's 33rd birthday. Tracy told me that he was telling a guy at work that he (Tracy) has got a real treasure for a wife (me). I fall in love with her more each day.
You said that?

Yes, because it's true. I DO fall in love with you more with each passing day. You're just growing all the time. You're not the same person I knew when we first met.
We are growing *together*.

July 6

I went a few days in May not throwing up. Then I went a MONTH last month. I haven't weighed myself in soooo long. I'm afraid to. But I did – 106 lb. on the nose. I'm pleased.

I was dropping Tracy off at work, he says to me, I need your help to make our dreams come true; I can't do it on my own. You'll get into school, don't worry, it's just I need you to at least get a part-time job while you're in school. And with that we hugged, I got back in the car ... and bawled, all the way home. I realized I'm afraid to work because I keep getting canned. I have no talents. I can reapply for the writing course. I *need* a job. I KNOW what a second income could do for us. I'm so stressed it's not even funny. I'm so confused. I NEED to make my life *happy*.

Aug 1

I go down to MRC to apply for the writing course – and it *isn't* offered in the winter! I cried all the way home. Tracy said everything happens for a reason.
Well, every time I try to MAKE it happen, it never works out!
We got a parrot, an African grey. A guy from CP wanted to give him to a good home and knew we take care of our pets. His name is Matusi, but they call him Matty. These parrots have a vocabulary of a five-year-old. Among other phrases, he already knows *good morning/afternoon/evening* and *would you like a beer?* This is gonna be fun! He's in a cage away from Babe, and I don't think they care much the other is there.

Aug 11

Mom came to Calgary *with* her two-year-old granddaughter, Chana. She looks like Levi. Mom kept saying she looks like *me*. Apparently, my father is going over to my aunt's, to visit his granddaughter.
I said to Mom, I don't want to be here when he comes.
You need to get to a place where he can't hurt you anymore. How do you feel about Chana?
It feels weird to see you as an *instant* grandmother. She KNOWS you; she calls you Bubby.

Aug 13

Over the past few days, Mom and I have been pointing out the similarities between Chana and myself – she gets a rash from eating tomatoes, she has a shoe fetish, loves the phone, has my mannerisms...

Tracy makes her laugh. It's very sweet to watch them together. She *tries* to say his name. She only speaks Hebrew so "Tracy" is weird for her to try to say. Mom said she sees how much stronger I am. I said, I'm not willing to be with people who don't give back. I don't need to play games. I've made new friends. I still half expect my father will pick up the phone and call. Instead, he chooses to push us away.

Sept 14

Mom said there's a *reason* why Tracy and I *haven't* been killed or debili-tated in our accidents. She knows now that he and I are linked – meant to be together. So many things *could've* happened to us, but we've re-covered. I've been tested so many times; for what purpose? There is a greater reason for all this. They haven't been *subtle* occurrences either. There's a message in there. Tracy and I need to figure it out. I was *meant* to meet Tracy, we were *meant* to be together and he was *not* meant to die in *his* horrific accident at 18 years old, when he was ejected from his passenger seat and squished between two cars, then dragged for a block. (Split his skull open, punctured lung, lacerated liver, and front teeth knocked out). We need to understand the message.

My itchy rash is getting *worse*. It's on my chest, right elbow/arm, back of my head, and neck, the left side of my bikini area. It's very odd. I'm not using any new lotions or detergents. A real head-scratcher. Literally.

Sept 28

I told my father I couldn't keep letting him bring me down. Mentally, I was being dragged through the past over and over – I couldn't do it anymore.
Well, if you're interested in reconciliation, you have my number. We decided to meet face-to-face next Sunday.

Sept 30

I went to the doctor about my awful rash. It has travelled to my chest and the backs of my legs; it's spreading like wildfire. She doesn't know *why* I have it *or* what to do about it. She needs to think about it and will call me later.

She called later and said she will prescribe a steroid. I need to get an antihistamine too.

Oct 5

I met with Dad, and we rehashed old stuff. I said, If you had no one to blame or be angry at, you'd have nothing.
I was in my own little world at that house.
You also began talking to me about Levi and Kyle all the time. I'm the LAST person you should've been talking to about *them*.
I know. It was very insensitive of me. Your mother even told me not to talk to you about them.
I can't go backward; I need to move forward.
We decided to meet at the same time and place next week. He asked me if we could hug. We did.

Later, I'm cleaning dishes and the phone rings.

Sari, it's Levi. I'm calling from Israel. Well, Ema (mother) was over for Rosh Hashanah (Jewish New Year) and there was definitely something missing – it was *you*. I saw all these pictures of you with Chana. She keeps saying your name.

Maria gets on and asked about my neck and back and when I'm coming out so we can all be together and be one big happy family. We love you. Levi gets back on. We hope we have more contact in the future.

I ran to Tracy crying. Tracy said, He's lucky *I* didn't answer the phone because I'd tell him *not* to call here ever again. I don't want him phoning you. I hate that they keep hurting you like this.

What's the story here, what are the chances I speak to my father AND brother on the SAME day? I couldn't just deal with what happened with Dad today; now, throw Levi into the mix? I'm drained. I think I used a whole box of Kleenex today.

Oct 8

After Bubbysitting, I sat in my car and bawled. I feel broken. When am I ever going to feel "normal," whole? I need my mother to put things in perspective for me. I need my therapist, and maybe I'll call Toby. I get home and Toby had called. Sometimes she can sense when I need her. I *didn't* call her back. I don't want to be such a basket case when I speak to her. I think I'll just keep this between Tracy and me. I just don't feel like confiding in anyone else. Myriam called, she said she's really worried about me since we last spoke.

I confirmed coffee with my father. He *won't* come to our house; he says he wouldn't feel comfortable. It's too soon for that.

Is this EVER going to work out?

Oct 11

Toby called. Everything okay with you?

I got your message the other day, but I didn't want to talk to you while I was a basket case, I needed to calm down first.

You *should've* called me.

I knew you'd say that.

So naturally I told her everything.

Then we talked about babies. She asked, What exactly *is* your fear? I listed them all.

I've known you longer than anyone in my life so believe me when I say, you'd be a *wonderful* mother. Maybe you'd be a little neurotic and eccentric, but what Jewish mother isn't?! I had the same fears.

I said, I've NEVER said I WANT one until *now*. I'm afraid my maternal instinct *won't* kick in. I'm afraid if I have one now, God will punish me for waiting so long and it'll be severely handicapped or deformed.

Boy, you really *have* analyzed this to death! It's ridiculous to think God would *punish* you. Go off the pill, live life. If it's meant to be, it'll be. Don't be so worried about it all the time.

Okay, like the dumb asses that we *are*, we are taking in a roommate. We need the money.

Oct 12

When I met with my father, I said, I know you said last time you *weren't* ready to come to our house, but I am proud of it, I *own* it! I *want* you to see it!

Well, if you put it *that* way, then yes. Do you want to see *my* place?

Sure.

We saw his place first, and then he followed me to mine. He really liked it. He said, Enjoy many years here. We hugged and he left.

Oct 23

The rash was getting SO bad – all over my stomach, halfway up my neck, on my bum and back. My doctor sent me to a dermatologist, who suggested it may be a form of eczema. He prescribed more antihistamines and a cream. He said that if it doesn't work, he'll do a biopsy.

I'm 105 lb.

Nov 4

I have an interview with a big communication company – Fifth Network Ltd (FNL). When I asked when the next training session starts, she offered me the job! I start Monday!

I feel overwhelmed and nervous about the new job, afraid I won't cut it. Hopefully I'll feel more confident by Monday. I need to pass a security check, do well in training and get good sales. If I *don't* make it past training, I've still made $4000! This could be "it." I just don't want to blow it.

Tracy said he's pretty sure he's losing his job; it's just a matter of *when*. Everyone *under* nine years at CP is being let go.

Nov 20

There are eight people in training and everyone thinks *I'm* so smart in class. They keep coming to me to see how something is done. I've been throwing up a lot in the past few weeks, working out lots – six days a week.
Toby's pregnant – again. Yay.

Nov 27

We had a quiz today. I bombed it. At the end of the day, the trainer announces, This test will be shown to your managers and then *they* will decide if they still *want* to keep you on. Huh? This was supposed to be a *little quiz*; suddenly it's turned into an all-or-nothing? I said to the girls, Nice to know you all; Friday will be my last day.

Nov 28

We're all on pins and needles. The trainer called us into the back room one by one. I was the second to last to get called in. Each person who came out was pleased about their mark. I felt sicker. My turn. I *told* her I was going to be sick.

I don't understand why you're so worried. She started telling me what an excellent command of the systems I have, and what exceptional potential I have for this job. You did *really* well on your test – you got 76%. You're doing so well.

Bubby had a few more mini strokes. Man.

Dec 15
We got our exam results. She said I did excellent – I got 80%. Others got 92% and 95%. Whatever; I'm glad I passed and I have a job!

1998

Tracy and I had gone to Montreal in December to meet Toby's new baby and to attend her one-year-old daughter's Barney-themed birthday party. The one-year-old IS the Campbell Soup Kid: a perfectly round face and those red, rosy cheeks!

Jan 30
I weigh 113 lb. I dreamt I had a baby; I was *so* happy.

The dermatologist did a biopsy on my right calf. He was hesitant about doing it because it'll leave a *scar*.
Look at you, he said. You look like you'd *care* about having a scar.
Do the biopsy! I told him.

Unbelievable. What doctor would perceive the patient to be so vain that they wouldn't dare mar their precious skin because HE thinks I'm pretty (he said as much)! I was pissed. Oh ya, you're right. Let's *not* figure out this rash, let me just go on being "sick". Idiot.

Feb 5
Results. Inconclusive, right?
Well, we know there's an inflammation of the fatty tissue. We can do *another* biopsy, take more surface area, but I don't think that'll make much of a difference.
Is it an allergy?
No, we can definitely rule that out. He had me get X-rays of my chest and bloodwork. I weigh 103½ lb.

Mar 8

Dad calls. I've been sick; I thought I would hear from you.

How would I know that? This is the first time I'm hearing this.

I don't expect you to be a mind reader; just have some common sense.

I don't believe this; I tell you I had a biopsy and you start talking about the weather, and THAT'S okay? We go weeks on end not talking and that's fine with you, suddenly YOU'RE sick and I have to just KNOW that and call?!

Maybe we need to leave it. Our relationship is strained, lots of tension. You don't seem to care enough.

I don't care enough?! How did YOU care about my biopsy?

When did you tell me about that?

Three to four weeks ago!

Oh well, I was sick then; I don't remember you telling me.

Okay, so YOU'RE excused, YOU'RE off the hook. I could have skin cancer but don't worry about it.

I live alone; I hadn't eaten in four days. If Marsha hadn't found me delirious, I don't know what would've happened.

If you had TOLD me you needed my help, I *would've* been there. We've talked before today, you said you were *fine*. Am I to believe that every time we speak, you're lying to me?

Well, the conversation may have seemed normal to you, but I was so sick.

HOW WOULD I KNOW THAT IF YOU DON'T TELL ME?! I apologize for not being a better mind reader, I'm a horrible daughter.

You're being so blasé about it.

I'm being BLASÉ?! I CAN'T WIN!

Maybe we should just leave this.

FINE, and I slammed the phone down. That's the end of that. It's over. He can excuse HIS actions, but *I* get condemned because I have no common sense. OMG. I have no father. No more trying to work at something that could never work. There's no reasoning with him.

I called Mom's friend for some therapist numbers because mine is too busy. It's months and months before I can get an appointment with her.

I called the one she gave me. She's *not* taking new patients. I called the hospital. You need a doctor's referral. I *already* asked my doctor and she has no names to offer.

I'M SO FUCKED! I can't stop crying, I can't get any help! I'm THIS close to checking myself into the psych ward.

Tracy came home because he took *my* keys by mistake.
I said I feel like I'm having a nervous breakdown. I have no control. Why would you *want* to procreate with me, so I can pass on my insanity genes? Have them turn out like the *males* of this family?
What can I do for you? Do you want me to call your therapist?
Why bother, she won't answer or get back to me or have the time for me.
He called anyway. She came to the phone and confirmed there is *nothing* available. She told him to check with my doctor and get a *referral*.
Thanks for nothing!
I said to Tracy, What the hell good is a therapist if they're not there for you?! You can go back to work now.
No, I'm waiting until you get your call from the doctor.
Well, it could take some time.
Tracy went back to work.
The phone rings – it's my father! Since this was the *first* time hearing about your biopsy, I would like to know what the results were. Is it cancer?
They don't think so.
Well, if it was, they'd tell you. Thank you for telling me.

Mar 9
I can't help but think he will be alone in the end. He's alienated EVERYONE. And he'll be stumped as to how this happened. He should ask himself, Why did it take a "friend" **four days** to finally go over and find him sick? Oh right, because he alienated her too. I could use HIS words: Maybe you THINK you told me yesterday you were

sick, but I was so consumed with thoughts of *my* test results that I was delirious with anxiety, and I just *don't recall* you telling me. You can't expect me to remember when I had so much going on in MY life! I can now be excused from ANY responsibility! Just like you.

I threw up three times at work.

Mar 18
I told Tracy I don't want a roommate anymore. He's not contributing, and frankly I need my space!
Tracy agreed.
And the therapist issue is dead. I won't need one. I'm done with them.
My skin hurts.

We spent the next few months either forcing the roommate to pay rent or trying to get rid of him, dealing with my lawyer about the settlement from my 1995 accident, and trying to heal my skin. I threw up a lot, but only took two laxatives since last April.

But the biggest news was that I interviewed at the end of May with the head of the Professional Writing Program at MRC. It's a very demanding full-time, eight-month course (condensed from two years), with only 25 students chosen from 400 applicants. There will be about 10 classes I'll be taking to complete the program. Apparently, the class publishes a magazine each year. I felt really excited about it when I left the interview, although I was worried about being able to work at the same time. One week later, I get accepted! During a team meeting at work, my manager asked me to share my news and everyone congratulated me. Okay, so work's on board!

For my "big" birthday, I've decided to get blue contacts for my brown eyes and dye my dark brown hair blond. I think I might finally get a tattoo. I feel a need for a major transformation.

July 23

Mom's visiting and tells me what a difference she sees in me from last summer – stronger, better. It's so obvious you've moved on with your life and left the past behind so it doesn't control you anymore.

I just looked at her, trying to figure out what *she* sees when she looks at me. I said, I don't feel it.

Something always reminds me of *it* and I feel like I'm relapsing.

How much time, from 0 to 100%, is spent thinking about it?

It's usually only a moment, and then it's gone, but long enough to affect me.

Before, it *consumed* your life. It's only *now* that I see you're focusing on *other* areas of your life.

I just thought, *Here I'm feeling suicidal and I have no desire to look ahead.*

She continued. You've done more work on yourself than most will ever, most don't. You're *only* 30 and look at all you've done!

Then we moved onto babies. I said that I'd regret it if I *didn't* have any.

I know you would. You say your biological clock is ticking, but maybe NOW you can think about it because you've freed yourself up to look at it.

I need to make a conscious decision to go off the pill.

Well, what if you did, *today*. You'd still go through the writing course. Lots of women do have careers too. You have a wonderful husband who is so good to you, he loves and adores you!

I thought, Ya, I guess I could do it. I'm just afraid.

Toby had her baby, another girl – 7 lb., 8 oz. I'm bursting with joy for her!

Aug 11

Tracy's mom had a lump removed from her breast; it turns out there is cancer in it. I talked to her about it; she's one tough cookie. She'll try to be strong for everyone. Why couldn't **I** have the cancer *instead*? She has too much to lose, so many people count on her, and they need her. She *has to* be okay.

I took Tracy's mom to her doctor. She will need six months off work. Another biopsy is required immediately. The cancer is spreading very quickly. They need to prevent it from going into the bloodstream – if it goes there, it'll kill her. She starts chemo on Tuesday. She will need a mastectomy if chemo doesn't work.

Aug 12
I had a horrid dream about Kyle. It was happening all over again. He figured he'd pick up where he left off. I was so angry. I had no control. I was 10 again.

I told Tracy that I choose to not dwell on the bad things in life. There are no guarantees – I could get hit by a bus today. ANYTHING can happen at ANY TIME. One just never knows.

Aug 27
My 30th birthday! I actually feel *good* about things. Most girls my age I talk to say they DREAD this birthday – I'm looking *forward* to life, because things can't get worse than the past 30 years! I'm excited for what's to come.

Tracy and I got our first tattoos today! I got a strawberry on the inside of my right ankle and he got Bugs Bunny on the back of his left shoulder. SUPER painful, but by the time I reached the door to leave I wanted *another* one! Tattoo, blue contacts and blond hair (Tracy loves it). I'm feeling good!

Sept 1
First-day-of-school jitters. Having a big course load is an understatement. It's going to be great though. I feel honored they picked me. Okay, perhaps I may have a *smidge* of skill. We'll see if I'm *really* cut out to be a writer. In the back of my mind I still think about Dr. Hasick

suggesting to me I write; he put the bug in my ear. I hope one day he gets to know this.

Oct 1
It's the first time since *July* I threw up. I weigh 106 lb.

Our roomie is *still* here. NOT once in the year he's been with us has he paid rent when he was supposed to. It's like having a child in the house whom we have to chase after. Sigh. I need my house back. He drank two bottles of wine that were 30th birthday gifts. Who does that??

Oct 11
I'm a coffee drinker now! I start college and drink coffee. It's SO cliché, but I get why people *need* it. School has been overwhelming. I'm learning about the technical parts of the writing process. So far, my interests lie in technical writing or brochure-making. This course has also made me realize there was a lot I DID know!

Aunty Paula's son Peter died. First Uncle Harry, now this. That is so sad. He was way too young, kind, and wonderful. He was a *better* big brother to me than *the others*.

Nov 21
Tracy's mom had a mastectomy and she's going home not even 24 hours later. What a thing to go through. I sure hope she heals quickly from all this.

I've been thinking about my life. Why didn't I ever turn to drugs? I was definitely depressed enough. I definitely hated myself enough. So much chaos in my life, so many memories I'd like to forget. I never repressed a single one of them. Maybe I have a chemical imbalance. That wouldn't surprise me with some of the thoughts I have. I feel so messed up sometimes. I think I was afraid to even TRY drugs because I think I would've LIKED them.

I went to Aunty Ruth's and Bubby showed me an updated family tree. I almost burst into tears when I saw pictures of Kyle's *kids*; I thought he only had *one*. I almost lost it, to see their faces. And, of course, there were pictures of *them*. Bubby goes on to say, Look at Levi and Kyle, their beards…

Aunty Ruth jumps in and said, Ma, okay, that's enough, and quickly put it away.

What a day!

1999

Jan 3

We went to visit Tracy's dad in the hospital. He had a stroke. He has some paralysis, and has to retire because he has no pain sensors in his appendages. He works in a steel factory so that makes sense. I sure hope he'll be okay. That family has been through a lot lately. Tracy's mom will now be looking after his dad as well. Not that she wasn't all along. That woman needs a vacation!

Jan 6

It's Bubby's 90th birthday! I'm so glad she's here in Calgary so we can go have dinner with her tonight. I love when she tells us the stories about coming to Canada from Romania when she was two, on a huge ship called the *Teutonic*. She would always say, *Not* the *TITANIC* but the *Teutonic*.

I got the second highest marks on the graphics exam: 86%. I couldn't believe it! I'm so proud of myself. I start a screenplay class next – I'm *so* interested in learning this form of writing. I've never written anything like that before.

Mom called. It was SO good to hear her voice. We only get to chat once every three months.

Jan 25

We had a big party for Bubby at The Carriage House on the weekend. SO many people came to celebrate her. She *loves* being the centre of attention. She was just glowing today. Of course, Mom flew in too, which was pretty great.

I haven't weighed myself since November. I'm 109 lb. I'm back on the treadmill, and it feels good.

I had my best sales day at work – 50 products!

Feb 2

My father, whom I haven't had five conversations with in two years, called me. Why *now*? I need to get my thoughts together *before* I call him back.

The creative writing teacher stopped me after class to get MY opinion on how things are going with the class. He said, I understand you're a quiet person, so I thought I'd ask you *privately*.
I told him what is and isn't working for me with the work he's given us. I suggested that we need him to dissect the process of writing for us. He agreed and thanked me and said to keep up the good work. He *listened* to me! I'm floored.

Feb 4

Tracy says to me, Your father called again. I got to thinking. *Why not* call him back? He can't shatter our relationship any more than it already is. If the conversation goes badly, there's *nothing* lost. I called.

I want a measure of peace between us.
What does that mean to you?
I got the feeling you divorced me too. I don't hate you. I love you, and you're my daughter. I didn't abandon you. I don't want to rehash. Let's just be civil with each other. Call me.
I'm keeping my heart safe, and I'm being more protective of myself. I won't be blindsided again. Yes, I DID divorce him. There are only so many times he can play with my emotions and be in my life, then yank himself back out again.
Huh, I didn't break down. No impact. I'm very pleased with how I handled it.

Feb 9

My school partner and I are interviewing the mayor for a feature in the writing program magazine! He was so gracious. He made the experience so uplifting and easy. What an experience. He is such a humble, generous, kind man. I can't say enough good things about him.

Feb 10

Our article on the mayor *wasn't* accepted by the STUDENT editor in chief for the magazine. It was all a go, and now he had a change of heart. How can a STUDENT decide that?! Isn't the WHOLE point of the magazine that EVERYONE contributes an ARTICLE?! I'm relegated to creating a millennium *crossword puzzle* for the issue. A crossword puzzle. I'm so angry. Disheartening. My partner felt just as snubbed as I did, but at least she has another article going in the magazine. I'm at a loss. I have *nothing* to go into my portfolio from this program. I'm always left out and ignored. The story of my life. I feel so slighted by everyone. And NO ONE cares. I want my money back from this program!

Feb 24

I have no peace. I'm fighting with everyone. I'm having another mini breakdown. I need to call my doc and say, Help me with my mood swings, my depression, my suicidal thoughts – you help me NOW! I scare myself sometimes. I'm not going to class. I'm not in the headspace for it.

Mar 3

Mom is talking about getting remarried. I told her I'll *never* go to Israel for the wedding.

I haven't thrown up since December. But I did today.

Tracy sees a tiny dent in the wall. When did you do that?
You see, I have these mood swings – they are either waaaay up or waaaay down, there's *no* middle ground.

Mar 11

They were taking a count for how many copies of the magazine people want, so I was asked.

None.

Then they were setting up for a group photo. Why *should* I be a part of this? I needed to speak to someone about my feelings on this course, so I went to speak to one of my teachers. I talked about how my work was handled. He said things like this have happened throughout the years, *not* every student can be published.

I told him some have ZERO articles going into the magazine, while others will have TWO published articles. He said, Write the teacher a letter, that way there will be documentation if you get a poor grade; you have recourse. Outline the experience I had from this course.

I told him I *won't* be using the magazine for my portfolio.

You've gained the knowledge this magazine offered, you WERE a part of it, your name is on the masthead, your picture will be in it…

He shared about a time a piece of his got changed – *two-thirds of it*, for millions of people to see. He said, It's *better* to have a piece *yanked* than *butchered*. I thanked him for taking the time to hear me out.

I still have a play to write and a creative writing assignment to complete.

I should mention the class has reduced to 20 people. Yes, they are dropping like flies. It is an aggressive workload.

Apr 1

So, there is a GLARING error on the publishing page – MY picture is *missing*. I was standing on the far right of the photo and I got cropped out! April Fool's, right?

The teacher came over to me and wanted to know if we should go ahead with the retraction?

Are you asking me if I think it's *worth* it if we *put* my picture in the magazine? Well, ya, I want my picture in it!

Okay, we'll go ahead and have an insert reprinted.

UN-REAL. I am *literally* invisible!

The first weeks of April I was able to recharge my batteries and resume a bit of a "normal" life – having lunch with friends, doing fun things with Tracy, going out…I wasn't stressing over assignments, which was a welcome break. Perhaps knowing school was almost over, I relaxed about it a bit more. Tracy was even more attentive and thoughtful than usual, calling me several times a day, and just being sweet. I think he sensed my stress due to school.

On the work front, I tried to get on full-time but didn't get it – again. They said my being quiet was a factor, then denied saying it. Uh, I think my stats speak for themselves! The union asked me if I wanted to fight it. I said no because I didn't want to rock the boat.

I received an A on a research paper, finished classes and studied for finals. In May, I was informed by mail that I passed!

June 7

Graduation Day! Only *three* of us showed up and walked the stage to get our diploma. I'm really glad I went. I'M A COLLEGE GRADUATE! I'm very proud of myself for having accomplished this. Before, when I went to college, it was just upgrading courses; this time, I completed an actual certified program and could graduate. What a feeling!

I called Dad, I heard about Uncle Benny passing, I'm really sorry. Toby told me. I know he raised you and was very special to you.
He died of natural causes, being 100 and all. That's all I wanted to tell you, bye.
I didn't say bye, I just hung up.

I got my settlement from the rear-end car accident of '95! IT'S OVER! I am so relieved!

June 28

It's been *three months* since I threw up. I did a bit. It's been *five months* since I've weighed myself. I'm 107 lb. Tracy bought me weights. I'm not eating as much and working out more.

Mom comes in tomorrow. I'm looking forward to her visit, and our talks.

On a great note, Tracy was discharged from his bankruptcy after two years. It stays on his record until after the seventh year, though. That's okay; we can live with that.

Aug 18

Tracy and I went to Montreal to surprise Toby and the girls. No, we *didn't* tell her we were coming. We rented a car and drove up to her house. She was sitting outside with her kids and as we got closer, she looked more confused. Once she saw our faces, she freaked out! It was priceless! How are you **here**? It was a perfect surprise. The kids are so fricking adorable! The oldest, 1½ years, has the blondest, curliest hair and the youngest, 11 months, has these huge brown eyes, just gorgeous. I may not love kids, but *these two* I do.

Aug 25

At work my manager said *other* managers are showing interest in me, vying for me. Your sales really stand out; you have the highest sales on the team. My manager said he'll talk to whomever and whatever it takes to *keep* me. He said I'm an excellent CSR, I have an excellent rapport with the customers, and I have incredible potential. I had no idea. I'm baffled.

They have handpicked me and a few others to head up the new High-Speed Internet Team while staying on the team I'm on.

At the beginning of September, Tracy was laid off from CP Rail, but already had an interview set up with a brewing company. He said not to worry about it, we'll be fine. We spent October being quite on edge with Tracy being out of work (no, he did not get that job).

We were watching the movie "Forces of Nature," when Tracy turns to me and says, I never wavered or had second thoughts about marrying you. I told him I didn't either, not once. Suddenly, we both burst out laughing and just like that – all the tension of the month dissipated. It was good to laugh.

We applied for a loan and got it! We could breathe again.

Nov 9

It's been four months since I weighed myself – 106 lb. I threw up a bunch – it's been five months. In all fairness, I have the flu, fever, chills that hurt, and a huge cough. It's been three days. Apparently, my whole team is home sick, too! Tracy took good care of me. The fact that he could look at me with no makeup and un-showered for days – it's nothing short of a miracle that he's still here. I guess he has seen me at my *worst* many times. *That's* true love.

Dec 10

I've been reading this book about positivity and making changes and I feel quite at peace, content and hopeful. *I* even had to re-read that. Yes, I'm feeling good.

I announced to Tracy, I'm changing my life!
You're getting rid of me?
Ha, ha. This thing I'm doing is for *me*. This is a *good* thing. I'm tired of dealing with certain people in my life and I need to DEAL with them in a *positive* way.

2000

Right off the bat, I set my sights on becoming full-time at work, which meant I'd get a raise, paid vacation and better benefits, and hours. From January to August, I went through a few rounds of interviewing, rejection, doubting myself, positive feedback sessions, dusting myself off, and interviewing again, and then rinse and repeat, until I finally got a full-time position at work in September. Around that time, Tracy got a new job at a car dealership as a warranty administrator. Weren't we fancy-schmancy! To celebrate my birthday and our new beginnings, Tracy surprised me with a trip to Mazatlan for November!

The latter half of the year kept delivering good things. In October at work, four of us were handpicked to start the new E-Commerce (E-Com) Department. We'd be communicating with customers off the FNL website, answering their questions via email instead of by phone. I WAS SO EXCITED! I felt so appreciated and valued and that the company believed in my ability to be part of this huge new endeavor. This was the kind of opportunity I waited for in FNL. Right up my alley – off the phones!

I went to synagogue October 9, leaving before the end of the service. Two girls approached me, from the A Channel, and asked if they could interview me about the situation in Israel. They set up a camera and mic and I answered their questions. Of course, they didn't know when they stopped me that I had a parent living in Israel; it was a bonus for them. With the situation over there being so volatile then (Israel handed over a sliver of the West Bank to the Palestinians, but the violence only escalated), it was a hot news topic.

And then there I was, on the 6:00 p.m. news. Not long after the broadcast, I got a call from one of the city newspapers: We saw you on TV and we'd like to do a follow-up interview. So, I did the interview over the phone. Could we send a photographer over to take a picture to go with the interview? Sure, when? Now. A guy came by and took pictures of me.

The next day, I got a call from CBC Radio – could they do an interview with me now? Sure. And then they told me that I was on the FRONT PAGE of the paper. Bizarre. So many people at work were talking to me about it and, after my manager saw the paper, he said, "It's the quiet ones that get the limelight, the ones who don't want it." It was so odd, like I was some sort of expert on what's happening in Israel for the media. The news people admired the fact that my mom lived there and how difficult it must be for me worrying about her all the time. Had I not left synagogue early...it could easily have been someone else commenting on all this.

And then a surreal set of circumstances during Yom Kippur led to me reconciling with my dad. My father left a message, saying he saw my picture in the paper. I was ready to reconnect with him. I couldn't wait to tell Mom. This was what she had wanted to hear for so long: that he and I were back on speaking terms.

And then, finally, we were off to Mazatlan! It was our first tropical trip ever. It was phenomenal. I can't believe we hadn't done that sooner. The culture, the amazing food, the brilliant colors, the exotic scenery, the fun shopping...it was all more than we could've imagined. Tracy had never been to or seen the ocean before. We had arrived at the resort late in the evening, but the second we dumped our luggage in our room, we headed straight to the water. Tracy was like a little kid; he was so giddy. I was too. Palm trees, sand, and a warm Mexican night – it was heaven.

Things got a bit more stressful near the end of the year, though. I started PMSing so bad and ate so much junk food. For the first time in almost a year, I made myself throw up. I weighed 125 lb. I hadn't been that heavy IN MY LIFE! It could've been muscle because of my workouts, but my body was changing and I didn't like it. Had my metabolism suddenly gone crazy? Was this because I went off the pill? I snapped, crying all over the place.

Goodbye 2000!

2001

Jan 11

I decided to get my hair chopped off. I was ready for a change. I was grinning from ear to ear through the whole process. Loved it! Then she colored it.

I called Dad. We spoke for 1 hour and 12 minutes. It was ALL good.

We told each other so many stories and not one single mention of garbage from the past. It felt good to be lighter with him.

Jan 12

I'm the new team lead! I start February 1.

Despite my new 'do and feeling good about where Dad and I are headed, I'm feeling quite depressed. And when I get depressed, I think of all the *wrong* things, *especially* in the middle of the night. I think about why I'm even here, and who would even miss me? Tracy would get over it. Maybe he'd even feel relieved to move on with a "normal" person. And life would go on. I'm chalking a lot of this up to sleep deprivation; I've been up for 48 hours. I'm 32 years old with low self-esteem, a horrible body image, I think about suicide, I have no friends, and I'm depressed. Pretty fucking pathetic. I feel like I've lost my mind. I feel invisible in every aspect of my life.

When we finally got up after my restless night, I told Tracy I felt insane this morning. He listened and I started to feel better about things. Off to work.

I was having lunch in the cafeteria with the girls; they were talking about *family*. One girl talked about how close she is with her brother. Another girl chimed in, I WISH I had a brother.

I just about lost my lunch. At first, I wanted to get up and run away, but I just sat there, feeling like it was written all over my face. I wanted to hide. It took great willpower to keep sitting there and praying they wouldn't want me to contribute to the conversation.

Mar 3

I can't seem to shake this depression. Tracy has his work, and a new part-time job bartending, friends, volleyball, darts, and baseball now – me, I have nothing. No one. I'm trying to convince myself it's *better* to have no one. Just to have them leave my life. And they always do. I'm doomed to a life of solitary. I don't fit in anywhere. Maybe I only THINK I want a confidant, it's what I KNOW, but is it what I NEED? I need a *different* kind of friend than what I've had in the past. Did I mention I'm sick again? Full-blown cold. Groan. I weigh 111 lb.

Mar 14

Since February I've been the team lead at work, and today I had my first managers meeting. I spoke up and I was heard! What a great experience. I handled many escalations, gave furlough – I was a leader!

I went out for dinner with Dad, and we spent about two hours together. We talked about many things, safe topics mostly. We kept the past in the past. We were both pleased at how the evening went, and then he insisted on paying. It feels like we are on the right track.

Mar 20

I went over to Mom's (Aunty Ruth's) and we talked about what had been depressing me lately. She said some pretty smart things about friends. She said maybe I don't need ONE friend to hear everything about me and for me to tell everything to. You can have the frivolous friends you talk about hair and makeup with, and other ones to talk about deeper things. That's when I realized I HAVE been doing that in the past few years. Then I started thinking about the people I DO confide in – Mom, Tracy, Toby, Myriam, the girls at work... I'm already doing it!

I *never* wanted to *be* everything to one person, so it makes sense I wouldn't want that for myself either. I've really been okay all this time and I just *thought* I needed more. I thanked Mom for being here, for her clarity and advice. Plus, I don't feel at this point in my life I *need* to divulge all that past stuff. I feel zero need to open up about that to anyone, especially not just for the sake of it.

Mar 23
It seems like the universe picked up on my vibes about friends because Tracy calls me at work and asks Are you sitting down? I'm sending you something.

I couldn't even imagine what he had for me. I opened up the email – it's from JANIS. I just about puked. It was a simple email saying hi and she lives in Dallas now. Maybe this is *finally* closure.

When I told Mom about it, she said, All these people coming back into your life – it's *not* by accident, it means *something*.
What, that I'm so memorable?
Well, ya. They all contacted YOU, they looked YOU up.

Neither Mom nor Tracy was surprised by Janis reaching out. It's been six years! I'm feeling a mixture of things. I need to sit on this and really think about *what* I'll do about it.

I had the girls from work over. We talked about first impressions. One girl said she was intimidated by me.
I said, I *know* how people see me, as a snob and unfriendly because I'm shy and quiet. But once I get to know you, I'll talk. If a person judges me and decides they *know* who I am *before* getting to know me, I can't be bothered to change their view. My favorite saying is *don't judge a book by its cover.*

We know NOW; you are soooo nice! You're completely different from what we ever imagined. Do you have siblings?

No, I'm an only child.

Thank goodness no more questions about that. The wine flowed and it was a great, great girls' night! Much needed.

<u>Mar 27</u>
I responded to Janis's email and she replied back. We pretty much hashed it out. I never thought I'd get an opportunity to ask her WTF happened out in Kelowna. We were very honest about everything. We had nothing to lose. I didn't hold back.
She said Don't leave me again, I just found you!
I always figured she just went on with her life, never looking back.

Toby called. Boy, was she mad when I told her about Janis! There is a code of honor with friendship; you *don't* break it! *Good* people don't do what *she* did.
I know Toby is being protective, but I'd already started questioning if I'm doing the right thing with Janis. Am I just being a sucker? Am I setting myself up for *another* big fall? Do I trust this? Are her intentions even genuine? Does she even deserve a second chance? My brain hurts. I threw up a little.

<u>Apr 4</u>
Our nine-year wedding anniversary! We are meeting our friends for dinner later.

I got another email from Janis. She said she needed to absorb everything, and take a break from it. We are so different. I tackle things head on, at the time; she doesn't. She's engaged. Whoopty-doo. I honestly don't know what to say back to her. I'll wait a bit before I respond, like she did.

I won an award at work for my newsletter! Validation! I finally got to use my writing skills, and it was recognized. My newsletter was distributed to all departments; it feels amazing to know that the positive feedback from everyone contributed to me receiving this award.

Apr 12
All the ladies in the office went for lunch – I'm the only one not asked. Wow. Invisible. Girls can be so catty and cruel. Is this high school again?

Work is so damn cliquey. The whispering and knowing looks back and forth. I feel like an intruder here. I've got to find a way to not let it get to me. I try so hard to fit in; it works for a minute (having them over for girls' night), and then I'm ignored again. I just have to pretend to be happy *all* the time and not draw attention to myself. I just want to fit in. But I hate pretending even more.

Tracy and I leave for Puerto Vallarta in nine days, for one week!

May 3
Mom said, You should go away more often; everything just rolls off you now.
I feel pretty relaxed. The weather was HOT, mid-30s, great food, and I mostly watched Tracy play volleyball all day.

Ebony's been sick for the past two days. It's either separation anxiety or she ate something bad. Slinky isn't well either, and the fish are dying. Going away seems to affect *all* the critters. The birds were fine. Tracy said Eb pooped in the basement; it looks like there's blood. We're going to the vet.

May 9
Ebony didn't come downstairs this morning. The vet called: her bloodwork *didn't* show anything. Maybe start her on antibiotics. It's the first day she *hasn't* thrown up. Slinky is doing SO well.

May 28

Mom calls me yesterday, Bubby's in the hospital again; she passed out during breakfast. I went to see her today. She thanked me a zillion times for being there. God should reward you for being so good to me.

Bub was discharged and she passed out again. Back to the hospital. Mom will be sleeping at the hospital in Bubby's room; they'll bring a cot in for her.

May 29

Mom told me there's a 13-second gap where Bub's heart stopped. They are putting in a pacemaker. So, it's her age, she's 91, and her heart. They are moving her to Cardiology.

Tracy asks me, So, you want a baby?
Ya, I think we should. We've been together 15 years – we could have had a *teen* by now!
We talked about where we'd put the nursery. Tracy said they'll be raised Jewish and go to Jewish school.
I said, We have to have a *girl* first so I can name her *Charli.*

June 2

I slept over to stay with Mom at Aunty Ruth's house; they've been out of town until tonight. Mom says to me, This week, with Bubby in the hospital, you gave of yourself, completely. You have a life, pets to look after, a husband, you work all day, but you spent *all* week with us, without apprehension. You gave with your whole heart; you're such a good person. I just saw you in this whole new light. She said Bubby was so aware of my visits – Sari doesn't *just* come to visit for a bit, she stays a long while!

I blushed and felt a little embarrassed to be noticed for loving my family. But I'll take the sweet sentiment. It's nice to be *seen* by others even though I wasn't doing it for the recognition. I'm relieved Bubby will be discharged from the hospital in a few days.

Tracy was offered the service advisor job at the car dealership.

July 8
Since Dad and I are making such good progress, Tracy and I decide to meet him at a bagel shop. We are clearing the air once and for all.
The two of them shook hands right off the bat. It was a very calm, constructive discussion. Everyone had the chance to be heard.
Tracy said, I have missed you dearly. The bad part is you missed five years of your daughter's life, so much wasted time.
Dad agreed.
When we were leaving, everyone hugged. It was wonderful!
In the car I said to Tracy, It's going to be so great having a father in my life again. I can't wait to have him over for dinner, include him in our parties, go for coffee...I'm soooo looking forward to the normalcy of it. I'm looking forward to the future!

July 15
Uncle Ruben's brother-in-law passed. I picked Dad up for the funeral. I sat between Mom and Dad. It's the first time since *my wedding* we were all together like that. Weird. For a funeral, we come together.

Aug 15
Dad's friend Marsha has to re-home her cat NOW! He's a two-year-old Siamese named Simon. I called everybody I know who might be able to help. I finally called Marsha and said, Regardless, *we'll* take the cat until we find him a home. Ebony and Gizmo both attacked him. I'm sure eventually they *will* all get along.

Dad came over for dinner. I look over and see Tracy's hand on Dad's shoulder as they're talking. I've waited SO long for that!

Later, Dad told me he had a talk with Tracy. He said, I told him I couldn't imagine Sari married to *anyone* else. You're good for/to him, he's good for/to you. Finally.

Sept 1
I weigh 125 lb.! All this eating three meals a day, no exercise and no laxatives crap, it's all making me *gain* weight!

Two of the bombs that went off in Israel today were RIGHT where Mom walks every day. The town where she lives was under fire. So surreal. I'm SO glad she is HERE visiting, and not in Israel. She said it's still business as usual there while these things are happening; you get used to it; you go about your day. We believe God will protect us. If it's your time, it's your time. Wow.

Sept 5
Janis came to town for a visit and I met her for coffee. She pretty much looked the same, and told me I've aged very well. We talked about her upcoming wedding to a guy she'd met in Calgary. Although they live in Dallas now, their wedding will be in Calgary. It was all pretty much chit chatty stuff. It's kind of exciting to think of going to her wedding. I didn't say that out loud. She WAS a bridesmaid at MY wedding, after all. She asked, If it's okay, I'd like to look you up again.
Well, ya!
We hugged.

Tracy's job is up in the air again. But when he came home, he said he has an interview for a pool and spa place on Monday. He'd be the foreman. And just like that, things can turn around for the better. I get an email that I'm due for a wage increase by October 25. Nice.

Sept 11
Planes crashed into the two World Trade Towers and the Pentagon today! Terrorists! Downtown Calgary has been evacuated. FNL is

beefing up security. A CBC Radio guy calls me: Can we talk to your *mom* about what's been happening in the Middle East?

I got in touch with Mom back in Israel; she said she'll do it, and gave me a rabbi's number as well for them to contact. She said, it's time to *Daven* (pray). Suddenly FNL is telling us to evacuate the building. Go home!

Sept 12

I'm just sick about the attacks. Everyone is so afraid. Those were *commercial* airlines too. Scary. *Thousands* of people lost their lives – right there in the States, not off in some other country. Tragic. No words. I guess people are just *now* taking notice of the awful things that happen in the world. This is all new for Canadians and Americans. People just don't understand the never-ending battles in Israel. And I get the REAL news straight from Mom.

Oct 17

I'm overwhelmed again. If Tracy doesn't get a job soon, we're pooched. He left the dealership a month ago because the work environment was too stressful. I think he thought he'd have gotten on with the pool place a lot sooner. He had that interview with them and they've been dragging their feet ever since. Either you DO or you DON'T need to fill the position! Tracy has also been trying to get back on with CP, talking to his old bosses. He just got word they've already *done* their hiring. It will be a while until they look again. Too bad; he sure loved that job.

Okay, I need to get real sick so I can lose the weight I've gained. I'm 120lb.!

Oct 24

I got my wish; I feel like crap. Careful what you wish for. Nauseous, sinus headache...

CP called Friday night – they *will* be looking for people; go apply! Hopefully by next week, *one* of the jobs Tracy's looking into will pan out!

Oct 29
Tracy called me at work. I got a job at the pool place; I start November 1! The pay is less, but we'll figure it out.

Dad called and asked me how I felt our relationship was going.
I feel things are progressing quite nicely. Is having you over for meals three times a week any indication?
Ya, you guys are spoiling me.
He had such joy in his voice. He told me he's going to a Jewish singles meeting.

Mom emails me, saying she's going on a *Shidduch* (an arranged date for the purpose of marriage). Ironic.

Nov 8
I had a meltdown walking to work. What is the point of my fucking life? Money problems, Tracy's not happy with me at the moment, people at work ignore me, and people in general dislike me. If someone came into the house this minute and shot me, they'd be doing me a *favor*! I've been tested and tested my WHOLE life! When the fuck do I get a goddamn reprieve? Happiness? Peace? Contentment? I give up. I'm suffocating. I have no *human* kids, maybe now's a good time to drop dead. I'll be missed for half a minute, and then life goes on. So many *amazing* people lost their lives on September 11 – why couldn't *I* have been taken *instead*? I've asked God for a sign that my life *is* worth salvaging – nothing. I'm still waiting. Mom will get remarried; she has her sons and grandchildren – she won't be alone. Tracy? He'll find someone in a minute. Dad – well, I'd feel terrible that we cut this budding relationship short. I wouldn't have to worry about growing older and getting more wrinkles than I already have, or worry about

being undesirable, which I am now anyway. The hardship would be over. Calm. Peace. I feel crazy. Unhinged.

I walk into work and no one has a clue what's going on in my head. Thank God. They think they know me. I just don't care about anything right now. I kept hoping a car would hit me and take me out. No such luck. I'm just exhausted, no sleep, crying, thinking, analyzing, on overload. When I think the worst though, things work out. We shall see.

Nov 28
I'm sick *again*. At work they think I have mono – I have no energy and am drained. I looked mono up on the internet: swollen glands, sore throat, fatigue... I just need my bed. I called the doctor; they're already closed for the day.

I've cut down on the amount I eat – I've only had soup and popcorn. My stomach feels flat for the first time in I don't know how long.

Dec 10
Slinky's not doing well. We're going to have to make some decisions. He didn't eat this morning. He seems to be in pain when he sits or lies down.

Mom called. She sounded good. So, I just got back from Jerusalem and the *Shidduch*. I'm getting married!
That's so wonderful! I'm so happy for you. I know these *Shidduchs* can work quickly, but I'm sure you found the right match for you.
Yes, I did put a lot of thought into this. We'll get married in four to five weeks. He's very kind, a real gentleman. He's a Rabbi. His brothers are big Rabbis in Los Angeles. So, you have to pack now.
Um, I don't know about *that*.

Dec 11
I woke up feeling sick again. Guess who just called me? Stepdaddy-to-be. He said, Your mother is a wonderful person, I hope to meet you. Your brothers will be at the engagement party.

I called Dad to tell him. His reaction was of absolute joy. He's very happy for her, thrilled.

I talked to Mom. *They* will be at the wedding. It'll be about three to four days of gatherings.
You wouldn't be *sitting* with them, but they'd be *around*, and the wives.

I don't believe I'd regret NOT going. I can't pretend. No more.

Dec 16
I kept thinking I *was* going to the wedding.
I'm really trying to be there for Mom.
Tracy says, If you're not comfortable going, don't go.
Maybe I needed permission to not go.
Why put yourself through that if you don't have to?
I know. I'd be going for Mom, but in reality, I'm not able to do it. I'd be SO stressed out. I'd be dreading *everything*, and for what – a one-hour-long ceremony? Things will run much smoother *without* me there. I'm a stranger. Is it worth all the shit I'll have to deal with? She doesn't need a basket case out there – it's HER day. I feel like throwing up, thinking about seeing Kyle. How could I avoid talking to *them*?

I called Mom. She was absolutely SHOCKED I was even *considering* going.

I didn't even think for a minute you'd actually come to the wedding; that makes no sense. Your support means more than you being there.
I just needed to hear *you'd* be okay with me NOT coming.
Of course! You always know what's best for you. I love you bushels and bushels, sweetheart.

I AM SO RELIEVED!

2002

Jan 8

Tracy and I are planning a trip to Puerto Vallarta (PV), Mexico, for our 10th anniversary; we want to renew our vows. We've got to figure out our anniversary bands. Tracy is getting a diamond put in his wedding band and I'm getting an anniversary band with 10 wee diamonds in it. Exciting!

Jan 14

Mom's wedding day! They decided they will live in Jerusalem, in *his* apartment. I'm truly happy for her. I hope she finds what she needs in this marriage. I hope he is good to her. I wish every happiness for her. She sounded happy each time I spoke to her since sharing her news.

Jan 18

I sure wish Mom would call – there was a suicide bomber at a Bat Mitzvah (a religious initiation ceremony for a 12-year-old Jewish girl) in Jerusalem yesterday.

Aunty Ruth called though, and told me everything is *alright*. I feel like such an outsider. Aunty Ruth and Uncle Ruben left from Calgary, and their daughter, who lives in Israel, *all* went to the wedding.

Slinky is not well – he's peeing all over the place. Fortunately, he still has a good appetite. Tracy and I talked about what we should do.

Jan 22

I'm still sick and rundown. We went to Aunty Ruth's for dinner and they had a friend over too. We saw the wedding pictures. Mom looked *stunning*! Then there was a picture of Levi and Kyle. I just about threw up. The friend kept asking me questions about them. That was SO uncomfortable.

Feb 8

I emailed Janis; I have nothing to lose. I put it all on the line. I wanted to know where we stood, and if she was planning on inviting us to her wedding. She answered back that we will NOT be invited to her wedding. Well, there it is: the *truth*. She was a bridesmaid at my wedding, but I don't even warrant an invite. I emailed her back telling her how hurt I was. She CALLED me. Don't cry. She feels terrible.

I didn't say too much. I was thinking I gave HER so many second chances, and that's *after* a falling-out, then for her to have the wedding HERE in Calgary (because her family lives here) rather than in Dallas and STILL not invite me. From once best friends to this. Another giant slap in the face. In light of this new information, I'm questioning the relevance of staying in touch with her. There's no point in continuing this. We said what we needed to. *I* did, anyway. That ship has sailed. I'M DONE.

Mar 4

I paid for our Mexico trip with variable pay, and I cashed in my shares – 41 sleeps!
Tracy got a 5% raise and my wage increased! We are rockin'!

I Bubbysat. We laughed so hard watching *All in the Family*. It's good to laugh. Bub says, Can I ask you a personal question? Do you want a baby?
Yes, I probably will have one.
She seemed satisfied with that answer, and moved onto another topic.

Apr 4

10 years married, 15 together! We had *two* outings to go to. Aunty Ruth had us up for dinner. She and Uncle Ruben really bothered, and made it very special. Afterward, we met friends at a pub for drinks.

I was thinking of our vow renewal, and I suggested we do the ceremony on the pirate ship they have in PV. Lots of people get married on the beach – who can say they did it on a pirate ship dinner cruise?

I've been sick so much, so I'm only getting paid 70% on those days. I have to work 65 days without being sick to get back to 100% coverage. I never knew that.

Apr 19: the 19th...9–1=8!

"8" **is** my number. So many significant events have happened on the 8th, or a derivative thereof. I hadn't noticed the pattern until I started looking back on some journal entries. The day we met – 04/04, for starters.

We've been in PV for almost a week now, and tonight is our vow renewal. A friend from Calgary is officiating. We knew he was going to be in PV at the same time as us, so we asked him. We also invited two other friends from Calgary to join us for our special celebration trip. I bought a cream-colored dress at the flea market and we bought onyx-colored rings. Tracy bought a white shirt and shorts. I'm so looking forward to it.

After dinner I said to Tracy, Let's do the renewal now. We had the whole upper deck of the ship. We had written our own vows, and Tracy went first. He started with a poem he had written me, and then continued.

"I offer myself and hope you will accept my hand to continue our journey together as husband and wife. As I stand before you today, I offer these words as a pledge of my continuing love for you. It has been 15 years since you first caught my eye, as you were dancing with your friends at Malarkey's. That thought will remain with me for all eternity. Being married to you for 10 of those years has been a wonderful adventure. In marriage, they say two people become one. I say in our case it is exceptionally true.

It is said after being with the same person for many years you begin to finish each other's sentences. You and I share and complete each other's thoughts. Each night as I lay next to you, I find it a true blessing knowing that when I wake up, you are there to begin each day with me."

I was so moved. He writes such beautiful words, from the heart. I love that man!

My turn.

"I have dreamt of this day, standing here with you, every day, for the past 10 years. I always knew that this many years later, we'd be repledging our love. What I didn't realize is how much more I love you today. I didn't know it was possible to love you more than I already did. So, 50 years from now, I'll be bursting at the seams! To be able to stand here today and TELL you how I feel is one thing, but there's so much unspoken pride within me. I feel so honored to be your wife. We connect like no other. We finish each other's sentences and unspoken thoughts. No one knows me like YOU do. I trust you with my life, my inner-most feelings, and deepest secrets. You're more than my husband -- you're my best friend, my partner, my soul mate, my fate. We were meant to find each other — in that crowded bar they called Malarkey's. I admire your ability to grab life by its horns and live it to the fullest. You are never too afraid to try new things, so you've taught me to take risks, because you only live once. And you can STILL make me laugh like no other can. You find the humor in everything -- just one of the many things I love about you. So, my promise to you today, is to continue to nurture our love, offer my unconditional support and grow very old with you. I am here freely, as I was 10 years ago,

and I rejoin you in our life of continued love, respect, and discovery, every day, for the rest of my life."

Tracy's gaze was fixed on me, listening to every word I said, with such love in his eyes.

We exchanged rings and kissed. So many people were watching and cheering for us. Then they played "Lady in Red" (we brought the CD with us). We danced to our song just as the sun was setting. IT WAS PERFECT!

Apr 25
We got a call in our room from our friend who's looking after the animals – *Slinky died today.* I cried for two hours. It's like he *waited* for us to leave for it to be okay to pass. He's finally at peace. My little Tinky bum.

Apr 30
Giz is SO happy we're home. He won't stop purring. Simon's been following me everywhere. I got more details regarding Slinky. They brought him to the vet *after* he passed, to make sure he wasn't just in a coma or something. They confirmed he was gone. Our friends said Gizmo knew exactly what was happening *while* it happened. He just sat there with Slinky while he died. When they put Slinky in a box to take to the vet, Giz kept rubbing his face on it. He knew.

May 8
I'm sick again; I got a cold from Tracy. I picked up Slinky's ashes. I've never seen that before: crushed bone. Depressing. I cried and cried – my kid is ash.

In the early summer, Mom came in for a lovely visit. After she left, we had a visit from a lady whom our group had befriended in. She had quite the story and we felt badly for the abuse she'd endured, so we took her under our wing. Well, we were duped. She was a nightmare guest: lying, as phony as they come, stealing, and pitting our friends we had along in PV against us. She started "dating" one of our friends and she never spent any time with us. This "friend" believed every word out of her mouth and would side with her. He was not thinking with the head between his shoulders. Suffice it to say, that friendship was beyond repair. We told her to get out and stay with those other friends.

Lesson of the day: Don't pick up strays from Mexico.

I felt under the weather off and on all summer. So tired all the time, had a few colds. And a bladder infection.

Sept 12

I'm sick *again*. What the heck is going on with me?

Tracy and I were talking about having a baby again. It's just gotta happen. Tracy asked me if Levi and Kyle are the reason I'm afraid to have one.

A big part, yes. I know *you* want one; you've been very patient with me, but if we don't do this *now*, we never will.

Tracy turned to the animals and asked if they want a *human* brother or sister?

So, what does this mean?

I guess you're going off the pill!

I started crying. Happy tears.

Tracy said, Are we going to have a baby?!

I guess we are.

He was SO happy.

Can we tell Dad when he comes over? He'd be so happy. Okay.

Dad almost blew a gasket. He *was* so happy. Is this what you *really* want?

We've been talking about kids for 15 years; it's not a spur-of-the-moment decision. We wouldn't be saying anything to you if we weren't *serious*. It may take a while, but we're doing it.

Sept 26

I'm expecting to see a *more* religious Mom next time we see her; being married to a rabbi and more immersed in Judaism. My stepfather gets on the phone with me when Mom calls and quizzes me on how I'm keeping the Sabbath.

I do, but not in YOUR way.

Tracy got a part-time job at The Carriage House as a private function bartender for now. It's in conjunction with working at the pool place.

Oct 3

TWO years on E-Com. I found my first THREE gray hairs! I mentioned to Tracy our friends are dropping like flies, Is it US?

He said, No, WE are just cleaning house, getting rid of all the negative people in our lives.

I just got a "Reason, Season, Lifetime" friendship email. I've seen it 100 times, but I think I was meant to reread it again *today*, to understand *not everyone* is meant to STAY in your life. And I'm okay with that.

Tracy and I made a pact that we do something different – well, not *every* day, but when we can. Live life! I'm eating healthy, on folic acid, going on the treadmill, going off the pill – we're REALLY doing this!

Tracy comes home and rubs my belly. He says, There's going to be a baby in there someday.

Oct 21

Tracy and I went to see my doctor to discuss having a baby. She said it takes about three weeks for the pill to work its way out of your system. Just go for it, don't stress about it. We're not panicked about it; we're just letting nature take its course. She said most people get pregnant a week after trying. I just wanted to make sure everything was okay after being on the pill for almost 20 years.

November was quiet; the only highlights were my five-year anniversary at FNL and Tracy's grandfather's 90th birthday.

Dec 3
Today at work we had a rumor confirmed about the E-Com department – it's going to operate out of Edmonton starting in June. Not a shock, we knew it was coming. It still sucks. All our hard work to create this team, only to pass it on to Edmonton. They tell us we'll be put back on the phones. *That* sucks. There could be something BETTER down the road though. Here's hoping.

I'm gaining weight from coming off the pill. Man.

Dec 13
I was sick last week and still this week. I have laryngitis and am feeling itchy today.

A co-worker just had twins and another girl at FNL just told us she's pregnant. While I'm thrilled for them, I'm a little sad for me.

Toby called – she said it sounded like I could use a friend. It's been a while since I heard someone say that to me.

2003

Jan 3
Our manager is pregnant now. Is there something in the bloody water here, and why is it *not* affecting ME? Tracy and I went out for dinner and talked babies. He asked me *what* I'm afraid of.

Is it BEING pregnant?
Oh God no, it's the *after* part. I'm afraid I won't be a good parent. I *know* YOU'LL be great.
You'll be great too. We'll have a boy first, then a girl.
I'm counting on having a *girl first*. Why a boy first?
So he can look out for the girl.
Um, the older brother doesn't always "look out for" the younger sister. Right.

Jan 28
I've decided I want to write a book. I need to figure out a topic. I *need* to write. I *want* to write. I just have to figure this out.

Tracy checked my back; I have this horrid acne/rash thing going on. He told me it's bad and to go see a doctor about it. They won't know anything.

Feb 24
Ya, I'm sick again. Something HAS TO BE wrong with me. My immune system is for shit.

I sure wish I knew where I was headed job-wise. Everyone is applying for other jobs, inside and outside FNL. Maybe I'm just meant to ride this out, *then* have a baby! I'll be on mat leave for a year, THEN decide. I know I DON'T want to be on the phones; I just don't know where I'll land.

I could write a book called *Just Going Through the Motions*? I could talk about what's *important* in life. Sigh. I sure envy people who do what they love. Maybe one day I will too. If I'm *meant* to write, I suppose I will. I just DON'T want to write about MY life. I *don't* want to divulge MY story. I need a different subject. But would it help *me* to be more forthcoming with *my* story? Can I even help others *without* telling MY story? Do people even *want* **my** help? I need the TIME to do it. Or MAKE the time. I just gotta write!

Then I had a brainstorm for a book! It would be about personal growth. We can stay stuck or we consciously decide to evolve! This IS a sign – don't ignore it, Sari. If I write this book, I will reference THIS day. It's like my hand was possessed, pen to paper, scribbling, it just poured out! I KNEW I had it in me. I finally gave it a VOICE!

Mar 11
My rash has moved to my shoulders. Itchy. Dammit!

I overheard a girl at work say she's *too old* to have **more** kids. She is MY age! And two more people at work are pregnant. I GOTTA get this water everyone's drinking!

I went to the bookstore and jumping off the shelf at me was a book about what I wanted to write about. I felt defeated. Of all the books I could see in front of me, THAT one stands out. Does that mean I can't write about the same subject matter? Go ahead? Forget it? See it as a sign to continue? WHAT?!

Mar 19

Dad bought a house! There's so much to celebrate – the house, Dad's birthday, our anniversary, and starting a family ... New beginnings. This is a sign of *great* things to come.

Apr 14

Tracy went to Emergency a few days ago; he peed blood. They have no idea why. He's like, How do you piss a quart of blood and find *nothing* wrong?! Fucking idiots! Man, doctors can be so stupid, wasting people's time. It's so frustrating he's not getting *any* help. I'm getting him in to see MY doctor.

May 16

I'm so sick again. I feel so unsettled at this age. I'm going to be 35! But it can only get better, right?

It *doesn't* feel like my life is *ahead* of me; it feels like my best years are *behind* me. No kids, looks are gone, body is shot, no money, no life, wrinkles, slow metabolism ... I've ALWAYS felt old though. An old soul. I think I've lived a few lifetimes already. I'm tired. And what do I have to show for my 34 years on this planet? A *great* marriage, otherwise...Is it too late for kids? Is this a midlife-crisis thing? I just feel so lost, like it's all over. I need to stop comparing myself to others and how THEY are having kids. Brooke Shields is 38 and she just had a baby! NO ONE says SHE'S too old.

June 11

There was a suicide bombing in Jerusalem – 13 dead, 65 injured.

Aunty Ruth finally got in touch with Mom. She was on a bus at the time of the bombing, a few blocks away; she heard it. She was *supposed* to be at the health food store, right where it happened, but she was too tired so she took a bus home. She's really shook up. But she's okay.

July 3

Mom's visiting and we got into it about religion. It got pretty heated and I stood my ground. Suddenly, Mom starts smiling and says, You stood up to me, you *didn't* back down; I'm just admiring you so much right now! I have such complete respect for how you handled it.

I'm sick and tired of feeling sick and tired. What the heck is going on?!

July 22

After a few job starts and stops this past year, Tracy started a promising new job, computer software stuff. I'm so relieved. But I hate my job. Well, I don't hate it; I just need a break or something. I'm grateful I have one though.
Tracy said be careful what you wish for.

Tracy and I both woke up sick. I went to see my doctor. I started crying. I think I'm mainly sleep-deprived and it's affecting my work, home, and life.
She said, Lack of sleep is a symptom of something else.
I told her, You can see by my history lack of sleep is nothing new, but I'm feeling extremely depressed. I just feel like I'm reaching my saturation point. I have good coping skills; there's really nothing I *can't* handle, but with not sleeping...I'm going batty.
Are you having major mood swings?
Oh ya! Major!

She wrote a note for work to be off for a few weeks. Come in for a complete physical, then we'll reassess. If you get some rest, everything else will fall into place. She prescribed a sleeping pill.

I spent the rest of July and August trying to tackle my insomnia, and my doctor extended my time off. Tracy and I were extras in the TV movie Hollywood Housewives *and we got to meet and shake hands with Farrah Fawcett, Melissa Gilbert, and Robin Givens. It was quite extraordinary. We had my birthday dinner with friends and then spent the weekend in Kananaskis. So far, 35 is looking up.*

Sept 4

I haven't slept in three days. My doc prescribed the same drug, only at a higher dose. She asked me, Have you ever considered counselling?
I laughed. Ya, I was in therapy for seven years.
I'm still off work?
Yes.

Sept 18

I told my doctor they want me back at work *Monday. I'm ready* to go back to work. I said I had a revelation – I realized I've had this sleeping problem for 25 years, so my expectations were a little high in thinking it would be *fixed* in a few months. I'm looking at it a little more realistically.
She nodded like, Okay, I buy that. She said she's going to refer me to The Sleep Institute.

It feels like things are looking up again.

Sept 22

My first day back. They put me back on E-Com! Yahoo! The department's move to Edmonton has been delayed until the new year.

The Sleep Institute called. They are going to give me a contraption to take home to regulate my sleep pattern.

I woke up with a sore throat, a cold, and a bad cough. I have a huge pain in my chest, with shortness of breath. Tracy noticed I'm sick all the time. Yes, it's true, I am.

Oct 8

I went to see a naturopath. I talked about the non-sleeping issue and how long it's gone on for.

Your body has a memory. I'll give you some herbs that will hopefully help with that.

If I can only sleep, I feel I won't be so depressed, anxious, and stressed. I can't shut my brain off; I think A LOT.

She totally agreed. Rest is the most important thing. She examined me. When she pressed on my lower back, I winced. She said, It's your adrenals – you're tapped out. No wonder you're always sick, you have nothing left for energy. You have to build it back up.

It was so validating!

You have to retrain yourself to *do nothing*.

I'm a Virgo, I can't do that.

You're probably the kind of person who when you get a bit of energy, you do 500 things? Yup!

Well, you're going to have to resist. Is the anti-depressant working?

Ya, it's to help me stay up during the day. I guess I don't burst out crying for no reason *as much*.

Your cold isn't in your throat; it's in your lungs.

It was so comforting to have an ACTUAL REASON for how I've been feeling for quite a while. What a relief! I'm not crazy.

Oct 15

I took home the sleep monitor. I need to see my doctor. I don't think I can bear this rash much more. It's spreading. I said to Tracy, I'm falling apart; just put me out of my misery.

He said, Careful what you wish for. He says that a lot.

My neck pain is so bad I'm crying. Unbearable. I made an appointment with a chiropractor at the clinic I used to go to. She said I've traumatized my neck; I'll need X-rays.

The X-rays show my brain stem is swollen; I had an adjustment and now the X-ray is showing it's aligned. Easy peasy.

Oct 27

At The Sleep Institute, I had a breathing test done. They said my sleep patterns are *not* abnormal. You *don't* have sleep apnea, but you *do* have insomnia. They will refer me to a sleep specialist. You are the worst case of it we've ever seen here. We do NOT recommend you come off the sleeping pill or the anti-depressant.

Tracy got a raise.

Nov 17
The chiro felt my swollen neck thingy. It's a swollen lymph node. It hurts, it's mobile and it's soft. If it was malignant, it would be hard as a rock and *not* hurt.
Okay, good. If you say there's nothing to worry about, okay. It just freaked me out.

I've got the worst cough *ever*.

Tracy comes up behind me and holds my stomach and says, Baby. Then he starts talking to my stomach, like there's a kid in there. It was actually very sweet. He's gonna be a wonderful dad.

The insomnia specialist's office called and booked me in for February 17, and they want Tracy to attend as well.

Nov 19
I'm feeling pretty good this morning. Dare I say, I feel like I'm in a *good* mood? Tracy even noticed. Then I weighed myself – BIG mistake! Over 125 lb.! It could be the Prozac, combined with being off the pill. I found *five* grey hairs – I flipped out! Okay, good mood – gone.

Dec 25
We got a new kitty – Gypsy. She's about six months old and has been abused by an evil man. It's a sad story. This guy had pit bulls and kept them in the basement. He would take the kitten and throw it down the stairs and let the dogs terrorize her. I want to find that pond scum and throat punch him! She's a tiny black cat and seems to get along great with our other cats. She was playing with Simon's tail. She hid under the bed later on. It must be her safe place. I can appreciate that.

My skin is killing me.

2004

Jan 8

Gypsy's making progress, being more playful and not growling at Tracy as much. It's understandable she hates men, but she'll see that Tracy is one of the *good* ones. She jumped up on my lap while watching TV and stayed for two hours. It was amazing!

I have a sore throat. My doc is increasing my Prozac dosage.
Is this going to conflict with my wanting kids? No.

Tracy took Gypsy to the vet. Um, *she's* a HE!
OMG! Good thing we gave HIM the name we did. His shots should clear up his respiratory and eye infections. In the evening, Gypsy snuggled up to Tracy's leg for about four hours, and then slept at his neck and on his chest. Aw.

Jan 13

I feel like shit. I'm coughing so bad, and nauseous. I looked up Prozac; it goes into breast milk; DON'T breast feed if on it. It *increases* appetite. I KNEW IT! First day I feel teary and like punching a wall.

Jan 23

Three days of being light-headed, a woozy feeling, and tingly weirdness. I had a dream my hair came out in chunks. I wonder what that means?

Jan 29

I've been dizzy for almost two weeks, nauseous, weight gain, tired all the time…pregnant? I'm fairly certain I'm *not* though. I'd be very surprised; I *have* had my period. It's just all the medication that's making me feel this way. Should I get a test? Whoa. I wonder if I'd be disappointed if I *wasn't*. This is crazy! I'm thinking crazy! It's so not the reality here. But I'm *not* freaked out – holy crap, could I be ready? OMG! This could be a really good time. This is probably the FIRST time EVER I've thought I COULD be. What if? I HAVE TO KNOW! Tracy would be so happy.

Tracy just texted me that he's on his way to Lethbridge: *"Bye my love and passion and reason for living."*

I took the pregnancy test – it's NEGATIVE.
I needed to know; now I do. I *almost* had good news to share with Tracy.

Feb 2

I get to work and they announce E-Com is *over*, officially. We are back on the phones. I'll start applying internally for a new position. I think I'm meant to pursue my writing. This is just a job, not my life! Unfortunately, my job and my life require me to make money. Sigh. I'm so stressed. The stress is going to kill me! Juicing and exercising.

Feb 19

I have a cold and am coughing like crazy. Our cockatiel, Babe, died; he was 21 years old. Sweet bird.

Feb 24

The sleep specialist asked 1000 questions, then said, You *don't* have a sleeping disorder. You have *anxieties* that prevent you from sleeping. Deal with the anxieties and you'll sleep better.

Oh gee, so simple. Why didn't I think of that?

Some brains are *sleeping brains* and require lots of sleep. You *don't* have a sleeping brain. You said yourself you can go for long periods of time without sleeping. Give your life to someone else and they wouldn't be able to function. This is who you are. You want to be able to sleep without the sleeping pill. I'm here to tell you, you will probably *always* need medication to sleep. That's your makeup. It's your choice if you deal with the reason WHY you're not sleeping. Until you deal with the problem, you'll never sleep. I can't help you. Are you a depressed person? Yes.

I can tell just by looking at you, you have *other* issues. What makes you happy?

My husband, my pets, my home. Being in the sun relaxes me; I'm not moody and my anxieties melt away.

You need to move to Mexico or the Mediterranean! You look ethnic – your body is being called by the Mediterranean. You should listen to it. You'd probably sleep soundly there.

Well, I DO sleep well when we go to Mexico. Are *you* going to pay for my move there?

He laughed. Are you suicidal?

I never tried anything.

I think you know WHY you don't sleep.

Tracy intervened. I *don't* think she wants to share that.

That's fine; I can only help you so much with the info you DO give me. Sounds like you've been through a lot and have done just about everything to help yourself.

In the car: So, doctor's orders, we *have to* move to Mexico! And get my brain fixed. I've *always* known WHY I don't sleep – it's never been a mystery to me. It's just the first time a doctor has actually called me on it, or saw the problem for what it is. It threw me off. Going to sleep for me is like going back to *that* time.

Mom said maybe I needed his bluntness. You have all the answers; you know yourself. You don't need to go to more doctors and keep searching for answers.

True. I'm always trying to be like everyone else, fit in, but I'm not like everyone else; this is me.

Sounds like you're starting to accept yourself.
Maybe I am.
This is a breakthrough!
Mom made it all better; she always does.

Mar 3

Tracy and I decided we've outgrown our house and we want to start looking elsewhere, especially if we're going to raise a family. We called our realtor. THIS time, we will get movers! We looked at a few houses. I think we found THE ONE. We had the same feeling we had when we first walked into this one – home.

I started my new job in Scheduling! I felt welcome right off the bat.

Mar 12

A girl from work died today – a brain aneurysm, 32 years old. How incredibly sad. I wonder why it takes a tragic event to see your *own* life in a new light. Why can't we put things in perspective *without* bad things happening? I supposed we need that reality check to jumpstart our own lives.

Lesson of the day: You gotta live each day; don't waste time! Waiting for the perfect time to do things ... it will never happen.

WE BOUGHT A HOUSE TODAY! Life IS on the upswing, I'm so grateful we *get* to live life, in a new home. Things are going to happen for us now. They put the *For Sale* sign up today. I'm happy, happy, happy!

Mar 19

I was just standing around at work, talking, when suddenly, I started choking my head off. I literally couldn't breathe. VERY weird! That has never happened before. It was scary.

Tracy and I are going to Orlando for two weeks – I'm *really* hoping the sun will ease the itchiness, and I can get some sleep. The itch has never gone away. It's so frustrating.

May 8
We moved into our new house April 30! I got a *permanent* position in Scheduling! I feel like if I think good thoughts, it'll jinx things with our new home; work is going so well, and we had a great vacation. Tracy enjoys his job... Things haven't been this solid and stable in so long. I'm going to enjoy every second of it. Well, it's May "**8**" today, so all is right with the world.

The garage door was broken and would only open half a foot from the bottom. Tracy was trying to fix it when some guy poked his head under the garage door, offered his help and introduced himself – Jim, our new neighbor.

The itch is back; I'm not sure it ever left, and it's getting worse. Crap! I can't stop scratching!

May 31
I am so not sure what is up with me. I feel like crying. I feel like I should be doing *something* – enjoying my life. I need time for me, and Tracy. I feel so weird. I'm so teary. Something must be wrong. This is an awful feeling. I'm *trying* to stay positive.

June wasn't busy, except for celebrating Tracy's 40th birthday. We had about 30 people over for a big bash.

July 13
I called Mom's naturopath to make an appointment. I also have an appointment for an allergy test – **_January 12_**! What a joke! As if I'm going to wait half a year to figure out what is wrong with me! I'm in this holding pattern with my health, fighting for answers. I called Tracy

to tell him. He sarcastically said, Good thing there's no panic for it. Cripes!

July 14

The naturopath says I probably have candida. We need to *radically* attack it. He also did some test with the irises of my eyes (Iridology). I went home with a load of supplements. He gave me a book and to follow the diet – it's a Swiss diet, eliminating yeast, dairy, sugar and many others. I looked candida up on the internet when I got home. It accounts for many things: chronic runny nose, insomnia, fatigue, ITCH, burning eyes, memory loss. *Finally* – an answer!

Dad disowned Levi and Kyle. He feels he can't keep pretending he's okay with how they treated me. It's taking its toll on him, and he needs to make a clean break. I told him to do what he feels is right for himself.

Aug 11

It hasn't been a good few weeks – Dad disowns *them*; I have candida; our utilities were cut off; Gypsy is sick, and Bub's in Emergency with fluid on her lungs. They think it's congestive heart failure.

On the bright side, Dad's tenant's cat had three babies – a *white* kitten was born and it's OURS! DIBS! We are going to call him Nike. We adopted a brown male cockatiel and named him Bailey. Our family is growing. Now we just need one of the human variety.

Aug 15

Bubby is back home at Aunty Ruth's now – she's on oxygen, not eating, and is very weak.

Tracy didn't get paid from the software job. Some bullshit about not enough sales so no money for payroll. We need money for the car payment. We may have to sell some of our belongings too. We *could* move into the upstairs of Dad's house. It would be cheaper for us. Tracy wondered what we have done that is so terrible, that we're in this predicament. Apparently, we're bad people. So much for our fresh start.

Aug 17

We got a loan. You couldn't *wipe* the smile off my face! Okay, enough with the bad stuff, only great things to come! This itch has GOT TO STOP! I don't want to be a grown-up anymore.

Sept 7

I get to work – there's an email from Levi and Kyle. At first, it didn't click in *who* it was from. And then I read it:

(Levi) "We received a disturbing call from Dad. You have gone through so much and we feel sorry for you! All these years of your suffering has eaten away at our hearts. But is it not possible your own choice is the real source of your pain? Do you not think had you refrained from marrying out you could have avoided so much of your emotional turmoil? Jews don't marry gentiles, but converts are welcome."

(Kyle) "Some 20 years ago we made a guarantee to never do such a thing. You promised me. Such a rift certainly echoes and reverberates in your conscience until today. We can understand. And feel sorry for you, how each day this eats away at your heart. Certainly, you realize this healing and happiness is not possible for someone who remains connected to the source of her internal conflict. The conclusion of the recent conversation with Dad was a request that the two of us 'say Shiva for our father' and basically cut ties. He will always be our father, you our sister, and a Jew forever."

"With warm wishes for good health and peace of mind, we permanently remain your caring brothers who love you and wish you only to be well and happy."

I could hardly believe what I was reading. I was in shock. I went to the bathroom to bawl. I was shaking. I finally had to leave work. Tracy and Dad rallied around me. We talked it out. Levi and Kyle have all this advice for ME? They don't even *know* me! And the **pain** they speak of –

is *caused* by THEM! But yet they know how to *fix* my pain. And they "love" me? I've had *enough* "brotherly" love to last many lifetimes! And they signed it – "permanently" your brothers. Cringe.

They devote their lives to God, and *they're* more screwed up than anyone! I find it amazing, after all this time, they're still *not responsible*. It's ALL **_Tracy's_** fault! Until there is an acknowledgment of the gravity of the situation, I will not be able to "get over it." Not until I KNOW I'm being HEARD.

Dad said he thanks God for Tracy. Tracy IS and always will be my sanctuary, my safe place. I will never think, *Oh if only...They are written off for good!* I have no doubts. This has given me great perspective. They are sicker than I ever thought they were. I have no idea *how* they got my email address. I have told both Mom and Dad, I have a great man, a good marriage – IN SPITE of them, a good life. My family was there for me unconditionally today, and *that's* what matters in life! Everything else is trivial.

What can I learn from this?

Lesson of the day: Mom said I need to figure out what I need from it, and let the rest go. Good advice.

Sept 14

I begged the girls at work for *any* ideas they might have to relieve the itch – ANY ideas?? An Epsom salts bath, calamine lotion, eczema cream...I told Mom to pray at The Western Wall for my itch to go away. How do I stop the itch?! She said I should be more forceful with my doctor to figure this out. I am going insane! I need something NOW for it – *not* six months from now! I've lost *12 lb.* on this candida detox. I'm actually NOT thrilled about it. I just don't feel well.

<u>Sept 19</u>

If this is the "bad" coming out from the candida, then the doctor will have seen this reaction *before* AND GIVE ME SOMETHING FOR IT! If not, then this is something *else*. I could be eating all the right stuff for this detox but what if the "good" things I'm eating are something I'm allergic to? Oh, give me the strength…

<u>Sept 20</u>

I am SO itchy!! I cried myself to sleep last night. I couldn't stop. I could be reacting to something – I just wish I knew *what* it was. I tried to get in to the allergist today. They said, No, you'll have to wait until your set appointment. Are they REALLY *that* busy? Argh!

<u>Sept 21</u>

The naturopath said my parasites are gone and kept telling me how *healthy* I was. He said I'm very stressed though – it took a long time to find my pulse. I have *mild* eczema – nothing a sauna, chamomile tea or oils couldn't fix. He introduced new foods into my diet – flour, dairy, vinegar and yogurt. He said, the itch is not a hygienic problem, but the opposite. I'm cleaning *too much* and drying out my skin. Its stress-related then. He had me show him my *worst* itchy spot. I showed him my belly.

That's not so bad.
It is though!
Oh no, I'm not saying it's not. I know the itch is bad, but it's not a rash. He couldn't tell me one way or the other the *cause* of it. It may be from toxins. Homeopathic products are best for the itch. He put me on acidophilus. He said, We have to kick things up a notch and treat it more aggressively. Generally, the itching stops when you aggressively treat it, and he had me on the "basic" plan. I thought I had been clear on how DIRE I felt up until now. I guess telling him I'm going INSANE with the itch was NOT a cry for help. It's just your basic, run-of-the-mill itch. Doctors.

Sept 23

In the past few days, my skin has been feeling like pins and needles. It comes in waves. I went to see my GP. He spent quite a bit of time with me. He said *from* the scratching, the skin has created a hard membrane – it's callous-y. He will get me in to a dermatologist ASAP. I gave him all my usual lines – I'm going insane; I can't satiate the itch; I'm not sleeping; THERE'S NO RELIEF! Is anyone listening? I showed him my stomach and he felt the skin on my sternum. I didn't have a rash *before*, but I do *now*, so now he's taking me more seriously. It's all about the rash, I guess. He said I MUST be going insane. He'd be surprised if he didn't start treating me for depression – as a *result* of the itch.

Sept 24

I'm so tired. The itching is keeping me up all night. I'm exhausted. I've used *38* products on my skin and NOTHING has worked! Yes, I counted.

Oct 7

Baaaaaad itching day. I broke down crying at the dermatologist's office. I couldn't help myself – I just couldn't. I felt so frustrated. He said, It's probably *not* an allergy, but all the same, it's good to rule it out. It would be easier to diagnose if my skin <u>looked</u> worse.

I know, that's what I'm told, but all the same, it's itchy and I NEED RELIEF! He looked over my body, at the spots that were the worst, and he said we need the bloodwork results from before.

Did I get tested for thyroid problems? Yes.
Do you have any allergy to wheat?
Well, I took myself *off* it and I see *no* difference. I was off sugar and dairy too. I apologized for my teariness. I'm just so frustrated and at the end of my rope.
We will test you to rule stuff out. It could be celiac disease. It's not common, but is easily treatable. He was surprised the roof of my mouth gets itchy too. He hadn't heard that one before.

Heat hurts my skin. No hot tubs or hot showers. Keep fewer blankets on. Take the Aerius in the morning, Allegra during the day, and Benadryl at night. You will need to take *all* three things; even if you start feeling better, keep taking them.

I told him about the pins-and-needles sensation. He kept trying to pinpoint my itchy spots.

It's from HEAD TO TOE! I scratch the itch until I *bleed and bruise*. I use a FORK to satiate the itch, to no avail.

Is your husband itchy? No.

I just feel so defeated.

Oct 21

I was selected for jury duty. I can't be around people right now. I can't stop scratching, itching, and coughing. People are probably disgusted with me. I don't exactly have a choice either. Great timing.

It's a drunk-driving case, and the accused hit a cop car. Today is the last of the deliberation of a three-day trial. Just as we had to go in and give our decision, I had the biggest coughing fit of my life. I couldn't catch my breath. I couldn't breathe. And they were all waiting for me. Only me and the foreperson were still in our private room, and he waited with me. I couldn't help it. After choking for about 15 minutes, and probably breaking every blood vessel in my face, tears pouring down my face, and more than likely wrecking *something* in my gut, I was ready to go in. I was so embarrassed. I tried to compose myself. The judge asked me if I was alright and able to continue? Yes. The cough lingered and I kept clearing my throat throughout. It was awful. Court was FINALLY adjourned! I couldn't get home fast enough. It was a mixed bag of an interesting experience and feeling sicker than I ever have. What the heck is wrong with me?!

Oct 27

My skin hurts so badly. I went to the bathroom at work and almost ripped my skin off. No fucking relief! Even now, as I sit here writing this, there is no relief. I can't take it anymore! I AM going crazy! I don't know what to do for myself anymore. I just spent a half-hour in the bathroom crying, and then I tried to go outside to cool off. It didn't work. I GIVE UP!! I GIVE!!I GIVE!! I pray for bedtime to come so I can take my sleeping pills and get *a* reprieve. I just feel at this point – I *don't care* WHAT is wrong with me, I just want it to be *labelled*, so it can be *treated*!! I am just so fed up – I want HELP!! Somebody, help me!!

Nov 6
I am sitting here in Canmore, at a pub, and I feel like I am living the dream; in this moment, I'm not itchy and Tracy is playing pool with a friend. I'm having a drink and *writing*.

THIS is the life I *always* imagined for myself. Doing EXACTLY what I'm doing at this moment – is *heaven*! I will always remember this feeling. I just don't think it gets better than this. It feels natural, good, and real. I'm loving this. I could write a book sitting here – it is so inspirational. I want to write about TRUE survivors, real people, inspirational people with real meat to their stories. It's about living, being here, but beyond that, beyond *just surviving*. Being positive about all the rotten crap you got dealt.

There's a reason for everything, right? We are dealt what we can handle. So, people who are dealt crappy hands…it's all for a reason. Even when faced with death, people facing the unknown – people can muster such unbelievable courage and the ability to see the *good* in their reality. It sounds hokey, but faced with a definite end, people have the unbelievable capacity to see the truth, the reality of the situation, and the goodness. To be able to view things in a different perspective. It seems to take something grave, before we can "see the light," to be enlightened about our lives. Is it too much to hope that people "see the light" even if they're NOT in a dire situation? Why does it take a tragedy, catastrophe, or a crisis to achieve enlightenment? Whew, that was deep. Unrealistic – I know.

This mountain air is *really* getting to me.

Nov 9

I knew that tranquil little bubble I was in *couldn't* last. **I CAN'T TAKE THIS ANYMORE!!** I'm bawling. I can't see how much longer this can go on before I do something *drastic*. I don't know what that will be – but I can't take the crying, aching, itching – **24/7!!! NO RELIEF!!!** AND NO ONE WILL HELP ME!!! Herbal drops ain't doing fuck all. Waiting *three more months* for an allergy test? How bad does it have to get?! I now have a rash under my arms that I never had before. I feel like my hands are going to break from scratching. I don't know what to do... I don't know who to call. Do I call the allergist? To call, to not call...Who? I need help TODAY!!! Waiting, waiting, more waiting. No answers. No help! I gotta wait for the blood test, wait...**IF SOMEBODY DOESN'T DO SOMETHING TO HELP ME**... Can ANYBODY do ANY-THING?! I should call my doctor. That thing we talked about me going crazy – it's *happened*! I'm *there*! I'm 36 years old and a sobbing mess. It's pathetic. I just can't wait any longer for somebody to do something... I'm curled in a ball, on the bathroom floor, rocking back and forth, and writing in my journal. Pathetic. I just called the dermatologist. Useless fucks. I hung up. I'm on the phone with my doctor's office. All I c,an do is call and pray they can help me.

Is it an emergency?
What consists of an emergency with you guys?! If I have to wait another *two months* before I get help... I hung up. I called the allergist.

What does it take to get in sooner to see the allergist?
We'll put you on a cancellation list.
I *AM* ON IT!
We'll make note that you called again. What is the best number to reach you at?

I hung up. I called the dermatologist back.

They said, Oh, the results of your blood test are in. We'll go over them *tomorrow* with you. I hung up. I then I called back to try to get in TODAY.

Is it just me, or AM I NOT BEING HEARD?!
I said, Sooner today, if not sooner tomorrow.
Nothing is sooner. There are no times available. None. We *can't* squeeze you in.

I hung up. Why is this happening to me?! Am I such a wretched, horrible person that no one wants to help me? And nobody seems to care. I feel completely alone. And the tests will show <u>*nothing*</u>. And *nothing* will be dosne. Do I need to kill myself for someone to notice I have a problem? Is this THE ONLY allergist in Calgary?! Can they not refer me to SOMEONE who DOES give a shit? I have never seen such a useless batch of doctors in all my life!!! It's really refreshing to know a person has to be *suicidal* before you get help – and even *then*! They call themselves doctors? They sure don't act like it!

It's taken me ALL morning to compose myself enough to get dressed. The itch is unbelievable. I OWN **NOTHING** THAT PROVIDES RELIEF. NOTHING! Except sleeping pills. Do I take them *all* for relief?

Hmm…

Tracy came home. I said, I need to tell you –
Ya, I know you've had a hard time today.
Actually – I had *a complete meltdown.* And *no one* will help me!

I feel at a total loss. I don't know HOW to help you.

Do you think it'll fly if, at my appointment tomorrow, if I say, What the fuck good are you?
Tracy just looked at me.
I've LONG PASSED my breaking point. Long passed.

Nov 10

I have my follow-up appointment with my regular doctor. How swell. A day late and a dollar short. Tracy told me to be positive. Here we go again, broken record. I'm getting worse. My skin is on fire. My bones feel bruised. It is affecting EVERY aspect of my life. There's no relief. It feels like my inner thermostat is broken. Heat hurts. Cold hurts. Clothes hurt. I have had this cough now for about five to six weeks. Shouldn't my mucus buildup be *lessening* after cutting out dairy, wheat? The cough is so bad. I have to hang on to something while I cough because it's so violent. I have to hang on to my chest so the pressure doesn't make me explode, and hang on to on object – a wall, a counter, an edge.

My doctor said, Well it's *not* liver disease, it's *not* kidney disease, you *don't* have lupus, it's *not* leukemia…
Well, I wish it WAS one of those things – at least *then* we can *treat* it! My dermatologist suggested it could be *leprosy* and gave me a prescription.

Are you kidding me? That's not the "label" I was expecting.
So, my doc couldn't offer anything new to help me. I'm fucked.

Nov 17

I went *back* to my doctor because I'm so tired of this cough. I need some antibiotics to just get rid of it. I'm dealing with the itch; I don't need to deal with a bad cough that won't go away, too! I'm spending a fortune on creams. The antihistamines are a joke. The inhaler is a joke. I'm just going through the motions. I got the prescription for the antibiotics and as I was leaving, I said, I *should* probably point out my swollen neck; my husband made me *promise* I'd *mention* it to you. I've had this bump for a few weeks now. I don't think it's a big deal, probably just a pulled muscle from coughing. He takes a look. He felt my neck and felt some other glands. He said he needs me to go for a chest X-ray and more bloodwork *right away.*

I get a phone call from the doctor's office later in the day at work: Can you come in at 8:45 a.m. *tomorrow* instead of Monday?
Yes, okay. Interesting. Maybe they *finally* found something.

Nov 18
My doctor said he's very worried about what the results show. Things showed up on the X-ray too. You may have lymphoma.

Which is what?

Cancer. You'd do chemo. Your lymph nodes are very swollen, and they are swollen behind your sternum. This is *why* you've been coughing, and this is *why* you're itchy. It is treatable. We have to get you to a hematologist as quickly as possible. I'm sending you to THE best in that area.
I listened; didn't say much; I just kept nodding my head.

My doc says, So, this may *not* be such good news.
But I think *it is*. We finally HAVE *something* to work with! A *label*!
The swollen gland was the kicker. That is *not* normal. He felt it again. The doctor will do a biopsy. It's malignant, but the specialist will confirm.

I left his office. I went downstairs to the lobby, and found myself walking in short circles, going in a circle, walking in circles, round and round. I couldn't stop. Shock.
I must go to work. I walked to the train station, where I called Tracy. Will you come get me?
I will wait to talk to him, *then* I'll go to work. It's important to tell him *face-to-face* – *then* I'll go to work.

On the phone he asks, Is everything okay?
I'll tell you when you get here.
Okay.

I called work. I just left my doctor appointment. I have cancer. Is it okay if I come in on *Monday* instead?

It's okay, Sari, work is just work – it'll still be here when you want. You take care of yourself.

Tracy arrived and I got in the car. NOW the tears come – *I have cancer.*

I knew it!

Wow, I didn't. No idea – not a one. I need to go to work now. They said I could go back on Monday, but I feel I need to go now. I just wanted to tell you what the doctor said in person.

No, you're not going to *work*!

I'm not?

No! He drives me home.

I called Mom when I got in. She was shocked. She asked if I was home alone.

No, Tracy's with me.

He's always there for you, isn't he?

Yes, *always*. She told me she loves me.

I called Dad to come over. I told him to his face. He cried.

I think I've ripped something from coughing. My chest really hurts. The pain is unreal.

Nov 19

My chest is really sore. Every muscle you can have in your chest – I think – is ripped. Most every reaction I received from the news was: quiet, listening, end of the call. They'd call back 5 to 10 minutes later. It just sunk in – delayed reaction. Then lots of questions. Everyone reacted like that. Funny. I cried when I tried to cough. The girls at work sent me flowers. A few friends have me dead already. I'll find out more info, like how far along I am, but *it is* treatable!

I guess it's not candida, allergies, or leprosy.

Nov 20

I had a HUGE coughing fit; I think I tore part of my belly. I think I feel more relief than anything. Relieved there IS something wrong with me and they can **_treat_** it now. This will all be good. They can finally fix me up. What a relief. But they better not be wrong about this. Wouldn't that be something?

Nov 21

I'm curious how long I've had this affliction. I cried this morning from coughing. It hurts so badly. This *isn't* a false alarm – is it? My doctor had me come to his office ASAP; he's sending me to a cancer specialist and said I *will* need a biopsy. He wouldn't use the c-word if he wasn't sure, right? I *should* feel certain they *didn't* make a mistake – right? My coughing fits are non-stop. They take my breath away. I can't breathe. As far as others at work know, I have a viral infection and I'm going for more tests. I need more info first. I NEED to know how far along I am. I just need to know that.

Nov 22

I was looking up lymphoma on the internet. There are four stages. The symptoms are **ITCHING**, night sweats, low energy, weight loss... But, I get to wait longer – wait for confirmation of it, wait for answers, wait for treatment, *if* it is the c-word, and also get to wait for *someone* to tell me I'm NOT crazy. My hair is going to fall out *if* I have chemo. Whoa, is THIS why I had that dream about my hair falling out? Did I somehow KNOW this would be cancer? Well, I'll cross that bridge… I'm so busy with the itch, I can't think about anything else.

Nov 23

I went to the hospital for 8:30 a.m. and had a consultation with the cancer specialist. He *confirmed* it was lymphoma, but didn't want to guess as to *what kind* it was. He examined me and asked a bunch of questions. He was going to have me *come back* for tests.

What can you do for me *today*?

We could do a bone marrow biopsy, and I will check with the surgeon about a neck biopsy. You could wait a week or two to get in to go under for the biopsy, or they could just use freezing *today.*

TODAY! TODAY!

Tracy asked him if there was anything I could do to relieve the itching *now*?

Yes, treat the disease. You've probably tried *everything* anyway and nothing worked.

EXACTLY!

He took me for my bone marrow biopsy. I have NEVER experienced anything like THAT! PAINFUL! I almost crushed a nurse's hand. The surgeon concurred, it's lymphoma. He examined me and said he could fit me in for a neck biopsy at 11:30 a.m.

Okay. The sooner the better – why wait?! Everyone was calling me a trooper for doing *both* biopsies today. I guess most people don't do both in *one* day. I just don't see why I should wait any longer. Let's do this! They'll have the results *next Thursday*. They have to send me for a CT scan as well.

My neck biopsy – I was a bit panicked. It was blowing my mind how my neck was all hacked up, moving muscle, tissue and nerves out of the way – with only freezing. A bit of a mind fuck. I could see why people choose the "going under" option. I even said *during* the procedure, I think I'm reconsidering my choice. The surgeon was like, No, no, you made the *right* decision – this IS the best way to go. It's all good. Then he called in one of his residents to help retract the gland. He said the neck is one of the *worst* areas to do this in; it's vascular – so it bleeds. The only way to stop it is to burn it as you go. I only felt it burn once. It spasmed the entire time. It took about 45 minutes. They gave me a prescription for Tylenol 3s. We went home. I was very sore, but feeling positive.

Nov 25

I'm putting pressure on myself to go back to work. I guess I'll be missing *a few more days* while I get all the tests done. My doctor had a letter for me for work. I told him about my visit with the oncologist. He was surprised I had the TWO biopsies.

I heard the marrow one hurts like hell. You're at a higher risk for depression now. It's important not to get stressed and perhaps another round of anti-depressants could help.
Well, maybe, but I'll wait until Thursday, when I get my results.

He gave me another prescription for sleeping pills and asked me if I was concerned about work.

Well, I figure I'll be off a day here, a day there, when I'm in treatment. Uh, no, you'll be off at *least* FOUR MONTHS. Oh.

My cough was so bad today. I told Tracy I may be in denial. I still believe the results on Thursday will say, oops, not cancer.
That won't happen.

Nov 26

What a horrid day! I was in tears for most of it. The itch, the cough, I couldn't bear it. My chest hurt. Everything hurt. I had my CT scan. They had me drink this lovely solution of *colon cleanser*. So now my bum hurts, too. No relief. My clothes hurt. At home, I changed 10 times to try to find the *softest* clothes to wear. It didn't matter – *everything* hurts to the touch. Tracy came home with a projection TV – for *me*. You need something to pass the time with when you're at home, a GOOD TV.

Riiiight, you got it for *me*.

Nov 27

I cried all day. I couldn't breathe. My chest, contracting from breathing, hurt. Cold, shivering, hot flashes. I couldn't stop the pain. Coughing. I think I'm falling apart. So much pain. Dad came over. He just kept hugging me. Even that hurt.

Nov 28

I talked to Mom this morning. She was telling me how strong I am. I've had so many challenges in my life; I meet them all head on. I'm an amazing woman with incredible strength. It's okay to cry and have meltdowns. You can't be 100% all the time. You're handling everything so well.

I said, When I have my meltdowns, it's not because I'm feeling sorry for myself or what's happening to me – it's not about poor me, why me? Nothing like that. I *still* feel positive. When I cry it's because I'm in *pain* – I can't get any relief. It's pure frustration. I'm going crazy with the physical part of it. I can't relieve the itch.
Do you want *them* to know?
What they think is of no importance to me. It's none of their business. I don't need them praying for me.
I figured that's what you'd say. The hardest part for me is not being able to be there for you.
I understand. I know you love me.

Nov 29

I went to work today. My manager said, Whatever you need from me, just ask. Should you even *be* here?
Probably not, but I had to try. I was crying; she was crying.
You have to take care of yourself. Work will be here. Not everyone knows.
Okay, it's best that way, until I get all the results.

I tried to work for a while, but soon went back to my manager and started to cry. I *need* to leave.

It's okay. Do what you need to for yourself – now, and after (referring to treatment).

I went home. My fear is that come Thursday, they will say, Nope, it's *not* what we thought it was and I'll be back to square one. I'll freak. I feel like my skin is on fire and pins and needles, hot and cold. I feel badly about work. But I tried. I looked at my neck for the first time since the biopsy – the incision area is bigger than I thought it would be. Tracy's not surprised. I had my *worst* coughing fit yet. It was baaaaad. He's worried about me and my cough. He said I stop breathing at night.

Dec 1
Results: Your bone marrow is clean; however, your biopsy *confirms* lymphoma – Hodgkin's. It's treatable.

I felt SO relieved!

Your oncologist will tell you what treatment you need. There are different kinds of Hodgkin's – he'll talk to you about that.

It is confirmed. There IS a reason. I KNOW my body! Wow. I *don't* have to start from scratch – we HAVE a diagnosis! Yippee!

Lesson of the day: Listen to your own body! You KNOW when something is wrong!

Dec 2
My oncology results: You're Stage 3 Hodgkin's lymphoma, and heading into Stage 4. You have tumors in your spleen, abdomen, under your arm, in your neck and a tumor the size of an eggplant in your sternum, thereby causing the pressure in your chest and the intense coughing. Either we'll go with six months of chemo or three months of chemo *with* radiation. There will be nausea, hair loss, fatigue, and possible infertility. You have a large amount of cancer. It is 70%

curable. You are very lucky; of all the cancers to get, you got THIS one. Because of the length of time it took to diagnose you, *years*, Hodgkin's is the SLOWEST progressing cancer of them all. Had you had ANY OTHER form of cancer, you'd have been long dead. The "chemo cocktail" is called ABVD; it will relieve the itch almost immediately. You can choose to be a part of a case study for Hodgkin's; this will increase the success of your treatment. You can stop at any time if you feel the study isn't working. You will go every two weeks for treatment. There's still a good chance the cancer could return down the road – in a different form.

Whatever. Let's get on with this. Let's get rid of the itch! That's all I heard. No more itch. Let's begin! There's better success on the study – uh, no-brainer – let's go for it!

Dec 3
I got a call from a lady at the cancer centre. They told me about a seminar Tracy and I need to attend, on how to deal with side effects of chemo. I'm starting chemo on Wednesday. Supposedly, I won't be bed-ridden – I will still have quality of life. They say I'm looking at *minimum* six months for treatment. I will need to go in next week for X-rays, a pulmonary test, bloodwork, and an ECG.

I called work. They didn't even flinch. They said to take all the time I need. That's a load off my mind. If you need to tell people at work something – it's okay with me. I do believe this is happening for a reason – I'm just not sure why yet.
I went <u>hat</u> shopping. I'm gonna have to cover my noodle once I lose my hair.

Dec 9
My first chemo treatment is today, but I had to go for a blood test first. They told me to be *very* careful about being around people who even have a cold – avoid it at all costs. My immune system is fragile and I can't get sick with other things while in treatment. I'm very susceptible

to germs. They had me sit in a reclining chair. A super-sweet 80-year-old man sat in the chair beside me, a very positive man. He survived lung cancer, prostate cancer, and intestinal disease and is now receiving treatment for kidney cancer. They hooked me up to a large IV bag of anti-nauseate drug, then they had four large syringes of chemo drugs. It burnt! My veins were on fire. And I'm *still* quite itchy. Tracy brought *Shrek 2* for us to watch to take my mind off the chemo. They had to keep diluting the drugs because it was irritating my veins. I felt foggy and out of it – kind of a drunk feeling. It took three hours to administer. We picked up my meds at the hospital pharmacy and went home. I definitely felt nauseous.

Dec 14

Four days after chemo, there was NO cough. None. I itched less. Lots of nausea though. I had my blood test, and then I went for my follow-up with the oncologist. They will weigh me at each visit. My blood count is excellent. The swelling in my chest is way down, and I will be in chemo for six months – with *no* radiation. Okay! I lost some weight. He believed the itch will go away since the cough has lessened. The histamines in my blood were out of whack, which is why it felt like my body's temperature gauge had broken. He felt my neck. He was quite surprised at how much it has gone down. The X-rays showed I had three fractured ribs from coughing. That would explain the intense chest pain.

People at work were told I'll be on extended leave. I'm told some think I just want Christmas off. Ya, okay. I'm faking cancer to get more vacation time. Idiots!

According to my mother's husband, Tracy has to convert to Orthodoxy to *prevent further* illness in me. MY Jewish soul needs him to do that for me; otherwise, it's IMPROPER.

He will NEVER respect us, OUR way of life, and OUR choices. And I don't care. How dare he say this is *Tracy's* fault – well, mine for marrying him. This sounds like two *other* people I know. Must be nice to have the inside track on *how* I got cancer! *Not even* my oncologist knows!

My husband is the most unselfish, loving, wonderful person – and *that guy* tries to invalidate all of it by saying none of that matters because he's not *Jewish*? WE have a better marriage than most *religious* people, and people who marry within the *same* faith. It's not foolproof, there's no guarantee that two Jews marrying will have a successful marriage. Right, Mom? We are happy and tired of being told to jump on board to THAT way of life. At 36 and 40, we're *still* being told HOW to live OUR lives? Can *we* give tips on how *they* can improve *their* lives? They'd be open to that? It's offensive. It's hurtful. It's *not* okay. We are not "searching" for anything and, if we were, it's for *us* to figure out, not *you*. And yet some observant Jews *still* get sick – what are THEY doing wrong?

Mom assured us that type of phone call *won't* happen again.
Tracy agreed, that conversation will NEVER happen again.

Dec 21
The past three days, the itch lessened quite a bit more and NO cough. I felt energized, but then the itch returned again. I went for bloodwork and a checkup today. My white cell blood count was too low so chemo was cancelled; it will be bumped to next week instead. I will have to start taking Neupogen injections to increase the white blood cell count – from now until the end of treatment, three days after treatments, for three days. Tracy *volunteered* to administer the injections. I will have flu–like symptoms from it. I may get fevers, and my body will ache. Oh joy.

Dec 24
I was very itchy today. I was thinking how great it is I *haven't* lost my hair yet. Maybe I *won't*. We went for wing night. I commiserated with our friend Ted about our respective cancers and treatments. He's not in chemo for his brain cancer, he takes *pills* once a month, for three to four

days. He then throws up for five days. It's real good to talk to someone who *knows*. Tracy didn't get paid. We're fucked. Yes, it sucks living paycheck to paycheck.

Dec 29

Chemo day. I got the "deluxe accommodations" this time – a TV, a *bed* and a warm blanket. It went fine except for that one drug – they had to keep diluting it because it was burning my veins. Tracy was shown how to do the injections; they demonstrated on an orange. Tracy's totally cool with doing it. If he wasn't, I'd have to go back to the hospital *each* time to have it injected.

Dec 31

I woke up this morning with a pillow full of hair. I went to the bathroom and tugged on my head – the hair came out in handfuls. Okay, time to shave my head. Tracy shaved it for me. GI Jane. Yup. I'm going to save a lot of money on hair products now! We picked up my injection kit – needles, three vials of Neupogen, bandages, and alcohol swabs in a pretty blue case. Thank God for coverage – the three injections cost $1800! *With* my coverage it's only $108. What do people WITHOUT coverage do??

I had my first injection – Happy New Year!

2005

Jan 3

Toby came to visit with me. It's the first time she's come to Calgary since my wedding. She's only here for six days – but I'll take it! What a treat. I am so excited to see her. She looks amazing! She asked if I'll be wearing a hat the whole time she's here (sarcasm). I took it off. We talked about the cancer and how I'm ready to snap because people say, Oh, it's JUST Hodgkin's. If there is a cancer to get – it's THAT one. The way I see it, cancer is cancer. She said people don't usually die from the cancer, they die from the treatment! The treatment is hell! It's so good to have my friend here.

Tracy and Dad shaved their heads in support of me.

Jan 5

So, if somebody were to ask me what's important in life now, I would say being with people you love, and to know *who* loves you. None of this "friends" and "family" labelling crap – just people you *know* you love and love you back. All I can say is, you sure know who your friends are when you go through something of this magnitude.

This new black fleecy hat has quickly become my new best friend. I LOOK like a cancer patient. I get the sad, sympathetic stares from people now. I'm *not* loving that.

Lesson of the day: When you are in treatment, it's harder to *blend in* with others.

Jan 6

It's Bubby's 95th birthday today. We are going over for dinner tonight to have her favorite: Chinese food. No itch. I had NO itch today. That is HUGE. I spoke to the nurse. I have an appointment with the Port (a device that goes under your skin and chemo is administered though it) doctor. The chemo is *destroying* my veins. They can't take it anymore. The burn is too intense and painful. After chemo, I feel like my veins are going to explode – and I can watch them, as they fill up with blood, bulge up from my hand, and try to build up enough pressure to explode. Ya, painful. I wore a bra today. First time I've worn a bra since last summer. There is no discomfort or pain from clothes. It's the first time in over a year I have *not* needed to put cream on my body *1000 times a day* either. Not even once. Wow, I think this chemo might be working! So, I have this vein pain instead. And quite frankly – I'll take IT over the itch ANY day!!

Jan 11

The surgeon for the Port told us the risks: punctured lung, severed artery, clotting... And you're really skinny so the risk is greater (I've lost 15 lb. from the cancer). It will take 45 minutes to do. It's day surgery. The device is plastic and I will have a tube going to my heart. I will see it under my collarbone. It's scheduled in about two weeks. I went for my bloodwork and checkup. My white count is good and the injections are working.

Jan 12

Chemo today. I gained a little bit of weight. Mom asked if she could come to Calgary for a visit. She just wants to come and give me a big hug. She wants to be here for me.

My savior, my guardian angel, my regular doctor, has *left* his practice. I'll never see him again to tell him he probably *saved my life.*

I have been getting my nails done – gel nails, and airbrushing. I figured I need to pamper myself during this time – to do something I normally haven't. Me time. Time away from cancer. And the nausea. I have been getting them done the day before chemo. It also covers up the ugly brown discoloration they are showing from the chemo drugs.

Jan 17
I met with my new doctor today. He asked me many questions.

I won't be doing much for you – your oncologist will be taking care of you for a while.

Mom is coming in tomorrow, for six days. She said she is here for when I need her, and not to worry about spending enough time with her. Just do what I need to for myself.

Jan 19
Tracy dropped me off at Aunty Ruth's for the whole afternoon. Mom was mothering, asking every five minutes how I was doing? Mom said to Tracy, You're such a good guy.

It's a bad day with vein pain – in both arms. *They haven't* heard yet. It's not a secret, but my only concern in telling *them* is I do not want them contacting me. I don't want anything from them. But otherwise, I told Mom to tell whoever she needs to tell.

Jan 21

I have my Port surgery today – at 7:20 a.m. Both Tracy and Dad came with me. I was so itchy. I was at the hospital for 10 hours! I was so sick. I was in recovery for two hours. Everything took longer than expected. I had **eight** hits of morphine, anaesthetic, two Tylenol 3s, and a bag of liquid Gravol – all on an empty stomach. I OD'ed. And I STILL felt the pain. Nothing helped. I'm immune to drugs! I was throwing up all afternoon at the hospital, and the whole car ride home. I was throwing up in a plastic bag that had holes in it. Oops. It'll all be worth it for easier chemo access.

Jan 24

Okay, I think I'm having a bad day. I'm getting a little tired of hearing, oh you have Hodgkin's, it's treatable. It's JUST Hodgkin's! Oh Hodgkin's – good prognosis. I get that they are trying to be encouraging. I get that. A diagnosis of cancer is a traumatic experience, even if the cancer IS curable!

Dad called. How are you feeling?
Great, because I ONLY have Hodgkin's!
I understand what you meant by that.
Cancer is just a highly, emotionally charged time, and people don't understand sometimes we just need to talk about stuff without others trying to fix it, or minimizing it. And, people, quit being so insensitive!

Jan 26

Bloodwork and checkup today. The doctor said Hodgkin's is the one cancer people quit treatment *early*. They feel it works fast, and if not for the chemo, there'd be no symptoms – so why continue? But those are the ones who wind up coming back. Then it's more complicated with treatment. I thanked him for telling me because my CT scan showed most of the tumors *are* shrinking so I thought, *Why go through 12 more treatments*? So good to know I need to follow through with the *complete* treatment protocol for the *best* results.

Feb 1

Mom said she is *so* glad she came to see me so she could see for herself how well I'm doing. She said I am so positive; my whole outlook is so great – she could learn something from me. I'm glad that's how I come across. I see the bigger picture. You do, you really do. The PORT I see as a hiccup. It'll help for the months to come.

Feb 8

Chest X-ray, bloodwork, and checkup today. Blood is good. X-rays show the tumors are shrinking still. I'm looking tanned. One of the drugs colors the skin – so I look healthy! Even my oncologist made a joke– so the chemo is going well, you're enjoying it? Funny guy.

This is the tough time with Hodgkin's – when the symptoms are gone and you still have to go through with the treatments. If we had caught it at the *beginning*, you could've been done by now; but as far along as you were, you've got to see it through to the end.

I told him I've had my period *all* this time – *every* day since chemo began. He was surprised. Women usually go pre-menopausal with chemo. He said, DO NOT GET PREGNANT! Okay! On the way home, Tracy said that had I gotten pregnant when we were trying, the chemo would've had to wait. I agreed. So obviously what was meant to be, was. I have a full-blown cold. I said to Tracy, I'm done. I'm sick of being sick. Done.

Feb 9

I woke up with all sorts of inspiration to write my book. If cancer doesn't inspire one to do *something*, I don't know what would! I'll get started this week.

Chemo day! I was a bit worried they'd postpone my treatment because I had a cold. I tried to hide the fact. They gave it to me. Phew.

Feb 16

I have such a bad cold still: a sinus infection and heartburn that is off the charts. Mom called and we were talking about friends. I said, This whole thing has been a test for everyone.

How are they reacting to you and what you're going through?

It's been a learning experience for me. But for me, the good and positive has far outweighed the negative and bad. Mostly, people have rallied around me, supported me and been there for me.

Those people don't have agendas with you. With the *others* – they probably don't know what to say to you; they don't want to bother you with *their* lives. And that's life.

Some people are giving me my "space" – I never asked for it. People make assumptions.

Lesson of the day: When in doubt, ASK a person what they need from you.

Mar 6

Mom asked me what my blessings are. I think this ordeal is meant to teach me to better deal with friends. I still need to work on that aspect of my life. Also, I've always wished for time to write. Well, I got it. Careful what you wish for – right, Tracy? So, I now have the time but not the energy. I think I'm meant to use this time to write though.

Mar 8

Bloodwork, checkup, and X-rays today. The tumor in my chest is *half* the size it was. Good news! I also gained 3 lb. Yay! This might be the first time I'm *happy* about gaining weight. He scheduled me for a CT scan in a few weeks. Those results will determine if it's still shrinking or just stable. It will also determine if I get only two more treatments – for good measure – or if I complete the full *eight* cycles. So... I MAY be done sooner.

I have decided to get a tattoo to commemorate this time – I want "Loyalty," "Survivor" and "Strength" put on my back. Tracy liked the idea.

Bubby is not well at all. She has a real bad cough, and her quality of life is non-existent. I mean, she has the best care possible – she's just not living life anymore. Poor Bub. She sleeps ALL the time at home.

Mar 22

Bloodwork and checkup today. My white cell count is low. I'm still having my period. It just proves chemo affects hormones and ovaries. My oncologist said, At your age, there's no reason to believe they won't go back to normal after chemo is done.

Mar 23

Chemo. I felt SO sick during the treatment. I never had that before. Bad heartburn, and so nauseous. Every moment felt like I was going to puke. This little "golden pill," as they like to call it – Zofran – is *not* helping. Nothing is helping.

Mar 24

It's Dad's 66th birthday and also Uncle Ruben's 60th today. Aunty Ruth said, I was telling your mom how I think the reason why you're doing so well is because of *Tracy*. He looks after you – you work well as a team. He takes such good care of you. He knows you so well, and vice versa.

He makes me eat three meals a day. He's amazing.

Mom said I sound so good. Not just positive about my situation, but positive about *life*.

I'm just feeling good to be feeling good.

Mar 31

CT scan day! I only had to drink that colon cleanser for an hour this time, not two. Note to self: *Don't* wear an *underwire* bra next time. The *female* attendant had to remove it, with one hand yet, because I was already hooked up to the IV. There's a first time for everything. I felt light-headed and nauseous after.

Apr 4

It's our 13th wedding anniversary! Tracy and I went for pedis, then are meeting friends at Malarkey's, where we met 18 years ago today. It's changed names a few times (Boomtown now), but it'll *always* be Malarkey's to us. We will have a drink there to commemorate today.

Later we got a round of free shooters for everyone from the manager. It was so nice to hang out with everyone on a GOOD occasion. I was very touched that everyone came out to celebrate.

Apr 5

Bloodwork, X-rays, and checkup today. There has been a "drastic" change in the size of the tumors, and *not* in a good way. I need to go for four more treatments, then they'll re-evaluate again. They say I may need radiation now. No surgery.

Apr 13

I know I'm meant to learn something from being sick. It would be shitty to go through something like this and *not* learn *something!* So, I know I'm being tested and challenged right now. I'm meant to re-evaluate friendships. I'm trying really hard to listen to myself and do the work. I've tried to get rid of the negative people in my life, but there are still a few stragglers.

Apr 19

Blood test and doctor appointment. My doc said he spoke to the radiologist – I will NOT need radiation. My tumors are below 5 cm. Okay, great news! I said the nausea is worse. He confirmed it WILL get worse. I queried about my skin discoloration and showed him. That will get worse too. People with darker and olive skin tend to get it worse, but it will *eventually* go away, when you stop treatment.

Apr 27

Bubby died at 9 a.m.

When Tracy and I got to Aunty Ruth's, I sat with Bubby, who was still lying on her bed. I stroked her hair and hand. The funeral home came to pick her up. We went with Aunty Ruth to make the arrangements to have Bub's body flown to Montreal for the funeral. We slept over so we can leave tomorrow morning.

Apr 29

Mom arrived in Montreal. Toby came to the hotel. It was so good to see her. The limo picked us up early for the funeral. I saw so many people I haven't seen in ages. The eulogy was unbelievable. The rabbi captured the *essence* of Bub: her zest for life. It was beautiful. Tracy was *allowed* to be a pallbearer. It was wet and muddy at the grave. I hate the grave part; it's so final. There was a luncheon afterward and I got to sit next to Aunty Sharon and catch up. She's a dear friend of Mom's, since they were 12. She has such a soothing, calming demeanor, and has such depth, insight and grace. She's a one-a-kind human being, extraordinary. I don't know another soul on the planet like her. She exudes warmth and goodness. I always feel uplifted and loved when we talk. She has an uncanny ability to make people feel like they are the most important person in the room. She has the gift; she IS a gift to this world.

Apr 30

Tracy and I went to Toby's for the evening. Her girls are getting so big. They went to bed, and we had an amazing heart-to-heart.

She asked me, Do you think we'd still be friends if you still lived *here*?
No, because of my track record with friends.
I think we WOULD still be. We don't judge each other. We always let the other say their piece.
I said, We are like night and day – *opposite* personalities. You're warm, caring and considerate – people gravitate toward that. I'm more standoffish, and keep people at a distance.
But you lead a calm, tranquil, quiet life – I live a chaotic one.

May 3

We got home yesterday; the flight was delayed. I'm exhausted. I can't believe I was able to make the trip. It was unbelievably tiring, but I wouldn't have missed Bub's funeral for anything.

I have a blood test, X-rays, and checkup today. I gained another pound.

May 10

I woke up *without* nausea! This will be a GREAT day! Mom called and said she could tell in my voice I sound better. I told her when I'm all better, I *will* appreciate each day I wake up feeling *good*. I *won't* take it for granted. She said how we take waking up and feeling "normal" for granted. This last treatment is not indicative of how it will be from now on. Your grandmother just died, you're worried about me, you traveled to Montreal, you saw me, you saw your best friend… They told you in the beginning not to get rundown. You were exhausted! It's no wonder you felt worse! But the time before that was okay. They say it's cumulative.

Checkup. Nothing is working for the nausea. I need to go for *five* more treatments – it's the best way to cure and be successful in getting rid of Hodgkin's. Blood counts were good, high. My weight is up a little more. The case study nurse said we'll assess things *after* the CT. The doc confirmed I *will* have to get the next five treatments. I began to tear up. The nurse said, You're just done with it all, eh? Eight cycles are a lot. It's tough; it's a long haul.

May 21

Chemo was okay. I didn't feel as bad. I was in bed ALL day. Last night I had heartburn for a few hours. I was crying and rocking, rocking and crying. It was bad. I thought I was going to die. It felt like my head and chest were going to explode. I couldn't breathe. The pressure was like I've never felt before in my life. Tracy didn't know what to do. I prayed the pain would go away, and my chest would just explode already.

May 25

Yesterday, Ted had a seizure and went into a coma. Today, he is out of the coma, and the cancer is back. It has grown four times bigger, with spider veins all over his brain. He may have two to six months to live. I can't stop crying for him, and his young son. I feel so lucky to have the cancer I have. I've *known* I'll be okay after this. I just want to celebrate what I *do* have. What I *will* have. All is not lost for *me*. It rocks me to my core. I AM so lucky. This will make the next four treatments tolerable – I WILL have a life after four treatments. I WILL be okay – he won't. It puts things in perspective for me. I will think of Ted when I go for those treatments.

Lesson of the day: Count your blessings, even if that includes going for chemo.

May 27

I went on the internet to read about life after chemo. One site said the effects of chemo can last up to a year after. I just assumed – bing, bang, boom – DONE! Back to "normal" when I'm done treatments. So, all this positivity I've felt doesn't feel so positive anymore. But it's still one day at a time. Someone else on the site said you can get hit by a bus tomorrow, but you don't sit around worrying about that! And you *can't* worry about a recurrence. It *may* happen, it may *not*. We waited to have children. Was I wrong to wait? No, I wasn't ready. Everything happens for a reason. Tracy's mom has been cancer-free for *years*! Now I'm freaked out. I want to be in the sun. I want to enjoy the outdoors again (you're *not allowed* to be in the direct sun with one of the chemo drugs because it will have a bad chemical reaction). I want to have children. I don't want to be sick anymore. I don't want the threat of cancer hanging over me like a dark cloud for the rest of my life. I need to see my future. I need hope. I need to know I still have a *quality* life worth living. Should I just be grateful I will HAVE a life? I'm thinking of Ted.

May 31

Bloodwork, X-rays, and checkup. My weight is down. The nurse said, You will always worry, for the rest of your life, when you cough. I know it's true. My chemo is cancelled for tomorrow. I should NOT be going for chemo BEFORE getting results of the CT – which I don't go for until Friday. If it shows no difference from the *last* scan, you're DONE. No more chemo. There are no signs of swelling in my chest from coughing. I'm relieved. So now we wait. He'll put a rush on the results. I left there going, RIGHT ON! There is a chance, a possibility I could be DONE already. Music to my ears! I needed this positive energy.

June 3

I got up in a really good mood. Potentially no more chemo! Dad called. My dad's cousin Bunny (Aunty Jenny's daughter) in Oregon has lung cancer. It doesn't look good. She's too far gone. Oh man. She never smoked a day in her life.

I have a CT scan today. I'm anxious for the results.

June 6

I received a call from the cancer centre. The results are in: there is *improvement* from the last scan so there *will be* four more treatments. Kind of bittersweet, right? Ya. I called Tracy and told him. I started crying. Four more. I just want to be done. There was a small window where I *could've* been done – and now I'm *not*. This IS the best way – to be sure. I just want it to be over. I just feel like I have more battles to come and I hope I'm up for it. I keep crying. It's the first time I'm being emotional about it all. Okay, Sari, stop crying and be grateful you had another good week. Deal with it – I'll be done soon enough!

June 7

I'm just an emotional wreck! I've been crying since yesterday. I feel like I'm having a mini meltdown. I feel I'm on overloaded, and overwhelmed. Very ironic – I feel sorry for people who don't have anyone with them at the tests or chemo, and there I will be, alone, because Tracy and Dad can't make it. Oh well. I just want this damn Port out of me! Get some normalcy back into my life! What the hell is the matter with me?! Aunty Ruth calls. Is Tracy able to take you? No, he's at work. Do you want *me* to come with you? Yes, please. She said she'll be right over. I suppose I was *not* meant to be alone today.

I went for my blood test. My doc is out of town, so the nurse went over my results. The tumor under my arm is *gone* – there is *no* sign of it on the CT scan. The one in my chest *hasn't* changed. Is that strange? No, not really.

June 8
Tracy came with me for chemo. I felt a little sick during. We went out for wings and Ted came with. His brother was there too, who said they wanted to pull the plug on Ted when he had his seizure because he's terminal; they figured, why bother?! I was noticing he's different now, after the seizure. He's quieter, slower; he's not the same – he's *not* himself. Ted said he's not sure WHY this is happening to him. He didn't stay long. When Ted was leaving, he hugged me and said, Take care of everyone for me.

June 21
I've gained weight. I just want to be done so I can look after myself again. My eyelashes are falling out. I'm freaking out! I have three left. I have less than a month to go. One month less a day. I'm being so selfish. Here Ted and Bunny aren't doing well and all I can think of is poor *me*. I just want to get off this rollercoaster and be "normal." Tracy asked me, Are you feeling lost? Ya, I am. I guess I *do* feel lost.

Blood test and checkup today. In the car on the way to the hospital, I started crying. Tracy says, What's going on in that head of yours?
I'm just fed up. I know I only have four weeks left – but I'm *done* with it all!

I couldn't stop crying. I just couldn't stop. I can't do this anymore. I can't. I won't. I had a total meltdown in the parking lot of the hospital. It was both physically and emotionally painful taking each step toward the cancer centre. I can't bear one single more treatment. Poor Tracy, he didn't know what to do.

The lady at the lab says to me, Don't be sad. Of course, I lose it and cry all over again. She says, God makes it so it all works out in the end. Tracy said, So God gives you this affliction, then he takes it away? I hope I don't lose it in the doctor's office. I probably will. The nurse couldn't make heads or tails of the CT results. We'll get the doctor in here and get this sorted out once and for all. He comes in and says, **_You're done_**. There has been no change since your last CT, so we can rule out any tumors left. It's just your normal lymph nodes that we see.

I start crying.

Well, you can have the three more if you want?!
We all laugh. It feels good to laugh. No, no, that's quite all right. He had sat back into his chair when I cried – as if not to race out the door, to let it sink in and not hurry out. He said he'll see me in three months and every three months after for three years. You're not done with us yet.

The nurse stayed when the doctor left, to answer questions. She said about my lymph node in my chest – it gets big, and then it never gets back to its normal size; like a deflated balloon. Your nodes are stretched and that's what we're seeing on the scan. Sorry you had to wait all this time, only to find out this.

I would've waited a helluva lot longer if it meant getting the news I did! I was just stunned. Shocked. I went from such a low to such a high. We finally left. I couldn't stop smiling. What a day. I called Dad in the car. He was elated. Then *he* started crying. I called everyone I could think of when I got home. Aunty Ruth and Uncle Ruben suggested going out for dinner – we have to celebrate! After dinner out, we met friends for champagne. We decided we'll have a gathering on the weekend to celebrate this news, and Tracy's birthday.

No more injections. No more chemo. No more drugs. No more!

I read an email from Oregon – Bunny died today.

Ted's not going in for surgery on Friday. It's been cancelled. He's too far gone. He will not survive surgery.

June 23
Maybe I can get back to a "normal" sense of life. Everything revolved around treatment – now it doesn't have to. Mom said people are saying I've been given this miracle. It's a miracle! And your car accident. You're just *meant* to still be here. You have a life to live. It's not your time to go yet, you're destined for *something*. I've been given a second chance. Unlike Bunny and Ted.

June 25
About 25 friends came over to celebrate with us. It was my "coming out" party – no hat. I had about 3mm of new hair growth. Written on Tracy's birthday cake it said, *"Celebrate Life."* When it came time for him to blow out his candles he said, It may be *my* birthday, but it's *your* re-birth. Very sweet.

I thanked everyone for their support: Because without all of you, I never would've gotten to where I am now. Everyone was crying. Later, Dad took me aside and said, I just want you to know, if you had *not* come through this, if something had happened to you, I'd have had no reason to continue on. I said, Well, good thing I'm not going anywhere! Everyone said how different I looked – less stressed, more relaxed, glowing. That's what a load off your mind will do! A pretty profound night. I'll never forget it.

July 1

I googled "recovering from cancer – feeling lost," "fear of cancer returning."

"Don't blame yourself for the cancer – people feel they got it because of something they did or didn't do – not true. After treatment you may feel angry, tense, sad or blue, irritability, moodiness, crying a lot, not being able to enjoy things more, feeling that you're "losing it." Feeling alone. Mourn your losses. Feel like you're getting less support now that treatment is over. Life has changed you forever. Nothing could ever be the same. Second chance to make life what you want it to be."

I printed it off and taped it to the wall beside my computer, to look at every day. That really helped me. I don't feel like I'm being an ingrate. It's *natural* to feel the way I have. We went to a party honoring Ted. He seemed better than the last time we saw him.

Aug 8

Ted died two days ago.
We are so heartbroken. It's devastating, but he's at peace now.

I'm so paranoid – I get a little cough and it scares the shit out of me. I get a huge itch...
I get so afraid I won't get a chance to do everything with Tracy that I want to.

Aug 12

Tracy's friend from school, her husband died today – of lymphoma. He was 41.
I feel scared – I'm still coughing. I feel lucky though too. Scared because I'm coughing, but lucky because I'm still alive,

Aug 27

My 37th birthday. We're having a Mexican fiesta for my party. I feel blessed to have seen my next birthday.

Sept 6

I'm supposed to be getting my Port out today – I called the surgeon's office.

I'm not comfortable getting it out until I've had my follow-up tests done.
Okay, no prob. Just call us when you're ready to reschedule.

Mom said it's *not* paranoia; you have a *reason* to feel concerned. Listen to your inner voice; listen to your body, like you have all along.
I started writing my book.

Sept 12

Toby called. She's getting divorced. She said, My life would be so void *without* you in it. We have the kind of friendship people dream about; a friendship people envy. Look how far back we go. People live their whole lives never knowing a friendship as ours. We've been to hell and back.

Indeed, we have. I love you.

Myriam is in town, and we're going for lunch tomorrow.

My cousin Bunny's husband died of a heart attack – only three months after **her** death. Tragic.

Sept 27

Today is my checkup at the hospital. They were all surprised at how much hair I have. I told my doc about the coughing, fever, and numbness in my fingers. He examined me, checked the X-rays and said, There's *no* sign of Hodgkin's. All clear. You *don't* need that Port anymore. Book the surgery ASAP!

I'm SO relieved my chest X-ray was clear. I can relax about it now.

Oct 4

I'm having my Port out today. They froze the area and *tried* getting it out. He was really tugging at it. My skin grew over it, so he had to make a bigger incision to get it out. He said other people aren't as lucky. I know it. Don't lift or do anything for 24 hours – you have a hole in your chest and it'll bleed if you do too much.

Oct 5

I've been doing some writing on my book. I'm feeling pretty gung-ho about writing MY story. I know I said I wouldn't, but I feel differently now. I NEED to tell my story. I just survived cancer, for God's sake!

I went on the lymphoma site and you can chat with people in the same situation. I found a woman, 29 years old and had cancer 12 years ago and STILL feels "paranoid." That doesn't give me much hope.

Nov 12

Tracy's good friend Norman's father-in-law passed away – lung cancer. We've lost so many people this year. Why do some of us survive the awful disease and others don't? I don't get it. It's devastating! Why am *I* still here?!

Nov 19

I had the CT yesterday. It's the very *first* time I *wasn't* worried about it.

Nov 29

I went for bloodwork; they took 13 vials! The CT looks good. Your nodes have gotten *even smaller*. There is minimal concern over the one in my chest. It's still 1.7cm, so they need to send me for a PET scan. It will detect *any* cancer cells, even those pesky ones that try to hide. The nurse gave me a card for a doctor who specializes in fertility in women who have had cancer.

Dec 12
A long-time friend of the family died today. We lost another one. Man. Enough!

Apparently six months is enough time to bounce back from eight months of aggressive chemo, the Long-Term Disability Board (LTD) at work has decided. They tell me to go back on *gradual* hours, then *full-time* **in a month**. I told the LTD rep that research says it takes longer to recover from the side effects than the actual cancer. I'm *still* dealing with the side effects. I'm the one living this; I have to do what's best for me. I saw my doctor. She's completely on board with me getting as much time as I need. I'm not afraid to go back to work, I'll totally go – but when *I'm* ready. Her recommendation was to not return to work until May 1!

Dec 21
I got an email from LTD: We're happy to report you have FULL coverage until Apr 30/06. I cried. Happy tears.

Dec 27
Tracy and I had appointment with the fertility doctor. Take 1mg folic acid for one month before getting pregnant. The chemo is *not* a factor, it doesn't pass the placenta. My age is apparently okay. The fact that I had my period all the way through treatment is an *excellent* indication that things are all good down there. He will monitor me extra, checking for cancer throughout the potential pregnancy.

What a year. I'm so grateful to be alive. I'm heartbroken for those who didn't make it. But we have many things to look forward to, and I'm going to live life to the fullest!

2006

Jan 6

We're off to a great start to the New Year – we're approved for overdraft AND a $5000 VISA. I put a deposit on a tattoo and booked it for February 14. I'm getting a banner that says, "LOYALTY SURVIVOR STRENGTH," like I said I would.

Mom said, Your life story is remarkable. What a survivor.
Yes, it has been quite the life and I'm still here to talk about it. All the people we HAVE lost recently to cancer – they *all* had kids. I'm the only one *without* children, and **I** lived. Maybe I survived so I CAN have kids.

Jan 10

PET scan day. It's very different from a CT with contrast. They inject you with a radiation and glucose mix. Then they put you in a room on a reclining chair for an hour. You can't move a single muscle! Then I went for the scan part. They also weighed me – 123 lb. O M G! But I'm okay with it. And now I get to wait a week for the results. A colleague from work died and the funeral is tomorrow. Yet another one. I can't bear it.

What if I'm getting ahead of myself? I get results next Tuesday; we're planning a trip to Mexico, a tattoo, and kids. What if something shows? That terrifies me. Nope, wait for results, *then* deal with it. Here I'm making plans for the future, for the first time in a *long* time, and that *should* be a GOOD thing. I hope I get to follow through with them.

Jan 17

Yesterday we booked our trip to Mexico! We did it, even BEFORE getting the results.

At the hospital, the nurse comes in and says she'll get right to the point. Your CT and PET scans show *NO* signs of lymphoma. There are *no* other signs of any beginnings of cancer either. There IS some fluid in your stomach, but I'll let the doctor explain that to you. He comes in – your PET scan is clear. The mass in your chest, the deflated tumor, we were concerned about it, but it's just scar tissue and we don't really know *what* the fluid in your stomach is, but it's nothing to be concerned about. I'll schedule you for a chest X-ray in March and a CT in May.

I'm relieved. This to me feels like I'm really done. It's over. Finished. Today my life begins. What a feeling!

Jan 20

I informed Mom. You'd be so proud of me. I have been forthcoming with people when things come up instead of letting it fester. I don't want one single thing bogging me down. I deal with everything head on now. It feels good! The new and improved Sari! I'm not going along with what *others* want. And I say *no* now!

In friendship, all you HAVE is loyalty. And yet nobody understands the value of it. Knowing WHO *has* your back, and who *doesn't*. People say they love you, and you'll be friend's forever, blah blah blah. SHOWING someone is worth more. Being loyal MEANS you love that person, you'd fight for them, you care about their well-being. To me, it's the cornerstone of any relationship. Knowing someone has my back means more to me than hearing them *tell* me they love me. And in my experience, loyalty is a concept few understand or are willing to go the extra mile for. It's loyalty *or* fickleness. Loyalty *or* fence-sitting. Either you are loyal or you're not. Period. Loyalty isn't some grand sacrifice, or compromise, or swear word. Either it's a quality a person possesses – or they don't. There's no middle ground on this one. It's in you, or it's not. It's having that much belief in a person; you value them and what they stand for. There's no better feeling than knowing someone is on your side. It's a foolproof way of determining who your REAL friends are.

My friend Paris needed me to *explain* what loyalty meant. I said, If I need to *explain* it to you, you *don't* get it. And she didn't.

Jan 25
I was watching an inspirational video about *telling your story*. When your life is over, you take all your experiences with you – *unless* you write them down. What could it hurt? I'm going to write my life out! I've kept a journal since 1981, my life has been documented; it's *all* there. I'm going to do it!

Feb 7
I announced to Mom I'm writing a book.

Are you going to write about…?
What *they* did to me has affected my entire life, so YES, it will be *mentioned* in the book.

What will you get out of it?
I'm done protecting people. My life is a lie. Everyone *thinks* they know me. They don't.

A lot of people will be affected by this.
Had *they* been honest about what they had done, it wouldn't be a surprise to those who may read about it in the book. THEY are living a lie. But it's so much easier for everyone to believe I'M the reason the family is broken. SARI is the unreligious one. SARI is married to a non-Jew. SARI is the bad seed.

You have *no idea* what goes on there!

Whatever "hardships" THEY have faced is NOTHING compared to what **I HAVE** had to live with. It happened to ME! They haven't paid nearly enough for the mess they made out of my life, and ruining our family. THEY are responsible for whatever they are going through. When I meet people, I tell them I'm an only child. It works. By saying I have two brothers, I get questions. This way, there are no questions. I didn't get a vote when they chose to trash my life. Why should I be concerned with what the book will do to *them*? Did they give a shit about me and the fallout I'D have to deal with from it? No!

I'm not doing this out of anger, but it's time for people to see them for who they *truly* are. I've dealt with it. I want others to know you *can* come out of it.

Feb 14
I'm thinking about a baby. I'll use the month of April to build up the folic acid and get pregnant by May. Great plan! The tattoo took about a half-hour. I was so excited! I love it. Dad said it's an important tattoo – you went to hell and back.

Apr 2
We are back from Mexico. Boy, did we need that. We talked about babies. I started folic acid today and I stopped taking my sleeping pill. Tracy had broken his ankle playing volleyball before we left but never had it looked at. Men – they seem to hate going to the doctor even when it's important to, like potential broken bones.

Gypsy hid under our bed for the two weeks we were gone and *barely* ate. I hope he'll come around.

Apr 3
Gypsy is *still* not eating. I took him to the pet hospital. He's critically dehydrated – stress-induced. They will incubate him. There is a problem with his brain; his sodium levels are so high. His brain is

telling him it's okay *not* to drink. So, when they give him fluids, his brain could swell and have seizures or go into a coma. My poor baby.

Apr 4

I called the vet. Gypsy had a good night; although he still has no interest in food, he is walking around the incubator. He's taking really well to the fluids, 12 hours of it. So, all in all, the same but doing okay. It'll be $900 to $1000 for three days in the incubator. They encouraged us to visit him.

Our 14-year wedding anniversary. Tracy came home with a fever and went to bed. I went to visit Gypsy. They asked me to help him eat. He ate twice while I was there! I scratched and pet him the whole time. He was very relaxed there, probably the first time since we left for Mexico.

Apr 5

Gypsy's bloodwork has improved and they increased his fluids. They'll probably send him home in the morning. But when I visited him later, he was restless, fidgety and uncomfortable. What we were worried about has happened – his brain has swelled. He's not responding to light. They'll have to watch him closely through the night.

Apr 7

I picked up Gypsy. He was being so affectionate, not hiding under the bed, wanting to be around us, and he ate lots!

Apr 13

Tracy came home with two boxes. He opens one – I realize it's all his office stuff.
You were fired?
Ya, they let me go. It's probably a good thing. I got today's pay and severance.

I feel relieved. The job served its purpose; it allowed us to get this house. He got paid and severance, I got paid today, we have Tracy's tax return and money in the bank. I also have my work shares. We'll be fine until he finds another job.

May 4

I'm freaking out. The LTD Board at work wants me back at four-hour days for the first week, then the following week at five hours, the week after, six hours and by July 1 *full-time*! What kind of *gradual* back-to-work plan is that?! My doctor TOLD them two MONTHS at four-hour days, then we re-evaluate. We told them I'm still dealing with extreme fatigue. I ended one battle only to begin another.

May 8

I get a call from LTD. They received my oncologist's work forms and he'd okayed me going back to work. How did he do that without even having a discussion with me about it first? I see him on Thursday – he couldn't wait? I called LTD back. I said his information is *inaccurate*. Why did I bother calling over there 1000 times to make sure he DIDN'T sign it before we spoke? LTD agreed they will wait until my appointment on Thursday before going forward.

May 11

I went for X-rays, bloodwork, and a checkup. They should be getting the results of the CT scan too. He says to me, I don't understand the problem, you're *clear* of Hodgkin's; therefore, you *can* go back to work. You're in remission, there's no reason to not go back to work.
Just *because* I'm clear, doesn't mean I'm physically READY to go back. So just deal with the fatigue?
Well, you're clear of cancer, there's no sign of disease. If you have *other* problems, you should see your doctor about it.

I WANT to go back. I get it, he *only* cares about the *disease* aspect, *nothing* else. I'm clear. Period.
Yay, I'm glad I'm clear. But it's not so black and white.

May 12

I went to see my doctor. She said she will tell the LTD Board that either they accept the 4hrs/day for 3 days/week for 12 months OR they can wait until you are *100% better.* I said I guess they want me calling in sick all the time because that is what *will* happen if I go with their schedule. I told her to submit that recommendation, they are waiting for it. It's out of my hands now. I'M SO STRESSED! I went to get my ankle tattoo – my Hebrew name with a star of David. The guy said, I know you, you're the one who had cancer.

Yes. I guess I'm cancer girl: my claim to fame.

May 16

I got an email from LTD before going to bed. They have *accepted* my doctor's recommendation. I go back June 1. I'm nervous, nervous about going to work and being so tired. I can't get out of bed before 11:00 a.m. each day. I'm exhausted. Maybe by showing I'm TRYING is a good thing, even if I may not be ready.

Tracy said it'll be fine; It's progress, the next step. So, you DO call in sick if you're not feeling well. So what?

I'm putting too much pressure on myself to be 100% BEFORE I go back. I'm grateful I STILL HAVE a job to go back to. I'm grateful I DON'T have cancer. Damn, I *just* got my period. I'm *not* grateful for that.

May 23

I went to see my doctor. I'm here because I'm completely freaked out about starting work in a week. I'm so completely unprepared. Everyone's telling me to go back, so I felt pressured to do so. But I'M the only one who has to work it. I get up and have a coffee, and from THAT I need to lie down. Let's say 45 minutes to get ready, then one hour on the train, be at work for four hours and one hour to get home. It's completely undoable. So, I need something to kick start this– like vitamins. I need to get through this fatigue and start feeling like a normal human being. I cried like a fricking baby. She didn't know *what* to do.

Are you depressed?

No, I'm frustrated. It's *pure* frustration. I'm NOT afraid to go back to work. I *want* to.

The effects of chemo don't leave your body for at least *a year* after treatment.

That makes sense; it's poison!

She's sending me for bloodwork and an ultrasound to rule things out.

For *years* I had people telling me NOTHING was wrong with me, and I almost died because of their negligence. Now, I KNOW how I feel. I KNOW MY BODY and I'll be damned if someone TELLS me, You ARE ready to go back to work. I know myself better than anyone so LISTEN to me! It had to get *so* bad before I was taken seriously. That *won't* happen again. We are doing this on MY timetable.

May 29

The union lady called. She will take the new forms to the Board, but they don't meet again until June 21. She wanted me to describe the fatigue. I tried to give as much detail as possible. The exhaustion, lethargy, no sleep, and waking up spent. I'll take the fatigue over cancer any day though.

She said, Well, we can't go against what your doctor has recommended, so she'll email all the people involved in my case to notify them of what we spoke about.

Tracy's been going on appointments with his buddy Derek for this new business that is helping us put *our* finances in order, as well as others. It's called Galaxy Securities. Tracy would get licensed so he could help families with their insurance needs. He would also put plans together to show families how money works.

Toby called. They need to remove her bad kidney. Lots of bad things could happen – kidney failure, septic shock… Her other organs are very swollen. Damn.

June 6
Toby called and said, The infection is spreading into my body and it *can't* reach the bloodstream. Her other kidney has to keep being strong. Life *without* Toby? I don't want to think about that. I hope it'll all be fine. She must be so scared.

June 21
Today is one year since my *last* chemo. Wow. Sometimes it feels like a *hundred* years ago, other times it feels like *yesterday*. My bloodwork and ultrasound are clear. The doc said *stress* is what's probably causing my irregular periods. It looks all good *in there*, no effects from the chemo. You can start a family now! How's one more month, then you go back to work? Okay.
Tracy had a few meetings with a guy from his last job, who owns a manufacturing company. Tracy is super excited about the work. He starts July 4.

June 24
Tracy's 42nd birthday. We had a big party and it was fun…until it wasn't. Ward, whom I've known since I've known Tracy, was out of control. He was following me around like a dog in heat. He kept trying to look down my pants and shirt. I went downstairs to get the hot dogs out of the fridge, he followed me – and shut the door behind him. He was coming at me. He was trying to see down my pants again. He's around 300 lb. I tried pushing him back. He didn't even budge. I got scared. He tried again to lift up my shirt. Yes, he was drunk, but that doesn't excuse his behavior. I was scared. No one knew we were down there. I finally got around him, whipped open the door and ran upstairs. That shook me. How far was he willing to take that? I'm glad I never had to find out. If only his wife, Paris, knew.

July 4

Tracy starts his new job today.

I called the fertility clinic and they said it's *not* a fertility problem until you've been trying for one year.

I'm feeling out of the loop with "that" group of friends – Norman, Ward, Paris, and the others. But it's fine. I DON'T want in. The *idea* of friendship is nice, but the *reality* is an ugly truth. It's Ward's birthday on Thursday, and we've been invited to the pub on Saturday. God help me.

July 8

Ward pulled the same stunt. He followed me into the pub bathroom, into the stall and shut the door.

I said, I came here to pee.

So, pee. Then he tried to lift up my shirt – I just want to see this.

Why are you doing this? You have a beautiful wife.

Because I'm curious and you're hot. I always thought you were so hot. This is our secret, right?

Paris saw us coming out of the bathroom together. I walked to the table, "laughing" it off. What else was I going to do? When we were ordering food, she made a remark like, Ward can eat off the Sari menu. This passive-aggressive comment indicates she knew things, but didn't let on. I just feel sick.

I have to think about telling Tracy or not. That's a long friendship to end if Tracy chooses to do that. But that's not being a friend, nor is it MY fault, so, come what may.

July 10

Ward calls me. "Are you mad at me?"

I wanted to know what he THINKS he did. Mad?

"I was drunk. I'm sorry. Because I flirt."

"I'd say it's BEYOND flirting. It's NOT okay!"

"I'm sorry. I promise I'll never follow you to the bathroom again. I didn't mean to hurt you or do anything bad."

July 24

There's a war raging in Israel. It makes me nervous for Mom.

I got a letter from LTD – 100% coverage until August 31.

I met our new neighbors, Dave and Erin; they also have an eight-year-old son. We saw the three of them splashing around on the street in the pouring rain the day they moved in. It was the darnedest cutest thing! They were laughing and happy, and seemed to not have a care in the world. They look like fun people. I'm hoping. We need that.

I go through many periods in my life where I believe I DON'T need friends. Sometimes it's so much work, too much hassle, energy and too many games. It's not always worth it to me. People I've known for YEARS were NOT there for me when I was sick, but are happy to hang out AFTER they knew I'd be FINE. I believe I went through what I did so I could weed out these people, and put my priorities in order.

Aug 1

Toby had surgery yesterday. She sounded AWFUL. She said the surgery was a bit more complicated; they had to open her right up! The surgeon told her that, at one point, she had died on the table.
OMG. I can't even…
She'll be in the hospital for a week. I had flowers delivered to her.

Aug 12

Our line of credit is now active – so we bought a used Porsche and paid off ALL our bills! It was a dream of Tracy's to own another one. I got to drive it. Now THAT was fun! We went to the Porsche dealership and bought matching Porsche hats.

Aug 19

Today is Tracy's niece's wedding. We actually aren't even sure they know we are coming. When we got there, his sister runs to him crying and hugs him – You came! You came! Her husband said I'm glad you came, I really mean that. His niece saw Tracy and hugged him – I am SO glad you came. I was so afraid you wouldn't. Tracy's niece is six months pregnant and looked beautiful. His other niece hugged us both. During the reception, Tracy got emotional. Being around his family touched a nerve. They were close a long time ago. And then they weren't.

Aug 26

Tracy and I met Dad and Marsha out in Canmore for my 38th birthday. We went to "our" bagel place for breakfast. The rest of the afternoon we walked downtown, stopping for a drink at outdoor cafés and then remaining at one for the rest of the day. Dad bought a beer so I could pour it for him, like old times.

It was HOT out! We nibbled on appies all afternoon. It was *so* relaxing and fun. I took a picture of Tracy and me; it's one of my favorites of us. It was one of the BEST birthday celebrations I've EVER had! No seriousness, no agendas, no schedule. What a great day!

Aug 27

We went to Chestermere around 2:00 p.m. Before heading to the restaurant patio, Tracy and I sat on the edge of the dock and listened to music on his cell. It was so peaceful. A few others joined us. We did that for a few hours. Everyone else came around 6:00 p.m. We had most of the patio; it was like having a private party room. Dad said, You have a real great group of friends here. All the *right* people came. It was just a wonderful weekend.

Sept 6

It's my first day back to work. I'm working 10:00 a.m. to 2:00 p.m. Monday, Wednesday, and Friday, for two months. I missed the 9:00

a.m. LRT. I felt like puking – I'm so nervous. I got upstairs – everyone hugged the heck out of me. New team members introduced themselves and said, I've heard so much about you. People commented on my hair growing in. I unpacked. By noon, I was sooooo sleepy. By 1:00 p.m. – exhausted! I'm getting another week of holidays because I've been there for nine years. Nice! My new manager came over and introduced himself. He said everyone is very excited to have me back. Seventeen minutes left...I...can...make...it! I lay down the *second* I got home. Tracy came home and said we are going out for dinner to celebrate my big step today.

Sept 19
I saw my doctor and told her this schedule is totally working for me, even though I struggle with being tired; it's challenging. I'm getting into a new routine, but I see it as a positive step.

Maybe reassess in December?
Sounds good.

We're picking vacation dates at work. People are pissed I *still* have seniority and get to pick prime dates. I guess all the happy, happy, joy, joy of me coming back to work is short-lived. Let the claws come out.

Sept 25
Maybe I'm not meant to have kids. This was my "fertile" week and now I just got my period. Five days late! WTF?! I'm regular my entire life, irregular for what six months, eight months? What is this about?

Oct 4
We bought our tickets for Akumal, Mexico. I can't stop thinking about the cancer coming back. I'm *convinced* it's coming back. There's this tickle in my throat that I only ever had when I got sick...it freaks me out. I WANT to have kids. I WANT to grow old with Tracy. I WANT to travel. I'M NOT DONE YET! A reoccurrence? Something else? Man,

that would suck. I must stay positive. It's probably nothing. I have a fear of getting sick again. I just *can't* get sick again.

Oct 10
I went to see my doctor about my concerns over a reoccurrence.

"What happened before when you were diagnosed? It started with a cough, right?"
"Yup. They sent me for an X-ray."
"I think we should do that."
"I don't want to be *paranoid*."
"How could you NOT be? Take Buckley's in the meantime."

Aunty Ruth and Uncle Ruben are moving to Toronto. I'm a little surprised, but they'll be closer to their children and grandchildren. That makes sense.

Oct 23
The cough is getting worse; it's deep in my chest. The doc prescribed an inhaler. Okay, I guess I won't worry.

Toby and I had a long talk, sharing our respective experiences. I said, It's amazing how the brain doesn't LET you know what's happening at the time. Only when it was *all over* did I realize, Holy shit, I had cancer! She said even though we live far from each other, we seem to live parallel lives. Look at us now, we both survived things that *should've* killed us!

Oct 31
I got an "8" tattooed on my foot, and it took 15 minutes! Dang that hurt! 18 sleeps until Mexico!

Nov 8
Tracy said he had a dream we had *seven* kids. I was up all night, thinking about the possibility I could be pregnant! I was so nauseous

yesterday and almost passed out. It happened again today. Food makes me nauseous. Hmm.

I went to my doctor about work – they are bumping my hours up by one. LTD had suggested going to six hours. Uh, no.
I told her I had a CT scan last week; I may have had a bad reaction to the contrast because I've been nauseous and almost passing out ever since.

"Do you think you might be pregnant?"
"It's possible. I've just been so irregular I don't know anymore."
"We can do a blood test. A urine test may not show anything yet."
"I leave for *Mexico* NEXT weekend!"
"I guess you'd want to know *before* then."
"Ya, I need to know if I should be drinking tequila or not."

Nov 9
Well...I wanted to know one way or the other. Now I know. I JUST got my period. I need this vacation.

Nov 30
One week in Mexico just wasn't enough. We had a wonderful time.

I had X-rays done. I tell the doctor about my cough and inhaler. Your CT is clear, your bloodwork is normal, your X-rays are clear. The nurse said, It's just a *normal* cold.
I can deal with that. Just a "normal" person with an average cold. Relieved.

Dec 15
I got a referral to the fertility clinic.

I took Gypsy to the vet. His eye was so goopy, it looked pretty bad. They took him to the back to run a few tests. They went to take his temperature in his bum and a huge chunk of puss came out. The infection is through and through. We can TRY to treat him, but we don't know what's wrong with him and the future outlook – we're not sure. He *will* get sick again. You have two options: treat him now and hope he makes it, or you can euthanize him.

I called Tracy. He's suffering. He can't breathe. We were both crying. Tracy said, I'll be right there.

They brought Gypsy in for me to spend time with him. The doctor told me we're making the right decision. I picked out his death box and we wanted the paw print. He's so weak. They put the IV in and gave him back to me. Tracy arrived and we said our goodbyes. Gypsy was all wrapped up in a blanket. I whispered to him how much I loved him. Go to sleep. The vet injected him. He slumped. It was over.

My little kitten. Gone. All the suffering is over. He had the best life he could with us. Three and a half years old. He had such a tough little life before coming to us. I will miss him SO much. That little guy got into everyone's heart. He remained such a tiny thing. He never really grew to a normal cat size. I'll miss him following me EVERYWHERE. Yes, he was antisocial and hissed and never purred, but there were *reasons* for that. We did everything to make him feel safe and loved. He was so lovable.

Dec 21

Tracy wants to get this kitten from the *Bargain Finder*. Fluffy (a.k.a. Nike) needs a little buddy because he's only two. He has the two older cats, Gizmo and Simon, but it's not the same. Yes, I want a black kitten, but I don't think I have the patience right now. Tracy pressed the matter; we *are* going to get him *today*. They had four kittens. We knew *exactly* which one we wanted. The lady said, She's a very *unaffectionate* cat.

Uh, okay, we *still* want her. In the car, she was so alert and kept looking up at me. Very fuzzy. Very cute, with the sweetest face. We are naming her Midnight. She slept with us on the bed, in Gypsy's spot to be exact. That blew me away.

Dec 22

She's a snuggler. I slept from 3:00 a.m. to 4:30 a.m. The other animals are not too crazy about her. Fluffy is the worst! Gizmo didn't really care. Ebony is used to all these new additions. We're NOT replacing Gypsy, we just thought Fluffy needed this, a play buddy. He will get used to her, in time. Tracy checked – it's a *boy*! Funny. *Three times* that happened we thought we were getting female cats. A house full of boy cats, I love it!

2007

Jan 4

I went to get kitten food so I stopped in at the vet. They had Gypsy's remains for me. In the car I looked inside – such a tiny pouch of ash. He was so small. I got home and cried. It's so final.

Jan 9

We booked our Caribbean trip yesterday for April. I'M SO EXCITED!
I took Simon to the vet. He has an abscess at the back of his mouth, an ear and eye infection. I got antibiotics for him. There's nothing we wouldn't do for these animals. They are our family.

Jan 16

NOTHING IS GOING RIGHT! I can't get pregnant – I'm a total fucking failure!
Tracy is so defeated. Derek had to come into town to perk him up, and get him excited about Galaxy Securities again. Tracy needs to get licensed. I think he's finally ready to give this a serious shot. Our neighbor, Jim, has joined the business as well, on Tracy's suggestion. I guess we can all figure it out together.

Feb 3

I received a big ol' apology from Dani, the friend I made through Tracy's volleyball. She said she was sorry for pulling away and distancing herself from me ,and basically being a shitty friend. I shared little of what's going on in my life. I figure, either you're my friend or you're not. I'm done playing games. I'm not chasing anyone anymore. I'm too old for this shit. I have found when I *stop* chasing, *they* stop our friendship. If I don't initiate or make contact, they sure as shit don't either, and the relationship fizzles. I don't have room in life for fickle people anymore. My circle is getting smaller and I'm *very okay* with it. I need unconditional friendships. People seem to only need me when THEY are going through tough times. They are around for MY good times. THEIR good times? Nope. It's exasperating, but I'm very clear about what I do and don't want. I've been thinking about this for a while – when I have a fight with Tracy or a friend, I feel the relationship is OVER. I have had lots of rejection and abandonment issues, so I feel, why drag it out? We're done. But then it's *not* done and things get worked out. But my first instinct is ALWAYS to believe: This is the end.

Feb 14

There's more drama at work. I overheard that somebody is pissed I took key December dates off and said, Sari got Christmas AGAIN?!
Am I supposed to ask HER when I'm ALLOWED to take my vacation time? I have seniority, sister. Deal with it. I actually heard someone tell her to shut up. I've discovered the secret to keeping my sanity here – EAR BUDS. Fa la la la la, la la la la!
I got another tattoo today, down the middle of my shoulders: butterflies. They signify *transformation and rebirth*. That's me. I feel like I'm starting a new chapter in my life; I'm in remission, weeding out the toxic people from my life, going back to work... The icing on the cake today: Tracy PASSED the first part of his licensing exam to become a financial advisor!

Feb 15

Oncology checkup. I'm 127 lb. Bullshit! The scale HAS TO BE wrong. I shouldn't have eaten lunch before getting weighed. I have 64 sleeps to do something about it before our trip to Mexico.

The doctor asks me to take my top off so he can examine me. He sees the bandage from the tattoo on my back. He was not impressed, even mad at me. He closed his eyes and shook his head. He explained there were medical risks in having that done after having cancer. Well, like he keeps telling me, he's there to deal with the *disease* – he has no say in *anything* else. I'm a big girl.

I begin *4 days*/week at 4 hours/day on Monday, instead of the 3 days/week at 4 hours/day.

Mar 2

Okay, so Tracy and I sorta did it in the Porsche (the car was *in* the garage, of course). I know, probably too much info, but there's a reason. We talked about *baby names*, if we conceived it in the car: a girl – *Charli Porsche Knock;* and if it's a boy – *Brandon Porsche Knock.* It was *so* much fun thinking about names and dreaming about having a baby! We talked about it for four and a half hours! It feels like the beginning of the rest of our lives.

Mar 5

Tracy PASSED his provincial exam! I told him how proud I am of him. This four-day work schedule is killing me.

I finally told Tracy about Ward. I was afraid of how he'd react, but he was great. He believed me.

Mar 8

No amount of positive thinking and wishing and hoping could mask the disappointment of getting my period today. How many times can I tell myself *it's not meant to be?* Tracy will be so disappointed.

Mar 28

We went to the fertility clinic. Tracy had to get a sperm test done and I had to have two blood tests before the appointment. The doctor asked a lot of questions about the cancer, treatment, periods… He was concerned about my AGE.

I'm 38; I did *not* think that was too *old* to get pregnant.

It *IS* an issue; I'd like to do an ultrasound TODAY. And a biopsy.

Oops, I forgot to wax.

He pointed out a few cysts, but he wasn't concerned about them. I have a thin uterus lining. I don't know; your bloodwork keeps coming back *normal*. They do show you DID ovulate. Tracy's sperm count is good, all normal – the doc tells him he can brag to all his friends. The biopsy result was it's all okay down there. He said. There is no cut-and-dried solution here. We'll run bunches of more tests and do many more ultrasounds.

Tracy asked, What about hormones to regulate the period?
Yes, we can try fertility drugs. Keep taking your prenatal vitamins; it's all about the folic acid. Come back April 18 for another ultrasound, and go to the lab now for more blood tests. And so, we went back to the lab and tried to stay positive. We want this so bad!

Apr 11
I told Dad about Ward. We don't want to be friends with *any* of them anymore. He was very supportive, as always. My dad really is one of my best friends. There's nothing I can't talk to him about.

Apr 18
The doctor said he saw three *viable* follicles. You can take hormones orally, or you keep coming here and we can inject you with fertility hormones. We can try to retrieve an egg, but it's not cheap. He wants me to go for an X-ray to make sure my fallopian tubes are *open*.

Tracy and I decided the egg retrieval is too expensive. If we could, we'd do it in a heartbeat. We'll see if the hormones that I take at home will help.

May 9
What an amazing trip. Sand that feels like icing sugar. Water as clear as ever. We will definitely go back to Akumal. The trip helped us both relax after all the stress of the fertility clinic.

My CT scan yesterday wasn't so great, two veins collapsed. Third time was the charm. Tests show I DID ovulate again. I start on a fertility drug today, Clomid, and then we'll move to injections. The drugs will make you moody and you'll have hot flashes. Pre-menopausal symptoms are a side effect of the drugs. It can't be worse than Hodgkin's. Also, there is a chance of having twins.

Bring it on! I *always* wanted them! And since I'm "old," it's better to pump out *all* the kids we want at once!

Tracy received his tangible, official license!

My work schedule is changing to 5 hours/day, 4 days/week. Groan.

May 24

My oncologist said, You're in FULL REMISSION. Music to my ears!

So, since your CT is clear, your protocol is seeing me every *four* months now.

He wanted to see my tattoo. Who IS this man?? Then he shared a *personal* story with us. Tracy and I leave his office and we just look at each other. What was that? He's NEVER been that way with us: friendly. Maybe he was being nice because he *knows* I'm *not* going to die. In his line of work, you keep it all business because he must lose A LOT of patients. I get it. He sees hope for me.

May 29

I started the antibiotic yesterday. As part of the fertility treatment. I've never been on them when I'm NOT sick. I wonder what kind of infections they think I'll get from this process?! I'm getting emotional thinking about being in remission. It feels good. I had my HSG test to see if my tubes are blocked. It made me feel nauseous, bloated, and crampy.

June 8

TWO years since chemo! We celebrated with some friends. It's a pleasure to surround ourselves with people who WANT to be friends. It's so easy with some people. They all asked if I was pregnant yet. Not yet.

June 22
Funny, as Tracy's birthday gets closer, people we haven't heard from in six months are fishing. They sure don't want to miss a good party. Ya, that's not friendship, assholes. We *do* throw great parties though.

June 26
Today – I was hit by a truck.
I was walking halfway across the street in front of work when a truck comes from around the corner at the lights. I can *see* he's *not* looking at me and I realize he **_wasn't_** stopping. I put my arms out, as if to stop him from hitting me, and braced myself for the inevitable impact. It tossed me back about five feet. I just lay there. He got out of his truck to "help" me and walked me over to the sidewalk. He kept saying, Are you SURE you're okay?
No, I'm NOT okay, I *never* said I *was*!
Can I get you some napkins (for the blood)? He gets me some. I'm really sorry. I hate driving downtown.
And then he left. Ya, he left.
Two guys come running over to me. We saw the whole thing! There's a paramedic at the fire station, you should get yourself checked out.
I *walked* over. I guess nothing's broken. I was shaking. It felt like shock. Dazed.
The two guys inform the firemen I was *just* hit out front and I need someone to have a look at me.
Did you hit your head? Did you lose consciousness? Blurred vision? No.
Do you want to go to the hospital in the ambulance?
I don't think so. I don't want to waste your valuable time on *me*. There are worse off people that need your help.
Well, you *wouldn't* be wasting our time. *Had* you lost consciousness we'd be *taking* you, we wouldn't be *asking*.
Right. I sat there thinking about it.
Well, if you don't go with *us*, go see your family doctor and get checked out.
I'll just get a ride to my doctor.

Okay, if you decide in 15 minutes you need us to take you, we will.

When the police arrived, I filled out my statement. The two guys who helped me did as well. Turns out we all work at FNL. They were outside on their smoke break when it happened. I kept thanking them.

I called Tracy. He was there in five minutes. Apparently, the guy who hit me came back because I saw him filling out a police report. I called Dad on the way to the doctor. He was practically hysterical. I love you. I love you.

My doctor said, You'll be sore for a few days.

I have scraped and bloody hands, knee, ankle, and thigh. There's a throbbing pain in my neck, lower back, wrist, and side. I probably have whiplash and muscle damage, *again*. She gave me a prescription for pain meds, and a note to be off work until next Tuesday.

It could've been worse – he could've run me *right* over! There could've been an oncoming car. My first thought was, Thank God I WASN'T pregnant! In one moment, *everything* can change.

I survived cancer only to get hit by a truck?! WTF?! *I didn't* need this as a wakeup call – having cancer *already* did that for me. I called Mom when I got home. I'm okay *but…*

Adding insult to injury – my car was broken into.

On a *positive* note, Tracy says, It's June 26: 2+6=**8**. And Dudie (a.k.a. Midnight, or the Dude) is **8** months old today.

June 27

Mom says, It's truly amazing the things you've been through and God is *still* protecting you. Obviously, you're very special to Him, and He wants you around.

I was starting to wonder, *Should* I get thoroughly checked out? What if there's internal bruising going on that I don't know about? I got banged up pretty good.

Tracy said, You know your own body. If things get worse, we'll go. The doctor said today you'd be feeling worse.

I'm concerned about my female plumbing, that everything is still in place. I'm feeling quite lucky though. I've been down this road before – I probably *would have* been better off *breaking* something – bones heal in a few months. Muscle damage takes for-fricking-ever to heal.

Tracy said, So I guess making a baby is out.

No. I'm going to be sore for a long time, so to wait for that to change...nah!

June 28

I woke up feeling, ya, worse. My arm was hurting, tingly in my fingers, a massive headache, ribs, hip pain…

I went to the doctor and she gave me a referral for physio. No sense waiting for more pain, let's get started on it *now*.

Mom asked if I want any of this info relayed to *them*.

What's the point? They'd probably only tell me TRACY is the cause for ALL my pain and suffering anyway.

July 4

Toby called. Her mom is in renal and heart failure. Shit! She shared with me about how she was feeling. I told her I am there for her in any way she needs.

I called work on Monday to say I won't be in yet. Neither work nor friends have asked how I am. Nice. I feel so blessed. I went to my first physio. He checked me out and basically said I'm a mess.

You definitely have whiplash and WAD III – Whiplash Associative Disorder. WAD III is a neuro-related injury. WAD III would be dislocation or fracture of the neck. You'll be off a MINIMUM two weeks. You should get a referral from your doctor to go get X-rays. You'll need treatment on your neck, arm and knee.

Is driving out of the question?

Yes, you'll just keep irritating the nerves.

He wants to see me three times a week. It's $90 per session, $350 for the assessment. Gulp.

We only did my "top half" and will assess my "bottom half" next visit. He didn't charge me.

July 9

I'm back at physio. He checked my legs. There's lots of swelling, and your ankle too. The ligaments are stretched in the ankle and knee.

I told him about the pain I have in my jaw, ears and the shooting pain down my back leg into my butt.

I contacted a lawyer. He emailed me papers to authorize.

July 19

I finally heard back from someone in LTD. My disability will be topped up until September. They decided since I'm off full-time with this accident, they realized I will need some income and they didn't want me to be without any money. They don't reconvene again until September. Do you know how long you'll be off?

I'm being treated for nerve damage at physio and I'm waiting for X-ray results.

Tracy came home and figured I needed a night out; we went for dinner. I could barely hold the fork or glass or cut my food and hold it. The pain billowed through every finger, my palms, forearms, and elbows. It was pretty intense pain. I can't even eat a meal like a normal person! Tracy says my body needs time to heal before we do the baby thing.

July 25

Mom called – she offered me $1000 to pay for physio. I started crying.

You're my *Zeesinke Maidele* (sweet girl) and I love you, and I want to help. I hate being so far away, and this is the least I can do. I don't want you missing physio, and worrying about not being able to pay for it. I'm so grateful.

Aug 7

Toby's mother passed away. I have no words. Mom is going to be devastated. They've been friends long before I was alive. Toby was six months old and I was a one-year-old when we met. Our moms would throw us in the crib together so *they* could hang out, since we lived across the street from each other. Our friendship is indescribable. The miles between us have never affected the quality of our relationship. We have this cosmically, otherworldly connection. We each can sense when the other needs them. She stood up for me when I had no voice, when I was bullied. She always looked out for me. I often wondered what trajectory my life would've taken had we *remained* in Montreal. Would Toby and I have stayed friends? But I never would've met Tracy, so it's a no-brainer for me – I was absolutely meant to leave Montreal for Calgary. My destiny awaited me here. And that incredible man stands beside me to this day.

Sept 8

I started with a new family doctor, Dr. West. He's incredibly thorough. I'm really going to like this one.

I've exhausted *all* my benefits. It's been ALL out of pocket. Then I received a TRUST check from the insurance company for the accident – $5500. OMG. I'm so relieved!

The fertility drugs ARE working well to regulate things. My period is a matter of *days*. It's amazing!

The Jewish New Year is coming up. It feels weird without Aunty Ruth and Uncle Ruben. I wish for good health, financial success with Galaxy Securities, living life to its fullest, still feeling grateful I'm cancer-free and that the accident wasn't worse, and could we please have a baby.

Sept 18

I told Dr. West physio wants me to start chiro and massage.

We have both, right here in the building – just around the corner. They are excellent, tops in their fields.

What are you taking for pain?

Nothing. I seem to have a high pain threshold. I deal with it.

So, pain-wise, you have sprained wrists, whiplash – anything else?

Extreme fatigue. Also, I have headaches *every single entire day* since the accident.

We can't give LTD a return-to-work date because we don't know when we are going to start seeing improvement. I'll just put "unknown."

Ok, wow. I could've kissed him I was so pleased. Later I was reading the Physician Assessment Form (PAF) – I was blown away; he was so thorough with such detail. I feel optimistic.

Sept 29

I got a letter from LTD saying I have FULL benefits until December 31. And that will be retro from the accident date. Tremendous!

I went through the usual history with my new chiropractor. I told him I have a higher pain threshold than I thought. Most women do – men are big babies. He examined me and said I have four vertebra/joints that are compressed and pressing on the nerves, creating all this pain. The C7 part of the neck directly affects the nerves in my arms.

SO VALIDATING! There IS a reason for my pain!

He said it *would have* been better to have *broken* something – you're in a cast for six weeks, then you're DONE. This is more serious and will take a lot longer to heal. But the good news is that it WILL heal. I'll need to see you three times a week, and then we'll get you going with massage.

He did my first adjustment. It hurt like hell. He saw me wincing, but I said, Don't stop, do what you gotta do.

This is it – I found a guy who CAN help me! I can't wait. I'm SO frustrated with not being able to hold stuff, I keep dropping things.

Tracy started his new job today, working with Jim at a security company.

Oct 15

I called the fertility clinic. The nurse said after being on Clomid, you need to be *off* it for a few months to give your body a chance to adapt.

Oct 26

Have seen my chiro six more times. There *is* some improvement. I also started massage.

Unfortunately, the dizziness and nausea are all part and parcel of what you're going through – no getting around it. He asked if I'd consider wearing a splint for my jaw? If it'll help, sure. I'll recommend someone to you.

Nov 10

Happy 10 years at Fifth Network Ltd. to me. Ya, that was sarcasm. No one remembered. No card, no calls, nothing. I haven't been to work since June. Out of sight, out of mind. Whatever, I'll cheers to myself from home. Forget FNL anyway, as we are SO busy with Galaxy Security stuff – a convention, training, appointments. It's really taking off. I support Tracy at events, and organize his office and paperwork. Maybe down the road I'll do more.

Nov 15

Mom is visiting and she announces she has gifts from "the family" in Israel. I have a gift from your brothers and wives and a letter from them.

I was confused and said I *can't* accept them.

It was sent because the wives care about you. They wish you had a relationship with them. They have no family. Family is everything to them. You're their sister-in-law. They heard about the accident. They love you.

I STILL *can't* accept these gifts.

Mom was irritated.

They gave me a bathrobe with my Hebrew name embroidered on it. I said, Since you're so busy defending them and making sure THEIR feelings aren't hurt, you can be kind and tell them I *enjoyed* the gift. I

DO think it's sweet and thoughtful of them, but the reality is things aren't so simple. In a perfect world, I'd love to be able to get to know them, but the fact is I want NOTHING to do with my brothers. And the letter – no good can come from me opening it. They will be telling me to divorce Tracy and go to *Yeshiva* and THEN my accidents will stop.

She said, No, I don't believe that's what they'd say.

Well, their LAST letter *was* like that. And quite honestly, if they did what they did to SOMEONE ELSE, they'd be in jail!

Levi too? For what?

As an *accomplice*! HE KNEW what Kyle did. AND HE DIDN'T CARE AND DID NOTHING!!

I was angry now.

Mom's demeanor changed, not defensive. She said she never once considered how I'd react to the gifts.

I need to wear a robe that will remind me of THEM every time I look at or wear it? Why would I put myself through that? If the wives actually knew WHY I'm distant, THEY'D FLIP! This isn't some *little* family TIFF. We're NOT going to be one big, happy family – EVER! Let us not forget, our family IS THE WAY IT IS because of **_THEM_**! Not me, THEM! I protected them for YEARS, never letting onto anyone what horrible people they were. I'm DONE with all that. I've played the good sister role for the last time. I'm done. They don't deserve anything else from me. I owe them NOTHING. If anything, I feel sorry for the wives. I feel badly they married into THIS family. *They* should be *thanking* Tracy for picking up the pieces of my life they trashed. I'm a BETTER Jew than those two! TRACY is a better human being than they are. He's NEVER hurt anyone the way they have. But THEY are the saints, the do-gooders?!

Mom said to Tracy, I'm grateful for you, the way you have been there for Sari and taken care of her. It's truly amazing, and I tell people that.

I said, *Tracy's* not holding me back (from Judaism) – I CHOOSE this life. Maybe tell them we are NOT looking for THEIR acceptance of us.

Mom hugged me. You have made yourself VERY clear. I understand a lot more now.

I ripped up and threw out the letter – UNREAD – and I told Mom to give the robe to someone who could use it; give it to charity.

Nov 19
Dad, Mom, and I sat at the kitchen table and talked. It's been 15 to 20 years since we've done that. Surreal. When he left, Mom and I talked about her marriage, my cancer, the accident...
We do dive deep when she comes out. It was good.
For my CT results, the nurse told me no abnormalities and nothing in the lymph nodes. You have cysts on your left ovary though. But it's nothing to worry about, you're good!
My oncologist came in and said, I'm here to tell you you're *still* in remission.
I headed for the nearest bathroom and cried. I was SO relieved.

Nov 26
I met my new dentist (the other one retired), who is referring me to an orthodontist, to discuss getting a mouth splint.

In the evening, I told Tracy I just got my period. Are you sad I'm not pregnant?
Of course I am, but try, try again. Tracy gave me a sly smile.

Dec 11
I went for an EMG (electromyography test – it can detect nerve damage). It sent shocks through my fingers and elbows, a most unpleasant test. The neurologist said, So, *no* nerve damage but it's all connected with neck and wrist injuries, and it'll take time. You're doing all the right things – physio, chiro, and massage – it's all you can do.

Dec 12
The fertility doctor gave us a few options: take the Clomid for four *more* months, try in vitro or do a procedure where they put me to sleep and look for scar tissue and other potential blockages in my uterus. We updated him on my accident, which delayed things. Tracy suggested

we should try the Clomid again. I told the doctor my mood swings are off-the-chart nasty. Tracy concurred.

Dec 14

My lawyer said that being an attractive person will make the other side NOT want to go to trial.

That's a weird thing to say.

Don't dwell on the pain, live your life; don't make ME your focus.

I assure you, you're *not*.

Did I mention he fell asleep on me four or five times? He said it was the "heat" in the office.

I said, Look, I just need some guidance. I've spent $5000 out of pocket already, and I need to know this *will* get reimbursed. And going forward I need help paying for all these doctors and specialists.

He suggested we see each other, face-to-face, every three to four months for updates.

Dec 29

Tracy told me he told a "friend" from *that* group about Ward. His reaction? I *can't* see that happening.

He should talk to the *three other* ladies, since we all have the EXACT SAME STORY! Well, that clinched the end of *that* friendship.

Ward doing what he did *could've* set me off, sent me back to all those years ago. He had no idea what I'd been through, and it could've propelled me into a traumatic place. Asshole.

2008

Jan 20

We shared with other friends from *that group* what happened with Ward. They said, Well, it only happened the *one* time, right?

No, three. I described each incident. If you tell the others, they *won't* believe me, so please don't talk about this with any of them.

Oh God no, it's up to *you* guys if you ever decide to say anything, it's not *our* place. Nobody *wouldn't* believe you.

Well, another friend didn't. He told Tracy that Ward never tried anything on HIS wife; therefore, it *couldn't* have happened.

I guess I'm glad these guys believe me because Ward did it to one of *their* friends too.

Later on, Tracy says to me, You don't have to worry about ANYONE believing you. You don't need to answer to ANYONE!

The only thing that DOES matter is Tracy believing me. And he does.

Feb 12

I have an Independent Medical Exam (IME) today. Yesterday I was sooo stressed about it. I'm so pissed I have to go through all this. I *refused* to answer a question on the form. I said it's too personal, and it has **_nothing_** to do with the accident. They already informed me there is NO confidentiality here, they WILL share the info. Well, *FNL* does NOT need to know things about me of a *personal* nature.

The doctor snidely remarked, Well, a car accident *is* personal.

No, it's *not*! That's not "personal" info. FNL does **not** need to know if I've been sexually abused and if I've been to therapy for it. How is that *relevant* in any way, shape, or form?! If they have a problem with that – fuck 'em! It's none of their goddamn business!

She asked me to list my pain. I had already said I have *wrist* pain, and then I said *elbow* pain.

She says, Well, your elbows are *part of* your wrists.

Since when? I showed her with my *hand* how the pain in my wrists travels *to* my elbows. (I'm pretty sure they are *separate* entities. I don't think your knee is part of your ankle.)

She took my elbow and knee reflexes. She said into her little recorder, She's **deliberately** not relaxing.

Unreal. The woman could barely speak English, and mumbled. I'm fairly certain she was being unclear *on purpose.*

I can't wait for *that* report! ARGH!

Feb 16

Mom called. Can I bring up a sore subject? I just feel like I need to clarify that I'm not here in Israel *because* of your brothers, or that we see each other a lot. I'm a grandmother, I have grandchildren.

I've *never* begrudged you any time you want to spend with the grandkids. I *know* you didn't move to Israel because of *them*; you did it for *you* and its home for you.

Thank you for understanding.

Feb 23

Tracy and I went with his friend John to Sunburst, Montana, to buy and pick up a used convertible Porsche Boxster. Our second Porsche.

I'm in pain but it was good to get out of the house. I went to Montana! When I "get out of the house," I *get out of the house*! When we got home, I drove it for a few blocks. Smooth ride. Much smoother than the 911. I know which car I'll be driving when I can drive again!

Mar 8

Tracy and I are feeling so good and positive. The Galaxy Securities convention in LA has inspired and amazed us. The speakers really, well, spoke to us. We had many conversations with fellow associates, who helped us realize we need to *really* commit to the biz. We decided for Tracy to make ***April 4*** his last day at his job at the security company with Jim and do Galaxy Securities **full-time**! April 4 being the day we met, got married and now our fresh start date. It's the right date for this milestone.

Tracy put it in his phone: *Apr 4/08: Last day of J-O-B, 1ˢᵗ day of the rest of our lives!*

Mar 10

We stayed a few extra days in LA after the convention, and then we rented a vehicle to drive to San Francisco. No schedule. We were just gonna wing it! Wherever we wanted to go, we would! We went to Beverly Hills and Rodeo Drive, then on to Venice Beach and drove through Malibu. Then we picked a place where we'd stay for the night in Santa Barbara and had some beach time. Aaaaa…

Mar 11

My spidey senses were tingling when I woke up. I listened to our home messages – yup, a message from LTD…your gradual back-to-work is starting March 31.
We walked up this long pier and had lunch and saw some harbor seals. We went for sushi in Carmel – the best we've EVER had! EVER!
Tracy said, You won't be at work much longer. We'll be busier with Galaxy, and maybe you'll even get pregnant.
Music to my ears.

Mar 24

The rest of the trip was fantastic. It was the break we needed before heading back to reality. Unfortunately, I lost 90% of the pictures I took on the trip. I was devastated.

The pain was always present. It didn't matter where I went, the pain was always constant.

I spoke to Mom – she's moving out of her husband's place, but on a part-time basis; she has another apartment in a different town.
Well, that's an interesting arrangement.
Mom said it's how I can manage things for now.

Tracy gave his notice at work. This is *really* going to happen!

Mar 26
My chiro *finally* had the IME report! The specialist said I WASN'T faking my injuries. She said my jaw was *fine*. So, my expert orthodontist who says my jaw is a mess is wrong, and SHE knows better?
She DID add in her report my *refusal* to answer that personal question because I felt it was no business of my employer. GOOD.

Mar 31
It's my first day back to work. A few people asked me how I was doing and said they were glad I was back. I was trained on all the new things since I'd been away. My ergonomic desk was NOT ready, so I had to sit at a desk all set up for a girl who uses a wheelchair. I'm sure she'll appreciate all the changes I made to fit *me*. Not! I'm in so much pain.

Apr 4
Our 16-year wedding anniversary!

So, here's a new thing – I went to eat a piece of toast and my bottom jaw slid forward instead of back. My bottom teeth clashed with the top and it felt like I broke my jaw. My top tooth chipped. So now even my *teeth* hurt! Ridiculous!

It's Tracy's last day at his job and he has a new recruit with Galaxy! We are building a team! Sweet. He came home with a bouquet of our wedding flowers (lilies) and white roses. Beautiful. AND a card! All our friends came over for an anniversary party.

Apr 8/08

What a gr8 d8 – 04/08/08.

I had a CT scan yesterday to "Assess Disease Status." I'm almost at the three-year mark.

I feel like I'm on the verge of a midlife crisis. NOT the "running out and having an affair" type, but the "what am I doing with my life?" kind. Are we having kids? Traveling? What AM I doing? I feel like I've *already* passed my prime. AM I too old to HAVE kids? I'm going to be 40! I never thought in a million years I'd make it to that age; I thought I'd be dead long ago. Clearly the accidents, cancer, and other factors **haven't** done *me in*. I should be grateful as hell that I AM here! I should be.

Apr 16

Tracy picked me up from work and says, THIS is what it's all about. Having the freedom to be able to pick you up and drop you off, to do the things I never would've had time for. We went to the Galaxy office for our Wednesday-night meeting. Tracy was asked to give a testimonial. (It's sharing what the company has done for you.) He talked a lot about me and how he has always had two full-time jobs since we've been married, and he never had time for a family – and *now* he WILL be able to do that. I'm so proud of him. I was just beaming.

Apr 24

Dr. West wrote a note to LTD to keep my schedule *as is* and NOT increase my work hours yet. He said just because they WANT to increase your hours doesn't mean you're healed.

My oncology checkup: Your Hodgkin's is STILL gone. There were cysts that showed up on your renal glands and your ovaries, but they seem to be "normal" for *you*.

Interesting way of putting it.

Since you're at the three-year mark, the clinical study is now *over*, so we'll meet every *six* months now, but for *bloodwork only*. We'll do a CT scan *only* if you're experiencing symptoms.

I said to Tracy, So I have cysts on my renal glands, that's kidneys, right? AND my ovaries, but they're not worried? Odd. I guess IF there is cause for concern, they'd say so.

May 11

My wrists are very unstable, my chiro tells me. They are moving in a way they shouldn't be. No wonder you're feeling tons of pain.

I will be seeing an acupuncturist in his clinic.

Tracy got paid from Galaxy. I'm thrilled *and* relieved. I paid bills – yahoo! Okay, so the money is starting to come in with this business.

I spoke to Mom and wished her a Happy Mother's Day. She said, God willing, this time NEXT year YOU'LL be celebrating Mother's Day.

I can only hope.

May 22

I feel like I should be more grateful for my life. I'm a cancer survivor; I've been in car accidents… I feel guilty because a lot of people who were sick at the same time as me are all dead. I'm not. I get mad at myself for not feeling and acting more grateful and thankful that I'm here. I don't inspire myself. I never felt deserving of *being* a mother. I feel like I'm being punished. I need to be okay with surviving, and be all that I can be. Goddammit. I WILL celebrate! So, fuck it, I'm done with NOT living my life! New me! I'm here for a purpose. Maybe I need to share my experiences with others.

May 27

It's been one year on Clomid already. Before the doctor came in, Tracy asked me, What's going on with you? Talk to me.

I'm feeling frazzled. I feel stupid being here. What are we doing?

The doc walked in – What did I just walk into?

I said, I think I'm in the middle of a mood swing.

You get those a lot?

Ya, I feel like I'm crazy.

Ya, but you were *before* you started taking the Clomid.

Yes, I was. Good sense of humor there, doc. I told him about my irregular periods.

Were you regular *before* taking Clomid?

Yes, I was on the pill for 25 years.

So how about we take you *off* the Clomid.

What are my options then?

Insemination, FSH, laparoscopy and IVF. He gave us the costs for each as well.

I said, Well, we're *not* panicked yet.

Well, you SHOULD be, get panicked! You're how old?

I'm still 39.

Chances decrease after 40.

Tracy turns to me and says, Take some time to think about it.

Yes, I think I need to. We leave. I said to Tracy, I think I need the summer to just let it be. If nothing has happened "naturally" by September, I'll double dose on the Clomid WITH insemination.

Mom called, wanting to know how things went at the clinic. She said she knows MANY couples who were older, married for years, tried for children, then they gave up and got pregnant! Don't let the doctor pressure you.

Tracy and I *are* on the same page.

She told me I have a good attitude and when *Hashem* (God) is ready to bless you with them, He will.

Yes, Mom. I DO believe if it's meant to be, it will be.

Look, with being sick and recovering, having the accident and recovering, and simply not wanting children – there is no way you COULD'VE had them *before* now. It'll happen.

I said, The fact is there are no blockages, all the plumbing is in the right place, Tracy is good, so now…

Mom shared with me that Sarah (of Abraham and Sarah) had a child at 99, when it seemed impossible to have one.

I said, Pray for me that I **DON'T** have to wait until I'm _99_!

Boy, did she laugh.

June 17

I had an acupuncture sesh. She put needles in my jaw, ankles, neck, wrists, and one on the top of my head. That was fun. It hurt like a son of a… Then I went to massage and chiro. Phew, what a day!

Nope, can't say I feel any better.

June 30

I got to thinking how I accept things, get used to things, I take it. Like the pain from the accident – I just live with it. Accept it. It's the way it is. I endure the pain. No sleep. Insomnia. It's the way it is. It's normal for _me_. I need more control in my life – and to _not_ be so okay with things. TAKE control. I'm going to be 40 – I need to take a stand.

Dad asked me if I miss Mom during times like this in my life.

I'm used to it – I'm used to things being this way. She's there, I'm here – it's the way it is. I accept it.

July 14

My manager TELLS me, Starting next week, your hours are going from three to five hours.

Uh, no. No?

Did your doctor say otherwise?

Yes, and he's already sent the forms in. Oh.

Just because they increase my hours doesn't mean I'm healed! Somebody should have TOLD me I'm "better" because then I wouldn't be going broke paying for physiotherapy, chiropractor, acupuncture, massage therapy, orthodontic specialist, reflexology…being busy with doctor forms, back and forth with LTD, lawyers…

July 22
Tracy texts me: My grandfather had a heart attack. We get to the hospital – he looked better than we expected, he was sitting up and glad to see us. We stayed with him through dinner and until he was sleepy. The doctors say he will be there for a few days for monitoring.

LTD is sending me for more independent testing. The humiliation. No one gives a shit if I'm in agony, in pain, and exhausted. I'M the one living it! I've done EVERYTHING that's been asked of me! Apparently, none of my doctors are "viable," but this IME lady is THE EXPERT on *my* health. Someone I see for an hour every six months knows *best*. Let's listen to HER! I need to jump through hoops because **I** asked for this?! Did the douchebag who hit me change HIS life in any way?

July 24
I was feeling quite fine about things, upbeat. Then I bawled. Sobbing. I just couldn't stop. I'm drained. I can't wait to enjoy my life when all this stress is over.
I went to throw a plastic bowl in the garbage, missed and it shattered, shattering a floor tile as well.
I flipped out. I feel psychotic. I have these bursts of rage. I hate it. I can't keep up with my mood swings. I feel crazy. I think crazy. I act crazy. So, I must *be* crazy! If it looks like a duck…
Tracy is like, Calm down; everything will work out.
I had a glass of wine…aaaah, calm. I should've done that *hours* ago.

Aug 3
I hate when people complain about their aches and pains. Boo hoo. You want pains?! When I had cancer and people would whine about an itch, and I'd think, YOU DON'T KNOW ITCHY! After the accident, people were saying, Boy, do I have a headache, and I'd think, *YOU DON'T KNOW A HEADACHE*! I get that people have their pains, but don't bitch about it in front of ME. Hello, mood swing.

Aug 5

Tracy's texting me: I love you with all my heart. I get a second text: I love you more today than yesterday.

Aw. I asked, How come? What did I do?

You woke up beside me.

AUGUST 8, 2008 – 08/08/08

It's only going to be the best day EVER! I had four *more* paw prints tattooed under the four I already had. I now have **8** paw prints. I love them!

After the tattoo, Tracy and I sat at an outdoor patio downtown, had a refreshing beverage and some appies. It was wonderfully hot out! What a fantabulous day!

Aug 14

I was figuring out how much money I have spent since the accident on therapies – $785/month!! This is so fucking insane!

Tracy came home with a dozen roses.

What are these for?

Because I DO appreciate everything you do. I know you think I don't, but I *really* do.

Aug 15

Ebony can't stay standing anymore, she falls with every step. She needs to be lifted and carried and I can't do that. I'm wiping up her shit. I clean her up and then she pees and shits all over herself again. She has no life anymore. I just finished washing out her bed and she now has diarrhea all over it. I can't do this anymore. There's no quality of life left for her. I told Tracy to look after her when I go out of town next week, and we will decide when I get back how to proceed with our pup.

Aug 21

I'm joining Mom in Toronto; we're staying with Aunty Ruth and Uncle Ruben. They had a birthday celebration for me. We all went out for

Chinese food, and I got a beautiful card from Mom. She said she's so grateful I'm AROUND for my 40th birthday. It's quite amazing all the challenges you've been through in your life, and here you are.

I spoke to Tracy in the evenings, and he told me Ebbie was about the same.

Aug 25
Tracy picked me up from the airport. He said he ran into someone from the "old" group, who told him that we no longer speak to the group because they're not interested in our pyramid business. WHAT?! As if! Tracy told him about what Ward had done. **_THAT'S_** why we no longer speak to them! The guy was floored. Well, THAT'S more of a reason. Let them think what they want.

I said to Tracy e need to talk about Ebony. She has no quality of life. Keeping her alive is not good for HER. Tracy was crying and left the room. After a while I went over to him and said, I know you don't want to talk about this, but we need to decide. Tracy gave in: Call the vet. I call. They can fit us in at 5:30 p.m. *today*. I lose it.
What do you have open *tomorrow*?
How's 8:30 a.m.?
I'll take it.
I bawled. I just booked an appointment to kill my dog. Just then Jim came over. I said, say goodbye to Eb. We all cried.

Aug 26
This is going to be a hard day. They showed us into a room right away. They call it "the death room"; that's where they do "it." They brought Ebony to the back for her IV. A girl brought in the consent forms and the different urns and boxes. They brought Eb back in. They did it right away. Tracy laid her on her side. She looked right into my eyes while she got her injection. I kept repeating, What a good girl, you're such a good girl. Her eyes closed and her diaphragm released. Gone. It was over in minutes. She lay there, looking like she always does. Peaceful. I

felt relief for her, so relieved. She doesn't have to struggle anymore. We sobbed. She was our 14-year-old kid.

Aug 27

My 40th birthday. We packed to leave for Vegas tomorrow with Dad, to celebrate. I can't wait. It'll be an awesome four days. All I know is we gotta hit the Coca-Cola store! I'm up for anything.

Sept 5

I updated my chiro on my aches and pains, and work crap. He worked on my wrists, which weren't doing great, extremely tight.

They've upped my hours again and are sending me for a Functional Capacity Exam (FCE). I'm crying at the drop of a hat. I'm so tired of being sick and tired. Enough! I watched *Stand Up To Cancer*– yup, I cried more. I guess I'm not as grateful as I should be, and maybe I had to see that show again as a reminder. I made it to my 40th birthday. I never thought it could happen.

Sept 21

I had *another* IME a few days ago with that same "expert." She didn't "challenge" me on things like last time. I guess we will see what she says in the report.

Tracy and I went to see Carol Burnett; I had bought us tickets for Tracy's birthday. A perfect night and I'm so glad we went. It was a real treat. What a gracious, humble human. It felt like a *normal* night, going out with my husband.

Oct 6

What did I do so wrong in this life that my childhood, car accidents, cancer, financial problems, and now *this* accident has not quite punished me enough yet?! I sit here at work – why am I here? I went to my manager: I need to go. I started getting teary. I'm just in too much pain. I've *never* shown her my pain; I never whine or complain at work, EVER. I'm kinda mad at myself for breaking down a little.

Oct 7

My chiro has the IME report. He said you are so strong and committed to getting better, and maybe you push yourself and overdo it, like going back to work. Basically, he was saying I should be recovering *before* taking on anything else. Well, I MUST be better because they keep upping my hours.

He said, Tell them it's no wonder you're in MORE pain. *You* know how you feel, *you* know your own body and what it's telling you; they don't. EXACTLY!! He gets me!! It's so frustrating that in 45 MINUTES an "expert" on MY life can undo all I have done in 1 YEAR and 4 MONTHS! I guess she knows better than me and all my doctors. SHE knows what's best for me, NOT the people giving me ongoing care since the accident. She makes these ridiculous recommendations and FNL thinks it's gospel. I, and *no one else*, have to live in this body and deal with the pain. Ya, I *chose* this. People can conduct any test they want on me – they'll still never know what I'm feeling. I need to stand up for myself and be heard. I made an appointment with a *new* lawyer.

Oct 9

It's Yom Kippur. So, all the talking to God and praying that I did THIS past year has done what? Will it do me any good to pray to him NOW for the following year? I'm supposed to have all this *faith* in…people, God, doctors, life…I'm so tired of struggling. I wonder what horrors I befell on this world to warrant all these "tests" I've had to face.

I just want to run away. Everybody gets what they want except us. Every year I get fucked in the ***money*** and ***health*** departments. THAT'S my Yom Kippur reflection. I feel like I have no control. Hopeless. Helpless. I have no direction. I have not stopped crying in *four* days. Tracy's trying to sell the Porsche 911 so we can pay our bills. A cop from Edmonton will be down on Sunday to get the car. They will be auctioning the car off, with the money going to a women's shelter.

Somehow, I felt better about selling it for less than our asking price – it's going to a good cause.

Oct 14

My lawyer and I covered a lot of ground. He asked if I belong to a union.

"Yes."

"You need to talk to them."

"I've complied, and they keep increasing my hours, and no one is listening to me."

"Your work HAS TO accommodate you."

I tried to stop a truck with my arms and now I'm in a job that requires the use of my hands. Does that not seem odd to anyone?? EVERY job requires using a computer or your hands.

I get an email from LTD–they have approved my schedule and will be increasing my hours EVERY TWO WEEKS! Shock. NO ONE IS LISTENING! Everyone has it figured out FOR me, yet I'M LIVING IT!! No one gives a shit. I'm overwhelmed with the hoops I'm jumping through. There is no time in this new schedule to go to any of my doctor appointments. All these battles, trying to recover – they are so counter-productive. *Both* reports state I'm progressively getting *worse* – so that is the signal for the Board to increase my hours?

Oct 15

I called the union. The rep told me it reaches a point where I do NOT get a say. I need to go see my doctor and get him to outline in *great detail* my prognosis; what I CAN handle, what I CAN'T, medications…

I get an email from LTD – they have approved… *"I urge you to accept the challenge with self-confidence and enthusiasm."*

What the fuck is that?! My worst fear came true – that this "expert" would dictate what happens in my life…and LTD listened. My life is not my own.

Oct 23

There were so many forms to fill out with Dr. West – we had our work cut out for us.

I said, I've been complying, but the truth is I'm struggling with the increased hours. They think increasing my hours will increase my productivity. And then they have me working only two hours on Tuesdays and Thursdays; what a waste of time and gas.

He completely agreed.

And the "expert" recommended anti-depressants – I have NO intention of taking those, just for the sake of appeasing *the Board*?

He agreed, and says he *does not* agree with that protocol. He also agreed that a 30-minute visit with me does NOT get to trump the *actual* doctors treating me on a *regular* basis. He is recommending more of a *gradual* increase in hours, and then reassess in one month. I feel relieved; someone IS listening to me.

Oct 26

Tracy suggested to me, if I help him with his business, and get licensed, he'll help me get out of FNL. So today I did the paperwork to join Tracy in business! I'm the **8th** person to join this month. It was meant to be. I hope I don't let him down. I can do this, and I will. Time to study!

Oct 28

I finally get a response from LTD regarding my schedule – *the specialist supersedes* any of my doctors and maybe working through the pain isn't such a bad thing.

I'm pretty sure I didn't *imagine* getting hit by a truck.

No one is saying you're not in pain.

Well, no one is listening either. No one is hearing me.

But I can't tell you, you *have to* work the schedule we give you. Try it, try the new schedule. If you can't, you can't.

I'm telling you **<u>NOW</u>** I can't. I've BEEN telling you. I've been saying so. I'M SAYING SO!!! I will have to cancel *all* my appointments next week. Increased hours mean I can't get my treatments.

Well, just think about it.

So, I went into work and told my manager that LTD is aware I will be following MY doctor's recommendations *instead of* the Board's. And that I keep being told I need to speak up if the schedule is not working for me – so I speak up and no one listens. They change it regardless.

Nov 4

I'm screwed. They screwed me again. Stick to the schedule. No deviation. No doctor's recommendations. Follow it or don't get paid. This is *not* reasonable! I'm bound to this! I'm crying at work. They *want* me to quit. They are trying to get me to quit! They want to have this power over me. I will go to my doctor and have him tell them I can't work AT ALL! They are fucking me over.

Tracy says, We'll go see the lawyer and call the union.

I'm listening to a girl at work whine about a headache and how she needs to go home. And she *is* going home. So, she gets to leave, but I have to sit here with *1000 things wrong* and THAT'S okay?! I'M supposed to suck it up? MY pain doesn't apply? WTF?!

I went to my chiropractor, acupuncturist, and orthodontist. They ALL offered to give me letters to give to the Board on my behalf. I have people on MY side. I cried at each appointment.

My chiro asked how things are going. I was crying. I kept apologizing for crying. I'm just so frustrated.

I can imagine. If there is anything I can do?

Do you know a good lawyer?

He gave me three names.

Wow, who does that?

Nov 7

I got a call from the union. There's a lady from Health Services who will be dealing with this. You'll be dealing with HER instead of LTD. SHE believes you should NOT be working what they told you to work; that schedule is way too aggressive. She's trying to sort this out. We'll have more info for you by the end of *today*. I just wanted you to know we're working on it.

Thank you SO much! I got off the phone and bawled. I couldn't stop. Someone is helping me. Someone from the union and someone from Health Services *are helping me!* Someone cares about what is happening! I'm so relieved. I can't stop crying. I've *yearned* for someone to hear me. I'm so grateful someone is listening. After 1 year, 4 months and 10 days – I'm being heard! I feel hope for the *first* time. I have hope.

Nov 12

Tracy and I met with my new lawyer. I filled him in. I gave him all the reports. He asked me what my previous lawyer did for me.

Tracy quickly spoke up and said he never remembered who I was *each* time I saw or spoke to him (hence the lawyer switcheroo).

I *just* received my section B forms.

Twelve months *after* the accident?

Ya, he won't answer my calls to help me with the forms.

Are you still shopping around for a lawyer, or…

No, no, no shopping around. If you can help me, *you* can be my lawyer. I signed the consent form for the other lawyer to release my file.

He said, Let's have a look at those forms – he *helped* me with them! Now THAT'S how a lawyer is supposed to be!

I'm frustrated and I just need some guidance. He said it will probably take another two years to complete the settlement.

He could hardly believe my lawyer asked ME to call the insurance people. Did you? Ya.

Among other things, we talked about loss of wages, and how the insurance company may be watching me. If you feel like you're being followed, call the police. I won't be your "official" lawyer for a few weeks, but you can call me and I *do* check my email, so if you have any questions, I'll answer them.

Tracy and I left feeling so relieved. I truly believe this guy *is* on my side.

Dec 5

I think I've gone crazy. My feelings are so extreme. I felt like ending it on Wednesday. It's pathetic. I'm pathetic. As if that's not enough, people at work are worried our jobs will be abolished and outsourced. It's only a matter of time.

Dec 16

I'm SO stressed out. The skin on my stomach hurts. I *can't* get sick again. I can't go through *that* again. What if…

My acupuncturist wants to send me for bloodwork – to rule out lymphoma.

I told Tracy. He just looked at me with love.

It may be nothing. It may be a virus, but it's *something*.

I called the cancer centre for some advice. They asked me to describe my symptoms.

I have these "lesions" or burn marks on my back.

It could be shingles.

I'll take shingles over cancer *any* day of the week!

Yesterday, I only had a few spots; today, it's a band of rash from the middle of my back to the front of my chest.

Dec 17

Dr. West confirmed it's shingles! It's caused by stress or injury.

Yes, and yes.

It can take up to three months to get over it. And you won't be going to work for a week.

I call my manager and tell her – Whatever you need, I'm on board. Uh huh.

Dec 20

The welts are so painful. My skin feels all pins and needles, wearing clothes hurts. It's hard to decipher what's shingle pain and accident pain.

The cancer centre called, Why did you cancel your appointment?

My shingles have been confirmed.

She said I could possibly still be infectious. Your oncologist isn't ruling out lymphoma. You probably have a virus and your immune system is compromised, so the virus will be different for *you*. We'll make an appointment for you January 6.

Dec 30
Yesterday was my first day back to work. It feels like razor blades in my gut, and like somebody kicked me in the kidneys, like a knife going in and out of my sides.

I got a letter from LTD: they stand by their *earlier* decision regarding the schedule.

Assholes! It's ALL about the *money*. *Period.* They will pay **thousands** of dollars for reports, but won't pay me what I'm due. Give me a goddamn package! I NEED SOME PEACE! I need to not be dealing with LTD, lawyers, the accident, illness, grievances... I'm beat. People are making decisions FOR me. I'd love to see any Board member or "specialist" go through what I've been through and continue to keep *their* sanity and work through the pain. They need a body in that chair at work, that's all. It's not about a person's health. They don't give a shit about that.

Happy Fucking New Year.

2009

Jan 6

My oncologist said, Your white blood cell count is a bit high, but that can be from your viral infection. I showed him the rash. He felt around my neck and armpits. It's *not* your lymph nodes; it's your carotid arteries. The shingles are affecting all those areas. We could do a CT scan for your peace of mind.

That won't be necessary.

Well, the bloodwork is no indicator of cancer. A CT scan goes deeper. We could do one of your neck.

On the way home Tracy said to look at it like, At least the shingles *will* go away.

Jan 21

So, I get to work and I see emails indicating that my manager has been corresponding with Health Services and LTD. As of January 22, I'm to work six hours, five days a week.

I'm so fucked. THIS is fucked.

My manager said she needs me to *work as many hours as possible*, that I need to get back on track.

I guess she's NOT on board after all.

I'm choking back the tears. They want me at work at ANY price – ya, at the price of MY health! All the work is *done*! There is NO work and they say they NEED me there?! Can you say *Stress Leave*? I am literally sitting here with NOTHING to do, trying to LOOK busy, going through emails.

I have Health Services AND the union telling me *their* hands are tied. Only medical professionals and advisors can make decisions on this.

I'm beside myself. I'm definitely on my own. *Something* is going to give. The shingles was the first thing, what's next? How sick do I need to get before they are satisfied?

My manager asked to meet with me. She asked about my schedule and I said I'm not okay with it.
Did you get the results back regarding your cancer?
No. I have THAT too to deal with. AND I have shingles. Oooh.
And the girl whose desk you're in – did you hear she'll be coming back soon?
Ya, I found out from someone else.
And that was the end of the conversation.

I'm at home, I can't stop crying. My body is healing, I'm exhausted, and jumping to five days seems rational to these people. And Health Services and LTD are saying ya, you have to. WTF?! Is no one hearing me? I CAN'T FUCKING DO IT!! Five hours every OTHER day is absolutely exhausting! I was talking to Tracy about it: I *work* the schedule, I'm fucked. I *don't* work the schedule, I'm fucked. They TOLD me I'm NOT alone. Tracy said to talk to Dr. West. WTF have I done to piss God off?! I've done something *worse* than my brothers? What have I done?! I am going crazy – again and again. I never thought this way during cancer, but I sure as shit am wondering why I deserve THIS. This is hell – absolute fucking hell!

Jan 23
Tracy came with me to see Dr. West. I said, You might like to know that they have totally disregarded *any and all* of *your* recommendations and doctor's notes.
Well, why bother telling you to come see me then?! If they want a fight, we'll fight back! I was worried something worse than shingles might happen.
He received a note from my oncologist saying he is sending me for a CT, and that I'm extremely susceptible to getting sicker from *stress*.
Well, I can't avoid stress with all this.

Tracy says, Uh Sari, you are breaking out *as we speak*!

Dr. West looks me over.

Great, just this *conversation* is making things worse. I pretty much had a nervous breakdown the day before yesterday. Am I supposed to go with their new schedule?

No, no, no. We know NOW you are not handling the current schedule, there is no way things won't get worse. You're going on *Stress Leave* – it's the *only* recourse. This is intolerable. We will keep you off for two weeks, then reassess. Don't even *think* about work.

Have you seen a psychologist?

No.

We have someone who comes in here Tuesdays and Wednesdays. I highly recommend you see her. No charge. He gave me my note and I made an appointment with her.

On the way home I said to Tracy, He's *really* on my side. I feel so relieved – from zero help to this. Last week I weighed 112 lb., today 107 lb. Tell me I'm not stressed!

Jan 30

Tracy and I are both in bed sick; I've also lost my voice, literally, *not* figuratively. I got an email from LTD – I will *not* get paid until my doctor gives them *more* info. Jump through more hoops. I go to the doctor; they get a letter from him, and they tell me it's not good enough. I was so relieved, and then they fuck me over AGAIN! Some Stress Leave. Maybe *Stress Leave* means MORE stress! This is intolerable!

While all this stuff with work, my health, LTD…is going on, two teammates, and ironically our best friends, from Galaxy have managed to sabotage our business. It's been bubbling up for a long while, but it all came to a head this past Sunday. We were completely blindsided, a baseless attack. We caught them in many lies, trying to discredit Tracy as a leader. They hoped we'd never find out. Disrespectful, backstabbing, undermining, attacking Tracy's integrity and character, and jealous of his rapport with the others on the team. Only when upper management at Galaxy got involved did they begin to "apologize." I think they are just sorry they got caught. They are not sorry for their actions, but these teammates are asking us to not give up on them. They're delusional if they think we can move forward from this. I'd hate to see how these liars would treat us if we WEREN'T best of friends. Words can cut through you and leave a lasting effect. The trust is gone. Trust is the glue of friendship. With friends like this…Things will *never* be the same between all of us ever again. You can't un-ring a bell.

Feb 3

The counselor asked me, So leaving here, what would you like to get out of it?
From Dr. West's perspective, with all I've been through medically in the past few years, I think he figured I needed someone to talk to about all of it.
Have you talked to someone about all this before?
Not for THIS, but I have talked to a therapist in the past. She was surprised I never spoke to a professional after I had cancer. We discussed my medical history and she asked many questions regarding Tracy.
We just want to get on with our lives. There are so many roadblocks and we are tired of not being able to move on. It's frustrating for him, too.
Don't you wish work would understand that if you *could* be better, you *would*?
Yes, and no one has to live this except me.
Would you be okay coming back to see me?
Absolutely.

The orthodontist adjusted my splint. What's going on since I last saw you?
I have shingles, the cancer might be back, and I'm on Stress Leave.
He just looked at me in disbelief.
But your work isn't giving you problems about it, are they?

I filled him in. He said, If there is *anything* you need from me, a letter for the union or *anything* that could help your case, please let me know. I might take you up on that.

Make sure you STAY on Stress Leave!

Feb 5

I woke up crying. I'm so stressed. Tracy and I went to see Dr. West. He said, Hear anything new from work?

I show him the email from LTD saying they need ANOTHER, *more detailed* diagnosis of me.

I just don't know what more they want from me. It would be good idea to get the doctors you are seeing to write letters for you on your behalf. Anything in particular they should mention?

That you are UNFIT to work.

When I go back to work, they have *no* ergonomic desk for me, anyways.

They *could* suddenly decide they don't need you. You probably didn't need to hear that. So, we will keep you off until the end of the month.

Several of my doctors even said how positive I was through the *cancer*, and how stressed I am *now*. I believe the company is trying to break me. I'm trying to fight for my rights.

Feb 6

I weigh 105 lb. now. I can't even eat. My counselor said she will send the Board a letter on my behalf. My oncologist has confirmed that the stress and pain is due to the *car accident*, not cancer.

There is no proof of disease, but I'm going to add "chest" to your CT.

I got an email from the union lady: *"I received your doctor's note. The Board is always willing to look at new info, so you can get paid and overturn their decision."*

Ya, right. I went to the bathroom and broke down; I fell to the floor, bawling. And out of my mouth came, Oh God, please; please, God, let us get through this month. Please. I beg you.

Feb 12

Dr. West is pissed. Why did they make you come here for a note, THEN tell you they need THESE forms? Why wouldn't they tell you they needed these forms in the first place?
I kept shrugging. This is what they do.

I got paid $66.51 from LTD. WTF am I supposed to do with *that*?!

Feb 17

Counselor visit – I talked about being invisible, having no voice, and not being heard.
You have strength in you, you're a survivor! She gave the analogy of the iron fist and the velvet glove; you look all pretty and nice on the outside, always done up, but you're strong underneath.
Interesting. I said, I'm tired of not being heard, I will not be invisible to the Board! I have a voice! They expect me to be quiet and go away. But I've done nothing wrong, and I WILL fight for myself!
She said, You've taught me so much about life, with all you've been through, and you keep going. It's an amazing quality. *She* was crying. I was stunned. She thinks I'M amazing?

Feb 18

This will be quite the day – I'm going for a CT scan, it's Toby's 40th birthday, and the Board meets today.

My orthodontist called me – I'm drafting up your letter to LTD and I wanted to know where to send it. If there is any way I can support you and get them on your side, I will try to help.

Feb 19

I get an email from my manager: *"How would you feel about working evenings and weekends so you can SHARE the ergonomic desk with the other girl?"*
Unbelievable. I was so upset. She even said, It's okay if you don't want to, I'm just covering *my* butt by suggesting it to you.

Unreal. I went to see my lawyer. I explained the current situation and that Tracy had to sell a vehicle at a loss so we could pay bills.

My legal advice then is to *not* settle now. They just want you to go away. You need to escalate this to the *president* of the union.

I finally responded to my manager's email: *"I apologize but I am unprepared to answer this email right now."*

I'm still dealing with those "friends" of ours from Galaxy too. Tracy said to me, It's like an abusive relationship – they are abusive, they say they are sorry, it's all candy and roses for a bit, and then they do it *again*. They continue lying and smearing Tracy's name. We keep giving second chances to the wrong people. They keep using the excuse – *we're a work in progress*. Well, aren't we all?!

Lesson of the day: Just because we are all a work in progress, doesn't make it okay to stab your friends in the back!

Feb 25

I'm bawling uncontrollably on the floor of the bathroom again. I can't catch my breath. Are we such bad people? We try to help others, now WE need the help! We can't redeem our investment that we have with Galaxy (it's locked in), I can't get money from the insurance company from the accident, work isn't paying me, Tracy isn't getting paid, he's trying to cash in his pension, we cashed in our cans and bottles…we're hooped. As I'm sobbing, both Nike and Midnight climb onto my lap, sniffing me to see if I'm okay. I laughed. I actually laughed out loud. Those amazing boys. It snapped me right out of it. Animals are so much more compassionate than people. God love 'em. I'm so tired, completely worn out, and exhausted.

Feb 27

I had an MRI yesterday and I see my doctor today. I told him about the evenings and weekends suggestion.

Your job description was never for evenings and weekends. They're really trying to make it as difficult for you as possible. I will tell them you are working three days a week, four hours a day, and they need to provide you with your *own* ergonomic desk.

I cashed in my FNL work shares.

Mar 2
My spidey senses were tingling again, so I checked our bank account. A deposit of $4000! Tracy got paid from Galaxy! I paid ALL our bills. What a relief. No words. Tracy came through, like he said he would. We go from one extreme to the other. My heart is in my throat.

Mar 6
At the LA conference this year, Tracy gets a call on his cell. It's Dad: We found Matty lying on his back at the bottom of the cage, so we took him to the vet. A few minutes later we get another call. It's the vet: It's not looking good for your parrot. We will keep you posted.

In the meantime, back in the hotel room, we're going around the room discussing what each of us has gotten out of the conference. When my turn came, I said, *sacrifice*. As of five days ago, we didn't know if we were coming. I'm really glad we did. And now I need to step it up and help Tracy and his business in *any* way I can. I looked over at Tracy and he was crying. I thought he was emotional from my speech – I go over to him and ask what's wrong? Matty's dead. We lost another kid. We had him about 10 years. He was a character. Loved him.

Mar 9
Sitting in the Denver airport on our way home, I said to Tracy, We are going to leave for the winters, for three to six months, and we'll be taking our cats with us. Tracy said, It's nice you're thinking ahead. I was! I haven't planned for the future *in years*. I try not to plan for *anything*. Life can change in a second. But it felt good to plan. I have to

not be so overwhelmed with life and get on with living. I'm 40! I have so much I want to do, and I feel my life is already half over.

Mar 10

I talked about going back to work with my counselor. I never had a problem with the job. I go in, do my job, and get out. I just feel dread when I go now.

Because of the people there?

No, because of LTD and them making decisions FOR me. I've always had good coping skills – I've dealt with what life has thrown me, but it's enough already.

How did it feel going away?

It felt good, getting away from...

And then SHE continued with: doctors, appointments…

Yes!

Have you thought about doing something *else*?

Yes, I'm realistic in thinking they *could* fire me.

Could they give you a package?

That *would* be the way to go. I'm thinking a home-based business would be ideal.

She was nodding in agreement.

People ask me why I *don't* leave FNL – I'm not getting paid, no benefits… I kept my vacation time because at least I KNOW for that time I'll get paid! It's just ironic – my husband helps people financially for a living, and we're used to helping others. Asking for help is not in our nature, but we've had to. We are not doing great, money-wise.

I was going to see Dr. West for my MRI and CT results, but he's away for five weeks. His replacement looks over the MRI results and says, They were looking for a pinched nerve and there is nothing like that here. They DID find on your C5 vertebrae on the back of your neck, a bulge. But there's nothing pressing on anything, and there are no blockages. Now, in regards to your CT, there is some soft tissue issues around the thyroid. They found a node in your left armpit that is larger than before; it grew 3mm to 4mm, but it could be a result of your viral infection. There are cysts on your kidneys but no significant change from your last CT. Other various lymph nodes *have* grown, but we're *not* alarmed about it. She examined my armpits. She said she DOES feel something in the lymph nodes.

I started crying.

They appear to *not* have scanned your neck.

What? THAT was the main purpose for the CT! We *added* the chest, but the neck was always the *main* reason for having it done. And they didn't MRI my wrists and THAT's why I went there for *that*!

She said, I don't know your history, but we could do an *ultrasound* of your neck? I realize this must be so frustrating for you.

Ya, it is.

Mar 13

We got the results from your neck CT. The lymph nodes ARE larger. I spoke with your oncologist and they want to schedule you for another CT just to monitor it.

I KNEW something was wrong. I could feel it. I KNOW my own body!

I sent the president of the union a letter.

Mar 18

Back at work, my manager hands me a new keyboard in a box. Am I supposed to assemble my own desk and computer?!

We had a team meeting where everyone spoke of team spirit. They took a team picture *without* me, on one of the days I wasn't there, and today the picture goes into the company newsletter, along with a *separate* photo of me, by myself. How does that keep happening to me? They're all whining about how they don't look great. I felt like saying, At least you're IN the picture!

Mar 19

I get to work and my new ergonomic chair and computer were all set up *for* me. Finally.

I have my one-on-one with my manager. I got 70% on almost everything. She said the team is picking up my slack, so that brings the percentage down. My return-to-work schedule *hasn't* been adhered to, so I got docked for that too. So how are your wrists going to be for working?

I don't know, nothing has changed, and it's still ongoing.

She seemed SO surprised. She asked, Do you have any questions for me? No.

No questions. You're a happy camper?

Oh ya, I'm a happy camper.

Mar 23

I get a response from the president of the union. He said he was on vacation and just got back today and will look into my concerns and get back to me. As I'm reading his email, the union chick calls. She was all sugary sweet: So ,what's been going on since we last spoke? I got a call from the president to contact you.

I thought, of course he did. I told her about all the pay issues. I think LTD thinks FNL is paying me and vice versa. I gave her the exact amounts I've been paid.

She tells me, You have exhausted your short-term disability, so now you have to work 65 consecutive days to replenish that. But obviously that's not going to happen. The Board met in January, February, *and* March and I've heard nothing. They SAY they are open to new info, but it has been disregarded each time. You need to call LTD to see what's happening. Swell.

Mar 27

It almost took one full year, but I finally got a headset. I received a letter from LTD – they stand by their earlier decision and the schedule that's in place. I actually *wasn't* worried because I feel soon, I'll be outta here!

Mar 28

We threw Dad a surprise 70th birthday party. I had a lot of help, which was so nice. He was stunned and surprised – he cried. I made him a picture board of his entire life. It was a nice crowd of friends, great food and lots of laughs. I gave him a toast: Think of someone who loves and supports you. Imagine that person, then times it by a *thousand*. *That's* my dad. There isn't anything he *wouldn't* do for any of the people in this room. *That's* how big his heart is. So, here's to my dad.

He said, I don't know what I'd ever do without you two. This is *not* my son-in-law; he's my son.

Wow, a declaration like that in front of all our friends. Boy, that meant a lot to us.

Mar 31

My oncologist said it's in the realm of possibility, within the time frame, for a reoccurrence. Three nodes have grown. I don't want to scare you, but we should schedule you for a PET scan.

I was talking to the union lady; the union *can't* do anything as my issues are *medically* related. The union aren't doctors. *Medical* professionals will have to change the Board's mind. Unless there is earth-shattering info from your doctor, is this where you *want* to work? I'm thinking, *is the union suggesting I quit?*

I got an email from a girl who helps with filing grievances against FNL. She said she'll be helping me with this process. When can we meet to get the ball rolling?

So, we met and I gave her every bit of documentation I could.

She said if I ever need to talk, she is available 24/7.

Apr 8

The grievance girl asked, Do you have a collective agreement? Yes.

When were you first violated by this?

I gave her all the details from the beginning.

Has your manager said or done anything that would violate the *Respectful Workplace Act?*

I smile. Funny you should mention that. *She* was the catalyst for my going on Stress Leave.

If your manager even ASKS you if you filed a grievance, she can be fined $50,000.

She explained the grievance process to me – it goes to three levels, the third level being arbitration. We will try to resolve this at the first level.

I'm flailing here. I have no idea what my rights are.

You have more documentation than most cases I have dealt with. What's the outcome, the main goal here? To get them to listen to your doctor?

Yes, that is all I EVER wanted, and to get back the money that's owed to me.

You'll get retro, plus money for undue hardship.

Apr 14

We get a utilities disconnection notice, scheduled for April 21. Alright, we'll be okay by then. I see an envelope from the insurance company. I open it: $3500! I never expected them to pay me *anything*. I'm beside myself. Tracy tells me to check our bank account –there's also money from his pension! We were right – it was ALL going to come in at the *same* time! Holy fuck! I paid ALL our bills, every last one of them, and paid *everyone* back we owed. We were *just* at the pet store and couldn't pay for the food because they don't take AMEX.

Lesson of the day: O*ne* day can change *everything*.

Apr 20

I gave my signature to move forward with the grievance. I just feel relieved more than anything. I said, From not knowing *what* to do…

And the grievance girl continued with: From feeling all alone to getting some backing.

Yes!

We will be fighting for "Denial of Benefits" and "Loss of Wages."

We hugged. I will be faxing in my "Respectful Workplace Complaint" tomorrow.

Apr 23

My oncologist said the scan came back *normal.* How long have you been out of treatment?

It'll be four years in June.

The likelihood of recurrence *now* is…well we *can't* "guarantee" it, but it's not seeming like it'll even come back; you're good; you're cancer-free.

That's ALL I need to know! Good enough for me!

His nurse comes in. *She* tells *him,* What about that *other* part? Don't you need to disclose *that* part to her? Maybe you need to explain the scan.

Suddenly, I'm not feeling so certain or hopeful.

There's a line, a benchmark, where they decide that anything *past* that mark is bad. You were *just* on the other side of it. There is some inflammation that shows, but it's *not* cancer. They're saying it's within the side that says it's okay. He leaves and the nurse explains the scan showed "moderate glowing" on the PET scan, and it's nothing to be alarmed about.

I don't have cancer. I'm SO relieved!

Apr 29

I heard somebody at work talking about her family – she has two older brothers who adore her, and they are so *protective* of her. She has what I was *supposed* to have: two older brothers protecting their baby sister. Instead, I had to protect myself *from* them. I'm happy she has that because the alternative isn't pretty.

I'm plain tired. I've struggled my ENTIRE life. I'm 40 years into struggling. I've still got a few fights to come. I need a good solid break in life. I need to not have massive challenges. Why can't I ride on easy street for a while? Everything I DO have, I have fought for. I'm tired. I'll still do what I have to… I just need some peace.

May 4

I was watching *Grey's Anatomy*. The Chief was apologizing to Meredith for *not* being her advocate. She was a little girl and no one protected her. No one fought for her. No one spoke up for her. The tears just streamed down my face. I had no protection, no safety zone, no one I could go to, to talk to. I couldn't hide; I couldn't say a word to anyone – for nine years. I was the one, starting at eight years old, protecting others. *I* protected *him*! So, I sat there listening to this fictional character being told all the things I prayed someone would have said to and done for me.

May 8

Friends can be so disappointing: fair-weather and wishy-washy. I get to listen to THEIR problems. I'm in agonizing pain and I'm still putting *others* first; I currently have *four* friends doing this to me. I'm mad at myself for *allowing* them to treat me this way. *Everyone wants to feel like someone cares,* as Nickelback would say. I feel like I'm being played the fool every time I let someone in. They offer big declarations of friendship, and then they just drift away. They do things to make certain we never want to see them again. They take it to a place of no return.

May 11

We went over a few things before we went into the meeting with my manager. The violation is *discrimination*. We feel Sari is being discriminated against because of her disability. It's been very *clearly* outlined by her doctors, her limitations. Working evenings and weekends isn't even slightly okay. When Sari provides documentation that she is temporarily disabled, and the company disregards it and doesn't accommodate it, *that's discrimination*. So now my manager has seven days to accept or deny our grievance. The union rep told me I'll be hearing from a lady who is a Human Rights rep. She's ready to fight for you.

June 2

I gotta get out of here. I have to. This place and the people in it are toxic. I started out in a good mood, then my lawyer is out of town until June 15. I'm composing a grievance letter for LTD, and Mom has left her husband permanently, and moved out. The second-level grievance meeting is taking place today, but my presence is not required.

My horoscope says: *Watch for stress. Your body can't handle this emotional rollercoaster*. No shit.

June 23

They *denied* us. Okay, so here we go…
My counselor notes, You're different from the first time you came to see me. You're feisty! You have strength and fight in you. You look slender and the wind could blow you over – but you're no pushover. Are you *dreading* the grievance?
Oh God, no! I'm looking forward to telling *my* side. My manager no longer speaks to me but, you know, I feel empowered.

July 12

The union rep called. Why did it take you so long to *file* the grievance?
I didn't know it was an option. I've been fighting for my doctors to be heard, fighting for the hours I need, and only recently did I figure out the kind of money I've lost.
Did you mention to anyone you were losing money?
I told my manager, Human Resources, and Payroll. I sit there in pain, with no work to do, my manager speaks of "resourcing issues" – it's ridiculous! It's never been about me *not* working. I've never had an issue with me working. It's about working with what I'm physically *able* to.
She noted, They can't see the bigger picture. They don't realize you need TIME to heal, and down the road it WILL be better.
Third-level meeting today. I fell *up* the steps at work. I think it's a sign – the building is trying to spit me out.

July 19
The union rep said that apparently, I did *not* provide the Board with the info they requested. She agreed that even she *can't* see anywhere that they have *requested anything additional* from me. I also mentioned to them your decrease in wage since October. They said it was *irrelevant.* Uh no, her benefits are based on her wage. If you have decreased her wage, it most definitely affects her benefits, which is *relevant.* They said they'll look into it.

I went to see Dr. West. They are telling me you *haven't* provided them with current medical info. I brought forms with me, not that it matters because they don't care what *you* have to say anyway. Their issue is there is no end date for increasing my hours and staying at the current hours and days.
He said, very matter-of-factly, That's because your condition hasn't changed. Why would I change your hours if your condition is the same?

July 21
My union rep says this thing with FNL isn't personal – it's about money. They have counsel guiding them and they are just trying to find where *you* are at fault. You shouldn't look so healthy!
The same thing happened when I had cancer, people didn't believe me because I looked so *well.*

July 24
I can't stop crying. I'm so dizzy I almost fell over. I feel so off today. I feel so down. I love Tracy, and I'm so grateful he puts up with me. I'm scared of everything – afraid of getting old, afraid I might never have kids, afraid Tracy will wise up and not put up with my insanity, afraid the cancer will come back, afraid I've pushed everyone away, afraid we'll never have money, afraid I haven't lived my dreams...it never ends. I've come so far in my life, yet it's having the opposite effect on me. I was grateful after I was sick, now...I'm just afraid to live. I can barely stand to be around myself. I need to hold it together.

My lawyer informed me by letter that I am in discovery in November. Apparently, it's part of the settlement process since it's been two years since the accident. I just need to live in peace.

Aug 11

I said to my chiro, Everyone is *telling* me I should be healed, so what's going on with me?

Everyone is different; people heal at different times. You are asking when is this going to be okay again?

You didn't sign on for this, you didn't ask for this to happen to you.

Is there anything *more* I could be doing?

You are doing all the right things; it's only a matter of time before it all works.

I spoke to a lady from the Human Rights Commission (HRC). We talked about my hours, doctor recommendations, accommodating me ergonomically, IMEs, FCEs and letters to the Board and union president. I just want to know if I have *just cause* to file a complaint?

Yes, you *do* fit the criteria. You have reasonable grounds to file a complaint. The issue began when you requested accommodations and they denied you.

Aug 24

I can't stop bawling. I'm so frustrated with my body not letting me just do "normal" things without pain. Doing the laundry, prepping dinner, showering, doing my makeup, needing people to drive me to my appointments… It's ridiculous. I just want to move the hell on with my life and have ALL of this *behind* me!

At Galaxy, Tracy is the #1 Associate in Canada! I'm SO proud of him!

Sept 2

LTD has "misplaced" my doctor form that was faxed in WEEKS ago. So, I re-faxed it. Un-real. It was completed in July, and just NOW they realize they need it for their meeting? More hoops to jump through.

I was talking to a friend who told me, You're so quiet, but when you DO finally say something, people listen. You get this fire in your belly; it doesn't come out nearly enough.

Sept 9 – 09/09/09!

I mailed in my HRC package. Oh man, there's no turning back now. Payroll screwed up my time submission at work. I'm *the only one* NOT in the system. They told me if I don't straighten it out and resubmit ALL of it *today*, they will *stop my pay*. Considering this was NOT MY FAULT. They only gave me access into the system Sept 2, while everyone else was in it by July! This just gets better and better. In our team meeting, my manager said, and I quote, "There's *not* enough work for one person for seven and a half hours." I rest my case.

Sept 17

Tracy got his promotion at Galaxy on Tuesday – senior associate! He has worked so hard for this. And no one on the team was there at the office to support him.

Today I saw my orthodontist for a splint adjustment. I brought up the $300 I owe and wanted to make arrangements.
It's not an issue, it's taken care of.
Taken care of? I think he incurred the cost *himself*. I was stunned. Who does that these days?

Work is clawing back $2000 they've *already* paid out to me so I will have **_zero pay_** for the *next few pay periods*. It just never ends. I called and cancelled *all* my treatments. I prayed to God – yes, I did. The tears are still streaming down my face. I said, I'll do anything, whatever it takes. I'll work harder on having a baby, be a better person…whatever you want! But, please, please, let Tracy and I get on with our lives. Let us out of this financial hole. Let us move forward. Get us through the next few months, but please get us through this.

Sept 25

Tracy got paid $7100 in commissions. Wha? I couldn't wrap my head around it. All of Tracy's hard work…OMG! Then I see a call from the union and one from my lawyer. Sigh.

Two *other* ladies from the union will now be handing my case. Work is asking for a NEW PAF. They say I *never* sent one in. Have you done one yet? Can you?

WTF?! What kind of goddamn incompetence am I dealing with?! This is a fucking joke! Is anyone paying attention to ANYTHING I'm sending in?! I just spoke to LTD! AND I faxed the PAF! This is insanity. I may need to speak to the union president again.

I said to Tracy, Maybe my next course of action is to go to the media and put it out there what this company is doing. It's a joke to them. *I'm* a joke to them. They just keep shuffling paper – it's *only* a person's *life* their dealing with, no biggie. Assholes.

Sept 28

My lawyer wants me to come by and sign an affidavit so they can show the defense my file.

The union rep called. I told her WHEN I saw my doctor, WHEN the PAF was sent in, WHEN I spoke to LTD and WHEN I *re-faxed* the PAF. It's pretty odd no one is receiving my forms. And if LTD didn't receive the PAF AGAIN, no one informed me.

She said there must be some sort of breakdown between Human Resources and Labor Relations.

SOMEONE there has my info!

I have to jump through *their* hoops, but when this gets important for ME, they screw it up. My faith is slipping in this whole process. How is it possible I have been sending those PAFs in since the beginning of time and NOW there is a problem?! Ironic? Coincidental? Suspicious? Because of this goddamn accident I have to keep dealing with all this shit! It's pure shit! NO ONE should have to deal with years of this garbage. I didn't survive cancer to deal with this crap!

Oct 1

How do you feel? my chiro asks. Like I've been hit by a truck. He did some digging with his thumbs into my neck. I sure wish pain meds helped, could've used some.

We get a tip from someone at Galaxy that our team is being poached by another company, a new competitor – our good buddy Derek, who started his own company. Ya, that Derek, Tracy's buddy he's known for 20 years, the dude who introduced us to Galaxy. The douche who was forced out of Galaxy because he tried to beat the system. A team member came by our house yesterday to tell us he was going with the other company. We tried to talk him out of it. He'll be handing in his resignation. Derek has successfully dismantled our team.

Oct 2

I get to work and the guy *just* finished setting up my new adjustable desk. Six and a half months later… I sent an email to the union vice president, cc'ing the president, asking for an update.

Tracy told me, I had a dream last night – that we had a baby. He was tearing up. Yes, I think we've put this on hold long enough.

Oct 6

The union gal calls me saying she got an email forwarded to her of the letter I sent the union president and vice president.
Maybe I didn't make myself clear the last time we spoke, she tells me. I have contacted Labor Relations regarding this matter. We are waiting to hear back. Then we'll have another meeting to discuss what they found out.
Did they find my PAF?
Yes. You don't need to worry. My partner and I are *quite* capable of handling your file and concerns.
Huh, so had I *not* sent that email to the president, I wouldn't have gotten this call now. I *wouldn't* have known they were even working on my case.

I get an email from an FNL co-worker, Gayle, – four people on our team have already found *other* jobs. That leaves the two of us. Our team is being dismembered, some by choice, some not. I'll see what MY fate is tomorrow.

Oct 7

My manager comes over. Can I speak to you and Gayle?
Gayle asks, So, are we getting our walking papers, the ax, since we *are* the only two left?
No. There *is* enough work for the two of you.
So, if Sari is on her day off and I'm sick...?
It's about a head count and you are both considered full-time. And there are more changes to come.

I get home – there is a letter from LTD. They will temporarily top up my pay until December 31 and they encourage me to work *their* schedule. And...I have to attend **multiple** IMEs! They will review my file again based on *those* reports. I felt sick. I almost threw up. The whole work situation didn't faze me, I was feeling fine. THIS fazes me. I swore I wouldn't go through *that* humiliation again. It's never going to end. They WANT me to quit. The union chick could've mentioned this letter to me *yesterday*. They will fuck me over again. Nothing will change. The report will say I'm fine. And this is *worth* the pittance they are going to throw my way? I can't take this anymore! They simply don't give a shit. I'm so tired. I feel so defeated. The IMEs are the *only* things they have left to do; they have nothing else. They are stalling. The top-up is for THEIR sake, not mine. They are being pushed to make a decision and this is what they came up with. They are in the business of intimidation.

So, what is my lesson here? What do I need to learn from all this? I need to use my voice. I need to stand up for myself. I am NOT a victim. I'm clearly not learning something I'm *supposed* to, because these circumstances keep repeating themselves, and they will continue to until I "get it." I need to GET IT! I'm fighting a *huge* corporation, I'm doing it! But I am living this, no one else is. Only I can dig myself out. In five years, am I even going to care about any of it?

Oct 13
The union called – we are at the mercy of the Board. After the grievance makes its way past the third level, it comes back to us. Labor Relations will do nothing until you go for your exams. We did NOT drop the ball, and I understand your frustration. Hang in there.

Sounds to me like they've given up on me; their "hands are tied." The Board doesn't listen to a word my doctor says, yet they keep telling me to go see him. The recommendation of an "expert" is nothing short of ridiculous. They'd rather pay HER *thousands* of dollars than pay ME. What am I missing here? Why is this continuing, and the Board is not settling with me? What is going to be *the thing* that tips this in MY favor? What documentation do they need that will be good enough for them and that will make them understand?! I wonder who the Board is at the mercy of? Who controls *them*? People are losing their jobs...all for the greater good of the company?

Two of our team members at Galaxy passed their provincial exams today! Things ARE looking up. Hallelujah! Screw you, FNL!

Oct 15
I called the HRC and was told that they have ACCEPTED my complaint. Now they need more info on the grievance process. You need to say whether you feel the union *can* resolve the issues or *not*. A copy of your complaint was sent to FNL – to the CEO and the senior consultant for the Respectful Workplace department. It's possible your manager will hear about it too.

OMG, they *accepted* my complaint! This is huge! And now FNL knows. I feel invigorated!

Oct 19

I received my two IME appointments – a psychiatric one and the other with "the expert" again – the day AFTER the Board meets. So, their decision will have to wait until January 2010, in their *next* meeting. Are they trying to buy some time? Does this have to do with my Human Rights complaint? I get a call from my manager – two people from the team have already left for their new jobs. But I'm not going to put the workload on *you* when you're trying to heal. I don't want to jeopardize your health with what's happening with the team; I couldn't do that.

Huh? She hasn't been empathetic, why now? I think she's saying what she needs to so I don't leave and go off sick too. Unless there is more info she's not telling me.

Zero pay for the __*third*__ pay period in a row.

Oct 26

Paul Haggis was talking about his leaving Scientology. He said, *Silence is consent.* Boy, did *that* hit home. If I'm quiet, that means I'm consenting to their treatment of me. By speaking up, I DO NOT CONSENT!

Oct 30

At FNL, we've been training the overseas people to take over our jobs and today most of our work was already sent there.

I have my psychiatric IME today. FNL gave me the *wrong* address. Nice.

He asked about: the accident, my parents, siblings, interests, to name a few news items, memory, moods, anxiety, if I'm suicidal, cancer, surgeries, my husband, kids, education, exercise, pets, and why I stay at FNL. They had me do handwritten exercises, draw shapes and tested my concentration.

Nov 5

Zero pay again. And Tracy gets $28 tomorrow. It feels like we're drowning again – still. The money is always "coming," but that doesn't help us right *now*. We had a meeting last week with our team at Galaxy about the new company and its poaching. It turns out all that talk about owing Tracy their loyalty, not leaving, not going anywhere and unity blah, blah, blah, was all bullshit. People are telling us to our faces they are loyal to US, then meeting with the new company. I guess it's okay they are messing with OUR livelihood – everyone else has jobs to fall back on. And when the new company screws THEM over, and they *will*, don't come crawling back to us. Tracy can look in the mirror and sleep well at night knowing he's done right by everyone. I'm not so sure anyone else can say the same. Loyalty means *nothing* anymore. I don't think I've ever seen Tracy this low or distraught.

Nov 9

I get an email from my manager – I just wanted to give you a heads up that we will be doing an *audit* of your sick absences in 2008 and 2009, and that can *reduce* your vacation entitlement in either year. If the audit shows you overtook vacation, then the shortfall would come out of your 2010 entitlement.

So, what little I have left, they want to take away. They have already taken everything, why not vacation time too! I can't imagine why I feel so unmotivated to work.

Nov 10

I haven't stopped crying since I woke up. It's scary when you just don't know what you're going to do. I'm just spent. I have no answers. I can't think anymore. I have cried for two days straight. I'm going through the binder of my life for the discovery. It's like I have to take this "test" on my own life! If it's IN the binder, it CAN come up.

Nov 20

FIFTH NETWORK LTD. OFFERED ME A PACKAGE! I will be accepting! The union told me if you accept the package, you can still *continue* with the grievance. She spoke with the VP, who confirmed that. My manager asked if I've gone through the package, and if I have any questions.

Are you going to take it?

YES! Now I can focus on my recovery. My health is my #1 priority and this would give me the opportunity to do that.

I wouldn't pray THAT hard for something, then NOT take it. I stayed the course and crossed the finished line!

Nov 24

The union rep said if I accept the package, I agree to *release FNL* from all claims and demands. This is their way out. It doesn't seem right they put you through all this, then you get nothing. As far as I'm concerned, you deserve that money and you should get it. When do you have until to decide?

December 7, but I've *already* accepted.

Nov 25

I'm taking on this *I don't care* attitude. I'm feeling better already. All I want is some peace.

I spoke to Myriam, who said, I want to enter your play in a contest and I want you to be a part of it. I'm good at producing and directing. Your play is brilliant and I want to cast and produce it.

How do you know it's any good?

I remember reading it and thinking that your writing was absolutely brilliant. Unless you're going to give it to *someone else* to produce?

Well, you're the only one who has read it in 10 years, so no, I think you have dibs.

I can't believe that after a decade, she wants to bring the play I wrote in the writing program to life. Way cool.

Dec 3

I *have to* go to the next IME, even though I'm taking the package; if I don't, I'll look "uncooperative." I HAVE been cooperative! They are going to fucking jerk me around until I give up. No human should have to put up with this garbage. I take a package and they STILL get to send me to IMEs?! FUCK THE GRIEVANCE! I want my life back! The Board, the union, IMEs, doctors, the discovery, money issues, pain, counseling, Galaxy…This affects no one but Tracy and me! No one gives a rat's ass about the outcome or what it's doing to me. I can't stop crying. It's unbearable. I don't know what I'm supposed to do anymore. Tracy took me by the shoulders and said, It's going to be okay. That's all I need to hear.

Dec 9

Five years ago today, I had my first chemo treatment. Crazy. The package due date has passed, and I will no longer have to deal with this place. R-E-L-I-E-F! Done! Done! Done!
Myriam said my play has been submitted to the contest. Would you like to oversee the play being made?
Yes, I would love to!

Dec 17

IME – this time it felt different. She wasn't as abrasive. It was way more casual and I already knew the drill. She genuinely seemed to want me to be okay and heal.

Dec 21

My manager calls me into her office. I have your package info. You need to fax it right away. I look down at it – It's stamped *ACCEPTED*. My End Date is December 28! O-M-G! It's a dream come true!
If you can get this done TODAY, you *won't* have to come back. You'll receive your money in February or March. I signed the papers. She sent out a department-wide email:

"Sari joined us in 1997 as an agent. Sari has had many challenges over the years which she has overcome with her positive attitude and persistence. She is an inspiration."

I said my goodbyes.

FREEDOM.

2010

Jan 14

Mom will be starting divorce proceedings.

I got my package money! I paid ALL our bills.

Myriam called – auditions are February 6 & 7. It's beginning, how exciting!

I don't think having my play produced would be happening had Myriam not moved back to Calgary. I'm so grateful she did, for many reasons. It's hard to believe we've known each other since Grade 7. She truly is special to me, and I know she will do my play justice. I trust her implicitly.

Jan 23

Tracy got to be a speaker at a Galaxy event. When he was asked *why* he joined Galaxy Securities, he answered, My big "why" is sitting right over there, my beautiful wife. Our dream is to have a family, but things happened along the way to stop that. My wife got cancer and we dealt with that. Then she got hit by a truck and we had to deal with that. So, I guess it's never too late, but that's my "why"-- to take care of her. You find out who your friends are in this business. The friends I have made here are worth their weight in gold.

Tracy was right. Even though a few colleagues have disappointed us, for the most part the people we met within the business have been wonderful.

Tracy received six awards for his performance over the past six months in business.

Jan 26

I went to see a new chiropractor. After an examination and questions regarding my history, he says, There is no doubt you are in pain. And you're probably frustrated and want to get on with life. Pain causes stress and stress causes pain; therefore, you're never without either. I hope to be able to alleviate the pain. You will not be like this forever. There IS hope.

I decided to go off the sleeping pill starting tonight. I'm doing all the other healthy stuff and we want kids, so getting the sleeping pill out of my system makes sense as the next step. I'm not sleeping well at all, though. When I do sleep, I dream the cancer is back – only terminal this time. I also dreamt I was pregnant.

Feb 9

Myriam and I attended auditions the other day in a church basement, and they went amazingly well. The people auditioning loved the fact the play is a true story about my grandmother and some of the trials and tribulations she faced with her friends. That even at her age, 82 at the time, she still experienced friendship challenges.
It's such a cool process. We picked the cast. Rehearsals begin tomorrow.

I talked to Mom. She asked, Do you ever think about coming to Israel? Maybe you'll think about it, instead of me coming out there this summer.
I would *never* do that trip for the first time by myself *without* Tracy. That would be soooo stressful. I don't know that I wouldn't spend the entire time worrying "they'd" show up. Suddenly, word gets out I'm there and they show up. At least when Mom comes *here*, THAT element doesn't exist. I feel sick to my stomach even thinking about it. Why would I put myself in that position?
Oh, it's JUST the grandchildren coming over.
Oh, it's JUST the daughter-in-law coming over.
Oh, they're JUST on the phone.

I would never go without Tracy, never. I'd be *stuck* there. I'd have no "*safe*" place to go to. TRAPPED. All the questions I'd have to dodge from "well-meaning" people: Why aren't you seeing your brothers? If they *hadn't* moved 10,000 miles away, I WOULD have. I have been able to move on with my life BECAUSE they live in Israel. I have no fear of "running into" them here. It's less likely I'd see them if Tracy were with me. They'd avoid us like the plague.

Mar 16
We are doing a dry run for the play, to see how it's coming along as a whole. Myriam kept asking me how I feel about it. I'm happy with it. It's pretty close to the original, no big changes; the characters are still true to how I wrote them. I'm *very* pleased. And having my play "come to life" has rekindled my desire to write my book.

Chiro says, Your body isn't handling all the stuff I'm doing. I believe that you're having adrenal issues. Your body has never recovered from the fight-or-flight from the accident. Imagine being in a state of increased adrenaline *all the time* – you couldn't function. I can't do much for you until that gets dealt with.
I started crying.
I'm not abandoning you. Let's go see the new doctor right now (he's across the hall) and see if he can get you in sooner; he's a naturopath.
There is a cancellation March 30. I'll take it!
You'll also need bloodwork, and to get your hormones checked.

Mar 18
PLAY DAY! But I had to get through my IME first, a Chronic Pain Assessment. I had to give details of every ache and pain, and each doctor I've been to for treatment. We discussed my work situation, then she gave me a physical examination. This doc believes there is worth in going to the Chronic Pain Clinic (CPC). I felt she was advocating for me.

We are finally off to the theatre! I can't believe today is finally happening. Ten one-act plays will be performed and judged afterward by two adjudicators: one public and one private.

Sixteen people came to support me in the audience. Myriam gave me a card and flowers. My play received MANY laughs! It was received in the way I intended, so yay! Bubby would've loved it, since it's about *her*. After, the *public* adjudicator commented: It was sweet and charming, a real crowd-pleaser. He enjoyed watching the audience's faces and reactions to the play. It reminded him of a Carol Burnett and Tim Conway skit. That's a BIG compliment in my eyes. HUGE. The *private* adjudicator remarked: Everyone had fun, playing off each other. It was much-needed levity, after the heavy play before it. He loved the dialogue. Myriam looked at me and said, Just tell him.
It's a true story, I said so quietly, I was practically whispering. But he heard me.
Are you the playwright? Yes.
From such a quiet person comes *this* stuff!
Well, it was easy to write because it actually happened.
I have no criticism for this play. Your intent was to have fun and you did! Is this your *first* play? Yes.
Everyone thanked me for a wonderful script. Patrons came up to me and told me it was their *favorite* play of the night. Tracy said, Not that I thought it was going to be *bad*, but it was just *bette*r than I thought it would be. Dad was practically in the aisles laughing. Incredible feedback. I just feel so blessed to have had this opportunity. Thanks, Myriam, for believing in me. At the reception afterward, I could hear small groups discussing MY play, MY work! It was pure awesomeness. I was beaming with pride for the actors. They really pulled it all together. Dad said it was a well-kept secret. He had no idea it was going to be so funny. What a night! Humbling.

Mar 29

I have another IME today. It's my first one with a *male* doctor. There were a lot of forms and a lot of questions. Then I had the physical exam. He didn't realize his report will be for the defense.

Mar 30

The naturopath explained that the body is made up of electricity, so he tested my body for energy. There was hardly any. The first thing to work on is getting the electricity flowing again. Your immune system is shot; a good fever would be best. Oh, and you may be allergic to your cats. You have a lot of histamines in your blood. At best, ONE of the cats is causing it.

Well, I'm NOT getting rid of them, that's NOT an option.

Oh.

Apr 1

I had orientation at the Chronic Pain Clinic (CPC) yesterday! Finally.

I have my pulmonary and CT tests today at the hospital.

I'm freaking out about money! Galaxy fees have doubled, and we have no steady income coming in. This type of work is obviously unpredictable when you work for yourself: some months are good, some are lean. We can't save families if we can't even save *ourselves*! We are about to lose our shirts. I knew the package would run out with no money coming in and paying down all our bills. Tracy told me not to worry, things will be fine, and it'll work out.

My lawyer says all my doctors are very supportive of me. The arbitrator will listen to both sides – your doctors and their doctors; it comes down to his decision. The issue is you getting your money back. He will wait for the reports from the IMEs.

Apr 20

It's official – I'M INVISIBLE. I've been waiting for an hour and 45 minutes for the oncologist to do my big five-year checkup, and then they turned off the lights. I poked my head out the door: Um, excuse me.

You're next, Sari.

Uh, can I get the lights turned back on? They flip them back on. Gee, thanks.

I'm down a few pounds from last time. He says, You are considered CURED! A clean bill of health. It's such great news, and I couldn't feel more alone. No one asked me about it; no one remembered. I *tell* people and they don't remember. I'll go home and toast myself with champagne. No, not even Tracy remembered. I'm sure he has other things on his mind.

May 4

The naturopath says, Your bloodwork is fine, but your hormones are causing you the grief. You are VERY low in progesterone; that's why you're tired and why your cycles are off. Even *if* you fertilize an egg, there are no hormones that can *sustain* it. Your DHEA is down. Go see your doctor for a progesterone shot and I'll start you on vitamin B injections. We'll give you melatonin so you can sleep. You need to sleep.

Wow, a real reason for not being able to get pregnant.

May 12

I saw Dr. West. He disagrees with the naturopath. This progesterone will put you in menopause! You still have your ovaries. It will *stop* your periods. He doesn't want to give me something that will *prevent* me from having children. He's referring me to an endocrinologist.

May 31

We are soooo behind on bills. We are doomed. All Tracy does is help people all day and yet WE are struggling. These plans he puts together for families take longer to come to fruition, with no immediate payout. I think this biz shows people's TRUE character; both in colleagues and potential clients. I think God doesn't want me having friends – when I do, they become backstabbers. Why can't I see these traits BEFORE I'm all in? I was crying. Dudie came over and licked my tears away. Loyalty galore. A *cat* understands more than people do!

On the bright side, I haven't had my period in **_two_** weeks! The other bright side – the Nickelback concert is tonight! We got tix for our anniversary.

Update: The concert was unbelievable! Just the best! I want to go again! I love those guys!

June 7

I woke up feeling JOY. Self-talk works amazingly! I've always known that if you give yourself positive affirmations, your outlook can change for the better. So, I really dug in and tried it. This week there is going to be so much promise, clarity, and new doors opening; I feel hopeful. Tracy got paid…YIPPEE! No relief from pain, but I had a great day!
We have a friend in Saskatchewan whose dog had puppies – do we want one? It's been two years since Ebony passed; ya, maybe. It turns out it's a litter of 14, and there IS a *female* runt.
Okay, we'll take her!

June 8

My five-year cancer anniversary! Am I expecting too much for people to remember? I only talked about the date coming up ALL week, so it's not exactly a secret. Things that are important to ME get forgotten, but I **get** to acknowledge everyone's special occasions? I make big deals about people's important dates. Am I an idiot?! Yup, I am. It's the small things that mean *so* much, but no one remembers. One *little* acknowledgment. I gotta pick myself up. Yay me, I survived cancer. It's a BIG deal.

June 22

I finally connected with the Federal Labor Program. I gave the rep the nutshell version of my situation – cancer, accident, grievance…She believes she can help me and will send me a package in the mail.

June 30

We received a picture of Coca wearing the red collar we sent. Yes, we have already named her. Jim is getting one of the pups too and naming him Cola.

I was telling Mom that the CPC *can* help me with my sleep issues.

You'll come *here* (Israel) and you'll be so at ease, you'll sleep better.

I have better peace of mind being 10,000 miles *away* from there. Being that much *closer* to *them* will never let me sleep better.

Ya, I realize that.

I'm not sure you do. I will never feel "at ease," nor equate getting a good night's sleep, with going *to* Israel. Just so we're clear.

July 16

Mom is visiting. She said she understands my apprehension about going to Israel.

Everyone would have good intentions and be well meaning, but word will get out I'm there and everyone will think it's a great idea if the whole family gets together… Like this invitation I received in the mail for an event over there. Was it YOUR idea they send it to me?

Yes. They don't have your address, so I wrote it in.

So, you'd rather *not* say no to *them* than send it to *me*? I almost threw up when I realized who it was from. There are REAL issues here, and it's *not* okay to put me in this position.

Mom apologized. She wishes things were different.

We talked about her eventual passing – do you want to be buried in Israel or Montreal?

Every Jew hopes to be buried in Israel.

How would I do that?

I wouldn't expect you to go to my funeral. You could sit *Shiva* (a period of mourning) wherever you are.

I'm glad to hear you say that.

July 21

I haven't slept yet. It's 4:25 a.m. We are an income-less couple. There's no money coming in. Our business has stalled. Plans take time and we are out of it. We can't afford the Galaxy office and we will more than likely have to vacate. We are drowning. Beyond drowning. What would that be? Lifeless at the bottom of a deep, deep abyss, sinking farther and farther into the depths, no end in sight, no light, drifting down, down, so far beyond the point of return. Dark. Empty. Listless. Hopeless.

The thread we've been dangling by has snapped.

Aug 7

We drove to Saskatchewan to pick up Coca! She's ten weeks old. She pooped in front of the outside stairs and peed on the carpet once inside. Now she's biting me. I hope this gets better. We haven't had a puppy in 17 years!

Aug 13

Coca's peeing everywhere. Then she violently puked for 20 minutes straight. Poor thing. I took her to the vet. She may have a virus. $150 later. We brought her home and she threw up some more, puking blood. I said to Tracy, Maybe she is our test for a baby. All the feeding, poop, pee, puking, clean up, sickness… This will prepare us for a kid! Jim is experiencing much of the same with Cola.

Aug 15

Coca is doing much better. I thought we were going to lose her.

Tracy's grandfather passed. We're going to the funeral home on Tuesday to make arrangements.

We have decided we *are* giving up the Galaxy office. We have sacrificed deeply and willingly, but it's enough. I've reached my saturation point. The tears are gushing.

Somehow, we've managed to survive financially until now by making things stretch, but the stretch is snapping back.

Sept 10

Jim sold his house. Tracy will have to get used to not having his buddy around all the time.

Business is picking up – we have more team members and some potential new clients. But still no income coming in. Our parents have had to float us some money to get by.

I'm in ridiculous pain – it's my new normal. I have my psych evaluation today at the CPC.

She asked if I have a support system.

Yes, my husband, parents, and a few good friends.

Clearly you have tried everything and do everything you're told and nothing is working. You will be seeing a doctor here who is by far THE best.

Sept 19

We were told by Galaxy upper management to pay the remainder owed for the office, resign, or get a job and make a payment plan. So, we packed up our shit and left. See ya! And to TELL someone to quit? An example of superior leadership. We set up our home office and we'll do Galaxy business from there. We made the right decision. When no one on the team is chipping in to help pay the $1,200 a month, no thanks.

Sept 28

The discovery.

I asked my lawyer, "What happens now?"

"Well, there could be talk of a settlement or trial."

"I'm not prepared to give this, three *more* years of my life, or take this to trial."

The other lawyer was late. She asked me how I am.

"Compared to what?"

She laughed. She requested to see my medical records from the accident of '92. We also need to establish your health *prior* to the accident of '95. She asked me about my cancer and wanted my oncology report.

My lawyer asked about the relevance.

"Well, ya, okay, I *don't* need that."

We talked about the CPC and discussed my pain. She asked me if I still want kids. "Yes."

"Do you feel in any way you *can't* get pregnant *because* of the accident?"

"I'm seeing an endocrinologist in November – she'll be able to determine that."

She brought up my grievance against my work. She wants my LTD file. "Where are you with that?"

We are going to arbitration. There's no date set yet.

I want my life back. I've complied.

Oct 20

Tracy and I borrowed money from an old boss of his. You do what you have to do.

I've been very excited all morning to be seeing a doctor from the clinic. This could be the beginning of the end. She examined me. She says that they need to control my nerve pain *first* and recommended two medications. She also recommended a few of the classes to take at the clinic. We are going to work on getting you more mobility – you're like an accordion, totally compressed. Your muscles are working overtime and there is no point where it's all relaxed in recovery position. Your muscles are particularly compressed at the base of your neck into your head. We will always work as a team and discuss your progress together. A full report will be sent to your regular doctor.

Nov 4

Tracy and I saw the endocrinologist yesterday. We provided the usual medical history. She's sending me for full bloodwork before we go any further.

Today I have my first physio appointment at the clinic. She will concentrate on stretching my obliques. From my shallow breathing and previously fractured ribs, there needs to be more movement there. The whole session made me nauseous. She said, Your body has been this way for so long, trying to change it will give you that nauseous reaction.

Nov 15

There's a guy coming to the house for a home assessment at MY lawyer's request. We went through the accident history, pain, social life, duties I have in and out of the home, CPC, coping skills, work, how it's affected Tracy, driving… He took pictures of the house.
I went to group at the clinic. It's a relief to talk to people who GET what I'm going through.
I am so disgusted and disappointed with my body. No muscle or leanness in sight. My body has failed me. I have failed it. I just got my period – that explains it. My body is just not me. And trying to get this body healthy for a pregnancy? Fuck me.

Nov 18

My vocational assessment is today. This is the home assessment guy's partner. He said he has binders of my info, so I don't have to go through everything again. We talked about my education, work history, and I did seven aptitude tests. Then we talked about the pain I was feeling *after* all the testing.

Nov 23

I got a call from the union – they want us all to meet to discuss a possible settlement or arbitration, which is in January. Did FNL make an offer?
Yes, but we need to sit down with your lawyer and figure out the amounts you came up with for lost wages, and go from there. If the offer is good, there's no need for arbitration.
I cried. This could be the end. They made an offer because THEY don't want to go to arbitration *either*!

Nov 26

I filed for financial hardship to get my pension released. My lawyer notarized my pension.

The Endocrine Clinic called: What *day* of your cycle did you go for the blood test?

Day three, like the doctor told me to.

Okay, well it came back showing you have a rare form of fertility problems, so she wants to send you for another blood test on day *eight* of your next cycle.

I cried. A rare form of infertility? Oh man. What does that mean for us? Will Tracy leave me for someone fertile? I wouldn't blame him. Could this be classified under things I wish I'd known ten years ago, so I could've *not* stressed about how we'd raise the kids...I feel numb. To go from happy about FNL making an offer to devastation. Happiness only lasts until the next bombshell. I wanted the *choice* of whether to have children or not. Levi and Kyle get to have as many as they want. It's so confusing how this universe works. I wonder how Tracy will react.

He's home. I tell him. He said, We'll figure it out. He hugs and kisses me.

Dec 6

Tracy came with me to the union meeting with my lawyer. FNL offered me *$4400*.

My jaw hit the floor. I felt so...defeated. Stunned.

My lawyer said it's a joke. I hope you will NOT accept.

Maybe I was being naïve, but I thought they'd do what's *right*.

No, they won't. He explained about going to arbitration, and he believes I have a case and could do better.

By my calculations, they owe me 40K – *they are missing a zero.*

We're all on your side. They've done this to others. You'll probably get your lost wages from the other settlement you have going, and you *can't double dip.* So, if we go ahead with this, it will jeopardize your other case. If the settlement covers the lost wages, great! If it doesn't, we'll still go to the mat for you.

So, we decided to adjourn the proceedings in January, and wait until after May, when the other settlement has concluded.

Ya, we had to borrow more money. Just going through the motions at this point.

I'm going to kick up my studies and get licensed. We still believe we can build this Galaxy team and get to where we want to be in this business. Things are slow now, but it'll pick up and it'll all be worth it.

Dec 15

I had back-to-back IMEs – six and a half hours yesterday and five and a half hours today. So not fun.

I was thinking in regards to Galaxy: sometimes in life you need to know which bridges to *cross* and which ones to *burn*.

2011

Jan 3

The endocrinologist revealed, There's an abnormality in your bloodwork. I tried ruling it out, but it showed up, *twice*. I want you to go *again* on day three and day eight, but in the morning. She weighed me – 137 lb. Never in 42 years have I weighed this much! I'm beside myself. It's not a *healthy* 137 lb., it's a flabby, disgusting, untoned, unfit 137 lb. This accident has taken way too much from me.

Jan 11

I have had a fever and been sick for six days now.
The Endocrine Clinic called. I couldn't imagine why; I haven't gone for any tests yet.
The receptionist said, I'll just read you what the doctor has written out here: "*I haven't been able to stop thinking about you since your visit here. I know we talked about you going for IVF, but I'd like for you to wait so we can rule out the rare hormone issue first.*" And instead of May, she wants to see you in March.

I saw the occupational therapist today at CPC. Among other things, I said, I need to drive again. *That* is my goal.

Jan 29

We had a conference weekend for Galaxy out of town. It was blindingly evident we were out of place there. We do not belong. When things are going *well*, they swarm you with praise and accolades; when things get tough and slow, you're on your own. No leadership, no mentorship, no office, no recognition, no respect, no support…we are lost. People's true colors *do* eventually show. Being alienated by the very people who said they'd do *anything* for us, would help us in *any* way, *you're not alone, we love you...* what does that even mean when you don't apply your words? Actions! Our actions, our values, our humanity...THAT defines us, *not* this business. If this business ceased to exist, who would we be? Strip it all away and whaddya got? Are you still a person of character and integrity? I would say no, most of *them* aren't.

This has made Tracy and me stronger, navigating these difficult times. I'm so proud of him and how far he has come without *anyone's* help. They could all learn about character, integrity, loyalty, and leadership from *him*. Tracy got a promotion, though: marketing director. That basically means he's built his team and has enough licenses to get promoted. We've been struggling to build our team and now we have, but still, no new business is getting put through to receive an income from.

Mar 16

A week ago, I passed the prequalifying exam and today I PASSED THE PROVINCIAL EXAM! Here we go! I KNEW it would be worth it in the end!

The endocrinologist said the marker showed *again*. You are a carrier of markers that show infertility. *Chemo* was the cause of this. The tests show you ARE ovulating, but *can't* get pregnant. If you want, I can send you to a geneticist for testing.

Damn you, cancer!

Mar 23

I'm on the computer and I read a headline: *"Explosion at Jerusalem bus stop kills 1, wounds 25."* They say the person killed was a woman. My heart sinks. I call Mom. No answer. OMG. Mom calls me back finally. I tell her about the headline. She says she was *supposed* to take the bus to her doctor that day, but was running late and missed the bus, so she wandered around the market instead. Thank God she was running late! This is the third time this has happened to her.

Apr 6

At our weekly meeting at the main Galaxy office, Tracy was asked to present me with my new license! He started off by saying, We talk about spousal support and my wife, Sari, has come to *every* event in this business. I have been with the company for five years and when I went full-time, she was *completely* on board. She has faced many challenges, first with cancer, and then she went back to work and was hit by a truck. So, it's taken a bit longer for her to get it going. But she did it. Her license has come in and I'm proud to give it to her.

I go up and accept the license, we kiss and hug, and I go to sit back down. They tell me I have to say a few words.

As Tracy said, I have faced a few challenges, but when you have someone who believes in you that much, who supports and encourages you that much, *anything* is possible!

Apr 21

I got a clean bill of health from my oncologist on Tuesday; I'm still in remission.

I received clarity today to say what I need to, to the people I love. I called and texted everyone I care about and told them so.

Lesson of the day: If you sense someone is toxic in your life, DO something about it. Don't wait for it to get better. It won't. Don't wait for them to change. They won't.

The team is talking about plugging into a *different* (better) office. We *need* to do what's best for OUR business. Everyone else is.

May 4

I want my body back. I want to be able to hold my husband's hand without pain. I want to drive again.

I met with my lawyer regarding mediation in two weeks for the accident. You are a spectator, you do not need to talk, be more of an observer. He's asking for loss of employment, pain and suffering, and all doctor and travel expenses.

I said, I want to be DONE on May 18. I won't settle for just anything, but I'm not prepared to keep on going with this. I need to move on with my life.

He said they might use my cancer *against* me, as a reason for my not healing; you were predisposed to injuring due to cancer and your previous accidents.

ALL reports indicate I'm *clear* of cancer and was *fully recovered* from *each* accident.

I desperately seek the end of this four-year poison fest.

May 18

At mediation, my lawyer spoke to me privately and said they seem to want to get this settled today as well. The judge arrived and explained the process. Each side needs to compromise; otherwise, no settlement can be reached, in which case we go to trial and the expense will be *yours*; it'll be stressful and not a pleasant experience.

After the ordeal, we left the room while the other side deliberated on a new amount. When we went back in, the judge said, There is *no* question of liability in the accident.

It turns out *THEIR* expert doctor was on *MY* side. He said my injuries and complaints stem SOLELY from the accident of June 26/07. The judge said, You deserve *every* cent you get. My lawyer said to the judge, I love this plaintiff; she's not your typical chronic pain patient. She *hasn't* given up on life.

The lawyers said things back and forth and the judge announced, *Settlement accepted*!

RELIEF!!

The other lawyer said to me, I don't know *how* you went through *two* discoveries and all those doctor appointments; I don't think _I_ could do it. I wish you well.

Tracy picked me up and we bought champagne on the way home.

May 20

While I am THRILLED to be able to finally pay people back, I'm freaking out all that the money will be gone again. There is so little income coming in. I know I sound selfish, but we have struggled so much for so long, to finally get a break and then it'll be gone. Back to square one. God knows I'm not ungrateful for the money, it just scares me to death we will be back where we were.

Tracy said, I won't let that happen.

Okay, music to my ears.

June 6

Tracy announces our team is moving offices (for our weekly meetings, etc.) and we'll be under different upper management! We have 100% support from the leadership there.

I was crying. This is so great. We are going to share a team office with someone who had to get out of the other office too. We've been in limbo and now we are finally back on track. I'm happy. I feel HAPPY.

Two members of the team are *not* on board with the move. They have the option to stay where they are, if they choose. If their morals, values, and ethics align with *that* office, great; ours don't. We are going to a more positive and supportive place, where they WANT to help us. If everyone is doing what is best for THEM, why are WE not allowed to do the same?

June 7

We went to our first weekly meeting at the new office. What a life-changing night! When you stick to your guns and use your voice and stand up for what you believe in, great things CAN happen. Never give up! I've never felt better about where we are headed. We are taking control of our business. It's FUN again!

June 22

I have $9 to my name and my lawyer said the settlement money was just couriered to their office. Come get it tomorrow. I burst out crying. R-E-L-I-E-F! I finally have closure on the past four years of my life.

July 16

Another reflective, heartfelt, milestone visit with Mom. Funny how we keep learning new things about each other. Mom said to Tracy, I've come to a point in my life where it no longer matters to me that you're not Jewish. I see Sari is happy, and all you do for her. *That's* what's important. I will never get tired of hearing her share feelings like this.

I went shopping for clothes. Three months of working out and I'm *still* fat! It's not my body in the mirror. It's been nine years, with the cancer and accident. I couldn't work out the way I'm used to. Tracy said it takes time.

Aug 20

Nobody from the team but us came to the Vegas Convention, so Tracy and I saw it as a great opportunity to turn it into a vacation. We played hooky from the lectures and did our own thing. We walked through Caesars Palace and the Bellagio. We found a quaint cigar shop/bar in Caesars Palace to hang out in. What a couple of rebels. We'd go have lunch somewhere new each day, then have dinner at various restaurant patios. One evening we took in a show at the Paris hotel. A real vacation.

Aug 23

Dad says, Not a day goes by I don't think about what Levi and Kyle did to you. And If I'M thinking about it every day, I can't even imagine what YOU go through with it.

There is always *something* that brings it to the forefront. It's always there. In every relationship I've had, every social situation I've been in, every movie or TV show I've watched with that type of content. But they don't rule my life anymore. It's a *moment*.

Sept 8

One of my nieces is getting married today and the family flew out to Israel for it. How nice for *them* they get all the support. Mom says, I wish you were here.

Well, I wish things were different. I don't have a family I can have those big celebrations with. And I'm fine with that. THEY messed up this family and I'M the outsider. Levi gets to celebrate his daughter's wedding. He HAS a daughter.

Yes, I can see how you'd see it that way, and feel that way. I'm sorry.

This is not a normal family. "Family," to me, is a *sad* word, an f-word. The truth is, it'll never be okay. I don't see you being in Israel as a betrayal. You are where you want to be, it's home. You are where you feel at peace. I don't begrudge you that. But you're trying to figure THE thing that will make this all work out perfectly. It won't happen.

What if you have a baby?

We'll cross that bridge IF it happens.

I'm feeling out of sorts. All our friends have failed us. All the people we thought were true blue weren't. The ones who pledged to be loyal weren't. The ones who vowed to always be around lied. It always has been and always will be: Tracy and me. We have each other. We love, support and depend on each other through and through.

Lesson of the day: People who are the quickest to judge, point fingers, and lay blame, have the *most* to hide.

Sep 19

I talked to the clinic psychologist: I think at this point, we can close the file. I think maybe I've gone as far as I can. I got a lot out of the clinic, but maybe I'm done.

If you feel you're done, that's a good thing! Congrats, you've just *graduated*!

I am finally FREE! No more doctor appointments, no more running around trying to find a fix for the pain, no more trying to find THE thing that'll help, no more dwelling on pain! I am free! What a feeling!

Is this what happens at 43? Is this when Bubby became assertive and outspoken? I always wondered when "the change" happens. It sure feels like a shift. Your tolerance shifts. You suddenly stop being a doormat. You stand up for yourself. And people start listening – people are listening to ME.

Of course, it's not to say the pain has miraculously vanished. It just means I'm not tied to a structured treatment plan. I go for treatment when _I_ deem it necessary.

Oct 4

I'm having a meltdown. Tracy got paid $85 and his office fees went up $50. Panic. I cried and cried and begged and begged God for help, to let us pay off debt and have an ample, *steady* income so we can have kids! I told Tracy and he said, It's coming; there's lots in the pipe. I haven't taken on my own clients now that I'm licensed. Tracy helps families out in the field, and I take care of all the paperwork and office management.

Nov 13

Tracy got paid $5400. He was right.

I found out our friend is having a 40th birthday party put on by *those* friends from *that* old group, and we *aren't* invited, and my father was told NOT to tell us about it. Her "friends" were OUR friends that we introduced them to, whom we don't speak to anymore. They didn't want to hurt our feelings by telling us about the party. Of course, we wouldn't want ANYONE feeling uncomfortable with OUR presence. We were their friends first and yet we'll NEVER be invited to a group gathering, ever again. Another prime example of people not understanding LOYALTY. No concept. Either you are or aren't. No middle ground. WE are the outcasts. They all deserve each other. I'd rather be an outcast and hold my head high than be around fake people who don't think twice about throwing you under the bus and stabbing you in the back. I guess standing up for yourself = losing people? Totally worth it! I realized something – the kiss of death in ALL my past meaningful friendships has been them declaring over and over that I'm their best friend and will be forever and ever. I can think of seven people off the top of my head who did just that. People who

KNEW I'd been burned before, and *swore they'd* never do that to me. I'm fairly certain I'll be more picky about who I let in to my life down the road.

Nov 16

For many of our "friendships," I kept the peace for the sake of our business. I sucked it up, stifled myself, bit my tongue, stayed silent, overlooked…but enough is enough. When trust is broken, it's difficult to move forward. I need to find a *different* kind of friendship: nurturing, reciprocal, loyal, not poisonous and toxic. People say you *need* friends in your life; you *can't* go through life without friends. Uh, ya, *I can.* There was a time I would do anything to hang on to people and chase them. If I get nothing back, if there is no interest or effort on their part – I'm done. I feel pretty clear on this. I'm using my voice.

Tracy and I are all fired up from a work retreat. Things are definitely on an upswing! We invited a new teammate, Harper, to come live with us as she was in a bad situation. Noah (a business partner) introduced us to her. We *vowed* we'd never do this again. God, I hope we don't regret this.

Dec 8

All the planets are aligning or something. Tracy said he doesn't want to jinx anything, but things are going well! Some people are coming out of the woodwork to make amends! POSITIVE things are constantly happening.

We went to a memorial service for Tracy's friend Norman's father, where all "those" friends were. Ward looked like he *wanted* to say something to me, but stopped himself. We paid our respects and *immediately* left. Tracy admitted he was feeling sick to his stomach and his anger was growing by the minute; the sense of utter betrayal by them all. We did the right thing by going to the service, but I'm glad it's over.

Dec 11

Tracy met up with Norman for a beer. Tracy asked him, Do you even know WHY we stopped being friends? Because of Ward.

No, it's because of Galaxy Securities. No one would invest with you.

No, not at all. All I wanted to do was *show* you guys what I was doing. That's what friends do, share.

I'm not buying it. Why wouldn't you have a private conversation with Ward and sort it out?

Would YOU if it was YOUR wife?

I would have at least tried. I don't think it warranted you not being friends with him anymore. I don't really believe it happened.

Tracy got up and said, I'm outta here.

Norman offered, *I'll* get the beers.

I'll get my own fucking beer. Tracy threw some money on the table and walked out; he still had two-thirds of a beer left.

FIVE years later and this douche is still the same. Zero growth and the same lousy attitude. So, in his eyes, it's okay for Ward to sexually harass me and be all kinds of inappropriate, so long as we "talk" about it? Oh wait, he doesn't even *believe* that happened. That chapter is closed forever. Thank God. Closure.

Dec 21

Tracy told "those friends" from "the 40th birthday party" fiasco about his meeting with Norman last week.

One of the wives said, Ward never tried anything on *me* or any of the *other* wives.

So that makes ME a liar because he didn't leech on to EVERYONE?

Tracy said, Why would Sari and Gina, YOUR friend, lie about something like that? What was there to gain by that? Being ostracized?

I said, Gina and I were telling the **_SAME_** story without having spoken to each other about any of it.

She still didn't believe me.

I guess we are done with *this* friendship too. Cleaning house, baby, cleaning house!

Dec 24

Our roommate Harper had a brain aneurysm at her boyfriend's house. Her mom is coming out tomorrow from the East Coast and staying with us. Harper is scheduled for brain surgery tomorrow.

Dec 26

Harper's mom and I went to the hospital to see her. She had a massive black eye, almost swollen shut and a swollen shaved head. She apologized for ruining our Christmas. You absolutely did *not*.

Apparently, had her boyfriend waited even ten minutes longer to bring her in, the aneurysm would've ruptured. We are grateful she is still with us.

2012

Jan 2

Despite the original potential diagnosis of infertility, we are still trying because nothing's been proven or ruled out yet. But our window is closing, if it's not shut already. Tracy saw I was upset. I told him why. I was reading an article about a woman who is pregnant for the THIRD time and dealing with "fertility issues." Boo-frickity-hoo! Does she even *understand* what *fertility issues* means? That means having ZERO children or struggling to have ONE. Not whining and bitching you can't have *three or four*. Oh, but we really wanted *more* and we're "struggling." My heart bleeds for you. Be grateful you had ONE! Be grateful you had TWO! Oh wait, you HAD a THIRD! Poor thing. Such struggles.

Jan 12

Okay, is it weird of me to think a house guest should ASK if their boyfriend can stay over? The boyfriend has been here for the past six nights, and *not once*, as a courtesy, were we asked. We have also accommodated her mother for **_three weeks_**; Harper has been here two months. No one is contributing and we are feeding, showering, hydrating, and heating four to five people. Our utility bill is DOUBLE. They come to the table *expecting* I've made enough food for everyone, and I'm just supposed to ASSUME he'll be here for meals too? It's like he's moved in and no one told us! What a great deal for them – no rent, no utilities or grocery contribution, free ride! I'm kind of shocked the MOTHER *never* offered money. Supposedly, they do well for themselves, and she couldn't muster a helping hand? Nice of us to take her in, a stranger…and support everyone! Tracy made $87 this month and WE have to figure out how we are going to support everyone?!

Wow, this time was supposed to be *different*. I am *through* being taken advantage of! Did anyone ask if this was manageable for US? It's still OUR home! But how do we kick someone out who is recovering from brain surgery? Catch-22.

Jan 14

I got my period today. Mom said, It must be so heartbreaking every time.

Ya, and it doesn't help when I've had a house full of people and I couldn't deal with it *privately*. I get all emotional and I can only cry in the shower, when I'm alone. At least Harper's mother left a few days ago.

Feb 12

We suggested to our friend John that Harper move into *his* basement suite: it's a self-sufficient suite, with a private entrance and all. He's open to it. I told him to watch for the boyfriend staying over nights and suddenly living there, and not paying rent. I told Harper that John had considered it, and said it would be okay. Don't fuck John around. He is Tracy's best friend. DO NOT fuck him over!

I promise, I won't. I would *never*.

I've never had an appreciation for my body. And now with this *aging, battered* body, I feel worse about it. I've been working out five days a week for three months, working my ass off, and I *still* look gross. I'm petrified to go to Mexico at the end of April for a Galaxy convention, and have to wear a bathing suit and summer clothes. I eat right and do all the right things…I just pray no one sees my body in the daylight. I was the skinny girl and *never* appreciated it. Maybe my body *is* perfect…**_under_** the cellulite and fat.

Feb 22

I feel like an idiot. We truly just wanted to help someone and got supremely taken advantage of.

Harper has zero regard or respect for us. She's making poor choices and lying. She can't be trusted. She has lost all credibility. She tells us she's just running to the store and disappears for days on end without a word to us. Selfish and unappreciative. She says we saved her life and she's grateful. She had an incredible free ride! We gave her everything and more. And now it's over. When she comes home, she's out!

Feb 24

Two days later, Harper came home. You're the *last* people I want to hurt. I'm so afraid I've wrecked our friendship.

I said, I never thought *you'd* be the one to screw us over *again*. Short of wiping your ass, we did *everything* for you. And all you've done is lie to us and play the victim.

I will leave NOW if it makes things easier. I'll do whatever you need me to.

I think you know we *aren't* those people. You hurt us. But we don't hold grudges; we aren't angry people. But we need to move forward. We are giving you until March 1.

No one, not even my own family, has helped me as much as you guys.

Tracy concluded with, You're damn lucky we are so nice.

Feb 29

No word from Harper. She hasn't packed or been home since our last conversation. So, I texted her: Any chance you might want to let us in on your plans?

I was *just about* to send you a text. Sunday is moving day.

Don't screw with John's good nature. He's doing this for YOU. Please don't do this to John. He said YOU are moving in, *not* the both of you. If you need to live together, go live in your boyfriend's apartment.

Oh gosh, Sar…that will not be happening. You deserve better from me. I love you.

I'm **_begging_** you to not take advantage of living there. Begging.

I can *promise* I won't as we've talked before, actions speak volumes. I *swear*.

I guess all that's left to give her is a kidney.

Mar 14

I'm amping up my workouts – doubling them.

John tells us the boyfriend has been there *every single night since she moved in.*

I texted Harper: You swore up and down that wouldn't happen. I don't get it. If John wasn't your landlord, I'd keep my mouth shut.

I'm speaking to John about that in the next couple of days.

Just keep your word. It was the *only* condition. If you can't stay apart, go live with him.

No need to worry, Sar.

Apr 4

Our 20th wedding anniversary! We invited everyone to Boomtown to celebrate. We met there 25 years ago, on April 4, when it was called Malarkey's. Boomtown *opened* April 4. It's just so cool. Everyone who we invited showed up, about 20 to 25 people.

Last month rocked – three new licenses and seven new business partners. We're growing!

Apr 17

I only have to come to this God-awful hospital *once* a year for a checkup, but it feels horrible *every* time. If I get the chance to forget that part of my life all year, coming here brings it all flooding back: every smell, feeling, thought…it's all present. While the worry and fear of a recurrence lessens, being here transports me back to that yucky time.

Your hemoglobin is low, your X-rays are good, see you in a year.

WOOHOO!

Tracy happily announced at the office, My wife is another year cancer-free! They applauded me. I couldn't help but think of this time last year when our "mentor" had said to Tracy that he should *not* be driving me to my cancer appointments: *It's not a good use of your time, it's not a priority.*

Tracy got in his face and said, Pardon? Are you telling me taking my wife to the hospital to see if she still has cancer or not is *not* a priority or important enough?!

Well…uh…er…what I meant was of course *that's* important.

Except you just said it wasn't.

I can't imagine *why* we left that office.

Apr 24

I got my period. Does it sound weird to say I was glad? My only reason is better to get it *this* week, if I'm going to get it, than *next* week in Mexico.

It's kind of a catch-22. Now I've confused the *Pregnancy Gods*. I may as well fold up my conception tent and go home. It may simply not be in the cards.

I have no idea how we will have money in Mexico. We leave in two days. Damn.

Tracy shows me a brown envelope, from Revenue Canada! I said, Holy shit, that looks like a *check*!

I rip the damn thing open. It's a check for $10,641. OMFG! It's *way* more than I ever expected.

It's a fricking miracle!

Being self-employed, I knew we'd get some form of a nice tax refund, but our accountant never shared the ultimate outcome with us when she filed our return.

Jackpot!

May 15

Los Cabo was incredible. It's easily our best trip EVER! We did some deep-sea fishing, hanging out with multimillionaires (they are people *just* like us, who knew). We spent a few extra days there, after everyone else left. I have to pinch myself. And I think I was in the *best* shape of my life. I was very proud of myself for doing it all *healthily*. Despite feeling defeated in February, I kept at my doubled-up workouts and it finally paid off.

John booted Harper, the nightmare tenant. I feel just awful bringing her into his orbit. You try to be nice to people and give them breaks we never had. Sigh.

Lesson of the day: Don't question your gut feeling about people.

May 19

We had a team gathering at home. We sat in a circle and everyone shared their hopes and dreams. One person asked the next person in the circle questions. It came to my turn. Noah asked me THE question – If you had one wish, and money was no object, what would it be?

I could feel myself quiver; my emotions were rising. I could sense all eyes were on me and I knew *instantly* what I was going to answer. Moments passed that felt like forever. With some prompting from others, I finally said, I'd have a kid. I lose it. I look up, and *everyone's* crying.

Noah says if it's God's will, and it's meant to be, you *will* be blessed with a baby. You two are the most giving, generous, big-hearted people I know. You open your home, your lives to everyone and you *never* ask for anything back. People have taken advantage of you, but I've never met more loving people. You always help me, check on me, make sure I'm okay, you want us to be successful… If I could find one ounce of love that you two share in *my* life, I'll be grateful. You have given more to me at times than my own parents ever have or could. Your success seems to depend on ours and I will do anything in my power to make that happen for you two.

His voice was getting shaky, and he was having trouble holding back *his* emotions. He spoke from the heart. It was so moving. It's kind of odd in some ways hearing what people think of you. I was humbled. I got up and gave him the biggest hug. For quite a while we stood there, just holding onto each other.

He said he loved me so much. Then we all group-hugged. It was quite a moment.

Tracy was the last one to be asked a question. He offered, Do you guys know *why* we want our own biological kid as opposed to adopting? We don't have anything against adopting, it's a wonderful thing but we want to be able to pass on our genes to someone. When you have a soul as beautiful as hers (pointing to me), when there is *that* much amazing beauty and goodness, you want to have someone to pass those genes and traits on to. She has the most beautiful soul, and we want to have a kid so they can share in that.

I was stunned by his words. *Nothing* can top what he just said. I'm deeply touched. I think this team turned a corner here; this group will never be the same. We bonded. What a gift today was.

May 20

Dad came over and I shared with him what happened yesterday. He reached out for my hand, looking at the ground, nodding, crying. I know you want a kid. I know.

After a few moments he said, I'm no longer angry at Levi and Kyle. I made the decision to not be angry anymore – not for their sake, but for my own.

I said, I agree. I feel no anger, I feel nothing. Indifferent.

He said, I wanted to kill them when I first heard what happened. One raped you mentally, the other physically. He started crying. And until the day I die, I have to live with the burden of knowing I *never* protected you. I didn't know. I didn't know it was happening and you needed protection. You have my word that they'll never hurt you again. I have your back. Always.

May 24

No period. Hmmm. Could I be pregnant? I'm ALWAYS on time. I know I'm just two days late but…I find myself daring to think this time could be *different*. Dare I…hope? What if I were? Would I even be a good mother? Wow, I can't go there. But it hasn't happened until now, why *would* it? Maybe I don't deserve to be a parent. As far as I know, things happen for a reason. Maybe there is a reason I've never been pregnant. Man, I could go nuts thinking about this shit.

May 27

No period. What is going on? I keep running to the bathroom to check if my period started. I had cramps this morning. I figured for sure it's my period. No, I just had to pee. I'm actually thinking, *This could be it!* It's terrifying, and exciting. I gotta pee again. *I got my period.* I'm surprised that I'm surprised. I *didn't* see that coming. The second I think a baby is a *possibility*, it stops being one. I told Tracy. Having my period is like a cruel joke.

May 28

Tracy comes home and tells me, I have a lump under my arm.
Does the doctor know what it is?
No, no idea, he's sending me for X-rays and bloodwork.
Okay, so it could be an infection? You didn't have that in Mexico.
No, I noticed it Wednesday. I'm having a complete physical on June 4.
Are you going to be okay? YOU'RE the healthy one!
Ya, I know.

He *can't* be sick. He's my rock. I need to be his now.

June 18

The doctor's office called Thursday to say the results are in and the doctor would like to talk to Tracy. There's no appointment available until Monday. So, we spent the past five days worrying about the results.
We *both* went to the doctor's office. It's your gallbladder; there are lots of stones. It could block things at any time. All your pain, months of it, and throwing up is from *this*. The lump is directly related as well. It's all connected. You have to lower the fat, spices, and alcohol in your diet. If you get an attack, go *straight* to the hospital and tell them you are prone to this and they will do the surgery right away.
We went home and researched the crap out of this, and came up with many things to do in the meantime to lessen the severity of the pain.

July 4

Five of us from the team drove to Vegas for a Galaxy convention. I was concerned about Tracy the whole time. He was in pain. What if something happened and we weren't close to a hospital?

Update: Tracy was okay throughout the trip and continued to try to manage his pain and symptoms throughout July.

July 16

Mom is in visiting. She said to me, I'm not sure if you're okay with me talking about people's babies, maybe I shouldn't.

No, it *doesn't* bother me. It's the comments from people *my* age, who *have* children, who say *I'd never have a baby at this age or start a family now.*

But you're parents in a *different* way, to your friends, to your team, to all your animals, and serving people with your business.

Yes, I guess that could be true. I have Tracy but no kids. Others have kids but no partner.

July 20

During dinner Mom says, I see you two have a wonderful life together. I SEE it. I know I've said this before, but it's worth repeating: I don't care anymore that you're not Jewish, Tracy. And, Sari, I'm *glad* you're married to Tracy. Mom definitely gets reflective when she comes in. She observes our relationship when she SEES us together.

Tracy starts crying. He says, All we ever wanted was for you to *accept* us, our life. It took you 25 years, but here we are. I had my walls up all these years. Why wouldn't I, when I *knew* you *didn't* accept us solely because I wasn't Jewish? I love your daughter.

The two of us were crying.

Mom asked me what *I* was thinking.

That my husband just poured his heart and soul out to you.

I know, I'm overwhelmed. For the first time, I'm speechless.

We all agreed we were okay, more than okay. She thanked us for making *Shabbat* a very special one.

Out of the blue, Gizmo's not eating much. He has taken a turn for the worse. I'm so worried. One eye is dripping with gunk and his mouth looked like some blood was in it. He's been lying in the sun outside most of today. Sigh. My sweet baby cat.

July 22

Mom says, You were the preferred child, the beloved one, the wanted and adored one.

I know, and I paid the price for it.

Your younger brother adored your older brother, *until* you came along.

Yes, and they BOTH felt I needed to be punished for being born, for the love I received from you guys, for being me.

Wow, what a clear way to put it. I don't think you having a relationship with them is at all possible or necessary. You have done so well for yourself; you're in such a good place. I'm grateful for that.

Then the conversation went sideways *fast*.

Mom asked accusatorily, Why don't you *ever* ask me how I'M doing with the whole situation?

I yelled, You know what? I deserve a medal for even *speaking* to my parents and having a relationship with the people who didn't protect me! I don't think an eight-year-old should have to be the one doing the protecting of the family.

I didn't know.

Well, you *should have* protected me! And yet I forged relationships with the two people who *didn't* help me.

You're right. Wow, that explains a lot of things. You were very resentful of me growing up.

How can you expect *me* to take on figuring out if YOU are okay with things? It may be selfish of me, but I'm too busy figuring out how *I* am doing.

You're right. You're absolutely right.

372

It's not up to ME to make sure everyone is dealing with it. I do what I need to for *me*. I don't envy you as the mother in this dysfunctional "family." I never thought it was an easy place for you to be. But I'm NOT the one to make you feel better about it.

How can you forgive me?

It's fine, we just need to move forward.

MY CONCEPTION

From the moment of my conception, I was wanted. The way my parents described their desire for a girl after having two boys is heart-warming. They were going to try "one more time" for a girl. Luckily, for *them*, that's what I turned out to be. From day one, I was Daddy's little girl and he called me his little princess (as my name directly translates from Hebrew). I have had friends who were "mistakes" – but not me. I KNEW I was wanted. I KNEW my parents wanted a girl and were over the moon when I was born.

One might even think I would go on to live a very charmed, spoiled life.

But *not everyone* shared in the delight.

The moment I was brought home, my oldest brother, Levi, hated me. He never even *tried* to hide his contempt for me.

In his eyes, *I* stole *his* younger brother from him, *his* buddy *and his* playmate. I would be on the receiving end of all Kyle's attention, and the bond between brothers was broken – because of *me*.

Because I was born.

Kyle lost ALL interest in being a *little* brother to Levi and was focused solely on being a *big* brother to me. I believe the jolt of going from two boys living a connected, bonded life for a few years to nothing was more than Levi could bear. It went from all to nothing.

Who knew a six-year-old boy could become so bitter, cruel, and resentful? These feelings of repulsion toward me would continue to grow as I grew.

Although what Kyle did to me was unspeakable, Levi would embark on a lifelong mission to make my life a living hell – no exaggeration. He was committed to causing me pain, hardship, and grief. He had a purpose. There was joy in that for him.

Only in later years would I come to realize the full extent of his deep disdain of me.

Aug 5

Giz is *not* doing well. At times he looks okay, but then he walks and falls over. It's the first time that he's *not* into food. I took him outside. He lay down, closed his eyes, and turned his face toward the sun, like he knew it would be for the last time. He sniffed the grass, the air, and his surroundings. I took some pictures of him; he looked so serene, content, and at peace.

Tracy and I brought him to the vet. I signed the papers, picked out his urn and paw-print box, then we sat with him while they gave him his IV. I gasped. Then they gave him his injection. We sobbed. Out loud sobbing. I forgot how quickly it happens. So fast. In seconds…gone. I kept apologizing to him. I'll never see his face again. His beautiful, sweet, round face. And those eyes. Our 17-year-old. Our little Chubby. He's finally at peace.

Aug 7

Tracy's on his next promotional run and no one is doing *anything*. There's no urgency from the team because everyone else HAS jobs. We have a mortgage too! It sucks ass when you have to rely on others. Things are about to change again; I can sense it. The fridge is empty and we have $33 in the bank.

Aug 27

This could very well be the *best* birthday I've ever had. Tracy surprised me and invited our close friends to the pub for dinner. Today, of all days, people paid us back money they owed. We went from being piss broke to getting $6500! Relief!! I expected nothing today and people made time for me. I felt special.

Sept 26

Tracy gets off the phone with his mom – there's been a death in the family, our brother-in-law died in a car accident.
What?! It just wasn't registering. Tracy's poor sister, this is horrible! OMG. OMG.

He called his sister. Tracy got off the phone and said they don't know *where* the body is. They don't know if it's in Crossfield where it happened, or Airdrie, or it's enroute to Calgary…

He was 56.

I said to Tracy, I feel like he lived at least. He got to see his kids get married and have children, travel, bought their dream home, bought a trailer, cars…

Tracy and I held onto each other for a while.

Oct 2

Funeral day. I have a cold, which is convenient because it will disguise the crying. This is going to be awkward. We haven't seen or talked to the family, nothing. Do we sit on the friends or family side? We weren't sure *where* we'd be welcome. It was standing room only. Tracy said he was a loyal, hard worker and beloved wherever he worked. It was a beautiful service, very moving. They even had his race car that he built parked outside the funeral home. We saw an old friend of the family. She asked us if we have any children.

Tracy and I looked at each other, pause, pause, pause…

I finally say, I can't have any.

We need to get better at our answer, but I guess we are still processing the reality of it, even though I know Tracy pretends it's still happening for us.

I hugged his sister goodbye and whispered, Call if you need anything. Call even if you *don't* need anything.

Lesson of the day: Live every moment like it's your last – because it *could* be.

Oct 4

I *get* that people don't know what to say when something tragic happens so they say nothing and give us our "space." Did we ask for it, though? For all the times we've been there for everyone else, we get nothing when we *need* people to show us they care. I guess so long as we are there for *them* in *their* times of need, there's no need to bother with us. I think for people like us, who give so much, bad things happen so it gives us a chance to see who gives back. It's the little things that mean the most, but that seems to be the *hardest* thing for people to do. There's no capacity to reach out.

A lady at the office, her husband died. Not another one. Shit! I'm so grateful I had a chance to speak to him a few weeks ago. He was very sick. I knew it would be the last time I'd see him. I don't know what I'd do if I lost Tracy.

I had two friends over to clear the air. One says, I didn't know you needed us. You're both always so strong and in control.

Huh. I guess I need to *tell* people what I need. That's not easy for me.

The other says, I should've just picked up the phone. I should've known you guys needed us to be there for you.

No matter how strong we *seem*, we are only human; we need help too.

I'm sorry, I'm so busy thinking about all my own bullshit. I get stuck in my stuff.

I said, I'm taking responsibility for my part in the breakdown of communication. I am admitting what I need to do better going forward. I'm just asking you do the same.

Oct 25

After all the potential job interviews Tracy has been on in the past few months, Jim and Tracy are meeting with a guy, Hunter, who wants to hire them to install security systems in 400-plus homes! Tracy would make $200 a day. OMFG. THIS is it! THIS is what we've been waiting for to carry us through. Things ARE coming together.

Tracy and Jim come in after their meeting. I'm searching for a sign that things went *well*.

Tracy begins, So…ya, we were offered the contract if we want it. And he wants *you* to man the phones.

So, I'd get a salary too? Yes.

Jim says, He'll come here and set up the system; you get to work from home.

OMG. This is so perfect!

Tracy says, We'll be making 12K a month and $350 for each referral, and he pays us on the first of each month.

There is a lot to be said for having faith. I've never prayed so hard. What a difference a day makes.

Oct 29

We met with Hunter. He will be putting an ad in the paper to advertise the security system. I'll be the only one manning the phone. I'm overwhelmed. Am I supposed to sit at the phone 24/7?

No. Rather than a salary, you'll get $10 per booking. You will make *more* money that way. If you book 35 appointments a day, that's $350. He says he has four *other* installers, but if Tracy and Jim want the bulk of the work, okay. He wants Tracy to do sales as well. There are no hours of operation. It's kind of disorganized and there's no contract to sign. Tracy said we will forego the next Galaxy Retreat because THIS is more important.

Nov 16

I said to Tracy, This isn't working out the way I'd hoped. We are putting in all this time and effort and we still have *zero income*. It was supposed to be all these installs and making all this money. He basically recruited us and we are no further along. Hunter calls and says the ad should *finally* be in TODAY's paper. He needs my help with the accounting stuff as well. Business is slow but it WILL pick up. I understand Tracy is frustrated with how things are going.

I said, The frustration comes from believing the sales were *already in place* and Tracy and Jim were just sliding in to do all those installs. We came into this *needing* an income.

I understand, but this is how you build a business. So, if I can just get you guys to hang in there, things WILL pick up.

Dec 1

Tracy got $1000 from Hunter. I'm not sure how that will cover being behind on *two* loans and LOC payments. I know we are going to get out from under this, but until that happens…it's just plain scary. I don't know how I still have hope, but I do. There were fourteen messages on my voicemail from creditors.

Dec 20

Okay, I have no hope left. Tracy tells me I give up too easily. No, I'm just being *realistic*.

I spoke to Hunter; he wants to meet up to give me a check. I told him I need *$5000*. He never even hesitated when I asked. I'll be less stressed *if* he comes through for us.

Later, Tracy came home – I got *$2000* from Hunter. It's okay, he said I'll get *more* by the end of the month.

Good God, I'm grateful we have SOMETHING, but I was irked because Tracy EARNED the money he's SUPPOSED to get and it's like pulling teeth to get it.

Dec 30

This is a foreign feeling – I've been *happy*, two days in a row. It's an unfamiliar feeling. I felt light-hearted, energetic, and I'm making jokes. I *literally* stopped in my tracks and had a moment. I'm gonna ride this feeling as long as I can. Am I just a naturally UNhappy person? I'm about to lose everything and yet I'm feeling happiness. Sooo weird. I have a feeling this is going to be a better year!

2013

Jan 2

I've struggled my ENTIRE life; nothing has ever come easily. I had those two days, but mostly only *smatterings* of moments of happiness throughout my life. I'm determined to make this year different. I refuse to spend the next 44 years struggling. I choose happy! Did I just say that? I want to get on with my life! I want to make a mark on this world. If procreating is *not* in the cards, what is? What's my legacy? I need people to know I WAS HERE! I existed. But how?

Jan 8

I called Hunter to discuss why we are not getting paid for the time and labor we've put into the company already.
I gave Tracy $3000.
Yes, he EARNED that money.
I explained that we understand it's a business and it takes time, but it sure didn't feel like we resolved *anything*.

Jan 12

Tracy was supposed to get money at the end of December, then this past Thursday. Nothing. We told Hunter to come over.
He said, I *overpaid* Tracy $3000, I gave him ALL the profit. I myself haven't taken any salary.
I showed him every detail of everything we've done since the beginning. I said, We *weren't* looking for JOBS.
If you can just bear with me for a few more months. Just hang in there.
With that, they left.

Tracy came home. How would you like to earn $150 per set appointment?

I guess I still have a job from home, fine.

Hunter gave Tracy a check for $500.

Jan 18

Hunter's check bounced! That means our loan payment bounced. I AM SO STRESSED!! I was on the phone all afternoon with the bank, utilities…making payment arrangements.

Feb 12

Hunter called Tracy yelling at him, saying *he's* taking advantage of HIM.

Tracy couldn't get a word in edgewise, so he hung up on Hunter. Hunter calls Jim to complain. Tracy told Jim he has nothing to say to someone who attacks his integrity, morals and character…

Tracy informed Jim that Hunter wanted to cut him out of the business. They are both done with Hunter.

Feb 13

Jim calls Tracy to tell him that Hunter is at the Galaxy office wanting to join our team. Jim tells Tracy he will NOT be processing Hunter's application into the business.

We've been friends a long time and he's pitting us against each other. No ethics.

Hunter tried calling Jim, then Tracy, and then me. *None* of us answered. Does Hunter believe Tracy and Jim won't talk and compare notes? Hunter is now texting me – you get your husband to call me. We all agreed we are done with him TODAY, and he will not get his inventory back until he pays Jim what is owed to *him*.

What was the lesson of the day? Maybe to make Tracy and Jim's bond stronger.

Feb 15

I woke up to *18* voicemail messages from that parasite, plus *109* texts. He also left Tracy threatening voicemails; threatening *our* standing at Galaxy Securities. It seemed like we needed to make it a police matter, so Tracy texted his police buddy to help out.

Jim met with Hunter to get his money. He had no money for him. Jim reiterated that Tracy had done nothing wrong: Tracy's integrity is FLAWLESS. People can't mess with my family and friends, my finances or my business and you've messed with ALL of them. Did you think I'd turn my back on my brother?

How about…

NO! How about you bring me cash and we call it a day.

Feb 20

Tracy says, I'm having a major anxiety attack. I feel like I'm going to throw up. I just need to do this, Galaxy. I need to commit and dive in so we can get ahead.

It scares the shit out of me when Tracy is freaking out. It's very unsettling. It's not good for his health and the gallbladder issues. I wake up every morning opening the fridge and being so thankful the *electricity* is still on. But I really feel like today is a turning point. I've prayed so hard for something to turn for the better for us.

Tracy came home. I couldn't get a read on him. He met with clients and has a lot in the pipe now. He pulls out a check for $5000. My parents didn't want us to lose the house, he said. Mom had said to me yesterday, *Everything* can change in the blink of an eye; that's why we have HOPE.

Feb 23

Hunter left Tracy a text to complete an install. The guy is fricking dense! He also thinks Tracy has his deposit book. He's blaming Tracy because he can't keep track of his OWN shit! Does this not sound like

Roger from Kelowna? Interesting how these patterns of people keep duplicating through our life. Jim is returning Hunter's entire inventory. Jim dryly joked, Shaving your head with a motorized cheese grater would be better than dealing with that guy.

Mar 4

A talk show was on TV. A young girl had been molested for three years by her stepdad. The things she shared resonated with me: *"I'll never know what it's like to have a life without this happening to me." "I can never get those years back." "I couldn't live my life as a kid. I was a prisoner in my own home."* The stepdad had snuck into her room eight times one night. Sadly, I can relate.

Two clients cancelled their insurance policies. We now owe Galaxy $7000. We are getting kicked while we're already down.

Mar 15

Tracy was asked to be a speaker at an event tonight. He talked about our dreams and facing tough times. He said, We had put all our dreams in a box, out of sight. We have only recently have taken out those boxes.

The next speaker said, Tracy's powerful message sums up the night – take your dreams out of the box. It's time to dust them off and dream again.

May 3

I'm having a meltdown at record speed. I've spent all morning looking for a job. I'm too old, fat and unskilled for anyone to hire ME. What am I doing here? So, I can get out of bed and face another day of hopelessness? I feel like I'm being punished. Everyone *else* gets to have an income, a job, make money…Tracy works his ass off at Galaxy and what does he have to show for it? Only irate business partners who seem to blame HIM for THEIR lack of business success.

A friend texts me: How are you doing?

How do I say I'm *not* okay? So, I lie. I will lie and say I am **FINE,** which right now means **F**ucked up, **I**nsignificant, **N**o worth, **E**xiting this planet. What's my epitaph? *She was damaged. She got into car accidents. She was always sick. She couldn't give her husband children.* Maybe on my stone they could put, she DID make a great seven-layer dip though!

Tracy could find a new wife and have children, my bros can sigh a sigh of relief I won't be around to reveal their dirty little secrets. My "friends" *might* have a sad reaction *at first,* but they'll quickly go on about their lives and forget me, like they did while I was alive. Dad might be sad for a minute, but he has his girlfriend now. Mom would be upset. My animals just might miss me…for a while, but they'd adapt. Maybe I should just succumb to the depression and put myself out of my misery. I regret I have no money to leave Tracy to make things easier for him.

Thank you, Galaxy, for running us into the financial ground, for being chock-full of multimillionaires who can't even pay for their own lunch and Tracy has to, who won't help the ones falling behind because…well – it's *not profitable.* And Tracy's fam, don't let this put a crimp in your plan to keep Tracy out of your lives. You've done so well with that until now, keep it up. Oh ya, and God, I BEGGED you for your help. BEGGED. I believed you'd help. I tried to keep the faith. You kept punishing me/us. I hope you delight in the fact YOU WON!

You sure showed me. *Mazel Tov.*

May 12

I was sitting with two friends. One was telling us their daughter's friend tried killing herself; she's 13. She's bawling. What would *possess* a 13-year-old to end their life?!

I looked away. I get it. At 13, or 44…sometimes the hope vanishes and it gets so overwhelming you feel there is no way out. Your only escape from yourself, and what you perceive to be the worst problems ever, is to find solace in imagining the pain stopping. Sometimes people will do *anything* for that calm. It's a comforting solution after you spend days, months, even years of endless torture inside your head.

I turned my head and cried. I so understand the continual hurting and aching to get over the seemingly insurmountable problems. Once you have "those" thoughts, nothing can erase the feelings; it's always there, in varying degrees, just waiting for the overload of challenges and obstacles to gear up again. I still consider myself as having good coping skills, but *everyone* has their saturation point – and that's when the darkness creeps in. You're vulnerable to the feelings and beliefs that this will *never* pass. I'm so grateful they didn't see my tears because I was not prepared to verbalize that a mere week ago...I was the closest I've ever come to carrying through with such a final act.

The one friend said, What I love about you, Sari, is how organized you are and how you remember *every* little detail. You're always sending me texts wishing me well on some important date. You remember EVERYTHING – every birthday, every appointment, everything that you think would be important to me. It's very admirable and it's an amazing quality you possess.
Wow. It's like somehow, they both *knew* I needed some propping up, to feel SOME worth and value. And it's Mother's Day.
Noah brought me flowers, a bottle of champagne, and a beautiful card telling me how I'm his second "Mom." I needed all this today. That touched my heart in ways I can't express. I told him I loved him.
I love you too, Mom.

May 16
Tracy is going to rebuild my father's bathroom for him. I thought I should go with him because I'm scared to be home *alone* to think and think and think… These pangs of desperation wash over me with *no* warning. It's horrifying. I feel out of control. In those moments, I'm afraid. My head gets bombarded with daggers of darkness, with no sign of lightness. *Everyone* can snap. The difference is some *act* on the panic. I wonder why I haven't acted. I always get right on the verge,

right to the edge, right there, where I'm going to do *something*, something I *might* regret.

I need to have a quiet mind and some peace.

June 8

Early on in the afternoon I realized, Uh oh, cramps. I'm gonna get my goddamn period! Damn, damn damn. I did.

Today's my *8th* anniversary of my cancer. Eeeeiiight. Eight on the eighth. Champagne anniversary.

June 13

Okay, so I've only been bleeding heavier and heavier with each passing day since the June 8. What the hell? It usually tapers, not gets heavier. I'm SO confused. Something has to be wrong. Mom called and, in passing, I mention this. It's day six of uncontrollably heavy bleeding. Mom freaked. Naturally she said, You need to call a doctor! Don't mess around with this. Ya, ya. I'm pretty sure I'll be fine after today. How do you know? You don't know that. Call your doctor now and get down to see him! This is no joke! I will call you back in a bit after you've had a chance to call. She was…frantic, adamant. I was flippant about it, even though I *was* concerned. Maybe she has a point. This *can't* be normal.

So, I call Dr. West. The receptionist agreed this is no joke. She said Dr. West can't do anything for you until your period is OVER. Swell. That could take a while at this rate. So, she gave me the Health Link number to call. A nurse mans the phone and she can answer your questions and tell you what you need to do. So, I call. I describe my symptoms. The nurse said, After *two* days of heavy bleeding, it's a problem! After *five*, get yourself to Emergency! Everything in the computer here is telling me that you need to get to the Emergency as soon as possible! If you're not experiencing symptoms yet, you will! And soon! You WILL feel dizzy; you WILL get short of breath. I feel fine other than the fact that this is pretty annoying and I have to keep changing my tampon so often AND use a pad, which I never usually use. She agreed my own doctor can't help me until I'm done my period, but she said if you go to Emergency, they CAN give you something to stop the bleeding.

She gave me something to think about. I called Dr. West's office back to make an appointment for whenever I DO stop bleeding – I made it for next Thursday. Mom called back. I told her I made an appointment to see Dr. West next week. I left out the part of my needing to get my butt to the Emerg. Why worry her? In the end, I was glad I called that help line, but I also just had a feeling it would be okay. Why waste time of the busy people in the hospital just for me when they could be spending it on REAL patients; they have better things to be doing. I hate to be a bother. So instead of going to the hospital, I went on the treadmill. Not too bright. I'm feeling unbelievably nauseous and I have a massive headache. I'll survive. I have survived worse than a bad period. It's 5:00 p.m. – I'm feeling stressed, rundown, no appetite, no energy…dwindling fast. Now it's 7:00 p.m. – sore throat. Oh man, I'm getting sick. Big surprise. But the bleeding IS slowing down.

June 15

Yup, I'm sick. Sore throat that kept me up all night, cold-y, flu-y. Not a good day. I'm so freaked out about money. I'm literally sick over it! I'm struggling with *everything*! Why am I here? At whose expense is all this for? I can't contribute job-wise. We struggle to make ends meet. I hate myself. I'm getting greyer hair. I'm getting fatter and uglier. What the fuck is the point! I DO believe sometimes Tracy would be better off without me. My life feels like it can't begin until debts are paid and settled. How can I move forward when it feels like 65 tons of weight on my shoulders? Our ship keeps "coming in." It's coming. It's been 26 years…I'm still waiting. I'll drop dead and then Tracy will win the lottery! Just my luck, but he'll be okay. He can go have kids. I cried all day.

June 16

I'm still pretty sick. I called Dad to wish him a Happy Father's Day. It's weird he's not here; he's on vacation with his new girlfriend, Dorothy, at her permanent trailer in Penticton. I shared a bit about my period and that I will get it checked out next week. I'm beyond happy for Dad. Thrilled. But normally he'd have been *here,* and I'd have bitched to him about all these things going on. I miss him. I miss that. He'd be mortified to know how I'm feeling right now. I'm not myself. I'm having thoughts you can't come back from. I feel at my wit's end. I feel alone. I feel like I've lost all hope. I look around my home and I feel terrified I'm going to lose it all. I look into Coca's face and I feel an abundance of love and trust. I'd miss that.

I was going to bed. I leaned on Tracy and I said, Can I ask you something? Okay. Can you lie to me and tell me everything is going to be okay? He obliged and said it *flatly.* Say it like you *mean* it! You want me to lie, but say it with *feeling*? Ya! He said it more genuinely: Everything IS going to be okay. Do you mean it? He rolled his eyes. No, no, say it again. I just need to hear the words again. He didn't. He must think I'm nuts. I am. I'm hanging by a thread. I need a pinhole of light. Something. Anything. So, I read this prayer Mom sent me in an email. I said it over and over and over. I pray *something* helps. I'm so overwhelmed. It feels so dire. I can hardly stand it.

June 30

I saw Dr. West. He said had I gone to the ER, there was probably *nothing* they could have done for me. He wants me to go for an ultrasound. It's scheduled for July 1. I picked Mom up from the airport and got her settled in. As I was heading to bed, I poked my head into her room and said, I love you, Mommy, and I'm glad you're here.

July 4

First thing this morning, I see my doctor's office calling. Your results are in. We have an opening at 11:00 a.m. *today*. Okay, I'll be there. Mom came with me to the clinic. Dr. West says, They found a cyst on your left ovary; it's 5.4cm long. On the *same* ovary, you are growing a large endometrial polyp. It's attached itself and that is what is causing the bleeding. You also have *numerous* fibroids. So, we need to send you for another ultrasound in 12 weeks to see if it's going to change in size. If it does, we will have to refer you to a gynecologist. They may have to remove the ovary.

So, I do nothing?

Right. Just make the appointment and don't miss it.

The next ultrasound is September 24.

July 9

Mom says, So I'm thinking I wish I could help you guys more. I don't know how. Suddenly, I remember I have this investment with Tracy from Galaxy; I have this extra money! I want to give it to you. *Hashem* has made it that I have this extra money to help you. I keep having nightmares about not being able to protect you. I think in some way, *this* is how I can.

She told me to take some time and figure out exactly what we owe. I figured it out. I was scared to give her the amount. I tell her. She never even flinched. She said, Maybe I'll take a little extra out for *myself*.

I started crying. I walked away from Mom and sat in the office. Overwhelmed. We won't almost lose our house *again* because of Mom's generosity.

A business associate passed away this morning, a brain tumor – he was 36. He had a wife and two young kids. It puts life in perspective. Again.

July 18

I dropped Mom off at the airport. We had some laughs. It was a pretty great visit.

Tonight, we go to Tracy's sister's to present her with an easel Tracy *made* in memory of his brother-in-law. It's for his race car showcase: a jacket and some pictures. I even had an engraved plate added to it.

She bawled when she saw it. It was a very touching thing Tracy did for her and a beautiful moment between them.

July 29

I have a full-on period. Heavy flow. This is never going to end.

It's my belief that people don't change. They don't. People become "aware" of their bad behavior and *can* consciously do things differently. But inherently, deep down, people ARE who they ARE. If you're a bad person trying to be a better person, you can consciously better yourself. Goodness won't come "naturally" to bad people; they have to work at it. They can CHOOSE to behave differently. Those demons are ever-present.

Lesson of the day: Beware of those people who "turn over a new leaf." They will always have the capacity to do harm.

Aug 7
Aunty Sharon's son died today. He was fifty years old and died from a blood disease. So heartbreaking. A travesty. I called her – she said, He's with me *now*, I can feel it. He never complained and was in pain, for two years. He's finally at peace. Even when tragedy strikes, she still manages to be so gracious and positive.

I called Dr. West. There is NO way I can wait until the end of September for another ultrasound. I need one ASAP.

Aug 11
Well...I had an ultrasound and there's *major* shit going on in there: there are massive cysts, polyps and fibroids on my left ovary and all over my uterus and cysts and lesions on my right kidney. The pain is outta this world. In the meantime, I haven't stopped bleeding since June 8! Tracy had me contact my oncologist as well.

Aug 19
Results: the tumor on my kidney is 10mm, I have an engorged uterus with numerous *new* fibroids, there's no sign of pelvic fluid (an indicator of cancer), but they can't say 100%, and one cyst has gone from 5.3cm to 6.3cm. They are giving me a prescription for pain, and I need to be careful of anemia/low iron – there is no treatment for any of it, except having a *hysterectomy*.

Wow. Again, I know my body and I KNEW things were NOT okay in there!

Aug 14

Last month, Cory Monteith died – by suicide. And today, a cast member from *The Bachelor* died – by suicide. Okay, so they're not personal friends of mine, but I can understand the pain! I would *like* to say I have *never* been in such a dark place – but I *have*. You feel, at the time, that you will never get through it. It feels like there is no other way out and no other solution for it getting better. It's a terrible, awful, hopeless, destitute place. You're a puddle of emptiness and grief. You don't think about "coming out the other side." I remember wanting to end things – and then suddenly *something* got better, *something* came through for me. And I'd think, Wow, I almost missed *that*. I *would have* missed that *good* thing.

Aug 16

Yesterday I went for my second ultrasound. It's tough drinking all that water so you have a full bladder. With all the things going on in there, there's barely any "extra" room for things like that! I'm unable to bend forward; the pain is everywhere. Eating hurts. Drinking hurts. Showering hurts. Lying in bed, sitting up...
I got a call today: the results are in! I had an instant knot in my stomach. I'm not sure how I found the room for that.

Aug 19

Waiting all weekend for results is not fun. But at least my appointment is first thing in the morning. Tracy took the day off to come with me. Dr. West basically went over the exact items from the *last* ultrasound. There is no treatment for any of this – only a hysterectomy. How do you feel about that? I just looked at Tracy like, Is this really happening? Uh, drastic, that's how I feel about it. He will refer me to a gynecologist to discuss options, but there aren't any. He asked if I have a preference for a gynecologist? *Female.* It'll be a wait for a female. I'll wait!
I feel like I have more questions than answers.

I asked Tracy, So, you'd be okay with me having a hysterectomy?
Whatever it takes for you to feel better; that's *all* that matters.
I was choking back the tears.

I was NOT meant to have kids.

Mom said a hysterectomy will make me feel 100% better. The flip side –
no kids. Bubby's life *began* after having her hysterectomy. I thought to
myself, What was the point of all these *years* "debating" about whether
to have kids or not? All those *years* of *having* my period. At first, I didn't
want kids, then I went on the Billings Method and went off the pill,
then we were trying, I had cancer (I had my period the *entire* time),
fertility clinic, hit by truck that caused a four-year delay, trying again,
endocrinologist, trying…now this, a *hysterectomy* being my *only* option.
Why have all those hopeful in-between times? This is crazy-making! It
could drive a person batty. I just want to know how this will all turn
out. I almost *didn't* marry Tracy *because* of the whole "raising kids
Jewish" dilemma and how difficult it would've been. But we'd have
done it. I told Tracy I feel like I have to apologize.
For what?
You wanted kids.
Ya, but I love you anyway.

So far, everyone I have spoken to who has had a hysterectomy *already
had kids* when they were told they needed the surgery.

I need time to let all this sink in…

Aug 20
I'm still torn today. I have so many emotions. I feel so scattered; not
knowing what should be done. I still feel like I'm cheating Tracy out of
the opportunity to be a dad. I feel awful.
Tracy comes home from a job interview. So, I start tomorrow at the
manufacturing company I worked at before, in conjunction with
Galaxy.

You got it! I guess the timing was just right for this to happen now. I'm so relieved.

I talked to Mom again – she said I could be *pain-free* for the first time in my life. Wow. What a thought. A new lease on life. And then on the other hand – no children. Ya, there's that. What's the point of all the hardships? Not wanting them, wanting them, cancer, fertility clinic…It just keeps swirling in my head. I said to Tracy, Did all that happen so we would be *sure* we'd be okay with it just being US, in the end? That we *still* want to be together? It's a predicament. Pain-free vs childless. Hmm…pain-free…

Aug 21
I asked Tracy if he imagined when he met and married me that I'd turn out to be such a defective model. I feel like such a big baby. I'm watching Tracy pack up his truck for his first day at work. He pulled out of the driveway, and I cried. I feel like our hopes and dreams are being taken away, one by one. This whole year has been a colossal mess! Things HAVE TO get better. They just have to. It's such an adjustment – first having Tracy home, and now not. I think my crying is finally a release from the past few days. I've only been contending with money, health, career changes…no biggies.

Aug 22
There are days when all you want is for someone to take care of you, to make decisions, to tell you everything will be okay. And when it *doesn't* happen, and you realize you ARE alone – the bad thoughts come barreling through. The earlier fleeting thought of wishing someone would care becomes more of a desperate desire. And then you realize people really don't care. They are too busy with themselves and their own lives. And the moment they DO look up from their own lives – it's too late. Then they are all like, Oh I wish I'd been there for you, had I only known. Feeling "alone" isn't about someone *physically* being there to say they care; it's about receiving a text or some small gesture – *that* can go a LONG way. It's about feeling like no one gives a shit. Wanting

the people you *thought* cared about you to *show* it. But you can't *make* people care. I've been ignored in many ways, shapes and forms my ENTIRE life. That's a deep hurt. You never get over that. You never get used to it.

Maybe I'm coming at this all wrong. What if I stop trying to give up on ME and just give up on THEM?! Huh. People will never stop being selfish and self-absorbed. People are people. It comes back to *expecting* people to care and to show it in the way *I* would. Few can show they care when it counts. I want to climb into a hole and die. Why bother? It's been downhill for some time – looks-wise, weight-wise, life-wise. I'll have the operation to make myself feel *better*? Then what?

Later, when I was talking with Tracy, he says, You need to just have the surgery and feel better.

I walk like a decrepit, 180-year-old woman, hunched over in pain. I told him I drive MYSELF crazy with these psycho mood swings.

Aug 23

I'm *gushing* blood! It soaked right *through* the pad. I told Tracy I need the operation ASAP. I think I realize *it has to be*. I *just* decided I'm having the operation. Gulp. It's just gonna be us after the surgery, no children. Not human anyway.

Aug 27

I called Dr. West to see where we are at with the referral to a specialist. The referral went in on the August 23; the doctors are reviewing your file to determine how important your case is against the other referrals. So, I wait. I'm alone on my birthday – weird. But for a good reason – Tracy's *working*! He came home, *with* a CARD. You DO love me! That meant EVERYTHING to me. His words were beautiful...I feel complete now. We got "our" table at the restaurant. It was a beautiful evening, just the two of us.

Sept 4

I get a call from the specialist's office: September 23 at 10:20 a.m. Perfect! I'll take it! It's a $150 if you miss the appointment. Oh, I **_won't_** be missing it!

Sept 10

I was watching a story on TV about *The Bachelor* cast member who committed suicide, Gia Allemand. It's the quiet, shy people. No signs. They keep things bottled up. Yup, you show people what you want them to see. You don't want the questions. Your dark place is just that – *yours*. It's not a place for others to sit with you in. People can see you in the light places, not the dark.

Sept 23

I have cramps from hell and a heavy flow. I'm in so much pain. The *most* pain from a period yet! I guess it'll get worse before it gets better. I'm so glad Tracy took the day off to come with me to see the specialist. She came into the room – she is so young. And so, the telling of my medical history began. She knew none of it, just the results of the ultrasound. We then basically went through my "options." There is medicine to shrink the fibroids; but they never go away. They only get worse with age. There's not much evidence to prove that works and you'd probably need surgery down the road *anyway*. Then there's surgery. I would take out the uterus and fallopian tubes, but leave the ovaries.

Tracy got a bit excited. If you leave the ovaries that means we could possibly *still* have kids?

Possibly, but Sari couldn't carry it. Even if there WAS an egg left, at your age, there's a 1% chance it would be a *viable* one. I don't want to be offensive, but the likelihood of a good egg at this point is slim.

You could always adopt, or use a donor egg. I could put in a referral at the fertility clinic?

Uh no, we've been down that road already.

In the meantime, I'd like to send you for some bloodwork, and I want to do a biopsy of your cervix to rule out anything cancerous. And I'll need an answer *before* you leave today to the course of action you'd like to take. You guys have had a lot of bad things happen; it's time for some good stuff!

Tracy left the room and I got into the gown. The doc asked if we have thought of adoption.

Yes, but we really wanted a genetic child. But as much as Tracy's always wanted a kid, he wants me to be out of pain.

She put the speculum in and said, Okay, you'll probably feel a "pinch," maybe some cramping. Well, holy fucking hellballs, that was some *"pinch"*!! I almost hit the roof. Tears were free-flowing down my face. It's a type of pain I've *never* experienced before. I thought I was going to pass out. I came very close. I couldn't breathe. I could not take any breaths. I stopped trying to breath. I put my hand on my forehead and braced myself as much as I could.

Please *relax* your knees, and take some deep breaths.

RELAX?! So, with **no freezing**, she made five to six scraping attempts for the biopsy, *with no luck*. The pain was so excruciating I could barely contain myself. She said, You may have to *come back* after I send you home with some muscle relaxants and medication to loosen the cervix. You've never had kids and your cervix is narrow and tight; I can hardly get in there.

I'm thinking, No way in fricking hell I'm *coming back* to do this AGAIN! No fucking way!

She announced, I'll try ONE more time. And she got it! She got the sample she needed. Thank fucking God. She then pressed on the outside of my abdomen to see where my sore spots were. She said, I'm feeling along the bottom of your rib cage, under your breasts – and your uterus is way up here. You have a very engorged uterus. Do you want some ibuprofen? YES! I cleaned up and Tracy came back in. I couldn't stop crying. So much pain. So much info to process. Both my body and mind were a jumbled frenzy of pain and rawness. I'm a heaping puddle of waterproof makeup gone wrong, burning in my eyes, streaming down my face.

A decision needs to be made – now.

I said to Tracy, I know she said she's leaving in my ovaries, but it doesn't mean we could have a "normal" baby. It could be deformed, have Down's…I just feel like this ship has sailed. I wouldn't want to have waited all this time to have a baby, then have one with so many problems and/or defects.

The doc came back in.

Tracy asks, When can you schedule the surgery?

So, you've decided?

Ya, there's no question; this needs to happen sooner rather than later.

I can do it laparoscopically, with a few tiny incisions, but if I get in there and I see I need to do more, you'll have a 3cm incision, like a c-section.

I don't care about scars; I give you permission to do *whatever* is necessary.

She told us the risks of surgery, anaesthesia, and hitting other organs. It's a quicker recovery and you'd be in the hospital for one to two nights.

So, what's the time frame? How long are we looking at?

Well, I believe I have an opening October 30.

I looked at Tracy for a sign as to whether that is *good* – too soon, too late?

Tracy said, We'll take it!

In the truck, I was still crying. Pain. Relief. Dread. Finality.

Tracy says, It's okay. All I need is you. We'll be okay, babe.

<u>Sept 24</u>

Mom told me to feel the feelings about the kid issue. It's huge! Huge for you. Come to terms with it in your own way.

What an emotional rollercoaster. I'm exhausted. I've gotten different things out of each "event": with cancer, it was an emotional journey; the accident, definitely physical but emotionally taxing; now this. With the whole kid factor – another journey. I do believe everything works out the way it's *supposed* to. There were too many signs to ignore – I wasn't meant to be a mother.

My heart has to catch up to my head now.

Sept 29

Dad has been in town since September 26, but he's sick as a dog and doesn't want to infect me. Mom wants to come out for the surgery, but I told her Tracy is around to help; he's home evenings and weekends.

Well, think about it for another week. I can look into flights.

She's not hearing me.

Mom, I love you. I love that you *want* to help me through this time. But what if I want to stay in bed all day? Or watch my soaps, TV, or movies? What if I want to listen to music? I won't be able to, yet that's what recovering people do. I know you'll want to help, but you can't run out with the car for groceries. Tracy will be busy doing those things for *you*. That will take away from what *I* will need. We won't be doing things together, like we do in the summers. What if *you* get sick here, have a bladder infection, or your Parkinson's symptoms flare up?

You've obviously put a lot of thought into this. It sounds like you're making decisions that are right for you. And Tracy's there for you. You're going through this together. Thank you for being honest with me. You seem really clear about what you need.

Oct 8

Mom called. There is something I need to bring up, but I just haven't known how, so I'll just come out with it. Your sister-in-law Maria, Levi's wife, is going to be visiting your cousin in Baltimore. She wanted to know if she can have your number and call you.

As I'm thinking, *Hell to the no*, Mom says, But it'll probably be at the exact same time you're in the hospital, so it's not even an issue.

I said, Fine then. Use *that* excuse and tell her no. I do not need to have a conversation with her when I'm prepping for surgery. I don't need the stress of *that* phone call.

Okay, I'll just tell her you're not feeling well and it's not a good time to call. She'd also like your dad's number. I'll ask him. It's *his* choice.

Oct 10

I now have a cold. Damn. Dad has stayed away for *nothing*. I haven't heard from him. I'm bleeding like never before. The toilet looked like a bowl of borscht or something. ALL blood.

I went to see the specialist. I have the heaviest flow *of my life*! I took the $500 injection at your suggestion, something you said I needed *before* surgery, and what exactly was it supposed to do I don't know, because it's only getting *worse*! I'm confused as to what was supposed to happen?

She assured me it should *still* work before surgery; it's supposed to shrink the fibroids.

I didn't pay half my mortgage so I could get this injection that, according to you, was supposed to STOP the bleeding IMMEDIATELY! It's gotten heavier!

She said, I didn't expect you to be bleeding again before surgery.

Me either! How about that biopsy?

It's all normal.

Well, THAT'S good news!

I asked Tracy if he loved me, like we always ask each other. We were watching a recorded TV show, he pauses it and turns to me and says, Let me tell you just *how much* I love you. While I was driving home yesterday, because I have a lot of time to think when I'm stuck in traffic, I cried on the way home thinking if anything *ever* happened to you, I'd be devastated. He was crying now.

I said, Aw, really? Because of the surgery coming up?

No, just everything.

Oct 13

The injection that *should* still work before surgery ISN'T WORKING! I went to take my tampon out and the blood forcefully gushed out, all over my hands, in the toilet and all over the new tampon. I've NEVER had *that* much blood free-flowing out of me. And it's not "period" blood; this is from a burst fibroid or cyst blood. I looked in the toilet and there was just a massive pool of blood. A big blot. And when I went to wipe – so much more blood came out and a clot. I think I'm hemorrhaging.

Oct 18

So, one of my worst fears will be coming true. The hospital tells me I *can't* wear ANY makeup the day of my surgery. Oh God.

I had my surgery bloodwork done and I got a hospital wristband. I received a letter in the mail saying my PAP came back *clear*.

I said to Tracy, Maybe we have to look at this surgery in a positive light; we can travel and do the things we've dreamt of doing because we won't have kids. This is the way it's meant to be. I *have to* believe this. He agreed. I'm an emotional wreck; I have so much on my mind. I'm thinking about money, the surgery, health, Dad, kids, recovery…I'm just…sigh. Maybe I should take a page out of my own family history – having kids doesn't automatically mean they turn out okay. Some people should never have been born, nor had kids of their own.

Oct 21

I hadn't heard from Dad since his voicemail last week; today we finally spoke. He's one of the only people I haven't talked to yet to address the fact I will no longer be able to have kids. He always worried I was too old and could have a child with disabilities. So, I didn't want to hear that from him. Not now. Not ever.

I started sharing with him, I'm very nervous. It's not so much the surgery itself, but the *finality* regarding having kids.

He said, I thought that the second you said you needed this surgery.

It's been an emotional process and it's been tough. It's one thing to DECIDE to not have kids, it's quite another to be TOLD you can't.

He wants to know what room I'll be in after the surgery so he can be there during the surgery.

I *felt* like saying, THAT'S when you want to see me? You're in town almost a month – I haven't seen you *yet*. I bit my tongue and said nothing.

He says, I still have a cold; can you hear it in my voice?

Ya, I gotta go.

Oct 23

Panic! Tracy works so hard and we still struggle. We're being kicked while we're down. Like God is trying to figure out just how much he can take away from us before we break. Financially strapped, trying to keep our heads above water, while HE claims my childbearing organs. How much do we have to lose before we get to live our lives? We're prisoners – things are being rationed out to us, doling out one thing at a time. We are "allowed" to pay only HALF our phone bill, HALF our mortgage, $50 toward this and that bill…And I pray we don't get disconnected from our basic necessities. I'll be going into surgery hoping and praying I have a home with electricity when I get out of the hospital. If the operation *doesn't* kill me, the stress of wondering if we get to keep our home *will*. We need a financial miracle! I've begged and pleaded with God. I hope he's listening.

Oct 30

Yesterday I waxed, colored my hair, did my toes – but no time for nails. I'm ready. I showered, then got to the hospital at almost exactly 8:30 a.m. Dad was already there. I go into a private room to go through a form and to sign paperwork. The lady says, They're *waiting* for you in the OR. You still need to go give a urine sample at the lab – to make sure you're not pregnant.

Wow, salt on the wound.

Go and tell them you need this STAT. I went, gave a sample and went straight to surgery admittance. They say, They're waiting for you in the OR. You can bring *one* person with you. So, I motion to Tracy to come follow me in. I put on my gown and lie down on bed. Tracy leaves and comes back to tell me my dad is *gone*.

That's weird. He said he was *staying* for my surgery. Huh. They take my blood pressure (very high), start an IV in my hand and give me a relaxer for anxiety. My doc came to talk to me before surgery. Do you have any questions?

So, no more periods but my ovaries will be left in, right? Right.

Will my ovaries be suspended?

She laughed. No, they will attach to another wall in there.

I said bye to Tracy and they wheeled me out.

They placed me in the surgery hallway, where I was greeted by about five people: the anaesthesiologist and his resident, my doctor and her resident and a nurse. What's your name?

Sari Knock.

Do you know why you're here?

Hysterectomy.

Okay, just making sure we have the right person and the right procedure.

In the OR they say, Please slide yourself onto the operating table.

Any dignity I had before now was gone. I have no makeup on, I'm buck naked under this gown, in mere moments my lady parts will be operated on, for all these people to see. I'm trusting these strangers to do *right* by me. I hear the anaesthesiologist say to the nurse, Sari will be feeling and hearing nothing in a matter of seconds.

Nope, I can still hea…

I wake up and the first thing I see is Tracy…and Jim. I'm realizing and feeling scared that my *insides* are now *out*. How am I going to feel? What is this recovery going to feel like, be like? I look over at the bed tray and I see three beautiful pale purple roses, from Tracy. People keep coming to check my incisions, giving me drugs, check my blood pressure, oxygen…

Any vanity I may have had is out the window. I thought for sure not being able to have makeup on would be the death of me, but I don't seem to care. Funny. It was brought to my attention I have these mechanical-type devices strapped to both of my legs: to keep the circulation going and to avoid blood clots. Tracy took a picture of me lying here and sent it to everyone. Jim left. Where's Dad? He never came back after he left when you were admitted.

I said, I don't understand; what do you mean *he never came back*? He was supposed to hang out with you until I was out of surgery, to keep each other company, to go eat…

He had some things to take care of at his house. I had six hours to kill so John hung out with me and took me out for lunch, and then Jim came.

I'm so glad you had *someone* to help you pass the time.

Tracy stayed as long as they let him.

The night was rough. Every time I was asleep, I was woken up to be asked how I'm doing. Really? I *wasn't* feeling pain *until* you woke me up, and now I need something! That happened about three to four times during the night. The morphine didn't help, it just made me nauseous, and so they gave me Gravol in my IV. I was told I had a catheter in so I won't have to get up to pee. I never had one of those before.

Also, they told me I had had a tube crammed down my throat during surgery so I may have a sore throat and may be a little hoarse. "Sleeping" during the night was very deceiving – what felt like "hours" of slumber was more like five-minute increments. I maybe slept an hour in total. But the daylight never seemed to break and the night went on forever.

Oct 31

I wanted to see Tracy so badly and it felt like he'd never get there. It's Halloween so when I'd woken up, my nurse was wearing all red with red horns on her head. Is this a dream? Am I in hell? Then I saw the floor manager was dressed as Gilligan from *Gilligan's Island*. My doctor came to see me. She looked like a little kid, in her street clothes, sitting on the bed like a close friend hanging out.

She described what she had done in the operation. She found a surprise in there alright – endometriosis, ALL OVER!

I got *most* of it, but I had to leave it on the bladder or you'd have a hole in it. I took your uterus out through your vagina so you will be experiencing *discomfort* from that. I made five incisions. You had a fibroid the size of a grapefruit and I took your cervix out. I'll try to check in on you later, in between surgeries, but I have no reason to believe you *couldn't* go home later today.

The *conditions* of being discharged – You have to have the catheter removed, you need to pee on your own, eat solid food, and you need to get up walking.
Oh, is that all? Okay!

So sometime after lunch they took the catheter out. I peed on my own, with some help from the nurse, into a toilet that sat in the corner of my curtained room. Not very much privacy. But if I gotta pee to go home, dignity must be cast aside. I peed out *many* blood clots. Tracy helped change me. We took three walks. I want to go home. Tracy called Mom to update her. Once Tracy started doing everything for me, the nurses stopped coming around. I think they forgot about me. Then a nurse comes in and writes *November 2* under the "discharge date" on the white board. I freaked out! I'm *not* hooked up to anything, no catheter, no IV, eating solid food, peeing on my own, blood pressure is good, I'm taking oral painkillers, I'm walking…Why keep me here? What can they do *here* that can't be done from home?!
It took a few hours to sort out, but the student nurse said, You'll be able to go TODAY!
Yay! Relief! And then *panic*. Careful what you wish for. Am I doing the right thing, Tracy?
Well, what more can they do for you?

I signed the discharge papers. They loaded me into a wheelchair. I got my prescription for meds, and we left. All the way down to the truck I was second-guessing being discharged.
The drive home was *brutal*. I felt every single entire bump, paint line and hole in the road. It was agonizing. *And* it was rush hour too, so it took forever to get home. That gave me *even more* time to think about what'll happen when we get there. I was scared to death I made the *wrong* choice about coming home so soon. We pull up to the house and Jim's truck is there; he must've come by to feed the animals. He helped Tracy help me into the house. I was SO scared about Coca jumping up on me. I got up the flight of stairs and sat down at the top of the landing. There, we let her sniff me and see I was okay. I was home and

she understood to not jump on me. I was panicking being home. I was analyzing what I had just been through. It feels like my insides are hamburger meat, I'm all raw inside, my organs have been removed – I'm a post-surgery mess! As we got ready for sleep, I lay there freaking out! I was worried I'd stop breathing during the night. I couldn't breathe through my nose, my throat was phlegmy, my head was about to explode, from all the oxygen they gave me and from having the tube down my throat, my throat was feeling tight, to my nasal passages being all stuffed up – I didn't think I'd last the night. I really didn't. I even said as much to Tracy.

What do you mean? Of course you're going to make it!

I wanted to be back in the hospital, where *should* I stop breathing, they could treat me quickly. I kept a pen by my bedside because if God forbid, I stopped breathing, I knew Tracy could use it to perform a tracheotomy. I loaded up on my sleeping pills so I *would* sleep through the night and not be awake worrying about not waking up, or not breathing. Visions of my carved-up insides floated through my head as I *finally* drifted off. I woke up *two hours* later. I had to pee. I felt like a Weeble Wobble. I managed to grab a part of the fitted bed sheet and heaved myself sideways, then up. I did none of this quietly, so Tracy turned his nightstand light on for me. This routine happened every two hours. Finally, the FIRST time since *June* there's NO blood in my pee or on the toilet paper, and no more tampons!!

Nov 1
When we finally got up in the morning, I was so grateful and surprised I had survived the night. It had felt like my body was going to completely shut down. But I made it through. My exceptionally heroic, loving and doting caregiver of a husband did that! I'm so lucky. I don't know a single other spouse who would do what he's done for me. He's a remarkable human being. He has seen me at my *absolute worst* – several times – and he's *still* here, loving me, caring for and tending to me. I love that man to pieces. He picked up my meds, fluffed my

pillows, held a straw to my mouth so I could drink, made me toast and eggs and later, quiche and minestrone soup. My nose FINALLY unplugged. Then I FINALLY pooped. And then it wouldn't stop! I said to Tracy, I don't know if I'm going to dart, fart or shart! It hurts so bad to laugh. We watched *The Notebook*. It hurts so bad to cry.

Nov 2

I'm rolling out of bed to get up to pee like nobody's business; I'm *not* a Weeble Wobble anymore! It feels like the inside of my left arm muscle has separated from the bone. Tracy said it could be from moving from bed to bed at the hospital…who knows; it hurts.

I have not seen Dad since Admitting.

I'm on T3s, but they're not working and I feel I am *meant* to feel every ounce of pain in this lifetime. Dramatic, but true. Since nothing has ever ebbed the pain for me, the only conclusion I have is that I'm *meant* to feel *everything*! I feel it all. I was shifting in bed and without any notice I suddenly felt the flesh ripping from the bone, on my left arm – again, followed by a burning feeling. Whoa. I'm not dealing with *quite* enough yet. Now it hurts to use *that* arm.

Tracy said he's feeling badly he has to go back to work on Monday. You don't need me anymore; you'll be fine without me.

No, I'll miss you – I miss you *already*.

Nov 4

On my walks through the house, Coca and Dudie would walk on either side of me, with me, every step. Such sweet children!

Dad texted and said he wants to come visit. We sat in the kitchen and I asked, Why have you decided to stay in Calgary for the winter and not remain in Penticton with Dorothy, since she's living out there permanently now?

Because I can't afford to have *two* places. The money I put out for you has drained me.

I started tearing. It's because of ME. I'M the reason he left Penticton.

It's getting serious. Dorothy and I now have each other as benefactors. She wants me to have the trailer we live in.

I was fairly quiet after that. I couldn't even look at him. I just kept crying.

I know you didn't expect this to go on as long as it has, that you'd have paid me back sooner. I don't want this to be something that comes between us.

I said, Well, it sure feels like another roadblock in our relationship. You don't know how to balance your relationship with your girlfriend and me. It's not just with her – it's with *all* the other ladies over the years. You never figured out how *not* to focus on just them. OUR relationship always suffered. Tracy and I are your *biggest* cheerleaders. We are SO happy you found someone that you are in a committed relationship with. We *adore* her! You could have moved to the other side of the world, it wouldn't have mattered – the fact is, you've missed so much. And not once have I EVER gotten a sense you even *care* that you've missed things. I started listing off events he's been absent for.

But I *do* miss those things, I tell *her* all the time.

Well, maybe you need to tell ME. You used to feel badly for me that Mom "abandoned" me when she left for Israel. I *never* felt that way, but if we are being honest here, I can tell you I have felt *more* abandoned by YOU in **four MONTHS** than I *ever did* in the **20 YEARS** of Mom being in Israel! I understand there has been an adjustment period to being in Penticton, living with your girlfriend, meeting her friends, and just focusing on your time there. We went from talking *every day* and telling each other *everything* to days and weeks with nothing. To adjust to that has been challenging for me. So much happens on a daily basis that you don't know about and that I don't know about you.

He says, So, we have to get better with that, maybe talk on the phone more. We'll work through this; we've gotten through worse.

I called Dad again to clear things up. You said you are each other's beneficiaries. So, if *you* get her *trailer*, does *she* get your *house*?

No, I'll probably sell it. And I can *live* in the trailer.

Nov 5

Day four with no poop. Lots of pain on my right side. The muscle on my left arm is still an issue. There are SO many bruises where the IVs were. I'm getting impatient that there aren't *big* improvements, but it hasn't even been a week! I can't believe I'm at *this* point – I was scared shitless of the surgery – and now I'm feeling more hopeful than I have since June! There is still a ways to go, but I'm not as scared anymore. I haven't really heard from anyone. People are so odd. Lots of well wishes *before* surgery but nothing *after*. I guess I'm being given my "space" again.

Nov 6

I went to the bathroom and peed blood, a watered-down version. I don't think that's good. The surgery was one week ago today. I've been in a lot of pain from noon until bedtime. It kinda felt like that first day home – all raw, I can feel every pain *inside*, pulling, throbbing and aching. Tracy is amazing. He worked all day, went to the pet store, grocery, cooked dinner, cleaned the cat litter, and tended to me. I tried to help by emptying the dishwasher – not my brightest idea.

Nov 8

It's November8 – five months ago this nightmare began. I'm thrilled to say it's being *dealt* with. I just had a poop! Such a huge deal that my plumbing *is* working on its own! Things feel a bit better than yesterday. I could roll over in bed without much pain.

Nov 10

I registered on a site for women who had hysterectomies; I'm hoping to find some support there. I just want to connect with *someone* going through a similar experience. I added my two cents:
"Day 12 of this 'journey.'
It's a crazy, lonely type of surgery to have to go through without the addition of wondering who your friends are, who is going to step up and who won't. Every single one of our friends knew we tried for years and years to get pregnant. Only ONE actually asked us, So, how ARE you with that? (Now

409

that you had a hysterectomy). My hubby is amazing, no question. I guess in the end it will only be us, alone together, so all that matters is HIS love and support and encouragement. For a guy, he's very sensitive about all this, and I get he's going through this too – not physically (obviously) but emotionally. This surgery affects him in every way also. So, to heck with those "friends"…we all need to just figure out what and who is best for ourselves and be around the people that DO care about us."

I went online to read *aaall* about the problems that can arise AFTER you come home from this type of surgery…hemorrhaging, trips to the ER…I was freaked out! If nothing else, it made me realize the importance of doing nothing and resting. It dawned on me at 10:00 a.m. that it's the *first* time I didn't take any meds the second I got up! It's 10:45 a.m. now and I JUST took my Ibuprofen. Progress!

I expelled an inch-long suture. Damn, I sure hope that was *ready* to come out.

Mom called. I told her I feel abandoned by my friends. Now that I'm finally on the *other* side of this, there is zero concern.

It's okay to feel disappointed. It's natural to want your friends to rally around you.

I shouldn't be that surprised though, because this is what I went through when I had cancer and with the accident. I need to find a way to *not* be bothered by it nor waste what little energy I have on it.

I have Parkinson's. I tell *some* people about it. Do you think they ask how I'm doing? They don't.

I said, With the Parkinson's – that's going to be a *lifelong* thing you'll be dealing with. In my case, it's ONE event, one that I *will* come through *after* a period of recovery. I get it; people get busy with their own lives. *Dad* hasn't even asked me if I need anything. Not even once. I think I expect too much.

Nov 13

I read this on the hysterectomy website (paraphrasing):

A hysterectomy is a major life-changing event and is a milestone in your life that changes your future path. It provides perspective since in recovery you have a lot of time to reflect. Don't miss the lessons. Some may be big, some small but be open to the learning.

It makes so much sense! It IS a huge deal and with it, like my cancer journey, comes so many enlightening aspects. I AM paying attention and I DO embrace what I AM/WILL learn about myself. Today IS a milestone – two weeks post-op! I'm actually proud of myself for once. I *doubted* I could come through this. The surgery was a remedy, and now I hope the outcome is a *pain-free*, better life. I'm optimistic that this life course will ultimately lead to a better place.

I read this online, yet another celebrity who *doesn't* think before they speak: *"Not impressed by a body that hasn't bore a child."*

You *must* give birth to be awesome like her? Some of us who WANT to bear children but can't: she's not impressed with US? Someone, tell her to shut the fuck up. Someone commented: *"Women who can't/don't/won't have kids, you're beautiful, too."*

Tracy said his boss came up to him and handed him insurance forms and said, We need to discuss your wage. They may give him a raise.

I almost cried! That extra money, coverage…that'll mean EVERYTHING to us. To the core of every human being is the desire to be valued and appreciated. *You* give that to the people you work with, and the powers that be see that in you, Tracy. I'm *so* proud of you. **I** always knew what a decent human he is. It's just nice to see others are seeing it too.

I sneezed five times. Killer.

<u>Nov 16</u>

Dad came by to help with paperwork, to be a sponsor and help me get a Disability Tax Credit through Revenue Canada. It was stressful, lots of number-crunching, but if it helps in the end, then it's worth it.

In the evening, Dad calls. I talked to my accountant and she told me to not even think about going there. I don't feel comfortable with all the questions from the forms.

Is this the same accountant that told you Galaxy Securities was a scam?

I'm not talking about that. She said Revenue Canada is telling you to declare yourself *completely disabled,* and I will have no part in being a conspirator in your claiming to be disabled.

Huh? A conspirator? Why would you think I'm claiming to be something I am clearly not? In no way, shape or form would I EVER be declaring myself COMPLETELY disabled! How are you getting that?

Well, I'm just checking it out.

IT'S RETRO TO THE YEARS **2007-2010,** WHEN I **_WAS_** DISABLED! Therefore, it has ZERO to do with making any declarations about being CURRENTLY disabled. And I'm NOT claiming to be disabled NOW – I had an OPERATION. I am NOT claiming 2013!

My accountant says this is a scam.

This is being done through REVENUE CANADA! Revenue Canada is a scam? Wow, since when? I've done my due diligence – do you honestly believe I'd involve you in something shady? If I can get a few bucks from the Canadian Government from the time I had cancer and chronic pain, great! Free money!

My accountant says they better not be charging me any fees.

They're not! No fees! I WOULDN'T HAVE EVEN ASKED YOU FOR YOUR HELP IN DOING THIS IF IT WAS GOING TO COST YOU OR ME MONEY! I'm glad you asked questions, but your accountant *doesn't* know what she's talking about. This isn't some Mickey Mouse company that's trying to *take* our money; they're trying to GIVE ME MONEY BACK!!! I'm **_not_** disabled, and *I'm not claiming to be.* And I've never been asked TO claim **_permanent_** disability with this.

I just don't want to have any part of this.

Ok, how about we forget about YOUR part in this. I can do this WITHOUT your help. I'm currently ripping up your forms.

Oh, okay, good, do that.

And with that he believed all is right with the world, and we were cool.

I'm left wondering, What in our history of EVER have I shown him I get into shady things? Scams?

Tracy said, You're his daughter and yet he automatically thinks you're doing something underhanded.

And how is this helping me heal?! I think I ripped a few stitches getting stressed by him. I'm tired of this bullshit – don't help me!

Nov 18

I'm perplexed about Dad. He INSISTED on being there for me at surgery time. Hmmm, I've seen him a total of two to two and a half hours in almost the two-month period that he's been back in town. He's just one more person too wrapped up in their own life to bother with me. I wonder if the shoe was on the other foot, he'd be okay if **I** were too busy? Our relationship has just not been the same since he went to Penticton. I'm tired of trying to carve out a place for myself in his new life. I feel stabbed in the back for being their biggest cheerleader. I just never imagined *I'd* be whittled out of his life as I have been. He has a new family now. I have Tracy – I always have and I always will. It's a lonely place when you go through a major life-changing event and you look around you, and you're standing alone, even when everyone "said" they'd be there for you. Words. Cheap words. *Actions* are all that count in the end. ANYONE can *offer* support, encouragement, and friendship but actually *following through* is quite a different ball game. I feel hung out to dry. But they'll all be around once I'm *well*. This part, the *tough* stuff, people check out and are unavailable for because it's difficult. People are people; people are selfish and self-absorbed. I remember when I met new people who became friends after having cancer – Oh, I wish I knew you back then; **I** *would've* been there for you, **I'd** have done so much for you, **I'd** have helped you through it. Uh ya, sure you would've. The "after the fact" concern.

God, people suck.

Nov 19

So, let's get real here. Maybe I need to concern myself more with the fact that the decision to have children is finally *out of my hands* rather than concentrating on *why*. All the YEARS of trying to figure it out, how we'll raise our children, when is the right time; am I healthy enough; do we have the money; am I ready; would/could I be a good mother? And if we hadn't conceived yet, were we even supposed to? Maybe I NEVER had the capacity to get pregnant. I've never been pregnant so maybe I was not supposed to ever be able to. And now it's done. A chapter we have to accept and close. All the years I spent agonizing over it. And now we agonize in a different way – knowing we'll *never* have a family. Kind of pathetic – I'm 45, not 35, not 25…wishing things turned out differently.

Or do I? Is there a part of me that *is* relieved? Maybe a part is, the part that wants to put this surgery behind me and move forward with my life. I'm with a truly amazing partner. I think a part of me *always* knew I *shouldn't* ever be a parent. I never had that "maternal instinct." Well, with the fur babies I have, but that is different, to me. Maybe that was God's way of *ensuring* I wouldn't bother trying to have a kid. But we *did* try and we experienced roadblock after roadblock after roadblock. I saw the signs. Was it a coincidence I never wanted children, then when I did, I got cancer? I was *never* given the option to harvest eggs before chemo. Once I got over cancer and we were trying again with the fertility clinic – I got hit by a truck? Once I recovered from that, I saw an endocrinologist who said I have "markers" showing the chemo killed any chance of a pregnancy? And now *this*. A done deal.

But damn, Tracy would've made an amazing dad. I feel *I* robbed him of that opportunity. I can only hope he doesn't come to resent me for it. And all the times we spent talking about what we'd *name* our children. But it was fun to dream about names. This is the first time I realized that won't ever happen. I won't be naming any kids of mine. We prayed the kids *wouldn't* get MY nose. I always worried about that one. They'd have had Tracy's amazing blue eyes and they'd have had my dark hair. It was fun to dream about what they'd look like. We could speculate all we want – the *reality* is *none* of it did or will come to fruition. I feel relieved I don't have to live through the "wrong" scenario. I don't have to worry about what defective features or traits of mine they'd get. I don't have to fret over whether my own children would even *like* me. I don't have to be concerned about whether they'd turn out well-adjusted or messed up like me. There are so many mixed feelings – unbearable sadness, relief, heart-heavy, inconsolable, resentful, grateful…

It's like, the decision to have kids against the decision to be pain-free and feel healthy. WE chose pain-free, so now we have to live with that. Tracy chose *me. I* choose him and me. I hope it's worth it.

Tracy texted me – he got a $5/hr raise! This is going to make a HUGE difference. We needed this! I went from having a sad heart to an elated one. I hope these mood swings aren't forever.

Nov 20

Checkpoint for third week post-op: *"You may be crying, frustrated, having temper tantrums. May totally feel discouraged with your progress. Be patient and kind with yourself."*

Well, nice to know I'm right on schedule with the crying and frustration. I really *don't* want to talk to anyone today – I need to just be.

Nov 21

I dreamt about Levi and Kyle. My cousin was trying to get me to call them by their Hebrew names, like they go by now. I said, No, those aren't their *real* names. They were born Levi and Kyle and it's ridiculous to call them anything else. When I woke up, I thought calling them by their Hebrew names doesn't make them *different* people. They are who they are. You can't convince me otherwise.

Well, I've thought this before, but now it seems more "official" – *they* got to have kids, and *I* didn't. What kind of world let's *those* predators procreate and spread *their* DNA? Or to simply experience the joys and tribulations of parenthood? It seems a little wonky to me. For most of their lives…they got to get married, have children, live in a country they love, doing what they love… Me? I got to suffer. Abuse, car accidents, cancer, infertility, financial despair, surgery…It feels a bit *uneven.* I love my husband, I love our fur babies, I love our home…but unfortunately it feels like we've dealt with so much tragedy. I'm 45 and I don't even feel like my life has begun yet! I have felt since the day I was born that I've had to deal with adversity, and HAVE dealt with it all, but when do I get to start living the life I've always dreamt of? When do Tracy and I get to live out our dreams? We have fought for everything good that HAS come into our lives. But we aren't getting any younger. I can only hope and try to MAKE the next 45 years what WE want it to be. I'm done with all these "tests." We've built *plenty* of character, we've never taken things for granted, we appreciate a great many things, but now we just need some **_quiet_** living: unchaotic, joyful, peaceful, enriching, fulfilling, and inspiring living. I want to be productive and respected, to contribute in *some* way. I want to experience happiness! I want to be remembered for something *positive,* not just as that weird quiet person. That's *not* who I am. I'll have no children to carry on our name, or to leave DNA to. No one to leave a legacy to.

The idea of writing my story comes back to me. A book is forever, my life isn't.

Nov 26

Follow-up appointment day! The specialist asked how things have been. I discovered a stitch sticking out of my belly button so she ripped it out. I told her today was my first car ride and first day out at the grocery. I'm sore and dead tired! She examined me. It's healing nicely. She said many times, Don't forget, you just had MAJOR surgery – there is a reason we say it takes *six* weeks to heal; you're at *four*, give yourself a break. Let your body heal.
I do get impatient and wonder why things aren't healing quicker.
But you're not bleeding?
No, that stopped the day after surgery.
I want to see you again in January, unless you need to see me sooner in December.
I told Tracy about the appointment – I guess January will be my "okay, go ahead, resume your life" appointment. I suppose my pain is just from overdoing things.

Nov 27

Dad came over. It was not good.

I said, Just so you know, we might lose our house in six days. I was bawling. He had *no* reaction.

He starts, I'm almost 75, and I hopefully *still* have a few good years left. I'm done helping you and Tracy. Any money I DO have/get, I need for myself to live on. I want to enjoy my life, doing the things I want to. As soon as the weather gets better, I'll be heading back to Penticton. I have nothing left to give you.

As he was leaving, he offered, Just stay healthy.

Nov 28

I woke up crying. I've been crying since 6:45 a.m.; it's 9:00 a.m. Not only am I grieving the loss of my womb, time, and ability to have kids, but also the abandonment of my father and friends. It's like the SECOND I went for surgery, everyone disappeared. Dad *literally* disappeared from the hospital and then my life. Gone. He didn't stick around for me. He didn't stick around for Tracy. Being there for us and to not think of himself was too great. It's like we were good enough to hang around when he had no one else in his life. We were good enough *until* something/someone better came along. Now that he has his girlfriend – too busy, no time for us. Let me know what happens, keep me posted, he tells Tracy later. I saw him *three* days later. The next time I saw him was *four weeks* after that. Dad would be heartsick if Tracy and I ever did that to him. Devastated. Tracy said Dad's **oblivious**. Perfect word.

Tracy and I made latkes (potato pancakes) for Chanukah yesterday. It's the first time EVER that Dad missed out. I'm crying also because when Dad finally met the right woman, the parent part of his brain dislodged. He's so wrapped up in himself, her and her family, that he does me a *favor* and comes to the hospital for a half-hour. He may as well have said to me yesterday: I have nothing left to give you = I'm done being a parent, I'm done being there for you, I'm done sharing important holidays and events with you. DONE. And his actions back

417

it up, because he has a new family now, so it's no great loss to him. I had no idea stopping being my father was an *option*!

Mom told me, Your father was there for you for that time after the accident. It's remarkable how he was there for you. He simply dedicated his life to you during that time, so remember that.

I got out of bed and I see Tracy has prepared my coffee...and I see a card. A card! On the envelope he's drawn a Star of David and a *Dreidel* (a spin top). I bawled. I couldn't open the card because I couldn't see through the tears. Here I'm upset over Daddio issues and my amazing husband goes and buys me a Chanukah card! I was so touched. It was beautiful. It's just a clear reminder of *who* I need to focus on and *who* **is** there for me. It's my husband. My rock. He works such long days, comes home so tired, and he went out of his way to make Chanukah special for me.

Nov 29

I'm freaking out! I get out of bed this morning to go pee – pure blood. The blood is pouring out. It's dripping in a steady flow. When I wipe, a clot the size of a walnut comes out. What does this mean? I know the pain I've been feeling meant *something*! I know my body. I'm scared. I remember in my take-home literature from the hospital they say to call your surgeon if you have a clot "the size of a walnut." Oh my God. I do nothing about it. I finish up in the bathroom and go to the kitchen – I have to feed the cats. There is *another* card from Tracy propped on the coffee pot. The outside of the card made me cry: *"The light of Chanukah reminds us to have faith that miracles are on their way."* I open it up – there is a bank DEPOSIT RECEIPT for $2000! I started bawling. How did Tracy do this? He never, not once even, let on. A Chanukah miracle is right! I BELIEVE!

Nov 30

I told Tracy that I decided last night, for my health, to *not* engage in talking or texting with Dad. He has done nothing but hinder my recovery. He has checked out. Disengaged. Disinterested. He thinks the worst of both of us. We are now irrelevant to him. He never asked how my surgery follow-up went. I went through this huge event in my life and he was far too busy to bother or care, but he *did* manage to make me cry, upset me and stress me out, and more than likely rip a few stitches – his parting gift to me. I'm done. I feel better already. Brilliant decision!

Dec 2

I saw Dr. West – he completed the forms for me for Revenue Canada to get the tax credit. I called my surgeon's clinic when I got home regarding the blood clot. Did you go to Emerg?
No, I wasn't positive if this was cause for concern. I tend to minimize things.
The clot probably got lodged above a suture. Can you come in Friday?

Mom called. She kept asking me if Dad's still in town and helping out? So, I decided to let her in on what's been happening regarding him.
Wow, that's cold. He's probably trying to distance himself from you so it's easier to have his new life and relationship in Penticton. He thinks you're "out to get him" so now he feels justified in leaving.

Dec 4

My horoscope today: *Be okay with just being right about ongoing drama with a family member. You've handled it with grace and compassion. Better to be happy than prove your point.*

Tracy gets home and he's emptying his lunch box, but he has his back to me. He turns around and he's holding this brand-new Menorah (Chanukah candleholder). And he's *already* put all the candles in them. I could not believe my eyes. Did you MAKE that?! I started crying; of course, he did. It's stunning. So beautiful. So thoughtful. That's one of the *nicest* things *anyone* has EVER done for me. I was blown away. He's so busy at work and he made the time to do this – for me.

Dec 6

The specialist examines me quite thoroughly and says I'm still healing fine. Sometimes blood gets trapped from the surgery, then dislodges and comes out.

You're only five weeks out. Be easy on yourself. Don't be in such a rush to "get back to normal."

I showed her where the pain still is.

If you're still experiencing pain, come back and I'll order you an ultrasound. I still want to see you in the New Year.

Dec 7

We had decided to go to Tracy's company Christmas party tonight. I'm exhausted after showering and getting ready but looking forward to it. It was a real posh place downtown. It felt nice to get dolled up and out of my PJs and dress like a "normal" person. Great to put faces to names. I was talking with a lovely sales rep when it came, THE dreaded question…*So do you have kids?* Uh, no.

No kids? No.

She stared blankly at me and the conversation came to a screeching halt. Awk-ward! So, I finally offer, Nope, no kids, but I *do* have lots of animals! Always a safe topic.

Dinner was amazing: intimate, elegant, and a lovely gathering. I was really glad we went.

Later at home Tracy said to me, I don't take you or your love for granted. One day you may want to leave me or not love me forever.

WHAT?! Of course, I will love you forever! On the other hand, YOU may want to trade ME in for a healthier, newer model.

No, not ever.

Dec 13

I checked our bank account. Tracy got paid. He also got his contract pay AND Galaxy pay. I cried.

Lucky Friday the 13th! I feel like our lives are turning a corner. I can face just about anything, and I *have*, but with Tracy by my side, it makes it *all* worth it. I have him. I *really* have him, and he has me. It's always been US. And that's all we need.

Dec 31

I'm putting so much pressure on myself to get a job in the New Year. Mom said to do that when your body is ready. But we need the money. Catch-22.

Another thought, *There are no coincidences*. Why did I have to have surgery when we were in financially dire straits? The timing of everything is odd. Please, please, please, let 2014 be THE year for us. Make it so we can help others because we will be doing so well for ourselves.

Please.

2014

<u>Jan 8</u>
We are going to make this the best year yet! We know where we stand regarding kids, and we have a plan. So now we gotta keep focused on the good, keep the negative out and start enjoying our lives!
THIS is the beginning!

I'm still in so much pain, like a knife through my abdomen. There's some light bleeding as well. But I feel like I'm ready to actually work through some of this crap. We need to concentrate on the people who ARE and WANT to be in our lives. I started off by thinking about all the oblivious people in my life. Friends who *have* been through this surgery, but I've yet to hear from. "Good" friends I haven't heard from even once since surgery. Friends who put some sort of virtual "expiry date" on my recovery. There are those who HAVE bothered and have called or texted. They didn't make me guess if they cared or not. Then there's my father. I was never supposed to be part of his new life. My own parent. It almost killed him when I had cancer. He was devoted to me throughout the accident. He was single in those two scenarios. Now I go through this…and he doesn't care so much; and he's not single. It's inconvenient to have a daughter now. He discarded both Tracy and me and hasn't looked back. Maybe he's realizing there'll be no grandchildren, so why stick around?

But you know – I REFUSE to let *any* of those people have so much power over me. I can count on *one* hand the people who supported me through this time. And yet, here I am. I am still standing. They haven't knocked me down and I am certainly not out! Plus, I've had more support from my <u>**pets**</u> than I have from most people. I have proven I can come out the other side of a major life event – *without* these people at my side, and I'm okay. I'm more than okay. I should write an open letter to the people who have drifted through my life, and they can certainly keep on going. They stopped along the way when *their* lives hit rough patches, then kept on moving when things got better for them. We are the pit stop along their road to better things. We are good enough friends until they get "back on their feet." Most of them disappeared with no explanation, simply vanished. So, this is the next phase of my life. Continue to use my voice and move through the rest of my life with dignity and my head held high.

Jan 9

My follow-up appointment with the specialist. So, are you feeling back to normal?

I laughed. Actually, I'm still wondering when I will feel like this surgery was a *good* idea?

The recovery part is tough on people. She examines me. Oh…well…there's a piece of tissue at the back that *isn't* healing and it's raw, and could cause bleeding.

Is that why I have pain in that area?

No, that wouldn't cause pain.

So why DO I have pain? Is that normal at this point and it's just part of the healing?

Well, no. I've taken out your tubes, but your ovaries are still in there. Maybe I'll send you for an ultrasound just so we can be sure. I'm putting silver nitrate on that piece of tissue. It'll break it down and you'll get rid of it.

Jan 16

I realized the "mystery" of our "friends" and some "family" – WE don't give up on *them*, THEY give up on *us*.

I've been bleeding since the cauterizing, I'm in so much pain. It feels like a knife going through my right side, stabbing pain. It took my breath away.

Got the ultrasound results today. It showed a cyst forming on my left ovary and the endometriosis could be causing pain as well. The doc suggested pain medication. She gave me two months' worth of free samples and a prescription, if it helps. Make an appointment for two months from now and I will order another ultrasound to monitor the growth of the cyst.

I don't know if I feel better from this appointment or not. I guess it's good to know there IS a reason for my continued pain, though. I came home and I cried at a Pampers commercial.

Jan 17

It occurred to me maybe the *ovaries* need to go. Maybe just "managing" the pain from here on ain't the way to go. It's no way to live. I may be better off having gone on hormone replacement therapy. It never occurred to me I'd need *another* surgery. I really want to get on with life. I don't want the constant "monitoring," ultrasounds, and watching…and waiting. Why keep an eye on things when we've been down this road and we *already know* where this leads? I'm so reluctant to take this pain medication. I read up on it – there's horrid side effects. Replace one problem of pain for a dozen others, on the chance it *might* help. I'm so confused. I did some cleaning and cleared my head. It's NOT worth it to me. All those extra nuggets to deal with. The two to three months to see *if* it works. And then what? It's crazy-making. Manage, manage, manage. Until menopause? Really? I need to talk to Tracy about all this. I need to just DO this and not have to deal with this in a month, a year, two years…

Tracy came home. You okay?

No, I'm not. I told him about all my thoughts today. He was fine with ALL of it. And you'd be okay with me having *more* surgery?

Why wouldn't I be? Why should you be in pain?

I thought you'd suggest I TRY the meds anyway.

No way, not if *you're* not okay with it – I support you.

Wow. I guess I need to go talk to the doctor now. I feel sooo relieved!

I received a letter from Revenue Canada. They say I AM eligible for the Disability Tax Credit! Some good news!

Jan 21

I was finally able to make a doctor's appointment – for February 12; she's out of town until then. I guess there is a reason for everything. I have more time to process? What if I have to go through another major surgery? Who is going to be around then? We've fallen off people's radar. Everyone "meant" to call or visit. But they didn't.

Jan 23

The National Benefit Authority (NBA) called – congratulations! They gave me all the invoicing info for when I *do* get the money. I can see your check is being issued *next week*. I'm just so grateful. And I did it *without* Dads help. Scam, my ass.

Jan 29

I woke up thinking I should get another tattoo with the initials of the daughter I *won't* have – CMK. It sounds weird, but I planned on getting my kids' names above my Hebrew name on my left ankle anyway. I'll keep thinking about that one.

Tired. Emotional. Stressed. In pain. I'm trying to remember WHY I had this surgery. My health, right!

Feb 1

At the grocery checkout, the cashier was talking about how she's having her first grandbaby. She asked Tracy and me, Do *you* have kids? I kept my eyes on the debit machine, ignoring her. Tracy politely answered, No, but we would have welcomed it.

I thought, That is the most *perfect answer*! I like that.

She said, You're better off, they're a lot of work.

Spoken by a person who DOES have kids.

Feb 2

I had a deeper epiphany about my father, some clarity. I realized it was okay for him to be in our life so long as he didn't have anyone. He met someone and then suddenly there's no room for the both of us – he *had* to choose. He *didn't* choose me. He disowned his sons and now he's lumping *me* in with *them*, in the same basket. Nice. Dad, you are more like your sons than you think. Is it just a big ol' coincidence that the second I tell him I'm having this surgery and won't be able to have children/give him grandchildren, he doesn't stick around? Are you purposely burning your bridges? Burn away. No father that I know, who supposedly loves their daughter and would never hurt her, would do what you've done. You will be alone in the end. And I'm done with you. We have successfully been phased out.

Feb 7

Tracy and I don't take each other for granted. There is no certainty in anything, and we know things can change in a second. When you're with someone as long as we've been together, it's important to keep making sure the other knows and feels loved. So, we took our *lovefest* to the *lobsterfest* at Red Lobster. We used gift cards from two years ago. It felt normal to go out and dine! We had to wait for a table so we sat in the lounge and ordered these monster Caesars. I said, I'd say I'm a "sure thing," but I don't know if I *can*. We laughed. It's good to laugh. You need to keep a sense of humor.

Feb 12

How did the meds work for you? the doctor asked.

They didn't. I struggled with whether to take them or not and I chose *not* to. But the pain is getting progressively worse. I can't do this until menopause.

We discussed where the pain is and when it happens.

I said, I know what you're getting at – it's *not* just a monthly ovulating thing. There is pain more than just a couple of days out of the month.

It's possible it could be chronic pain and that's something surgery *doesn't* fix. You could try acupuncture; otherwise, there is this Lupron injection. It will make you feel menopausal, but if the pain is related to endometriosis, the pain goes away. The Lupron will essentially shut down your ovaries and prevent estrogen production.

So, what is the point of my leaving my ovaries in? What's the difference?! The cysts HAVE grown back, and we keep "monitoring" them? We did that already for four months, and then I had surgery! I'm glad you DID leave them in; I have no regrets. We tried that, and it's *not* working. If I'm going to take meds that put me in menopause *anyway*...I'd rather deal with hormone treatment than with this pain.

My concern is doing another surgery and you *still* have pain; then we've taken out your ovaries for no good reason. I just need you to know, if I take them out, and your pain *doesn't* improve, it's a possible scenario.

I understand there are no guarantees. I understand there is a chance after a second surgery that I could *still* have pain. However, I'd be shocked if the pain DIDN'T go away. It's too *coincidental* that my pain is EXACTLY where my ovaries are.

I know you know your own body; I'm just trying to get you to consider other options first. If you want your ovaries removed, I'm happy to facilitate that for you. But try the injection for a month; if your body can tolerate it, we'll give you another month after that. If it doesn't, we'll discontinue it.

Is that the same injection before my surgery? Yes.

So, we ALREADY know it *won't* do anything.

But that was for the bleeding.

Ya, and *nothing* changed.

At any time, you want to bail on this plan, you just tell me. We could also book you for surgery, give you the few months' trial, if it's *not* working, at least you have a surgery date booked. If it *does* work, we can always cancel the surgery.

She left and came back with the prescription for the injection and said I have to come in and get it done. I'll give you a surgery date *then*.

I came home and read anything I could on this injection. I'm so confused. It says IF it *relieves* the pain, the ovary removal is *good*; therefore, the Lupron is to see if the pain *will* stop. Everything in me says NOT to take it. I feel I'm going in circles again. When Tracy got home, I filled him in. He said I should take the injection since I have to wait anyways. If you have to wait a few months for surgery anyway, you may as well see if the injection does anything.

True. My brilliant husband.

Feb 26

So, I finally decided to do the injection and picked it up on Sunday. Thank God I have coverage *this* time! I went to see my doctor. I was in baby hell! Let's take a woman who JUST had a hysterectomy, is possibly facing having her ovaries removed, and dealing with the fact she will *never* have children, and plunk her amid newborns and parents bringing their babies in for their first checkups. Are you kidding me?! The nurse brought me to an exam room and administered the injection in my butt. The doc came in. How are you?

About the same since the last time I saw you.

Did you have the injection?

Yes. But I'm not happy about it; I did it for YOU. She laughed.

Well, good, I do want to feel like we've exhausted *all* our options.

Are we booking a surgery date?

No. Come back and see me in a month and I PROMISE you, I'll book the surgery date THEN. I just want to give this one month, and then go from there.

I've talked to my husband a lot about this, and it just seems *inevitable*.

There may be *other* reasons for your pain – like scar tissue in the abdomen.

Yes, you're right, it *could* be. I still find it too fluky that the pain is *exactly* in my ovaries. They throb and feel like they're going to burst. Don't get me wrong – in no way am I *eager* for a second surgery, it just feels that's where I'm headed, and I don't want to keep "monitoring" this. I GET there are no guarantees.

So, I'll see you in a month.

I laughed and shook my head. What else was I going to do, cry? And with that, I left. I've been petrified to take this injection. Now that I've done it, I'm not loving it. I have no clarity with this. I'm so confused.

Feb 28

I'm still waffling over the second surgery, to have my ovaries removed or not. I can't live with this pain, but now I'm scared of *other* problems stemming from *surgical menopause*. Or the pain not going away even *after* another surgery. I need a crystal ball, stat! Everyone is different and while it's *helpful* to read other people's experiences, it's still no way to know how it will affect ME – until I do it. Sigh. Too many decisions.

Mar 8

Okay, so my body is "tolerating" the injection, there are no horrible side effects, so by all intents and purposes, we could assume this is how my body will react by having the ovaries out and going into menopause. I *could* be fine!

Our business has taken another turn. We are *transferring* our team to another financial agent for one year. It's a win-win all around. Our business continues, but someone else can be there on a day-to-day basis for the team.

Mar 17

I feel like I'm searching for a lifeline. Not that anyone can make this decision FOR me, but I desperately need to talk to someone who knows *exactly* what I've gone through, continue to go through, and what I *will* be going through. I feel alone. Like when I had cancer, when I was hit by a truck… At the time it just feels like *I'm* the only one who had gone through it. I keep reaching out on sites; it helps to a point. I need to feel like I'm making the *right* decision that this is all routine, and I'll get through it. That it'll all get *better*.

Mar 26

So, surgery, is that what we've decided to do?
Well, I'm here to discuss if that's the most viable option. I took your injections – I felt no different. Nothing. The pain didn't change.
She asked me to describe the pain. Does anything make it *worse*?
Nothing makes it worse or better – the pain is just *always* there.

That was my concern. I just don't feel convinced it'll be resolved after I take your ovaries out. It could be nerve pain. Did we do the nerve test? No. She does it. We rule it out. Any hot flashes? No. No?

Isn't that a GOOD thing? You said if my body tolerates the injection, and I've had no reaction, isn't it fair to say...I just don't know why we're assuming the surgical menopause will be so horrible.

As if that was the first time she had considered that outcome: Ya, you might be fine.

The hysterectomy DID what it was supposed to – I stopped bleeding! You merely go off what your patients tell you – YOU'VE never had a hysterectomy, have you? No.

You were surprised I was still in pain, yet the ultrasound PROVES I have more cysts – there was a REASON. I'm *terrified* to have another surgery...but I KNOW my body.

Okay! I'm happy to do the surgery. I just want you to be aware if your pain doesn't improve after the surgery, then...

You'll be the LAST person I tell!

You HAVE TO tell me!

I have *agonized* over this decision; I'm *not* taking this lightly.

Did we discuss your family history?

Yes, that there is ovarian, cervical, and breast cancer.

I did not know that. Ya, okay, it makes sense. I'm already filling out the consent form. You still have the endometriosis too – I'll try to take out as much as possible while I'm in there. I'll use the same incisions. It might not be until summer.

Okay, then I guess I have LOTS of time to think about all this.

I feel very calm now. The decision has been made.

Apr 7

OMG, OMG, OMG. My doctor's office just called. They have *April 22* open for surgery. That's like THE only day I *can't* – I have an oncology appointment that day.

No prob, we also have April 25.

I went silent. Shock...horror...relief? Okay.

This second surgery will eliminate any *proof* I am a woman! And it makes me 100% unable to bear children. But I DO have this amazing man by my side. There are still so many unknowns – job, life after this…. I've *never* been a go-with-the-flow person. It's hard to be all *flowy* when my life changes forever on April 25. I hope I get to experience *stress-free* living before *I* die. I also hope to make peace with this body before I die.

Apr 8
Starting this week, I've experienced a hot flash and I had a night sweat yesterday. I think the ol' ovaries may just be shutting down on their own. A hot flash hit, nausea came over me, and I had to sit on the floor where I stood. It came over me so fast. Good God.

Apr 22
I felt totally okay about going to the cancer appointment today; I'm here by myself too. That dread and sick feeling whenever I come – *wasn't* there. Nine years in and I FINALLY feel okay about it. No thoughts of gloom and doom; just a routine checkup. The oncologist comes in and announces, You're still cured. He asked me questions regarding the hysterectomy and upcoming surgery. Okay, good luck on Friday. I guess I'll see you in a year.

I'm *still* feeling good about the decision to have another surgery. The sooner I do this, the better I'll feel in the long run. I told Tracy we had 100 kids in a *previous life* together and in THIS life, it's meant to just be the two of us.

Apr 25
I'm a bit anxious driving to the hospital with Tracy. I get to the unit and into a gown. My doctor came to see me in the hallway outside of the OR. She says she'll be doing a bilateral laparoscopic oophorectomy with resection of endometriosis. As I lay in the operating room, I had some doubts and was feeling nervous. I had both my arms spread out and strapped down, my gown lifted to my chest with a blanket over me…it doesn't get any more vulnerable than that! I just kept repeating

over and over to myself, This is my new lease on life, this is all going to go smoothly. Then I switched to:
MY LIFE CHANGES FOR THE BETTER TODAY! MY LIFE CHANGES FOR THE BETTER TODAY!
MY LIFE CHANGES FOR THE BETTER TODAY! MY LIFE CHANGES FOR THE BETTER TODAY!

They had trouble waking me up in recovery. They couldn't get my heart rate down and my blood pressure was very high – they were quite concerned. They brought Tracy into recovery, which is *not* allowed, but they did, and my blood pressure finally came down. Mission accomplished – thanks, honey bunny. There was lots of pain right off the bat. The pain was too much so they kept giving me morphine. They went *way* over the maximum amount so I was essentially OD'ing. They changed my pain meds, put me on oxygen and I finally stabilized. They gave me ibuprofen, then Tylenol. That *finally* took the edge off. I had three nurses look at my chart and say, Uh oh, you've had a lot of narcotics; no one *ever* gets *that* much. My doctor came to see me. She agreed that I had A LOT of drugs in my system and they may need to keep me overnight to monitor that – we'll keep you here until you're stable. Then she told me how things went – she *couldn't* find my left ovary; it was *behind* my bowel and it was FULL of cysts. Gee, no wonder I had pain! She was finally able to remove both ovaries. She also said the scar tissue and adhesions from the hysterectomy were *abundant*. It's not an issue with laparoscopic surgery, but again I seem to be the exception to every rule. Again, a *reason* for all the pain I was experiencing! She even said she was *very* surprised by how much scarring there was. The endometriosis on the bladder was so dense, she could not remove it without wrecking it, so she cauterized all of it, but without ovaries, I won't be producing anymore and it *should* go away. I have four incisions. She will send me home with a prescription for estrogen – it's up to me if I choose to take it. After *four hours* in recovery, my pain stabilized and they brought me back to the Day Unit. Tracy kept feeding me water so I'd go pee. When I finally did get up to pee – I was light-headed, nauseous, and three incisions bled. They gave me Gravol in my IV and then I felt I was okay to go home (with my doctor's permission).

On the way home, I gushed blood out of my belly button incision, through my shirt. The incisions are bigger than last time. I got settled into bed, took Gravol and a sleeping pill while Tracy ran out to the pharmacy. While he was gone, I got up to go pee and I puked! Tracy came home; we re-bandaged my belly button, took some Tylenol 3s and called it a night.

See, I *knew* I was right, *I know my body*. There was lots going on in there that was causing pain. I'm guessing my surgeon's "concerns" were probably alleviated after SEEING all that WAS going on in there, the cause of all the pain she *didn't* think was there. I now have *zero doubt* that this was the best thing I could've done for myself. I won't second-guess myself again! That 2% of doubt I felt, gone! I'm 2000% relieved I made the *right* choice. Can you imagine if we HAD left it, no surgery? Holy crap! I was doubting the surgery even as I lay in the operating room ready to go under. All that wasted anxiety. I'm just glad it turned out this way. To be on THIS side of it now…I'm just so relieved and justified! Me and drugs – they just don't work! I wonder what happened in a previous life that they don't work in this one? This time feels opposite with the pain – last time was all inner pain, with *no* incision pain. This time it's *all* incision pain. Normal.

Apr 29
June 10 is my follow-up appointment. There's bruising above my belly button. Intense pain. I'm not taking the Tylenol 3; I'm sucking it up. Tomorrow is six months since the hysterectomy and 10 years in our house! Mom is talking about moving to Toronto. I'm pretty excited about that. I don't have to worry about going to Israel – *ever*! Mom wants to call my father regarding my surgery. No, no point. He doesn't hear me, he sure won't listen to *you*, his EX! Right.

May 4

I'm cranky. All my "close" friends haven't even once asked me how I'm doing. It's just another day. Nothing changes with people. I feel like everyone knows EVENTUALLY I'll get better, and they will speak to me *then*. I'd never do that. Two surgeries, six months apart. I'm a strong woman! I don't need anyone not willing to give me support and friendship. Fuck 'em.

May 11

Mother's Day. I'm sending greetings to people who haven't even asked me how I'm doing since my surgery. People aren't THAT busy. For the first time I thought of something in a *different* way. I'm the queen of worst-case scenarios. I imagine the worst so that the reality of things and the way things ACTUALLY turn out seem manageable and better. I got to thinking that thinking about the worst-case scenario is *negative energy*. I'm putting it out there, all that bad stuff. It doesn't "prepare" me; it only puts those horrible thoughts out there into the universe! Instead, I should try expecting the BEST outcome, to plan for everything TO work out. I *never* thought of *that* before. Huh.

Lesson of the day: Stop being Johnny Raincloud and be more *optimistic*!

May 21

It was 3:00 a.m. when I heard an "explosion" type sound, then a *crash*. Tracy ran out to see what it was. All I heard was, God no, no, no, no…The saltwater fish tank blew. He was scrambling to get the fish into *some* water. It was pandemonium. Flooding of the dining room, with water cascading down the stairs, the basement floor, through the ceiling. What a fucking mess. I couldn't *not* help. I didn't do myself any favors. Pain. It was 4:30 a.m. when we finally finished cleaning up. Tracy went to work; I crashed and went to bed. One out of ten fish survived. I need a vacation.

May 22

I cut my finger and foot on the broken glass; I suppose I didn't realize last night. I called our insurance and started a claim. They will send someone to assess the damage.

The support of people is *under*whelming. A text? A bowl of soup? If they put an *ounce* of effort they put into looking at their Facebook…If I dropped dead today, they'd all be like, We loved her so much! In YOUR time of need, I wish you all to feel as alienated as you've had me feeling. Shame on all of you. Such little effort it would take to stop thinking about yourselves for a *second* and think of someone *else*. You make zero effort while I'm alive, but I would probably get flowers or a card in death. Or not. People can't even be bothered *then* either. Oh, there was a funeral? Damn, it took me a month to remove my head from my ass and see what's happening in the world out there. You mean *other* people have problems too? Wha?
I get a text from a *friend*: Sorry, you got lost in the shuffle.
It's always nice to hear you've been forgotten. That's my favorite.

June 10

I had my follow-up from surgery. She examined my belly but not inside. Well, there are no other organs in there *I* can deal with, all your lady parts are gone so I *can't* help you with anything more. Good luck, my friend.
Huh? I was BAFFLED! Dropping me like a hot potato, really?
There IS a doctor in the clinic here who deals in chronic pain. Would you want to see him now? YES!
A nurse comes in to get more info about the surgeries and pain. How many children do you have?
I don't have any.
You didn't *want* any?
Yes, I *wanted* them, but I had cancer.
I don't understand.
The chemo made me infertile.
I see.

The *real* doctor came in. A very nice man, Dr. Nepal. He pressed on my belly in different spots and said, I found the source of your pain; it's a hernia.

Is that the case for the right side as well?

He checks. Yup, there's a hernia there too. He gave me four trigger point injections (TPI). He told me I'll need injections twice a week and needs to send me for an ultrasound right away.

I spend *five minutes* with this new doctor and he's *already* helped me more than the other one in a year! Holy shit.

The injections will help break down scar tissue. He gave me the requisition for the test. Tell them my name, they'll get you in *right away*. Come to the office on Thursday and see me for your next injections.

That's in two days.

Yes, I'll get you in. Just so you know, there is a two-year waiting list to get in to see me. If it wasn't for your doctor asking me to see you, you would not have gotten this time. I won't give up on you. I CAN help you.

I cried. Did I luck out or what!? To get this man's help, I was dropped and then I was scooped up; it was serendipitous. I feel blessed.

June 12

I went to see my new, wonderful doctor. I asked, So, what *caused* these hernias?

It's from your surgery; she had to dig pretty deep and on angles.

Yes, my ovary was hiding behind my bowel.

It's *not* a coincidence that the hernias are right at the incision sites.

SO validating! He gave me two injections and wants me to come every Monday and Thursday. I went for a few groceries after – I was in crazy pain. With every step I lost my breath. Burning, bursting, stabbing pain.

June 24

My honey bunny's *50th* birthday! We had a lot of people over. His birthdays are always pretty special. I had a bit to drink and was crying to a friend: He's 50, he could STILL have a family, with a *different* wife. There is nothing wrong with HIM. *I* can't have children.

No, no, he loves you too much.

He COULD though. What is the point of going through these surgeries? There's nobody to pass *anything* on to. Why try to get better? Tracy can do better. I'm holding him back. Tracy wanted kids, I can't give him that, and I have nothing to offer anymore.

You know people love you.

Silence.

July 21

I told the doc about that *bursting* feeling I get.

You have *another* hernia. Does it feel like it's tearing?

Kinda. It takes my breath away. It's happened a number of times.

Yup, it's a hernia. He suggested I try platelet-rich plasma injections (PRP) – it breaks up scar tissue. Oh, and it's $500 an injection. Your bloodwork shows your adrenal glands are only working at 20%.

Well, that would explain the fatigue.

You are deficient in vitamin D, magnesium, cortisol and testosterone. We will test for estrogen and progesterone in ten weeks. The bloodwork shows you are in FULL menopause.

Just to hear those words. It's official.

I went grocery shopping after. I'm feeling these emotions rise up in me. I'm choking back tears and was going to leave my cart and flee. I wiped away the tears and kept on. I'm in menopause. It feels so *final*.

Aug 10

I get to cross off a bucket-list item – our neighbours Dave and Erin are taking us to the Stampeders game, and we're staying in the VIP Suite! We took a *private* elevator to the suite. OMG. I couldn't get over it. I took a picture of the *elevator*. The doors opened and my jaw dropped: beautiful seats, tables of food, air conditioning, bars, bathrooms… We found our section overlooking the 50-yard line. I couldn't stop thanking Dave for inviting *us*. None of us were ready to call it a night, so we went to the pub. By the way, Calgary won 38–17! The icing on the cake of an amazing, unforgettable evening! God, I love football! I guess this is me living my life, finally.

Aug 13

We went to the hospital for Tracy's dad's biopsy on his lung. I did so much walking I was in tears from the pain. I had to put sunglasses on to hide the tears streaming down my face. The doc spoke to Tracy privately and told him he thinks it's lung cancer, but they probably got it in time, so he'll get surgery and be done with it; he's getting a CT scan tomorrow. To pass the time Tracy's parents asked me if I've heard from my father. No.

Tracy said, He *doesn't* want to be part of our life; he hasn't spoken to Sari since after her *first* surgery.

Is he in town? I dunno.

I was thinking, I've lost one father and the other is sick. Tracy's really had a lot to deal with – his mom had cancer, his dad had a stroke, I had cancer, our accidents, his brother-in-law passed, my surgeries, and everything else – and now his dad again.

Aug 19

I went to bed thinking about how I never have been, nor ever will experience being pregnant. I had two possible "false alarms" the whole time Tracy and I have been together. But they were never anything, just late periods. I could go round and round about whether I'd have been a good mother or not. We'll never actually know. So last night I dreamt I was pregnant. I was happy. Tracy was over the moon. I was healthy and about five to six months along. At least I can have the things I'll never have, *in my dreams.*

I asked Mom if she told *them* about her move to Toronto?

Of course. They said nothing negative. They just wondered *why* I wanted to be closer to *you.*

Uh, *that's* not negative? I only ask because I want to know if they've been *helping* you pack.

Yes, they have been helping.

Aug 25

The doctor said to Tracy's dad, There's good news and bad news; it's lung cancer. The *good* news is it *hasn't* spread to the lymph nodes. You'll need surgery. Any questions?

Tracy leans forward like he's going to say something…and keeps going. The doc catches him. Tracy's eyes roll back into his head and the doctor lays him back on the exam table. He starts convulsing. He's not responding to us calling his name. Nothing. They ask his parents to leave the room. I stay. Tracy's eyes *finally* open; I thought he was dead. He's looking confused. He's drenched in sweat. They take his blood pressure and put a cold cloth on his forehead. They give him juice and cookies. Tracy just keeps looking at me. Are *you* okay?

I am *now*. I thought you were dead. I was scared. We agreed **I'd** go first. We were here for your dad and you stole his thunder.

On our way home Tracy says that the news of hearing his dad has lung cancer caused him to pass out. Then randomly he says, August 27/68 was the *best* day of my life.

I said, No, April 4.

No, August 27/68 – the day the love of my life was born. Who knew *that* day a Yid (Jew) was born in Montreal, and I'd meet her.

Aug 28

Tracy came home; we were relaxing and he's about to go into the hot tub. He gets a call. I gotta go! My mom called and said I have to get over there ASAP.

Did your mom sound like she was crying? Yes.

I went with him. Privately, his mom tells us the PET scan results show the cancer has gone into his bones; therefore, surgery is out. The surgery is way too extensive and he *wouldn't* survive it. We went in and joined the others. Tracy says to his dad, What's going on?

I don't want to talk about it.

So, we talked about it *around* him. His dad finally says, It's done. The doctor even said *nothing* can be done.

Tracy said, There's always SOMETHING, don't give up. You've *got to* fight this.

I'll do whatever the doctor tells me to do.

Tracy's mom thanked him for not fainting this time.

At home, Tracy's clearly shaken. Terminal lung cancer – oh man.

Aug 31

I'm just feeling so blah; my head is so full. I'm thinking about how *age* is just a number. I seem to have let my age limit me. I feel there is no point in planning or making dreams come true because I'm too old and unhealthy to bother. I have to change my way of thinking. People *older* than me are accomplishing so much more; I limit myself. I keep thinking everything's *too late* to try. Just now I realized *it's not*. It IS a number. I'm still me. I need to plan. I need to make Tracy's and my dreams come true – until my last breath.

Sept 10

I was scared to tell Tracy I had a lump in my neck, but I told him. He looked so worried. I went for an ultrasound and X-rays. Dr. Nepal looks at the ultrasound results. In light of your history, I think we should biopsy it. My uncle is a retired surgeon. I'm sending you to see him.

I went to bed tonight and these thoughts kind of stopped me dead in my tracks. It hit me; I will *never* have a child of mine look up to me in *any* regard, or respect *anything* I've done. To *never* have offspring that would or could say, *I'm proud of you, Mom. My mom has been through a lot and I'm proud of her. I have such a strong mother and I admire her.* I'm 46 now. There are no children or others to say, Hey, she really did something special, people looked up to her. It's just so disheartening. I'm feeling emotional and all over the place.

Sept 29

The uncle-surgeon looked at my lump and says, Oh ya, it's *a lot* bigger than I thought. Is it bothering you?

No, not per se, but it is growing and my history with lymphoma...
You will have a *scar* if I remove it.
I don't care about that! (What is with these doctors and scars!)
I'm going to give you a local anaesthetic.
I'm thinking, I met this man two minutes ago and now he's doing a *mini surgery* on me, *in his office*. Is that weird? I didn't feel much, mostly pressure. There are six stitches in.

Our neighbour Jim's having surgery to remove a blockage in his intestines, 30cm worth. Man, if it's not one thing...all at once.

Oct 7
The sutures are *not* ready to come out yet; come back Friday.
I changed the bandage when I got home – it *doesn't* look great. There are one-inch-long stitch threads everywhere. Yuck. The *good* news is he said it's NOT lymphoma.

Tracy's Dad starts chemo in two days. He said it's better than doing nothing.

Oct 27
My father left a message; he sounded *angry*. So now I'm *supposed* to call back ASAP? It's been *11 months*. Oh, there *was* the day he dropped off our cat crate – no note, no call, nothing, just the crate. Apparently major surgery *isn't* an important enough reason to warrant keeping in touch. He has no clue what has been happening in our lives. I don't believe he *even* cares to know. Discarded like garbage. To give so much of ourselves because we loved him. He was interwoven into *every* facet of our lives. He made his choice. He treated *me* worse than I'd witnessed him treat his *tenants* who screwed him over. I just feel sick to my stomach. Maybe I'll take 11 months to answer. Tracy said, Just call him and get it over with. Tell him you're still recovering from your *second* surgery.
And share details of my life? YOUR dad is what's important now. What *he* wants is irrelevant.

He could just be reaching out. Just call him.

I called. What's up?

I sold my house. The worst thing *you* ever said to me was *sell your house and live off it*. YOU said that.

Huh? I did *not* TELL you to sell your house. YOU said you were going to sell your house, *not me*. YOU brought it up. If anything, TRACY told you to KEEP the house as a good *investment*. And really, that's the WORST thing? What YOU'VE done is far worse!

Nothing is ever your fault.

I could say the same. You picked your girlfriend over family.

Why did YOU stop talking to ME?

I had surgery, where was your fatherly concern? I *cried* to you, in my house, *four days* after MAJOR SURGERY, that we could lose our house in six days.

What surgery?

What surgery?! You don't even remember I had surgery?! For months and months before, you said you wanted to be there for me, to come into town and be there when I have surgery.

I bought you flowers, so I did *something* right.

So, you *remember* the flowers but not WHY you brought them? YOU WERE AT THE HOSPITAL WITH ME! You CAME to the hospital and was there while I was being admitted! Are you calling me a liar? I'M the liar?

Yes. Have a good life.

You too.

Click.

Wow.

That was some logic. Selling his house is MY fault? He blacked out my entire surgery? So much blame, no responsibility, pointing fingers. Oh ya, how many kids do you have? And how many do you talk to? And all your "family" in Montreal? You're currently speaking to…? Right, NO ONE. They have ALL wronged YOU. I KNEW he wasn't just "reaching out." I guess *his* truth is the ONLY truth. How convenient. Zero recall. He never even *tried* to apologize for "forgetting" my surgery. He just said, Oh, that's how you want to remember it? What am I dealing with here? Something isn't firing on all cylinders. His "reality" is a little – no, *a lot* – skewed. I'm sure there is hospital video footage that can actually place *him* there. Nurses and patients that he spoke to. But I'M lying. Who would lie about that?

He can't hear what anyone else is saying. He's so busy thinking of the *next* thing HE'S going to say, he misses everything else. If you're talking, you're not listening. Maybe it's a GOOD thing I didn't pass those bat-shit crazy genes down to a kid.

Oct 30

Tracy's dad has his second round of chemo today. It kinda puts all that stupid shit from before in perspective. THIS is what's important, not the rantings of someone who forgets who I am. Mom's coming next week, then moving to Toronto. We are so excited. Tracy and I were talking about Galaxy Securities. He's really *done* with it, he's SO tired of making a financial plan for someone and they take it somewhere *else*, tired of relying on others for our livelihood.

Nov 4

I see I have a voicemail but no number on the ID. It's *him*. He sounds more like "himself."

Message: *I've had some time to think about our last conversation. I'd like a chance to further discuss things, to talk again. Have a good day.*

Hmmm, another chance to degrade, disrespect, and devalue me? He threw it all away and for what? Was it worth it? Last time it was *bitter, angry father. Who* is it going to be today? So…"have a nice life" *until* you need to get something *else* off your chest? You'd think I'd feel RELIEVED he was being "nicer" in his voicemail; I'm not feeling relieved. I'm supposed to, what, stop everything for you? Accommodate YOU? A courtesy, return call? I know he thinks he renders some sort of priority in my life and I'll drop everything. Nope, not even close. I've got my mom coming for a visit.

<u>Nov 5</u>

Message: *Okay, ah, it's your father, second time I called. I'll leave it up to you. If you want to call me back, fine. Ball is in your court.*

I have *lots* going on here and he's clueless. I went out for some groceries. He calls *again*. I answer.

Hello, I just wanted to go over a certain thing. You said I *didn't* call you when you were sick. It was when you were bleeding.

I had a hysterectomy.

Right. I kept asking how your medication was working. You got home; I came over with flowers.

So, you DO remember? I went on to explain to him our situation. We are *not* living high on the hog; we gave up Galaxy Securities; and the debt is mounting; and Tracy works three jobs while I'm NOT working.

You *don't* owe me a penny; I'm forgiving you for that. I *didn't* LEND you the money. *It's a GIFT.* I don't need to carry around the anger. You don't need the added pressure. I hope things turn around for you.

Now that *that* is settled, how are you?

I hemmed and hawed.

You don't want to tell me?

I'm not good, not good at all. I'm still recovering.

For what it's worth, my heart goes out to you for that.

What would make you even question us? You said I *lied* about having surgery!

I never said that.

What in my 46-year history with you would make you think I'd lie to you? What do I have to gain by that?

Let me be clear. Dorothy *wasn't* chosen over you. I don't want another five years to go by without speaking.

I've said everything I need to. I don't plan on rehashing this over and over.

I'm done with it too. Okay, so be well, Sari.

I filled Mom in when I got home. It sounds like your father *really* heard you.

Nov 9

I see my father has left a voicemail: *Hi Sari, just wondering how you're doing, how you're feeling?*

I could hardly believe it. So, I called him back. I shared more about my hernias. He asked about certain friends. Well, keep us informed on your doctors. I just wanted to see how you were.

Thank you for the call. That was nice.

Nov 10

I was talking to Dr. Nepal regarding the hernias. It's not improving. What's our plan B? He examined me. Okay, make an appointment with my uncle again and I'll go *with* you.

I called my father to give him the update; it seemed like the right thing to do.

Wow, you have a full plate.

Nov 13

Mom and I were very busy cleaning. She vacuumed most of the house. We were heading downstairs to do laundry – and Mom *fell*; she missed the last few steps and hit the concrete floor. It's still uncarpeted down there from the fish tank flooding. Tracy was JUST getting home from work, and walked in to see her at the bottom of the stairs. It was frightening, for all of us. I called an ambulance. I guess in a *medical emergency* it's okay for the *male* helper to assist Mom, to *touch* her (otherwise, it's a big no-no). They scooped her onto a stretcher chair, then onto the gurney. We spent many hours at the hospital. She *didn't* break anything but badly bruised her back, side, and tailbone. It's gonna hurt for a while.

Nov 15

I understand her needing more time to recover here, but MY recovery is being hindered. I had to lift Mom at the hospital, she hangs on to me…my body can't take the extra weight. The pain is astronomical, but I can't show that to Mom. She needs me even more now. Mom said, God must want us to spend more time together.

I don't know *what* he's thinking right now, to be honest. She said nothing.

I said, I don't think his intention was for us to visit *like this.*

I just don't know why this is happening – we had a *great* visit, we looked after her, then the fall. And this was Mom *helping* ME after my surgery. Funny how things work out. It occurred to me, I'M probably in MORE pain than she is. And I can't take care of myself properly.

The furnace is broken and we have no heat.

Nov 18

This morning Mom said, I'm glad you've been *healing* while I'm here.

Who said I am?

You haven't gotten worse.

I'm looking at her like, Says who?! You *see* what you *want* to see.

The left side of my gut is beyond bursting. Burning and bursting, if that's possible.

She said, I know you've put all that aside to look after me. I'm so grateful. We have to talk "straight."

You and Tracy need to get on with your lives, and I just don't know how to get on a plane right now.

What if I help you get on the plane? You're only going to Toronto this time, not Israel.

I called Aunty Ruth, and she asked how *I* can travel with Mom?

I hadn't thought that far ahead, I was only thinking of Mom.

She said she'd come *here* to get her.

Mom said, I am very aware of you and Tracy and all you've done for me. She hugged me. It's the biggest Mitzvah (good deed) what you are doing, THE biggest.

Maybe God will bless us with a new furnace!

The furnace guy came to give us a quote on a new one. So overwhelming.

He's not sure WHEN it can be done. It's only WINTER in Calgary, no rush.

We watched *The Blindside.* I told Mom it's one of Tracy's "go to" movies when he's feeling overwhelmed. After the movie Tracy said, This is all we ever wanted, to be able to do this with you – *watch a movie and eat popcorn* (kosher, of course). It was so nice.

Nov 19

Mom said it was a *good* day, she's feeling better. Today was one of THE *worst* pain days for me. Unbelievable, non-stop pain.

I simply don't do well with *big* purchase items – it freaks me out. I just wish we were *allowed* to SAVE money instead of things always happening. I told Mom that Tracy said his contract work *will cover* the cost of the furnace.

Tracy's dad has round three of chemo tomorrow.

Nov 21

My surgical consult is today. Do you have pain all the time? Yes! You have holes in your abdomen from the scope. It seems surgery would be the only thing to help repair the hernias, but it's not my first choice. I will confer with another surgeon and see what he suggests for the tears. Mom is feeling like she needs to get on with life, to go to Toronto and find a place to live (she'll stay at Aunty Ruth's until then). She said she'll call her sister and tell her she's *ready* to go. It's up to her if she comes or not.

The best way I can help YOU is to leave, she said and laughed.

I'm glad you still have your sense of humor. As you got better, I got worse.

I'm so sorry.

Don't apologize. You're where you needed to be to recover. We're glad we could help you. But now I need to help myself.

Thank you for being straight with me.

Aunty Ruth got Mom a flight out on Monday.

Dec 1

Our new furnace and water heater (*free* with a furnace install) were put in. Phew.

Dr. Nepal went over my bloodwork. Your hormones are *not* in the happy zone. I *don't* want to give you estrogen because there's the likelihood of getting breast cancer and you have a history of lymphoma, too. You're also very low in magnesium.

Dec 7

Dudie is just not himself; he's losing weight even though he's eating. Him *not* being in our lives is NOT an option. It's gut-wrenching. We talked about taking him to the vet – but the cost. I'm just beside myself. I followed him to the litter box each time – all is normal. He ate one and a half cans of food and is drinking lots. He's jumping on and off the bed okay. So, what's the deal?!

Dec 8

Dudie is eating like nobody's business. I don't know what's happening with him, but I'm grateful he's doing better. I'm taking him to the vet tomorrow – for peace of mind. I was talking to Mom – Aunty Ruth's best friend's husband died yesterday. Our neighbor *across* the street passed, and the neighbors *down* the street, their son died. It never ends. It's too much. Overload alert.

Dec 9

Ten years ago today, I started chemo. Holy crapballs.

The vet remarked on how *great* Dudie's teeth look for his age – usually they're *plaque-ier* and rotting. Cats have ways of *concealing* their diseases. We will need a urine sample, bloodwork, and an ultrasound. Leave him here, and get him by 6:00 p.m.

I felt so relieved he was finally being looked after. It feels like he's in good hands. Then we took Tracy's parents to the hospital for his dad's bloodwork and consult. Tracy recognized the nurse and asked if she used to administer chemo?

Yes, I remember you (to me), I do. Wow, has it really been ten years? Ten years ago, *today.*

Tracy's dad's oncologist came in. The bloodwork shows problems with your kidneys; you're probably not drinking enough. The CT scan shows some issues with three blood vessels from your heart to your brain; one is almost closed off. It would now seem that having another stroke is more at forefront than the cancer.

They want to do another CT scan, but the dye they use thickens the blood, as does the chemo, and it is a problem. So, the cancer has become secondary to fixing up your kidneys; chemo is *canceled* today. We've ordered fluids for you; it'll take about one to one and a half hours. Tracy's dad was ONLY stressing about the fact that he knew we had to pick up our cat at 6:00 p.m.

I call the vet. Dudie just had a pee five minutes ago. His bloodwork is all over the board – high liver enzymes, high blood sugar, very anemic, blood glucose should be at 4-9; he's at 22, RBC very low, WBC very low – we are positive he has *diabetes*, he's genetically predisposed.

Is that *treatable*?

Absolutely! We close at six and no one is here after that so you *need* to get him *tonight*. I'm going to have a pathologist look at his blood, I'll call you back.

I can't stop tearing up, which is only upsetting Tracy's dad more, so I left the room. Its 4:45 p.m. and he *still* has an hour to go. I'm so stressed I could throw up. I call the vet to say our neighbor Erin will be coming to pick Dudie up.

Okay, we want to send some of his blood to another lab so they can check for viruses and feline leukemia, etc. You might have to bring him back in the morning.

That same nurse from before came out to talk to Tracy and me and said, IF you need to go pick up your cat, I'll give your parents a ride home.

We *really* appreciate the offer, but we have someone picking up our cat. Just then Dave texts to say that Erin is at the vet. RELIEF.

Today – was simply too much.

Tracy even said, I don't know how much more I can handle.

Dec 11

Dudie's *not* eating. We went from feeling so hopeful to being scared again, and there's *no* plan for the diabetes. I can't take this waiting and doing nothing! His tummy is shrinking and that is no good. I've got to keep believing they can help him TODAY! So, I called the vet. I'm still waiting for them to get back to me with the bloodwork results. We gave Dudie the medication they gave us and it's having the OPPOSITE effect. The vet said he'd be *ravenously* hungry. He hasn't eaten properly since Monday (it's Thursday). I'm afraid by the time the vet figures out what's wrong with him, he'll have a whole whack of *other* problems. The vet calls me back – based on the bloodwork, he needs an ultrasound. Fine, I'll be right there with him. This is breaking my heart. He said the bloodwork still shows elevated liver enzymes. He agreed, yes, it's diabetes but we need to check his liver. Sometimes with diabetes, it will go into overdrive and create fatty tissue around the liver. We'll have to give him a feeding tube. We *can't* give him insulin without food so we will use anaesthetic, use forceps to get the tube down his throat and nick him at the neck to put the tube through. It will be very easy at home.

I couldn't stop crying. Are you giving him insulin *today*?

Yes, right now.

I left Dudie there overnight. I gotta believe the Little Dude will be okay; I just don't want him to suffer. I feel like a zombie. I don't think I've ever felt this overwhelmed. I'm ready to pull the pin.

The vet called this evening – he's already been given a half-can of food, they brushed him and he's doing well. That's my little guy.

Dec 12

Depending on how things go, they'd like to send Dudie home this evening. Tracy picked him up on his way home and got the feeding instructions. Dudie runs *straight* to the scratch post – to let off some steam. His neck is shaved and there's a bandage all the way down his arm, and a tube sticking out of his neck. What have we done to him? There are *four* things he has to take – three of them are two times a day. Thank God it's the weekend so I don't feel like I'm alone in figuring this out. $1900 for his past two visits.

Dec 15

I told the vet how *well* he's doing – eating, drinking, grooming. He was so happy he's well and *shocked* that he's been eating like he has. He has lost muscle mass on his spine. The trick is for him *not* to *gain* more weight. His glucose read is 22.3, that's high. We need to increase his insulin from two to *three* units. We need to get a glucose kit for home. They will need him in for a *full day* so they can monitor the glucose curve.

Dec 16

I went to Tracy's parents to give his dad a haircut. He took his sweater off and showed me the radiation mapping he just had done. Tracy's mom says, He has *maybe* a year.
Oh crap. The radiation *could* give some pain relief?
Maybe, but it won't *stop* it from spreading. There's nothing more they can do. The waiting is the worst part.
I said, You just take it one day at a time and call if you need *anything*.
As I drove away, a profound sadness came over me – this is the beginning of the end. This is going to kill Tracy. I now have the dubious task of telling him the doctors are more certain the cancer is spreading rapidly through his dad's bones.

I was watching a soap and someone said, *Bad things happen really fast and we have to live through them really slow.*

Dec 26

Yesterday I had an old memory I'd forgotten about. I was 10 or 11 and home alone with Kyle. You can imagine the rest. Perhaps the memory came from having watched a TV show where the woman said, *He stole my innocence.* I'd never thought of it other than: he screwed up all my relationships regarding trust, with men (including Tracy). I always say once you're an adult, you *can't* use what's happened to you as a kid as an *excuse* anymore. You're an adult; you can make choices and do things *differently*. But when things happen at a young age and it molds you into this *different* person than you would've been had it NOT happened, how do you *not* allow it to affect your life? There are *always* reminders, the memories don't dissolve; it's part of you and makes you who you are. I was never meant to become a person *without* the abuse. I AM a person OF abuse. It happened, so it shapes you. This is me. It's HOW you deal with it, react to it, allow it to affect you, your life, your relationships, your physical state…it's all-encompassing.

I went to Tracy's parents and did a puzzle with his dad. Tracy and I are thinking this is a special holiday – it could be our *last* with his dad.

2015

Jan 9

Dudie is not himself; he hasn't eaten since 9:30 last night. He threw up, pooped twice, drank lots and then slept. He ate tons after and *now* he seems okay. I guess he just had to get something out of his system.

Tracy says he's very emotional, up and down. I'd be surprised if he *wasn't*.

Feb 7

I received a voicemail from my father: *I'm just calling to see how you're doing. Okay. Give us a call when you can. Bye for now.*

I get a *sick* feeling, not a *happy* one, when I see him calling. There is no connection, no *Hey are you watching the Super Bowl*, no *I want to see you*, no chitchat. It's *nothing* like before. He wants to know about my health; it's nice, but that's it. It just feels so weird, forced, and awkward.

Feb 15

Dudie had the *best* day ever yesterday, but in the evening, he peed on the dog bed. He ate well at night. Today he *hasn't* eaten and is only drinking. I get a glucose read of 24.5. I was able to give him his insulin after him having only some salmon broth. Then he peed on the cat post and is now hiding in the basement. He came upstairs, went outside, but upon coming back in, he almost fell over and lost his balance. I gasped. No, no, this is no good. Tracy! I need Tracy to figure this out with. Damn. We have to do something NOW. This is no good, this isn't good…

I brought Dudie to the vet hospital. I'd been crying. I couldn't stop when I realized this could be *it*. I called Tracy at work and he said no way it'll come to *that*; his insulin is off and they'll give him something and *fix* it. At the reception desk they asked *why* I was there. I was still crying but I tried to explain. I think she understood right away this was *dire*. She took Dudie back *right away*. The vet gave me the lowdown, then left and came back with the cost – $2400. I sat there with my mouth dropped open. She continued, He will need to be here at least three days to check his glucose every two hours and get him eating again.

Wow, do you have a *payment plan*?

No, we don't do that here. She left the room.

I was freaking out. Who has $2400? But how do you *not* go ahead. I texted Tracy. He wrote back, Ya, go ahead. He didn't even flinch. The vet came back. I said, Yes, go ahead, do what needs to be done. Is this treatable? Absolutely. We'll need a $500 deposit now. We are just running bloodwork now. Would you like to wait? Yes.

She came back after about ten minutes. Yes, it's what we thought. There is acid in the ketones. He's not getting enough insulin, so his body creates these ketones to compensate so we need to remove them from his body. There is nothing you *could've* or *should've* done differently; it's not your fault, nothing *you* could've done to *prevent* this. I'm guessing that's why your vet increased his insulin last week but it's still not enough. We need to keep him here tonight and tomorrow, and we'll play it by ear.

Tracy said, Dudie *deserves* the chance to live.

OMG, that is a great way to put it; yes, he *deserves* it. I called the vet after 9:00 p.m. Dudie's doing really well. He's very comfortable and maintaining his insulin with the dextrose. He's not interested at all in eating, but it's not surprising considering that's one of the reasons you brought him in. Dr. April will call you in the morning with an update on how he did during the night.

Such an emotional day. Holy bananas. I'm all cried out.

We watched *Step Brothers*. We *desperately* needed to watch something *funny*. All the animals are on the bed, but it's glaringly obvious Dudie is *not* there. All the rituals and extra things we do for him, and we're *not* doing any of it tonight. I'm so relieved Tracy *isn't* worried about the money. I said I can relax then if YOU'RE not worried. And hearing from the vet he's doing well. I think I can sleep now. Well, I hope I sleep. We have two to three days to come up with $1500.

Feb 16

I spoke to the vet. Dudie *didn't* eat this afternoon. He's going for bloodwork and they are giving him potassium chloride and checking his ketones. He still has 24 to 48 hours to get them down. He's *not* out of the woods yet. He's very comfortable.

I told Tracy, He's *not* getting any better. I'm afraid to say it or think it but…

He'll be okay.

Feb 17

The vet called. Dudie is *not* responding to treatment, he's not eating and he has high glucose.

Is he in pain?

No. His temperature is normal and has a normal pulse – he's stable.

I bawled, hysterically. Poor Dudie, he doesn't deserve this! My sweet little baby. I can't bear where this is headed.

Feb 18

The vet called. They started him on steroids. He's eating a little, pooping and walking a bit. So, a few positive things but not enough to send him home. There is intense inflammation on the pancreas. His liver enzymes are high and he has hepatitis. We just need the meds to start working Maybe a visit would help, bring a toy he likes.

Feb 19

Tracy and I went to see Dudie. He had an IV on his leg. He was calm and nuzzled up to me. He seemed more like himself. His glucose is at *20.* Yay!

He ate really well today. The steroids we are giving him for his liver makes him insulin-resistant. A biopsy of his liver would tell us *for sure* what is going on.

No, we *won't* put him through *that.*

Okay, we will work with what we have.

I'm so glad we went to see him.

Feb 20

Dudie did well overnight. He didn't eat his last meal, and he's being weaned off fluids. We can pick him up at 7:00 p.m. They gave us five million instructions and meds. Oh man. Insulin. Steroids. Antibiotics. And a $2700 bill. I just want him to be okay. He peed on the dog's bed again. Sigh. We need to be getting Dudie all different food, syringes, needles…

Feb 28

I'm in bed and Tracy's coming down the hall to the room, clutching his chest and breathing hard.

I'm not feeling so good.

He goes to the bathroom and throws up. He says the pain has lessened. I get him a cold cloth and, no sooner, the pain is back. He's practically hyperventilating. I keep asking him if he needs me to call an ambulance. No, it could just be something I ate. We ate the *same* things today and *I'm* okay.

He kept rocking and going into the fetal position. He scared me. I didn't know *how* to help him. HE looked scared.

Do you think it's your gallbladder? He shrugged.

My mind raced. *He can't die.* We need him! I begged God to take Tracy's pain away. As the heating pad heated up, he fell asleep. The rocking stopped. His body relaxed. Thank God. Poor guy exhausted himself out. Very frightening. HE is the rock here, *my* rock, and the one who *always* knows what to do.

Tracy wakes up, sits up and says, It's happening again. Out of nowhere, it's starting again. He lay on his back and fell back asleep.

I'm so worried.

Mar 2

There is too much going on – *five* people we know have been in the hospital with serious things, then with Dudie, now Tracy. It's enough! Let's be talking about *good* things happening. All this doom and gloom is overkill. My hernias are killing me, but I'm the obvious choice to take Dudie to the vet. Tracy is still feeling crappy from those pesky gallbladder symptoms. I went to warm up the Jeep and I slipped and fell on the ice. Just what I fucking needed! I don't know if I broke anything or what's injured; I just know I have to get Dudie to the vet. As I'm trying to concentrate on what the doc was saying about Dudie, the pain was setting in – head pounding, neck, wrist, jarred hernias, my ass…

Dudie's weight went UP. Yay! High glucose though. Shit. We discussed the conundrum of the steroids whitewashing the insulin. The vet took a pee sample and gave me a thumbs up. We need to increase his insulin to SIX units.

I got home and filled Tracy in, and suddenly I get that explosive hernia thingy happening. I irritated them in the fall. The pain is just radiating all over. And now I have to go to the pharmacy to get Dudie some things.

What A Day!

Mar 13

Lucky Friday the 13th! Dudie is on SEVEN units now. He has a spring in his step. Dudie is flying around the house like nobody's business. My sweet little man. He has to go for bloodwork *every* week for the next *two* months. He's now on a "liver cocktail." And, Tracy is still having symptoms and not doing great. I pleaded with God, if *I'm* not worthy, smite *me* down where I lay, but *spare* my family. My family is everything to me. Give me a freaking sign, or kill me where I lay. Help us, not in *years*, but NOW.

Mar 21

I went for my oncology checkup. He comes in: Your bloodwork is all good. So, this looks like our *final* visit. It's been ten years? Yes.

People get anxious knowing it's their last visit, but you know if you need to call us you can.

Yes. I've gotten *more* visits than most because of the clinical study, so I *can't* complain. I'm 135 lb. Groan.

You were going for a hysterectomy and an oophorectomy the last time you were here. Did you have those done? Yes.

Was there a lot of endometriosis? Yes.

Did they get it all?

No, not in the first surgery, but most of it in the second.

I see here you say you have pain but not cancer-related.

Right. They are surgical hernias. I told him about the lump in my neck that turned out to be nothing.

He examined me. Okay, so barring any complications, you're *done!* He put out his hand to shake mine and said bye.

Thank you for *everything*. I hope I *don't* see you again.

You couldn't wipe the smile off my face! I walked back to the Jeep, in the sunshine. Happy, happy, joy, joy. Today I didn't have a smidge of doubt. I *knew* I had this.

Apr 30

Tracy tells me he was up all night with *another* attack; it was *worse*. The pain woke him out of a dead sleep. I went into the kitchen so as not to wake you up, then went back to bed with the heating pad.

Wow. And I slept through it *all*. The person, who *doesn't* sleep, *slept*. I asked him why he won't go to Emerg?

I may not get paid to be off. I can't afford to be off.

You still have to look after your health.

Tracy is peeing orange – it means a bad liver, and the gallbladder is getting worse.

I called Dr. West but he's not in. The nurse said to go to the ER.

Tracy says he's fine.

My pain is getting worse. It feels like an inflated balloon; everything feels like it's *expanding* and ready to blow. It's been a helluva week – I had a meltdown: I had my *last* oncology appointment FOREVER, three of our vehicles are kaput, Tracy's dad had a CT scan, issues with my father, Dudie is up to EIGHT units of insulin (and doing SO well), Tracy's gallbladder attack…

May 6

I'm anxious. I've been to so many doctors with various problems only for them to say *nothing is wrong* with me, when each time *there clearly was*. I went to a specialist regarding my hernias; he was the *same* surgeon who put my port in. He asked about my surgeries, where and how much the pain is.

I said, Even just sitting in the waiting area now, it felt like my innards were about to burst like a balloon.

He examined me. You need a blood test and a CT.

May 12

It's Tracy's dad's 75th birthday. We went over and had a beer with him. I took of picture of him and Tracy holding their glasses up. It felt like an important event to capture, like it could be the *last* time they get to do that. I'm so worried about Dudie. He's *very* sick again. I spend all day with him, I know what is "normal" and he's *not* himself. He keeps going to the faucet but won't drink. He's crying in the bathroom downstairs. He's a bit wobbly. I don't know what to do. His meds *must* be off. I'm worried about Tracy, my little baby, Tracy's dad…it's too much.

May 13

I said to Tracy, *If* I'm taking the Dude to the vet, he's *not* coming back out.

I know.

Tracy did a glucose read: **30**! OMG. That's off the charts! I gave him an injection, but he won't eat. I'm losing faith. Why would God make everyone sick in this house? Great test, God. Thanks.

I said to Tracy, We have *three* options: 1) I get him to the vet and spend money we *don't* have, 2) we do *nothing* and he suffers, or 3) I think you know the last option.

I feel like my grip is slipping. Every aspect of our lives is in peril: our health, finances, family, friends, work...it's exhausting.

May 14

Tracy stayed home with me *just in case*...Dudie slept then got up and *ate*! And I didn't have to force-feed him. I never imagined I could feel relief again. Dudie ate a full bowl of food during the night and another during the day. My sweet little boy.

May 19

I dreamt I was screaming and yelling, but had no voice. Nothing comes out when I scream, just air. It's a recurring dream. What an awful feeling.

I got an email regarding renewing our Galaxy licenses. I cried. I realized, We *are* done with them, it's best. It was unrealistic to think we *could* keep moving forward with it. My tears are for the YEARS we put into it and got nothing back. It's drained us – emotionally and financially. Since 2013 with my surgery and giving up our office, transferring the team to another leader and all the office drama, we pulled back and just let the business die down.

Tracy said, I have regrets for *joining* the company; I have zero regrets *leaving* it.

May 26

Tracy has been missing work because we have no working vehicle. But a guy from his work did come by and drop off a check – $3250! All the money owed to him for contract work! A miracle! We had $21.76 in the bank.

June 8

I'm having dark thoughts again. Sometimes I have this overwhelming feeling of being better off by *not* being around. It would be good for *everyone*. This *constant* struggle to make this life work.

Tracy told me to cancel his doctor appointment this Friday because he can't take the time off. Yet he needs the time off to get checked out! A vicious cycle. Round and round we go. Everyone else gets to enjoy the merry-go-round of life – ours is broken. It's getting tricky to feel hopeful.

July 5

I feel like I'm mourning my father. The day he left for his new life, that person I knew has ceased to exist. The relationship we used to have is dead. This new person is a complete stranger. My *real* father passed two years ago. I've worked through the anger, betrayal, sadness, confusion, hurt, and the disappointment of it all. My father is gone.

July 7

Our licenses expired and *we* fired Galaxy, we *resigned*! All we ever did was help others while everyone helped themselves. In OUR time of need, there wasn't a soul in sight. Nobody held out a helping hand. And without a dime to our name, we STILL talk about having money and helping others!

We were *completely* on our own. We were the lowest of the low in the pecking order, the scapegoats. We took the brunt of anything and everything that went wrong. Left out in the cold. Ironically, without us, the team fell apart. We became stronger and literally fought our way back up. We decided to prevail and not be a punching bag any longer.

It's also a metaphor for my life – fighting my way back.

Aug 1

At Tracy's parents' house, THEY sound hopeful. I think his dad is starting to live again.

We decided I need to start looking for a job. I agree we need the extra income, but Little Dude still needs me. I'm afraid for him if I'm *not* home to monitor him.

A few days ago, Tracy came home with our new few-months-old truck from his work. We have a new vehicle? Can we actually afford this?

Yes, all my contract work money will go toward it.

We sold our other truck today. Okay, we got this.

Sept 15

I had my follow-up with the surgeon. You have scar tissue, but there's nothing we can do surgery-wise. It would probably make things *worse* and create *more* scar tissue. I wish I could do surgery so you'll be fixed, but it won't be. Maybe your next step is the Chronic Pain Clinic for injections.

That was my FIRST course of action – it didn't help.

What sometimes happens is where the holes were made to do the surgery, some endometriosis can get inside. Go back to your doctor and see what he says. Best of luck.

I feel defeated. While I'm thrilled I DON'T need more surgery, even though I'm still dealing with daily pain, there's still NO solution!

Sept 17

I saw Dr. Nepal and I told him I had my CT – they said they *can't* help me.

He was getting pissed right away, shaking his head. You *absolutely* need surgery. I JUST had a guy in here in the same position as you – he had to see *four* surgeons before they finally did the surgery and he feels 100% better!

He validated all that I'm feeling and the cause of the pain. I got teary, I'm back to square one. I feel like I'm going crazy.

NO, you're NOT crazy. We need to break down that scar tissue. We'll figure this out.

Tracy called me *tough*. Mom said, Not only are you tough, but with all you've dealt with in your life, and you *do*, you're not only sweet, but amazing too.
I needed to hear that.

Sept 22

Tracy's dad has one tumor that's *still* growing, and one that *stopped* growing. His next checkup is in October, so we shall see then.

Horoscope: *Have you repeatedly asked the universe for a favor? Have you pleaded with the heavens for an answer to a prayer? Are you feeling ignored and abandoned by the forces above? If so, it may be because you are expecting something very specific in response. It may be that you believe that you know better than the universe what is best for you, but you may be wrong. If you just trust that the best will be, and you remain open to what the "best" really is, that's what you will receive.*

Lesson of the day: Mom always told me to pray for *specific* things and don't ask small, go for the *big* stuff. Put it out there you want more than *just* to pay bills. Think bigger. Ask bigger. So, I do. And with it being the High Holidays, I prayed and prayed for a better year for Tracy and me. I spent Yom Kippur looking for a job! I was thinking about happiness and what being happy means to me: having a positive outlook even when you are going through challenging times. Inner calm. Feeling good about yourself and the people around you. Living with no regrets, and accepting your choices and decisions – good or bad. Making the most out of your life, even if it's not exactly what you planned. To be able to live in the moment, the present, and not look back and not look too far ahead either. I want to be happy. I want to live a contented life. I want that.

Oct 13

Tracy's had his surgical consult: his gallbladder surgery and post-surgery recovery is set for January 13 to 16! Finally, some relief for my honey bunny; I hate seeing him suffer.

I went on an interview for a cleaning company and I *got* the job.

Oct 22
I'm in so much pain I almost drove myself straight to the hospital; I went to see Dr. Nepal instead. I told him I cried for two days from the pain after I took the cleaning job.
Why don't you get a *desk* job?
Apparently, I'm *over*qualified. I feel like I'm in a vicious cycle.
Yes, you need to get those hernias repaired.
I went down to work and quit. They told me I'm welcome back *anytime*.

Oct 26
I prayed to God all night for help, for money, for a proper job so we can get by. I'm such a big fat loser. Why am I here? What is my purpose on this planet except for being a waste of space? A waste of skin. A waste of time. A waste.
Tracy said, I don't hang with losers, so you can't be one.
You must have made an exception.
Nope, that rule must never be compromised. It's okay. Life is good.
Life is good?
Are we together? Yes.
Are our kids here?
Yes. It's Dudie's birthday today.
Then it's okay.

Boy, he sure knows how to yank me out of my negative thought processes. He's my light.

I must have put feelers out to a hundred people to keep an eye open for a job opportunity for me. That's all I can do. It's *who* you know. I need a job, no joke; one that will work around having to give the Dude his meds. I think God has stopped listening to all my begging and pleading. I see us losing it all, bit by bit. Why aren't WE allowed to work, pay our bills, and move on with life, *like everybody else*? Has God cast us so far aside it's not even worth the effort to reel us back in?

Oops, negative thoughts again.

Nov 2

The people who HAVE *don't* help the HAVE-NOTS. At Galaxy, we were *have-nots helping* others. The good ones go to their graves with nothing, waiting for the good to happen; the bad ones get more and more and more...

Tracy's hours have been cut, less pay, and his company is almost going under; I'm looking for work; no money for food or gas; and I took our cans and bottles in to pay for Dudie's meds today. I rolled our change so I had money to put gas in the car. Tracy had to empty the lawnmower gas tank into his truck so he could get to work.

Nov 6

I had an interview yesterday for an *at-home job* and I *got* it! I will be in training for the next few weeks. I hope it's not too late – we are *three months* behind on *everything*. Disconnection notices are coming out the wazoo! We are a few weeks away from losing our home *again*. I have no pride left – we need help. A friend is telling us to sell the house, go on welfare and get food from the food bank. Great plan, thanks.

I get a call from Mom – she wants to pay three months for the internet so I can do my new job. And I'm giving you $250 to buy food and gas.
A friend calls me and says, Tracy is coming over later, I'm giving him a check for $2000, will that help?
OMG. Yes. Absolutely.
Aunty Ruth said they will help with one mortgage payment.

From one extreme to the other. I'm so grateful for all of them. I'm bawling.

Dec 1

I got an email from work – training has been *delayed* until January. I'm not sure what to think. Do I look for *other* work? I got a call from another place I applied to – as a merchandiser. It would be five to six hours twice a week. You set your own schedule. Next week they'll be doing interviews. I can do *both* jobs. Or pick one or the other. It's nice to have choices!

Dec 5

I got the merchandiser job! I start online training next week.
I went to check our bank account because I needed to go buy milk and veggies – $5230 was deposited from our tax returns! I instantly cried. Are you kidding me? I lost it. I just can't believe it. I can buy groceries! I'm so thankful. We truly ARE onto better things. I have <u>*two*</u> jobs, Tracy's back to a regular work week, AND he has contract work…it's a miracle, truly. We are on our way! I'm humbled.

Dec 14

I just got an email from the first job – they are committed to bringing me on. Training starts January 4 for a week. I'm overwhelmed and had a meltdown about easing back into the workforce, and now I have two jobs. How will my body react? Well, at least one job is from home. I can make this work. Okay, I'm feeling better about things. Online training is complete for the second job; I start training at an actual store tomorrow.

2016

Jan 12

I had another surgical consult with a different surgeon. It's possible some endometriosis is *still* fused inside. I can't say for sure they are hernias. If it's random and there is no real rhyme or reason for the pain, it's hard to diagnose. The bottom line, for the type of surgery you had, the pain could be around for about two years. It could still go away on its own. Have you considered the Chronic Pain Clinic?

Yes, I laughed.

He could get Dr. West to get me pain meds. He said even if it's scar tissue, he *wouldn't* do surgery. I was happy about that. Well, yes and no. It's good to have surgery to *fix* things, yes; but if it *won't* change anything, then no. That thought didn't hit me until I got home – and I cried. I couldn't imagine how I was going to work. I was a mess. I talked to Mom before I went on the phones for my first job. There is SO much on my mind. Dudie is *off* again. I'm worried sick about him, and all this the *day before Tracy's surgery*; what timing. I prayed that God would be merciful and not let Dudie suffer. If this is *it*, please let him go in his sleep. My little angel. Tracy thought I'd pick staying home with the Dude rather than go to the hospital with him. Nope, I'm coming with you. What a stressful night. I feel sick to my stomach. So, falling asleep was fun – worrying about Tracy, Dudie...my brain is very full.

Jan 13

Tracy had his gallbladder surgery. Coming out of surgery his blood pressure was 180/120! His liver was fused to his body from adhesions from his car accident when he was 18. His gallbladder was thick and inflamed; there was NO question that gallbladder HAD TO come out.

He had to have his first pee before they'd let him go home. *Hours* ticked away and I needed to get home to give Dudie his shot! I called several people to go over and do it for me, but no one was available. By 6:00 p.m. Tracy had *finally* peed. He was severely dehydrated, which caused a few problems. We got home and I got Tracy settled, I fed Dudie and gave him his meds; it was *hours* after he needed them. He was *not* doing well. Here we go again. I'm just sick about it. Fortunately, once we got Tracy hydrated, he managed to rest. He just needs to watch some of the foods he eats and he'll recover relatively quickly.

Jan 20

I'm stressed about the jobs. I feel like I'm at a point where I need to pick *one*. They are increasing my hours with the at-home one, but the pay is terrible. What to do? I called my manager at the merchandising job to see if they could give me *another* store, so more hours and the pay is better. If they *can*, I'll stick with *that* one; it's no evenings or weekends.

Jan 24

It's Tracy's *first* day out of the house since his surgery. I don't think he was expecting it to be going to the hospital to see his dad. His dad wasn't feeling right, and then it got worse – problems with breathing. I think Tracy was supposed to go back to work today, too. The tumor on his dad's lung has suddenly grown from 4cm to 8cm. The pressure of the tumor is not allowing his lung to breathe properly. He's not getting enough oxygen. He's only on oxygen, no painkillers. They believe the cancer is spreading into his head. Oh God.

Jan 25

Tracy's *second* day out, he went to the hospital again. His dad's tumor has grown *again*. Carbon dioxide is *not* expelling from his body. He's still having trouble breathing. All of Tracy's siblings were at the hospital. Tracy's dad slept the entire time we were all there. It was awful to see him choking, coughing, gasping for air, and jerking around in his sleep. It's so not him. I felt badly for all of them to see him like that. The once strong, stoic man is now an unconscious shell of himself. They moved him to a private room because there were so many of us. Everyone stayed long after I left. I had to get home to Dudie. When Tracy got home, he said his dad woke up a few times and hugged Tracy. Oh wow. That is pretty special.

Jan 26

I feel so badly for Tracy. He hadn't slept and he's out the door by 5:15 a.m. He has no coverage for the time he has been off. I pray Tracy will be okay. He hasn't exactly had time to recover from his surgery. He came home and said his dad *isn't* getting enough oxygen to his brain. He wasn't making any sense; he was talking gibberish. They have to make a decision about his DNR.

Jan 27

I'm at work and I get a text from Tracy: Dad's gone.
OMG. I couldn't think. I called Tracy. He's crying. Are you at the hospital?
No, I'm on my way now.
I'm heading there right now.
I'm in the middle of my store and I burst out crying. OMG, he's gone. I called my manager. I don't know what to do… My father-in-law **just** died. I don't know if I'm supposed to stay here and finish or…I think I need to go. I'm so sorry.
I called Mom to tell her. I FLEW to the hospital. I drove so fast! I get into the hospital and I RAN! I get to the room – Tracy's in there alone, holding his dad's hands and crying. What a sight. His Pops. They say he took *one* deep breath at 8:32 a.m. and died. How do we say goodbye? I held Tracy, who held on to his dad, and the three of us just stayed like that. Tracy missed seeing him alive by half an hour. I said I'm relieved he doesn't have to suffer anymore. Tracy agreed. We had 45 minutes alone with him before the others arrived. We all sat and talked, even laughed, and then made plans. Cremation. No funeral. His mom will have an open house for people to drop by and pay their respects. Tracy's mom said, I want to bring him home where he belongs; it's what *he wanted*. She was very calm. I think she's relieved

he's not suffering any longer. It's awful to watch someone become something they're not. To live a whole life with dignity, then get this cancer shit and become something different. Everyone said their goodbyes. We all stayed with him for about two to three hours and then went back to Tracy's parents' house. She was looking for a picture of Tracy's dad for the obituary. It was a picture *I* took of him. It was taken on our deck from our last house, celebrating Tracy's birthday. His dad looked happy. We all had a beer in his honor and toasted his life. While we sat there, I *texted* Tracy: He loved you. He trusted you. If he wanted help with *anything*, he called you. If he needed to go out, he felt safe with you. I know Tracy needed to hear all that. It's the truth. They had a very special bond. Tracy will miss that.

Feb 7

I feel like it's been a nightmare few weeks: Tracy's surgery, Dudie getting sick that same day, Tracy's dad in the hospital, Tracy getting better, Dudie getting better, and Tracy's dad passing. What an emotional rollercoaster. Overwhelming. Then worrying about money. Tracy didn't get paid for the time off from his surgery, but they *say* he'll get bereavement pay.

Today's the open house. I made a picture board of Tracy's father to display. I could hear Tracy's mom telling someone: It hit me yesterday, but I keep thinking he's going to walk through the door. They were married for 56 years!

Mar 1

I couldn't fall sleep last night. I was thinking about money. The struggle is real. It's so difficult when we try to MAKE our dreams come true and try to give ourselves a better life – only to be back at square one. Thirty years of chipping away at life, at believing – it makes one wonder *why* we keep believing. Or maybe we *don't* any longer. Tracy *doesn't* talk about his hopes and dreams anymore. Our plan to go to *Paris* is a non-discussion. I LOVE our home, I'm grateful we *have* one, and I hope we'll get the chance to repair it before it completely falls apart. We have no fallback vehicle so we *can't* ditch the *money-pit* truck. I think we'd be in a better place if we *didn't* have that payment. That truck takes away from being able to pay half of our interest payment, or two to three bills. It's maddening, yet we have no alternative. The contract work that was going to pay for the truck *never* came through. All our best-laid plans…When is it OUR turn? When do we get to simply NOT live paycheck to paycheck? And those paychecks *don't* even cover expenses. We are mid-life. Our health declines, no money, in debt…We need a huge-ass miracle. A fricking miracle. There's no other way to put it. Tracy works so hard and he gets sick. I hate watching him not be able to take sick time. It sucks for him. It's not right, but here we are. So, I get that he's frustrated, and he becomes unwell, and has to work *no matter what*. We're living the dream.

Mar 4

I went to Dr. West. I'm not feeling like myself. I need to consider hormone replacement therapy (HRT). It's been three years since my hysterectomy, and I'm thinking that going the natural way may *not* be working. He can help with that. I was tearing up. I said I have the worst acne I've had in my life.

We can put you on a low dose of HRT; see me in two months and we'll recheck.

Tracy has a lung infection. He *didn't* get any bereavement pay. Why can't people keep their word?

I got paid $117 for two weeks' worth of work. God still believes we aren't worthy of a fucking normal life. He won't be satisfied until he's run me right into the ground, completely beaten down. I BEGGED for a sign that things will be okay, that things will turn around for us. Silence. As long as Dudie gets his medication and my sweet babies have food, I'm good. But for Tracy and me, we have to keep suffering. But I'll do it quietly, right, Bubby? I'm *quietly suffering* while all I want to do is scream and yell and punch walls. All these life lessons: I will be the *smartest* person on earth – in my grave.

Horoscope: It is always darkest before the dawn. You may feel that you are at a dark point now, and you may be cynical about the above-mentioned adage. No, this is not a sign that the dark will get darker, or that there is more of the same to come. You really do have a bright dawn to look forward to, and very soon.

Well, that couldn't be a better horoscope at a better time.

Mar 14

I can't stop crying. I've been awake for almost 24 hours. I wonder what life would be like in a *lighter* place? I've never *not* had dark thoughts. I went into my contacts and blocked all my friends. I just feel like there's no friendship anywhere. I text people and get *nothing* back. Forgotten. If you *don't* let anyone in, you *can't* get hurt. My fear is being ignored when I'm vulnerable, like *now*. People don't think of how it would feel if the roles were *reversed*. It wouldn't feel very good and they'd feel as devalued as I do. I *unblocked* everyone.

Mar 20

I woke up thinking we all have "expiry dates," like on a milk carton. In some ways I wish we *could* be stamped on the bottom of our feet with our expiry date, and then I think in some ways maybe it's best *not* to know. I feel in my case, I'd appreciate life *more* if I *knew* how long I had. If I'd known I'd be okay after cancer, after the car accidents, in the throes of dark thoughts... In the movie *Arrival*, Amy Adams asks, "*If you could see your whole life from start to finish, would you change things?*"

Today must be a thinking day because I was also thinking about menopause, of the women who *have* had kids, they whine and bitch and complain about menopause symptoms when they get them. Then there's people like me, who *don't* get to have kids, suffer through every nightmarish period, go through the gut-wrenching conversations about how we'll raise our children, go see one million doctors only to learn I will *never* have them, have surgeries to remove ANY hope of ever having a kid, then deal with *forced* menopause. While the childbearing mothers cry over the fact that menopause means they'll never get to have ANOTHER child. Boo-frickity-hoo. My childbearing years are over. The finality of never getting to have *another* baby while they already have one or two or three, while I get to deal with the emotional wreckage of having periods that didn't mean **anything**, then going into menopause when it means your body will *never* have had the chance to have a baby. It's cruel. It's just plain cruel to put a woman through all that – and have nothing to "show" for years of menstrual agony.

Mar 22

I took my first HRT. Instant headache and nausea. *Nothing* goes smoothly. I'm petrified my eye appointment today is going to be bad news. Petrified. I'm thinking of canceling it. I keep hoping *they'll* call *me* to cancel. After the doctor's examination I braced myself, here we go…

She says, Your vision is *perfect*; it's 20/20. The bubbles on your eye are quite common. People living in Calgary, with the dryness, these dead cells build up on the eye. She suggested Restasis; it helps you create better tears. I could've kissed her. The relief. I'm so relieved there's nothing serious, my vision is great…All good! PHEW!

Mar 24

Why do I get out of bed? For what? *When* does this get better? Before I *die*? My task for today is to try to *not* drive into a tree or oncoming traffic, to try to *not* think these thoughts. To think of one or two people who would actually give a shit if I were no longer here (and that would be Tracy and Mom). My task today will be trying to snap out of this funk, and pretend like life *might* get better. To try not to think about how tired I am of this challenging life. I'll try to think of Tracy, the greatest man, human, and person I know. And to remember we're in this shit *together*. And our fur babies need us. Ya. I'll try to remember all of that today.

<u>Mar 27</u>

I'm not sure this positive thinking is *working*. This is too common a thought and feeling lately – the urge to "call it a day." Everybody we know who ever had a rough stretch, they ALL got to get back on their feet in spades! Us...we get to fucking be in the trenches *indefinitely*. We get to have our heads juuuust underwater but never above. We get to watch everybody *else* move on with life, and we get to figure out how to pay for pet meds and food, bills and how we will try to keep the house for another month. We are not worthy of being like all the others. We aren't special enough to warrant a thought from God to fix this. It'll be too fucking late and every person we know will be like, *Had we only known. Oh, gee golly gosh, I'd have done* something *had I* just *known.* Bullshit. That's what people say when they feel *obligated* to say they *could've* helped. Ya, but you *didn't*. You simply didn't because your heads are so far up your own asses. We are screaming for help, but no one is bothering to listen. Instead, God piles on more shit and buries us deeper until we are so out of sight that we are so out of mind. We are nobody. We could all be dead in this house and probably my mother, calling every day as she does, would be THE only person with an inkling something isn't right. It would be weeks until a "friend" would text or think of us. Tracy's work *might* wonder where he's at, but would anyone call or try to find him? Doubtful. My work? It would probably be a few *weeks* before they realize. People are too self-involved. People like Jim have their own health issues to focus on. Again, until *they* need something. People only ask about what's going on in *your* life if it affects THEIRS. Fuck 'em. People suck. When we need help the most, we are on our own. Left behind. And for all those people who may not sleep at night wondering if they *could've* done more – you *could* have. People distance themselves in hard times. But wait, wha? You're having a party?...we'll be there! EVERYBODY'S rough times were OUR priority, our focus. You can hear the crickets when times are tough for *us*. It's exhausting being in my head.

Mar 28

I was saying to Mom, Why can't it be *our* turn? Why do others get a break? We help others and this is our reward?

I believe there will be a turnaround soon.

I *don't* believe that anymore. I've lost all hope, all faith.

You've given up? Ya.

Your time *will* come. Be patient.

I think I'm running out of patience – I think that's what's happening.

Do you feel you're being punished for something?

Not punished, just not rewarded like others. It seems those who think of *themselves* get *more* and have more.

You need to hand it over to God. He needs for you to believe in Him. He's waiting to hear you. We are His children, and He is here to help. You just have to realize you can't do it alone, and He'll take over if you wish.

So, I said, God, I'm handing it over to you. Tell me what to do. I pleaded and begged for God's help.

Pleading. I have nothing left to offer or bargain with.

Apr 11

I had a major meltdown; I felt so hopeless. I got angry at God. I said, My mother told me to pray to you. I understand you have a plan for us, and I need to give it over to you to handle, that you'd hear me and help me. So why *haven't* you heard me? Why does all my praying land on deaf ears? You're supposed to help those who ask for it. I never asked you "Why me?" when I had cancer, when I was hit by a drunk driver, or when I was hit as a pedestrian. I took it. But NOW, I'm asking, *Why me*? Why do you continue to keep your thumb pressed down on me, on us? Why do you keep putting up roadblocks to our success, money, and health matters? You make us struggle and we wonder if we'll lose it all today, tomorrow…WHY!? Will you be satisfied once I have a gun in my hand pointed at my head? Will **_that_** be enough for you, and finally satisfy you? When I'm dead and buried, THEN you'll help? All we ever wanted was a *chance*!

I've been *force-feeding* Dudie since Sunday. Today he turned a positive corner.

Apr 13

I feel…happy. It's a strange word for me to use. I told Tracy my heart feels *happy*. It's amazing how productive I can be when I'm not worrying about money or Dudie. I'm feeling hopeful. I feel…alive. These are foreign feelings to me. I feel light. I slept really well, too. I think that's a HUGE part of this new outlook. We even received a utility disconnection notice, and I dealt with it A-OK.

Lesson of the day: Don't worry so much. Dudie is still not out of the woods and money is still an issue, but maybe, just maybe, having a conversation with God, or the universe, helps unload the burden.

May 21

Out of the clear-fricking-blue, my father texts me: Truly hoping this text finds you guys in good health. It has strongly occurred to me that there is from your accident payout a shortfall of a large sum still owed to me…which has nothing to do with the rest of the money that I forgave. I'm sure you will find this to be very fair. A reply would be greatly appreciated.

I answered: Our last conversation you outright called it a "gift," so you can move on from it. Clearly, it's not, and you aren't. If you are finding *other* monies owing, money we still *don't* have, how is that moving on? So, what exactly is it that you want?

He replied: You paid back a big chunk of money and left a shortfall of some…and this was way before I decided to keep you guys afloat until his promotion…that's what you told me with bitter tears in your eyes and, if I didn't, your house would be lost. YOU KNOW THIS TO BE TRUE. What I want is the shortfall still owing to me from your accident insurance payout.

I said, I will get some banking verification next week on that. My records show I paid you that big chunk, then I also paid you smaller one. YOU KNOW IT TO BE TRUE that we have no money. You said you believed me.

He answered, You just made me a happy camper. I'm so happy that you will verify the TRUTH of the matter at the bank. So happy.

May 24

I went to the bank and they had a copy of the check! I could've kissed the teller! VALIDATION! **The TRUTH**. I texted him back and said the bank had a copy, faxing you a copy.

He replied: My bank has no record of a check being deposited…it *does* have a record of the smaller amount. I have no proof that you might have written the check this morning so I'm walking away from this too. FOR ALL THAT I HAD DONE FOR YOU BOTH THAT RUINED ME FINANCIALLY WHICH DIRECTLY LED TO THE LOSS OF MY HOUSE…AND NOW I UNDERSTAND WHY YOU DON'T SPEAK TO ME. TODAY YOU LOST THE BEST FATHER I TRIED TO BE…AND WAS. I WISH YOU BOTH WELL.MAY G-D FORGIVE YOU…I'M DONE…YOU OWE ME NOTHING…HAVE A WON-DERFUL LIFE. To conclude this matter…just for my record, send me the backside of the check with my endorsement signature on it.

I said: The fax I sent SHOWS the back side of that check. Impossible for me to stamp it with an RBC stamp. Interesting reaction, when I PROVE I **actually gave you that check**. You are not only questioning me but you're now questioning your own bank who could not have stamped the back of that check *without* you physically depositing the check. Why don't you call my branch and verify I was actually there today, and an Asian teller lady gave me that printout. There is 100% going to be video footage of my being there today as well as the proof you asked for. I'm sure her computer will also have evidence of her plucking that info from the TD database – and not a fabrication on my part. If you don't believe the check is real, or the back of that check, stamped by YOUR bank, not sure how seeing anything else will change that. You'd probably think I endorsed your name too. But I've already faxed you the front and back of that check. The proof is right there and you're choosing to still believe I've made it up. You lost the best children (Tracy and me) you ever had. Yes, we owed you money, NEVER disputed that. I still said we'd pay when we had money, but I can only say we don't have money so many times. Lending money *doesn't* make you a father. If there was any shred left between us, you destroyed it. I will forgive all of *your* transgressions as well. We can call it monetary compensation for my childhood and not protecting me from the two monsters *you* created. You be right. We'll be happy. Done.

UNFUCKING BELIEVABLE! I'm a liar *and* a criminal now? Nothing in our history of EVER would warrant him thinking I *could* be that person! He *actually* believes I can manifest a check with a bank stamp on it? Really? What a crock of shit. Gee, if I calculated all the money WE shelled out during HIS hard times, meals we made, carpentry/electrical/paint work Tracy did for HIM all those years, EVERYTHING we *ever* included him in...I think that we'd be on an even footing. But apparently, he has conveniently forgotten all that. I wish *I* could *forget* the shitty-ass things HE did, that *I* forgave *him* for. The man is NOT a saint like he probably thinks he is. It's everyone ELSE'S fault. *He* is perfect. He has an overinflated sense of self. Blame, blame, blame. The fact is that I DID PAY HIM THE MONEY HE'S GRIPING ABOUT, and he *chooses* to believe *otherwise*. He asks for the *proof*. I *GET it* and he thinks it's *phony*. I'm not dealing with a full deck here. There is no reasoning with him. Whatever, we are SO done! No more chances. Finished!! I'm not going to invest in hatred, bitterness, and anger anymore. I'm *done* with this tumultuous, emotional battlefield. It's all very clear to me, finally, that we *are* through, as we've been down this road before.

June 1

I had me another stellar meltdown day. I'm *not* sleeping, and I'm worrying about money issues. I freaked when the Keurig wouldn't work. I put oven mitts on this time and harangued on the kitty condo, punching it until I was exhausted. Major pent-up frustration. I had to get Dudie meds and both his wet and dry foods, with no money. No money for groceries and no money to pay bills. Whatever.

I said to Tracy, It's not too late for *you, you* can **still** have kids. He just looked at me with the saddest eyes. A light bulb went off in my head – I WASN'T MEANT TO HAVE CHILDREN. It's like it **FINALLY** sunk in. Genetic markers, endometriosis, cancer/chemo, hysterectomy, car accidents…A MILLION SIGNS! It's just *so* obvious *now*. The universe DID give me the most remarkable, extraordinary life partner though. I received a great love for all my life. I do *not* take that for granted. So, I get the love of my life, but no kids. It's like a one-or-the-other deal. I wouldn't trade Tracy for all the children in the world. So, I need to stop second-guessing if I should've "tried harder" to get pregnant. Tracy will have to come to terms with it in his own way, as well. I can't say this epiphany is a relief; it's still sad to me. I *have* found an acceptance of it, is all. Maybe I'm not in denial over it anymore. Maybe.

Lesson of the day: There's something to be said about analyzing something to death – you *can* finally get clarity…when the time is right.

June 28

Mom called: I have something to tell you; it's about one of your brothers. Levi has pancreatic cancer. He has a very large mass on both his pancreas and liver.
I said nothing.
I don't know if you have questions or not. I've been holding on to this information for about *three* months, not knowing *how* to tell you.
Well, now you told me. I have no questions.
All I could think of is karma is a bitch! Did YOU get cancer because YOU married a non-Jew? Hmmm?

July 22

Mom is visiting. She says she sees Tracy looking at me sometimes, and it's a look of: I can't believe I have her.

I feel the same. I'm very lucky.

She told me the last time she was here they had a conversation where Tracy said he saved my life when I had cancer. He would have to spoon-feed me, make me eat, coax me, cook for me...

Wow. *That's* why she said she *now* understands all he did for me during that time. She said your gift was to look so good, you *never looked* sick; you looked stunning. You were in treatment and you were still gorgeous. You look amazing *now*. You'd never know you and Tracy had any troubles. Why do you suppose all those awful things happened to you?

To appreciate my life. I AM grateful for many things; I need to express that more.

She read me an article on God's miracles we *don't* see. He's working behind the scenes and we are completely *unaware* a *good* thing happened because of something he did. It was interesting. Mom said this visit felt easier because it didn't feel like we had any unfinished business, just relaxing.

July 29

It's Mom's 75th birthday. She gingerly said to me, I never call over *there* when I'm *here*, but Levi is having surgery on Sunday, and I want to call him.

That's fine, make your call.

Really? I've agonized over talking to you about this. Thank you for understanding.

It's *not* about *me*. If you need to call, it's okay.

My thoughts? God's going to give him the ass whooping he deserves when he passes, for being a quiet bystander during my childhood.

We had a lovely Shabbat/birthday celebration for Mom. She told me she's privileged to be my mother, that I'm someone special beyond others.

I love our relationship. I love that she can be insightful of my life and can share that with me. And she often tells me how my insights into her life are so clear and helpful.

Aug 18

I saw my new foot doctor about two weeks ago regarding my left foot. It's a pain I've had in my foot for months that I've chalked up to being fractured. He said my left toe *is* fractured and I need X-rays right away. Today the results are in – you have a lot of bone spurs and arthritis. The bone is degenerating; it's not broken. I'm going for a bone scan.
Tracy got paid ALL his contract work money AND he got a raise. I cried. I was SO relieved. I do believe my prayers *were* answered. Better late than never?

Sept 14

Yes, I'm *still* writing my book. It occurred to me, I have been thinking I *had to* figure out how to write a book like OTHERS do. There's no ONE way to write a book! This is MY book, MY experiences, MY format, MY content. Why would it *have to be* like others? Why did I think that?

Lesson of the day: You are you, and your unique way of doing things is okay! You don't have to be like everyone else.

Oct 12

I'm really struggling with Yom Kippur this year. If God wanted me dead, he had *many* opportunities to do so, but here I am, only because he *wants* me to struggle *more*. Bad people get good things; good people get bad things. Either kill me or let me *live*! I mean *really* **live**. All I've been doing is **surviving**. I'm so tired of fighting the fight. I want an abundance of goodness to offset the past 43 years of crap (I'll say the first five years of my life weren't so terrible). Is that too much to ask for? I've paid my dues. A lifetime of struggling EVERY day...it's NOT okay anymore. It never was. You've given us all the negative stuff, let's do something *different*, something *positive*. Give us *good* health, *enough* money so we don't have to live paycheck to paycheck, give us *success* in a business and let us be *fulfilled* people! God likes to keep me in a place of helplessness, begging for our basic needs to be met. If he didn't get *something* out of it, he wouldn't keep doing it.

All that aside, I've decided I will get my book *done* in my 50th year! I am going to reclaim my power, no matter what!

I was going through my jewelry box and I have some nice things that were *passed down* to me. I have *no one*, no children to hand things down to. If I die, it all goes into the *garbage*. Suddenly I'm reminded of the quote from the movie *Star Trek Generations:* Jean-Luc Picard says, "*What we leave behind is not as important as how we lived.*" I think I need to make a deal with myself – not to self-loath for the next half of my life.

Nov 4
Dr. Nepal was with me to see his uncle-surgeon. It shows here on your last ultrasound you have cysts on your *kidneys*. Did you know you have 1x2cm cysts on your kidneys?
They may have mentioned something about it when I was going for my surgery. But they were more concerned with the cysts and fibroids on my ovaries and in my uterus. Why, is it serious?
Oh yes! You have polycystic disease.
That *would* explain the pain. I feel like I've been going crazy. Did you say the cysts were on just the *one* kidney, or *both*?
Both. We need to do a full blood scan on your kidneys, and you'll need an ultrasound. I need to send you to a kidney specialist.

Again, does this not confirm that *I know my own body*? The millions of times I've said I don't feel like myself. There's a reason! And now the cysts that were 1x2cm have had a year or two to grow, depending on which ultrasound he was looking at.
Tracy says, Out with it. Tell me what happened at the appointment.
Well...I have kidney disease.
What? Is that some *guess*? No.

482

Wow. Another hump to get over. Tracy grabs us some champagne: Here's to getting over *this* hump.

Ya, I guess God *hasn't* tested me/us enough.

Nov 13

In other news, I was thinking that the accidents, illnesses and such – they make you *stronger* in ways you never thought you were capable of. It strips you to your core. There's no in between – either you fight OR you give up. Either you persevere OR you quit. It's so easy to quit, to give up on yourself and the people around you. So easy. So, you dig deep and find *something* to live for. It's a constant battle to keep moving forward. You're never the same person you were *before* those experiences happen. Good or bad, a part of you changes.

Lesson of the day: You can't live through a life-altering event and remain as you *were*. A new you emerges; whether it's a positive or negative new you. It's inevitable.

Nov 17

Dr. Nepal asked, How are you doing? Enh.

He tenderly touched my cheek and said, I hate seeing you like this. It was so sweet. It's the first bit of *fatherly* "love" I've received in YEARS! He gave me *nine* injections!

When do you start the PRP (platelet-rich plasma injections)?

January 5. If I could do it *tomorrow,* I would.

Does the pain keep you from sleeping?

You know, I've been in accidents and had cancer and THIS is the *first* time the pain actually wakes me up and keeps me awake.

Nov 23

I feel like Tracy needs to move on to having a wonderful life, with kids and a healthy partner. A passionate life. We watch our dreams float away. This is not a life. I love that man with my every fiber. I just want *more* for him. I feel like I hold him back. I've been on this emotional rollercoaster for years, beginning with the pain and the ultimate decision to remove my innards. It's been gut-wrenching (literally), with a few minor breaks in between. I get a handle on one thing, and then I get thrown another. I'm in the middle of so many of them – hysterectomy, no chance for kids, no one to pass things down to, a second surgery, pain that never ends, a cancer scare, hernias, bone-on-bone toes, kidney disease, scar tissue, and lack of money. I need to stabilize my hormones and "fix" the scar tissue that's mashing my organs.

There are reminders every day, everywhere, that we *don't* have children; it's a constant presence. Yesterday we were watching TV and a commercial said, *If you don't have children, you have no idea it's the best feeling in the world. You have something worth going home to.* WTF? I said to Tracy, There's *nothing* worth going home to if you DON'T have kids?! There couldn't be anything else a person could have that would be worth coming home to?? I was disgusted. Everyone MUST have children? Women can't NOT have children and be considered a value to society? Well, that clinches it – I have no children; therefore, I can't possibly have a life worth living! Asshole commercial. The way the world is going with having to be *all-inclusive*, one might consider including PEOPLE WHO CAN'T HAVE CHILDREN AND STILL WANT TO BE CONSIDERED A VALUED MEMBER OF SOCIETY!! How about that? Maybe people who DON'T own pets should be ostracized because they have no clue what it means to be privileged with having one. It's ridiculous. I feel like if I live long enough, facing old age with crippled feet, pain, complications...I'm finding it more and more difficult to find the silver lining. What's the incentive? Dire finances, health decline, emotional breakdowns...sounds like a dream. Well, a nightmare. It's a fucking nightmare.

Dec 15

Another stellar meltdown day! My morning started off with snapping the mirror off my Jeep getting out of the garage; then the garage door wouldn't close. I cried all the way to work. By making me late, God, you probably *prevented* me from getting into an accident or something? But you could've saved yourself the trouble and *let* it happen. God, would it kill you to give me ONE fucking EASY day!? You're up there having a good laugh. Laugh it up, Chuckles.

Wow, I'm just NOT myself. If the docs don't get these goddamn *hormones in check*…My chest is wheezing, congested; my cough is back in full force. Bronchitis. Tracy has *another* lung infection. It also feels like I broke a rib coughing. Dang.

Dammit, can this year be over already?

BODY IMAGE

All my life, I had body image issues. Not shocking, or a big revelation for someone who has been violated. Since I was eight years old, I've been aware of my body, of *others* being aware of *my* body. I hated my body my entire life. I wanted it to go away. I ate little, exercised a lot, I never wore revealing or form-fitting clothes; I wore dark, loose and baggy ones. I didn't buy a pair of jeans until I was 37 years old. I had a pair of jeans that I had in high school that I wore maybe twice, and they hung in my closet until 2005 – when I threw them out.

People would often tell me how skinny I was and what a great body I had. I never believed them. I figured they had to be pulling my leg or trying to make me look stupid. But they weren't, they meant it. I just *never* saw myself in that light. To me, MY body was gross and disgusting; it was an *abused* body. At eight years old, my body was the object of someone's desires – how does a child of that age process that? They don't. So, I carried all those feelings of confusion and repulsion into my adulthood.

The first harmful things I did to my body were throwing up and taking laxatives; I started both on the same day, when I was 28 years old. I purged *intensely* for three years, but on and off for seven. I averaged four laxatives every single day for three years. It gave me comfort knowing I was ridding my body *of myself*. It was a tool to control my body. I *needed* control over the body that let me down. My brother was a predator, but my body *didn't* stop him either. That was when I purposely began to religiously monitor my weight on the scale. I didn't stop until I was 33 years old.

I felt like I was wearing an ugly suit – if I could just unzip the tainted, revolting me and reveal the REAL me, the body I was MEANT to have.

Years later, when I had cancer, there was no way to *not* eat. For me, food kept the nausea at bay and was a necessity with all that poison in my system. Tracy made me gourmet meals to keep my strength up. I wasn't *ever* hungry, but he kept me alive by *making* me eat. I never once threw up or used laxatives when I was sick. I had a different battle on my hands without worrying about the other stuff. I hoped maybe the chemo would kill all the ugliness I had on the inside.

That was the end of the bulimia and laxatives, but my body image issues remained. I realized that if I was trying to have a baby, I had to take better care of my body.

I tried desperately to *accept* my body and KNOW it's the only one I get, so I needed to treat it with respect and do no harm. I looked back on pictures of myself when I was slimmer and I couldn't believe I *ever* thought I was fat! I understood I had the brain of an abused person and that distorted what I saw looking back at me in the mirror.

2017

Jan 16

The doorbell rang. It's Myriam! She said, I've been thinking about you lots and I took a chance coming by. My car just kind of brought me here. You are home to me. I've imagined coming here so many times. We caught up and I told her TODAY I booked a procedure for my belly, a last hope. Her wonderful husband, Darren, is a saint like Tracy – they are so supportive of their wives. Bless them.

Jan 18

A "loving God" would *help* me. But no. My ENTIRE life, my body has let me down. Combined with everything *else* on my plate – it's a recipe for giving up. What's the incentive to keep on? I hate myself. God hates me. I don't see a light. There's no light! I see more struggles ahead. I see Tracy working his fingers to the bone, with no payoff. I see emptiness. I see nothingness. I can't even say I "see." Fucking blurry vision. I FEEL no light. No warmth. Dead inside. Dead outside. I feel failed. I failed myself. Failed by people. I feel so done here. Another 50 years of this fucking hell? Marrying Tracy was THE BEST thing I've EVER done with my life. But what kind of life did *I* give *him*? A childless life. A life with struggles and issues. Day after day. Year after year. It's no life at all. All our hopes and dreams – gone. There's nothing left but the bad stuff. It just doesn't end.

It. Just. Doesn't. End.

Have faith. HA! I'm 48 – when does it *start* getting good? Everyone else gets it. I don't see it. I don't feel it. God despises me. Sometimes I think I can't "leave" Tracy, to leave him alone in this world. But he *could* still start a family if I *do* go. There's *still* time for HIM, he's 53. Jeff Goldblum, he's 65, his wife is pregnant with their SECOND baby! Then there's my precious Dudie. He needs me to survive. He's my fur baby.

So, I keep moving forward and searching for those thin threads of hope.

Jan 19

Dr. Nepal looked at my blood results. He's putting me on a higher dose of estrogen.

Your mood is good?

No, it's in the toilet.

When we get your estrogen up, your mood *will* get better too. Menopause *is* correlated with depression.

I told him about my cough and I thought I cracked a rib; I heard it crack.

You can't always see the fractures on X-rays; sometimes they're too small. He pinched my cheek again, You poor thing.

It's comforting to me when he pinches my cheek. He's my unofficial fatherly figure, and I trust him implicitly.

He gave me adrenal shots. He got me in to see a doctor to check my lungs.

Tracy says, You seem to be in a *good* mood today. I'm glad. I like it when you're feeling that way.

I think maybe because I saw Dr. Nepal? He gives me peace of mind.

Jan 25

Yesterday my horoscope was about having faith. I think the universe is trying to tell me something. I heard on TV that each thought you have manifests physiologically. Again, the signs are knocking me over the head to get an attitude adjustment and start believing in myself and the universe.

Feb 2

Today's the day; I'm getting my PRP procedure. I'm so nervous and anxious.

Dr. Avery examined me and said, It takes three to six months to see any improvement; we are *regrowing* your tendons, they are so degraded.

I started tearing. *This is my last chance.*

He took ten vials of blood. What are your hopes or concerns from this?

To have no pain. To live a day with *no* pain.

Dr. Nepal came in for a quick peek and to offer support. He anaesthetized the area, then began. Indescribable pain. When Dr. Avery punctured the hernias with the needle, I hit the roof! Excruciating.

Do you have a good support system?

Yes, my husband is in the waiting area. He's amazing.

How old are you?

Forty-eight.

Too young to have to deal with all *this.*

I hit the roof again. I couldn't breathe, I couldn't talk.

And then he was done. Do you drink wine? If you partake, it can help today. I laughed. Come see me in three to four months.

That pain was in my top-three things of most painful. We went home and Tracy took care of me.

I'm so glad it's over. I so hope it works!

Feb 4

Tracy asked me, Do you need to see a therapist? You're *not* happy.

He's on to me. I felt like he can *see* me, *really* see me.

I said to Tracy, Not that I think the procedure was some miracle cure, but it's frustrating that I had a bad day. It takes **months**, not days, months. Knowing that the low dose of estrogen for the past few years gave no relief of my menopausal symptoms didn't help either. Dr. Nepal says if I can just get that balanced, it'll make a *huge* difference. I very much look forward to that.

Mar 2

Dr. Nepal asks, How are you doing?

I'm in as much pain as I was *before* the procedure. He pinches my cheek: You poor baby. I know it takes time. You may need *another* procedure. Its three out of ten that it *doesn't* work. Are you going to be one of the three?
Probably, I'll be the anomaly, again.
No, don't say that. You need to have hope.
Yes. Thank you for reminding me.

Mar 9
I went to see an eye doctor. My eyes have been watery and blurry for *so* long, I need answers. They froze and dilated my eyes. He said, It's an *easy fix*. There's inflammation and the left tear duct is completely closed and the right one is partially closed. He prescribed drops and said to come back in a month. I'm SO relieved it's *fixable*. I had visions (no pun intended) of this being bigger than it was.

Apr 4
Our 25th wedding anniversary. Tracy came home with a bouquet of our wedding flowers – lilies, and roses. GORGEOUS! I had T-shirts made that said *April 4, 1992*, with our names. Tracy loved it. We wore them all day. We looked at our wedding photos when we went out to Boomtown. It's been so long since we've gone out; it was so nice.

I was watching a talk show – a brother molested his sister two times. She's confused. She wants to hang out with him. She sits at the dinner table and everyone pretends. It started with him watching porn, his dad's porn. Check.

Do *all* these scenarios start out the same way as mine? And our family...it's almost like we never existed. We were a "family" so long ago, for such a short period of time, it's like it never happened. In fact, it really doesn't feel like I EVER had a family. The one we had for a while was all pretend – parents who fought behind closed doors, I had to pretend I liked my sibling, the other sibling left the home because he couldn't pretend or hide his contempt for me, Kyle pretending to be a good older brother...

May 4
Dr. Avery examined me thoroughly.

Do you find the pain gets worse with mood changes?

As of a month or so ago, I finally *am* in hormonal balance.

I explained that my job requires me to be on my feet all day and do heavy lifting.

He suggested an SI Belt to stabilize the pelvis. I think your job is counterproductive to things regrowing and healing.

Are we saying the procedure DIDN'T work?

No. We are at *three* months and it takes *six* months to tell, but if you keep going down the road of this job, nothing will change. You have a lot of stress in your pelvis. I suggest you DON'T DO ANY core activity. Your body is *not* ready for that. You can wear the belt at night too but looser than in the day. Come back in three months and we can decide if the PRP is worth trying again. We might do it at the year point. Your body is so unstable. Surgery *isn't* an option; fusing things together poses a greater risk than not. We need to stabilize your body *before* we take the next step.

June 3
There was a discussion on *The Young and the Restless* regarding suicide: *"A permanent solution for a temporary problem."* In my case, I feel it's a *lifelong* problem. It's not just ONE thing, it's not TWO things...it's an entire life of things. No break. No end in sight. So no, it's not a "temporary" problem – it's 40 years of problems. I don't know if the good stuff will ever come. I'm waiting. I've been waiting. I'm a good person; I work hard and help others. And the universe blocks us. Bad people get things handed to them, or so it seems. They get to get ahead. I have no money to buy milk for Tracy.

June 8

My *cancerversary*, as Tracy calls it. I want to cry. Tracy got paid today, but the money is already all gone, and now it's two weeks until payday again.

June 19

Blood means nothing. Under that *umbrella*, it means people can hurt you *more* and then say, *But we're family.* To have the same family blood running through your veins is just that – linked *genetically* but not in life. In life, you get to *choose* those people you can't live without, and it's *not* genetics, it's a REAL bond.

You *don't* get to pick who is in your bloodline, but you *do* get to pick who actually means something to you, who has your back. Family has nothing to do with biology. Blood means poison, the poison is deep within your body, but you don't have to live with it. Expel the poison and choose GOOD blood, good family. A REAL family means people you can trust. People who have PROVEN you can trust them with your secrets, your heart, and your life. And you fight for those people you call family. People you would do *anything* for. I'm at a point in my life where if I don't speak to friends and family, I'm cool with that. I won't chase anyone. I never have and I never will. I don't chase people for their loyalty or friendship. I will never *force* someone to *want* to be in my life.

"People will stab you in the back, then ask why are you bleeding?" I just read that. Sooo true.

June 24

I guess I'm only *allowed* to feel good for two days. I have no money to buy needles for Dudie, get gas or buy a few groceries. THIS FUCKING SUCKS. I cried all day. All the fear and uncertainty. I got a text from Myriam – that brightened things up. She told me the reason she reached out to me out of the blue in January was because her "soul told her to." Wow. I need her just as much as she needs me – reciprocal friendship, what a concept.

June 27

It was Father's Day. It's a sad day with painful reminders of what Tracy and I have both *lost*. For me, letting go of a parent changes you, but the alternative is detrimental to my well-being. I told Tracy I didn't sleep very well last night. I was hoping he'd tell me everything was going to be okay. He didn't. In the evening, we noticed that water was starting to seep through the basement ceiling. I thought the ceiling was going to cave in, what were we going to do? How much was this going to *cost*?? I cried. I stood under the ceiling where it was soaking through and just stood there, and waited, and cried. Then it occurred to me – THE FRIDGE! Tracy pulled the fridge from the wall. IT IS THE FRIDGE! It was all flooded in behind there, seeping through the floor, from the icemaker. Tracy turned off the water to the fridge and reassured me the ceiling **wouldn't** cave in. It'll be okay.

June 29

I can't stop crying. I cried all morning, teary during work, cried all the way to my car after work, and I'm STILL crying. I'M SO STRESSED. I'm going to fucking snap! Our last $10 in our account got sucked up by fees. Just fucking shoot me. We are drowning in debt. Drowning. I can't breathe. We owe so much, working our asses off, getting nowhere. I see no future. I can't bear this. I can't.

EVERY day is day by day.
EVERY day there's a setback.
EVERY day I have to figure out a way to believe I should be here.
EVERY day I think I'd be better off gone.
EVERY day I have to give myself a reason to stay (living).
EVERY day I have to find the strength.
EVERY day I have to convince myself Tracy and the fur babies *need* me.
EVERY day I wonder if I made the right decision.
EVERY day I wonder how I'm going to do this all again tomorrow.

July 12

We had drinks with Dave and Erin on a rooftop patio downtown and Erin states, You're the strongest person I know. With all that you've had to deal with, you DO. When I feel down, I think of *you*.

I never knew you saw me like that.

She hugged me and said, I love you.

We four bar-hopped for a bit after. It was so much fun, and then we cabbed it home. It was a nice reprieve, to be having FUN!

Lesson of the day: Don't forget to have fun!

July 25

Mom came to visit. Things went well, until they didn't. The three of us had one bizarre blow-up.

The next day Mom said that with Parkinson's, she can't process thoughts quickly, it muddles her thinking. Brain fog.

I said, I *don't* see you as a disease, I see you as my mom. I always have and always will.

Don't stop loving me.

I won't. You've been really good about not discussing *them* while you are here.

I know, but he IS on my mind.

I understand that. I was thinking to myself, He's been on death's door for a year now? He's had *a year* to make amends? To feel remorse? To make things right before he...I guess it's just not on his radar.

I *need* to call Levi. He's very sick and I know *you* don't care but I need to keep tabs on the situation.

That's fine. I can separate the two. My issues with *them* are completely separate from you and them. You do what you need to do.

She was so relieved. I feel for you as the mother in all this.

Aug 22

I was talking to Mom about the internet; she said, A child sees things on there they can't UNsee. I knew she meant porn. True, but they can see inappropriate things **anywhere**...billboards, magazines, bus stops, newspapers...Bad things aren't *just* on a *computer*.

A child sees sexual things and they don't know how to process it. It's like an addiction.

Oh boy. Boy oh boy. I bit my tongue. I forced myself to NOT mention her darling child. Loooong before children had access to the internet, there were porn movies and magazines, of which *he* looked at *relentlessly*. He couldn't UNsee what he saw. *He* couldn't process the images. So, he used *me* to "experiment on," to "figure it out." If a *ten-year-old boy* has difficulty processing that, imagine how an *eight-year-old girl* CAN'T either! It's not children OUT THERE; it's *her* child!

Sept 12

I feel like I'm failing life miserably. I begged to live when I had cancer. I survived. Now I don't feel like I appreciate my life. I appreciate and am forever grateful for Tracy and our marriage and our fur babies, but the nonstop challenges and stress and fear are taking their toll. I feel like life is passing us by and we have no means to getting back in it. On the train of life, everyone is on it, passing us by, not even glancing out their window to see us standing there. And there's nothing and no one to grab onto, to lift or pull us on to the train. No one sees us.

Lesson of the day: Life IS a train. Either you find a way on or you get left behind. I have to find a way back on.

Sept 19

I get home and Tracy's already there. Your mom just called me. Your brother died.

My heart skipped a beat. Interesting reaction. Not how I imagined I'd react. I'm not feeling "elated." I mostly feel badly for Mom.

I said to Tracy, In my entire life, I can count on one hand the amount of times he was nice to me.

He deserved to live a LONG life to think about the awful things he did. Instead, he died weeks after turning 55. Shame.

I didn't even have one tear. Nothing.

496

Tracy said, They already had the funeral. How are you feeling?
Ding dong, the witch is dead.

Sept 20

It's the eve of Rosh Hashanah. I've begged and pleaded with God every year for good health and financial stability. Despite some high points, it seems like every year my health and our finances get worse. So, God, do whatever you want. My helping others, living this life in pain, worrying about losing my house every month, watching my sick cat die in front of me...this is what I get. And the bad people of the world continue to prosper. So, asking for health and wealth because it's Rosh Hashanah seems stupid. I've reached out to people this year, I've been the bigger person, I've given people 100 chances, and what do I get? Nothing. Are we not *allowed* to have *regular* struggles like everyone else? To have the typical ups and downs? Instead, it's down, down, down. What is my crime? Am I supposed to pay and pay for the crimes of my brothers *forever*?! Will they *never* be held accountable? Can we not shift the blame to where it belongs? Is the *next* 49 years going to be much of the same? I give up *now*, if that's the case. I surrender. I'm done fighting. I want to be free. If we're given what we can handle, why am I not handling it?

God, don't make me beg for the life of my cat, only for you to keep him in pain and suffering. Don't make me beg for my home, only to keep the threat of it being taken away dangling in front of us. Don't make me think I can get through a million different doctor appointments in the hope my health will improve, only for it to get worse. You dangle things in front of us, with seemingly great pleasure, knowing it's *always* going to be just out of our reach. With all the hurricanes happening now – Irma, Jose, and Harry – suffering is your game. Yes, *you're* the boss, we get it. But you still want us to beg. You will do as you please, regardless. My amazing, NON-Jewish husband baked Challahs (braided bread) for the High Holidays. That's a Mitzvah, but there will be *no* mercy or reward for that. I've apologized to this world for having me in it. It's never apologized back to me. You take and take. I have nothing left to give. Happy New Year.

Sept 29

I took Dudie to a holistic vet. She checked him out meticulously: ears, mouth, eyes, chest, weight…The cold is *not* in his chest – it's all sinus and upper respiratory. First off, he's on the *wrong* food.

But I get his food from *here*, a VET!

I know, but it doesn't mean it's the *right* food. Kibble is high in fat and carbs. His little body is working so hard with the insulin to break down food that is all sugar! A cat's body is *not* meant to eat or digest grain; they need to eat *meat*. If the *first three* or four ingredients on the pet food label *aren't* meat, it's *no good*.

I felt awful. How could I know? I got his food from a *vet*! I am essentially killing him.

You'll need to *reduce* his insulin immediately, from eight to six units. Get him *off* the kibble, *only* canned food from here on. If the cold gets worse on the weekend, you don't need to bring him in; I'll have antibiotics on file and enough for you to pick up. So, change his diet, reduce his insulin, research the new food, get probiotics, and I'm giving him some Chinese herbs. You should see a difference right away – not in days or weeks.

Wow. Overwhelming. So many changes, but it makes so much sense. Poor little guy. I thought I was doing right by him. And this is why I changed vets; someone with *solutions*. I'm so relieved, he's in excellent hands.

Oct 4

Here's some irony. I guess with Thanksgiving coming up, I wanted to make a list of what I **am** thankful for. There's been a lot of negativity in my life and it clouds things. I needed to refocus and bring some positivity back in. The bad stuff can really bog you down, but wonderful things *have* happened in the last little while, and I need to acknowledge that. I thanked Mom for a beautiful video reminder she sent me, about our journey in this life. It's like a train – people get on and off, some you'll remember, some you won't recall ever sitting next to you. Be kind, and show your best self to everyone.

Funny, *I* was just saying life is like a *train*, my *own* analogy – it seems to be a meaningful one.

Oct 12

I think I'm going to have a stroke. Tracy said the owners at work don't want to pay for parts and paint, and that he's probably *not* getting paid tomorrow. Are you fucking kidding me? What the fuck are we going to do?! I'm trying not to lose my shit. I'm sure those owners *aren't* having trouble making ends meet. *They* don't care about all the people who *depend* on that paycheck. It's a game to them.

Oct 17

Tracy comes home and says they are closing the shop. They won't pay for the vehicles at the paint shop, so there is no work for anyone. They haven't paid rent either. I doubt I'll be getting paid *next week* either. I'm going down tomorrow to get my tools. If the landlord closes the doors, I won't be able to get my stuff. I have no words.

Oct 18

Throughout my youngest of young years, when most girls *get* a chance to figure out their sexuality *naturally,* on their own, the process was vastly *expedited* for me. Now at almost 50, I feel like I've *still* been stunted by that forced acceleration. I feel I never properly experienced enjoying a first kiss or a boyfriend because the back story was always there, lurking. Yes, I had a first kiss; and yes, I had a first boyfriend, but the beautiful experience it *should have been* was tainted by being exposed (literally) to very adult situations at a very early age. I can never get those *firsts* back. I couldn't enjoy my first kiss without knowing I'd experienced far more than that innocent event.

Oct 26

Dudie's 11th birthday. Thank goodness he made it. I love that little man.

I swear, if I hear one more person say, "*...but they're family*" one more time...So "family" can treat you in ANY way they want, and we have to forgive them because society deems them *worthy* of that – THEY'RE FAMILY? WTF DOES THAT EVEN MEAN? *Yes,* they mistreated you buuut, they're *family*! Seriously?? Yes, your father/brother/sister/mother beat/assaulted/humiliated you BUT they are STILL *family*, go make peace. Do people hear themselves? Ya, but I'm their kid/niece/sister/mother and that makes their actions *worse*!

Lesson of the day: One CAN find peace in their life WITHOUT having to compromise on the truth. If a person can and does come to a place of peace in their life, moving forward, how does an outside person have the right to suggest otherwise – in order for you to be able to forge on, you NEED to *forgive* and *not* rock the boat? Do it for YOUR *own* sake, not *theirs*. I've made MY peace and I'm good with that. It did NOT consist of me making inner or outer declarations that I have *forgiven* them. I don't think these blanket, generic statements from TV doctors or therapists or celebrities or anyone who deems themselves to know *better* than you do, about your OWN life and experiences, can say you NEED to do this for your own benefit. I will do what I feel is best for me, thank you very much. They could speak to 100 traumatized people from the same plane crash and **_every_** story and perspective would be *different*. It's **_their_** experience. No one else can feel the way that feels – to them. A doctor is not going to come in and say, Okay, EVERYONE needs to move on, forgive the event or person, get past this, chop, chop. And to follow the cookie-cutter way of moving on from trauma is ridiculous. EVERY person and situation is unique. Everyone has to do what is best for *them* and not what an *outsider* feels is best for you based on what, a psychology textbook? talking to other people? To each their own. Person by person. Nobody has a right to even have an opinion on MY experiences. I will deal with my life, in my own way. It's beyond inappropriate to have someone tell you how you should move on from something. No one is the authority on their life except themselves. Even if someone "walked a mile in your shoes," it would STILL be THEIR experience, not yours. We can show empathy and compassion, we can sympathize, and we can say this is how *I* felt when a *similar* event happened to *me*.

Everybody got that?

Oct 29

Horoscope: *The dark clouds above – those scary things that have been hanging over your head and following you around – are not dissipating. You may not have noticed though, because you have been afraid to look up. You have just kept your head down looking at the ground. But that is all about to change. Be brave. Take a look around. If you do, you will see that things really are getting better. Conditions are improving, and soon, you will feel more carefree. It's about time.*

Fluffy peed on *my* side of the bed. Is THIS how things will get *better*?

Nov 1

I *know* there is *something* for us out there. I know our whole lives have been steppingstones to *something*. Everyone on this planet is looking for purpose. I get it. I just keep waiting for the good to start happening. We make our own destiny, I believe. But what does that say about you when you give it your all, trying *to make* things happen, thinking outside the box, trying *anything*, and we are **still** in the position we're in? Is our fate doomed, no matter how hard we try? It feels so futile. I try to believe. We finally get the loan *paid off* and we *still* run the risk of losing our home. One step forward, one hundred steps back. We are in the epitome of limbo! Do all, be all, try, try, try… And in return, deeper debt, deeper doubts, and no hope for the future. Life is a test. I feel I have failed miserably, and I don't know what I've done to warrant it. *Everyone* has challenges. But abuse, car accidents, legal woes, on the brink emotionally, childless, massive health issues, business flops, deaths, some of the most toxic friendships…Some people go through *some* of those things, we get it *all*. Therein lies the confusion. One test, two tests – okay, that makes sense. But we've had *more than* our fair share. It's exhausting. My husband is **the** best part of my life. He's everything that really matters to me in this world. I wish for him the world. We **are** fortunate we have each other. I cherish that. So, some people have money, we have love. I just *don't* believe people can't have *both*. It's difficult convincing yourself the universe *isn't* out to "get you" (or is it?).

Nov 6

Mom calls me, I thought you should know...Rabbi Fineberg is searching for your father. Kyle didn't want the task of seeking him out to tell him his son is dead, so Rabbi Fineberg took it on.

Cut off is cut off. We don't pick and choose *when* it's okay to be in touch and every other time we ignore each other? He didn't care about my surgery or Tracy's dad dying. Why the heck would I tell him about this? It's not my problem.
I bought champagne tonight because I told Tracy I'm tired of feeling sad and scared.
It's about time! Anything can happen at *any* time. Things can change for the GOOD!

Nov 10

Dudie has poopy-bum issues and he's not eating again. Tracy's going to call the Labor Board – his work won't lay them off *nor* will they pay them. I'm pretty sure that's illegal.
And our friend Jim has cancer. It's melanoma, but is treatable.

On the pain front, it hasn't improved much. I'm still at a job that is counter-productive to healing properly. I think I will leave it be for now as I need a job more than I need another PRP procedure.

Nov 11

I was up all night with the Dude. I force-fed him and wiped runny poop off his bum.

I feel completely saturated and inundated with Hollywood's sexual assault allegations and the ME, TOO movement. It's a *very real thing*

502

because I've been through it, *but I can't get away from it*. It's in *every* news feed and headline. It's a serious matter, but *I* need a break. It *triggers* all kinds of shit for me; and with everything *else* going on in MY life, it's one aspect I *don't* want to keep in the forefront. Every day is *already* emotional for me; to have to mix that in too, it's overload.

Nov 14

We basically have no income. The job thing is taking so long. Even though I'm still working part-time at the merchandising job, my income is hardly making a difference. I'm putting out the résumés and using word of mouth for both Tracy and me. No income. No savings. No investments. Nothing. It's freaking the heck out of me. I don't know what's going to happen. We need a HUGE break!

Nov 15

I asked Tracy if it's time to start panicking yet. He just looked at me like, That's *not* helping. I prayed all last night and tonight for tomorrow to be THE day Tracy gets an *amazing* job! I get that we *make* our *own* luck and *make* things happen for ourselves. We've worked hard and never expected handouts. I just don't understand why everything we try *doesn't* pan out. All our "failures" or lessons or tests will mean *something someday,* but when we are weeks away from losing it all because we have no income, it makes a person wonder, Why me? What have *I* done that the universe thinks is so unforgivable that it will keep taking from us when we literally have nothing left to give? Why can't WE make it? It feels like the whole family is cursed. Frick and Frack are monsters. My parents struggled financially and emotionally. They had two children with cancer, one who died from it. This "unit" never had a chance, and I feel I keep paying for the mistakes of a *previous* life because I can't think of what I've done in *this* one to deserve all these years of major crap.

Nov 20

Tracy asked the accountant at work for a Letter of Employment. They haven't laid anyone off though.

Well, when there is *no* work in *seven consecutive days,* I'm entitled to EI. The bosses will be in today, and I will ask.

At the end of the day, the response Tracy got was that they will *think* about it.

I said to him, Uh, you're not asking for *permission* –it's your RIGHT to get it. Asses. They are playing with people's LIVES! It's the most ridiculous situation.

I accidentally broke the last vile of insulin. I have no money to replace it.

Nov 29

Tracy started his *new job* yesterday, at a security company. Yay! I got another store for merchandising – I have four now. I texted Jim and asked how he was feeling. He goes for surgery on Wednesday.

Dec 5

Why are we killing ourselves to "get ahead" when it feels like we *never* will?

What. Is. The. Fucking. Point? Truly?

Those fleeting moments of hope – when I feel *so* good and *anything* feels possible – they last about a second until the next bomb explodes. Minuscule moments of hope compared to gigantic long stretches of pure shit! It's sooo defeating. I'm defeated. The world beat me down. Us down. I'm beat. You win. I don't know what I'm fighting for anymore. I'm so tired of feeling vulnerable and asking God and the universe to be kind to us and HELP us...and there is silence...deafening nothingness...it's time to take the cue.

And yet I still believe there is something better out there for us.

I couldn't wait any longer. I had to bring Dudie to the vet. His eye is almost completely sealed shut. Our regular vet was in surgery so we had to go with another one. She said his eye is related to his abscessed tooth.

I *can't* afford the $2000 surgery. I can't even afford *this* visit!

I can give him medication for the swelling and stuff to put on his gums for pain.

When we were done, I had just paid and was leaving when my *regular* vet comes out. Sorry I was in surgery. Is Dudie okay? She goes over to his crate and takes him out. She sees his eye and asks me if the fluorescent light test was done. No.

She grabs him and brings him *back* into the exam room. He's on *the* best antibiotics. Cats hide pain well; they can go on for quite some time with a bad mouth. Eventually, the surgery will help him. It would probably make the diabetes better too. An *inexpensive* way to get rid of tartar and saves cat's teeth, try chicken neck bones.

After trashing the universe all day, I had two little miracles – Dudie getting meds *and* being told it *will* heal. I'm so relieved. And the vet visit only cost $156. Dudie received **two** vet exams for the price of one.

I think we might be okay.

Dec 18
Eye specialist. Why are you here?
For a second opinion.
He checked my eyes. It can only be *three* things: 1) Tear ducts – yours are clear. 2) Eyelids – yours are fine. 3) Allergies or the environment – there is *something* in the air causing this. Do you have a cat?
Yes, two and a dog.
You need to remove the thing that's causing the problem.
Actually, it gets *worse* at *work* and that's nowhere near animals.
I have drops that are *preservative-free* and it acts like a sponge; it draws in all the garbage and it doesn't burn. You can use it 1000 times a day. You have a lot of inflammation and swelling that we need to reduce right away. Check back with your doctor in two months, but this stuff should clear things up pretty quickly.

This means 20-20 vision for 2018.

2018

Jan 17

Tracy and I were watching *The Good Doctor*. A woman breaks up with a man because she doesn't want kids and she wants *him* to have them. She doesn't want him resenting her later on. I'm sitting there bawling. Tracy said, That was pretty intense. Are you okay?

That episode hit a little too close to home. Tracy saw I was still upset so he says, Don't sweat it. Then on TWO other shows, the *exact same theme*. I even said to Tracy, Okay, Universe, we get it! Geez. Tracy said, I know I haven't said this in a while, but you're my love and passion and reason for living. I think it all the time, I just haven't said it lately.

Jan 20

Jim came by. I think it's been over a year since he's been over. We talked about all that Galaxy stuff and how we will *always* be in each other's lives regardless. It was great reconnecting. For years he's called me *Lil Sis*. He's like the older brother I *never* had.

Jan 29

Tracy calls me, Where's the *closest* walk-in clinic to our house? A ladder took off on me and I ripped my hand open. I found one in our area and they took him right away. He's recounting the story of how he was drilling a hole in the ceiling and the ladder starts leaving. He grabbed on to the ceiling T- bar and it gave way. It ripped the flesh open on his palm all the way back. They might have to cut his wedding ring off. It bent and cut into his finger. I took a picture. They stitched it up with FOUR stitches and put a pressure bandage on it. It looked like he needed WAY more stitches.

Jan 31

Horoscope: *You may wind up getting attention for your efforts that could result in a raise, a promotion, or even a better job.*

I got an email at 4:30 p.m. from my boss saying she's pleased to inform me I've been given a $1.40/hr raise. Sweet.

Lesson of the day: It's the small things that make the biggest difference.

Mar 13

Dudie is having issues with his mouth, drooling profusely. It's so upsetting to watch. If I take him to the vet, they'll only want to extract his teeth and I STILL don't have $2000 for that. I gave him pain meds and an oral numbing medication. It seemed to help. The drooling stopped and he ate well.

Apr 14

Chicago Med: What a messed-up episode. Waaay too close to home. There's a young character named *Kyle*. He likes to watch girls and is afraid he *will* hurt someone. He walks into a hospital room of a *sleeping* patient. I almost threw up. TV is supposed to be *entertaining*. Tonight, it was just traumatizing.

May 8

It *should* be a good day with all those **8**s. Dudie had a *great* morning. He was in my face waking me up because *he was hungry*. Excellent sign. He ate solid food and was up the scratch post when I left.

May 9

Dudie is not doing well. I tried to make an appointment with my vet. *May 28* is her *first available* appointment.

May 28? My cat will be dead by then. The thing is, he's *not* eating, so I think that'll be way *too late*.

I can get you in at 3:30 p.m. *today*. I'll take it!

Dudie kept *trying* to eat, *wanting* to eat but *couldn't*. He didn't hide like sick cats usually do. He kept following me around and looking up at me. *I've* been crying for hours. He's alert, excited by the birds flying around outside, not sleepy, running up his scratch post, and grooming. He seems "normal." I don't know what to do anymore. I KNOW he's suffering, yet he's NOT lethargic and *has* energy. WTF?

3:30 p.m. is a long way off from now – it's 9:20 a.m. I'm at my wits' end. My little baby. He's mouth-breathing too. His tongue's hanging out. He *finally* fell asleep on the bed. He stretched his arm out to touch the dog. I took a picture. He woke up and was meowing at me for food. And he *can't* eat!! Fuck! My heart is breaking into a million pieces. I just gave him what could be his *last* injection. I lay on the bed with him. I need to spend time with him. The last bit of time. He flipped on his back and I rubbed his belly. He then got up and curled right up to me. My baby is sleeping now. Every part of my life revolves around him. Everything. My job, my schedules, our outings...everything we did, we had to consider if it would affect him. Getting up at midnight to give him his shot. I'd have done *anything* for him. This sucks so bad. My sweet angel. Brutal. He woke up a few times looking for food, realizing he can't eat, then went back to bed.

I *finally* went to the vet. It's the one and only time he *didn't* make a peep going to the vet. Not a single sound. Not one meow. It was eerie. Like he knew. She checked him out. He didn't fuss for even a second.

Cats with bad teeth can live a long time without issues, but his diabetes makes him worse than others. I'll bet if I took a urine sample, we'd find ketoacidosis; that is VERY serious. There's not much you can do at that point. So, have you considered the "other" option? Yes.
Are you prepared to do that *today*? Yes.
You're making the *best* decision here. I would do the same. I'll get the paperwork started and we'll have to get an IV in. You can spend as much time with him as you need. One girl came in to take him for his IV and another came in and brought with her...the box of boxes for me to choose from to put him in when he's gone. Damn. I picked the cedar box to match our *other* ones.

They brought him back into the room. While I waited for the paperwork, I texted Tracy – he agreed he's *got to be* put down. I talked to Dudie the whole time. He nuzzled his head into my chest and purred, as if to console ME. It felt like he was trying to tell me it's okay. He seemed "ready." I let them know I was ready for them. She began. I'm going to give him a sedative first so he gets sleepy; it's very gentle and quick. His head slumped a little. Then "THE" injection. And it was over. My sweet little angel. My precious boy. I spent more time with him. That tiny little body that endured so much can finally be at peace. I kissed and kissed and kissed him and gave that belly one last rub. I told him how much I loved him and will miss him. I wanted him to live forever. He was so special. One of a kind. My heart hurts. I did the right thing, no question, but damn it hurts.
Tracy texted me, Is he gone?
He's gone.

I'll miss that sweet face looking up at me. I'll miss *everything* about him, but I'm grateful he's no longer in pain. I don't think he had an angry a day in his life. A happy, friendly, lovable baby. We were so lucky. Go play with your other brothers and sisters in heaven. Be free. And then there was one – Fluffy. He'll be lost without his *twin*. His life buddy. Man. I think I have nothing left to cry. Tracy just texted: I am so sick to my stomach. I *should* be with you.
Bad timing is all. It can't be helped. I got home and threw out all his meds and needles. I threw out his little ceramic pot of grass. I was looking at his food dish. I cried. Fuck me, I miss him already! Tracy just texted again: I never got to say goodbye.
I'm sorry.
I knew this day was coming. There's just no way to prepare. My 11-year-old. Tracy came home and I shared the details. He was crying. I told him I was comforted by Dudie's *readiness* to go. Fluffy is looking in all the usual places for him. Our house is a sad one tonight.

May 19

This morning we were talking about kids. All the hormones I took were for naught. Cancer killed *any* chance of that. Nothing was ever said to me regarding harvesting my eggs *before* chemo. Today, people get that option; I didn't. I think they just had to get me in treatment *quickly*. Fucking cancer.

I told Tracy, YOU can *still* have kids.

What's your point?

YOU CAN. Just saying.

So damn weird. Tracy and I go to bed and there's a noise coming from Dudie's box area. A noise *we've never* heard before. It could have been the door hinges. It sounded closer to where the Dude's ashes were. I said to Tracy, Is he trying to get *out*? It freaked the hell out of me! I pat his box. So bizarre. At least we BOTH heard the noise. I could see Dudie's face clear as day beside the bed, with those beautiful wild eyes, jumping on the nightstand, then I'd say, Hi baby, my little baby. I'd feed him, and then we'd snuggle. Fluffy *has to* be wondering where his sleeping buddy is. He must feel lonely.

May 30

Three weeks today. I can't bring myself to clean Dudie's food bowl or put it away, out of sight. I leave it there for Fluffy, so he doesn't feel so alone when he's eating. We cried last night watching videos and looking at pictures of the Dude. God, I miss him. I dream about him every night. There are big empty holes in my heart. It's hard to ease into a life that doesn't revolve around him. There was no *weaning* him out of my life –he's just *gone*, one day to the next. Fluffy has become more social. He still searches for Dudie though. Coca seems to have adjusted better.

Lesson of the day: Life is a series of goodbyes. We are always saying goodbye to people (and animals). They come into our lives and some make a deep imprint, then there is a gaping hole when they are gone.

Tracy's working so damn hard. No kids. Pets dying off. Turning 50. I keep praying for some *levity* in our life, for enough money to breathe and perhaps enjoy a thing or two. But no – tears instead. A few regrets. Sadness. Struggles. I'm tired. And I'll go out with a whimper-y, quiet fizzle. Unremembered.

May 31

I came home from work and Fluffy shit all over himself, in my closet, and on the floor. I cleaned it all up, then wondered if he went on the bed. Yup. He peed all over the bed. A reaction to Dudie being gone?

Mom called. Her ex died. She seemed relatively okay about it since she knew he had been sick. I think she feels closure regarding that part of her life.

June 10

It's truly no wonder that when people get depressed they FEEL alone – because they ARE. My horoscope says things are turning around for me. Ya, more like going in circles. Friendship to people is a convenience. When it's *convenient*, we can be friends. When it takes some *effort* on their part, it's *inconvenient* and the friendship lapses. Until they need something. But hey, as long as everyone gets what THEY need, to heck with you! We all know people *wouldn't* have helped, but they gotta live with themselves and need to say they *could've* saved that person. They *couldn't* have. They wouldn't have even tried. But they sure look good in front of others SAYING how selfless they *would've* been. How they *would've* done *anything* for them, had they only known. There were no signs, they seemed so "normal" and happy, always in a good mood and strong. You see what you want to because it makes YOUR life easier. You really *never* know what's going on behind closed doors. People don't WANT to know. They'd have to stop being selfish and give a little more of themselves. It's innately embedded in people's nature to *be* selfish.

I went to bed crying about Dudie. It's my new normal. I get into bed and think about him and miss him. Dudie was nicer and more amazing than most people I know. He was sick – and he never once "complained," and he was in pain. He had so much going on in the little body of his, and was more positive and loving and giving than most people I know. Truth.

June 27
At Galaxy Securities, it was drilled into our brains that you NEVER QUIT and if you *did*, you were the *devil*. I just read that sometimes you *have to* quit in order to succeed. That statement just undid *years* of bad "mentoring."

Lesson of the day: Sometimes you have to quit a toxic, life-sucking environment.

July 17
I've been up since 2:00 a.m. Is anyone *else* struggling like us? It doesn't seem like it – people are buying new vehicles, going on trips, eating out...People's *versions* of debt vary greatly from ours. People have pensions, investments, savings...Some people really *do* get to have it all. At least it appears so. You can't get blood from a stone. The cost of living outweighs what we bring in, and that's that. It only takes getting behind *one month* to never catch up. And now, we are working feverishly to get everything ready for Mom's visit.

July 28
Mom said I seem content, content with Tracy and the house, etc.
Huh. Looks CAN be deceiving, I thought. She said it makes her feel good knowing things are *going well* for me. And I guess that's why I *portray* that to her – she doesn't need to be upset by how I'm REALLY feeling and doing. So, she sees contentment. Interesting. You've had so many challenges and near-death experiences and you've come out the other side. You do it. You simply do it.
I guess I do. But some people have *more* challenges than others and sometimes I feel like it's enough.

So, you ask *Hashem* for help, and say help me deal with these challenges in the best way I can. People admire you for a reason, celebrate your strengths. God gives us what we *can* handle. When you feel challenged all the time, it's because he knows you *can* handle it. And you always look like you've come out of a salon, all done up.

My *outside* appearance doesn't match the *inside*. I still haven't felt like myself since the surgeries; it's been four years. I need to focus on myself and get rid of the negativity and toxicity; it takes too much energy. I understand I *do* have Tracy. And I deal with the continual pain the best I can.

I'm so proud of you and your accomplishments, and I don't mean work or title. You work so hard, it's no easy task. I mean, for all you've been through in your life, I don't know anyone who could go through all that and come out being as pleasant and mostly positive as you. You have so much character and goodness.

I always find it interesting how she puts a positive spin on my life and what I've been through. I need to take a beat from her and try to see myself more through her eyes.

July 30

Mom was telling us a story about the middle child syndrome. A family she knew, three daughters, two of them died of a skin disease the father had. At the Shiva for the youngest daughter, the middle girl, who was a quiet person, snapped, in front of everyone. She went on about the parents never having time for her because they were so busy with the other two. She said, I needed attention too. I needed to be able to share my problems with you as well. I had no one. So, I got into drugs, drank, was promiscuous, and had an abortion. She said all that happened when she was 14.

Mom said, And that's how it is with a middle child – the parents don't know what they don't know.

I looked at Mom and said, Uh, that was OUR family dynamic. You *assumed* Kyle was fine and he took *full* advantage of that.

You are right.

Aug 1

I came home from work and Mom was on the phone with Rabbi Fineberg regarding my father. He is going to try to call him. The grandchildren really want their grandfather in their lives. They can't try to make a perfect family out of a very *imperfect* one. Every time Mom referenced our "family," it was like nails on a chalkboard. We are NOT a family. There has been no *family* since forever!

Aug 8

Mom called from back home in Toronto. So, do you want to hear the update? Rabbi Fineberg spoke to your father. He asked the rabbi, Why didn't my ex call me? I said, He cuts off from everyone and expects them to be obligated to fill him in on things? He lost that right. I called Levi's wife and daughter to tell them he was reached; they were SO happy, they called him right away.

I said, Nothing will change. They'll have high expectations, but he *won't* deliver.

Mom said, It's just a giant fairy tale for them now. How are *you* with all this?

It doesn't affect me in any way.

Right, you sound okay. If you ever want to connect with the family in Israel, I could help you with that. Nope.

I guess he is now the "grieving" father. What's it been, 20 years since you SPOKE to your son? About 30 years since you'd SEEN him?

Aug 16

Mom tells me, I just spoke to your father. He yelled at me for half an hour about *everything* I did wrong in our 25-year marriage and HE said he should've left 25 years ago. That took her by surprise.

Well, that was uncalled for! That's what he does. That's what he says to make *himself* feel better. The blame-game. He blames everyone for everything.

Right, he has no responsibility or ownership in ANY of it. Everyone *else* did wrong by him.

I told her what I'd said in my *last* text to him. It is a dead issue and that chapter is *closed*. There is nothing more that needs to be said or done.

Is there anything you need to say to *me* about your childhood?

I thought, This conversation is FINALLY happening?! This is my chance to ask.

Yes. You were far from perfect parents. I've often wondered why you never told your sons' wives. It's still this *big family secret* and I don't know *why* you never said anything.

I just didn't know where I'd begin; what I'd say; how that would look.

I feel like they got to have wives and kids, and no one is the wiser. And I felt *angry* when he died because he will never have to face the consequences *when* his family knows the truth. She agreed.

But maybe it happened this way because the *other* has lost his *ally*.

Yes. But they never had it easy. In fact, it's hell.

Good, I find comfort in that.

Chana wants to know WHY her grandfather and her father stopped speaking.

She needs to be careful what she wishes for.

Right. So, I told your father he can tell her whatever he wants about it. I'm just sorry *you* don't have *that* relationship in your life.

Right, it's the *principle* of it, but I don't need his toxicity in my life. I won't have a relationship for the *sake* of having one.

He asked if we can speak again. I said no. He said he was sorry I had Parkinson's. Well, part of having that is I can't have stress in my life so this call is over, and I hung up.

I hope he *doesn't* call you.

Tracy asked me, So, how are YOU doing with all this?

I was more concerned about my mom. I knew she'd wind up calling him. I just feel badly for her.

Aug 17

Mom called: I just want you to know I'M ON *YOUR* SIDE! I'm holding YOUR hand; I'm beside YOU all the way. Things are going to keep coming up with your brothers and you need to just have a good cry, let it out. Be emotional and let it happen when you need to.

I know, that's what I've been doing my WHOLE life. I cry if I *need* to. But yesterday I didn't shed a tear over any of it, not even over my father.

Good, I'm glad to hear that. *Kol Hakavod* (well done)! You sound good. I love you bushels!

Aug 25

The morning flew by. There's a lot to do and my 50th birthday party starts at 5:00 p.m. I was trying to embrace turning 50, so I put out a lot of decorations that had "50" on it. Groan. I'm not certain it worked.

There was tons of food, many guests, and lots of laughs. We had no money, but Tracy bought me a *card* and a cake. A photo cake. Our fave photo from my birthday in Canmore on my 38th. It had burgundy icing and it read: *"Happy 50th Birthday Punchie."* (our nickname for each other). I loved it! I love that man of mine.

Aug 27

It's my *actual* 50th birthday today. I never imagined I'd be top side up, but here I am. Tracy and I got a tattoo – our initials with our wedding date. I got mine on my left wrist, Tracy on his chest over his heart. I told Tracy, NOW we are bound together *forever*, stuck with me, there's *no* going back.

I wouldn't want to.

Sept 10

It's the Jewish New Year. My prayer: A year of health, prosperity, love, and happiness and making our dreams come to fruition. No more putting things off. Life can be over in the blink of an eye.

Sept 17

Tracy is getting $500 *less* on his pay. He did receive *another* job offer though. It sounds amazing. I'm changing my outlook and it DOES feel better. Tracy *didn't* get a call for work tomorrow. I'm not panicking. I'm changing my thinking – THINGS ARE GOING TO GET BETTER. A LOT CAN HAPPEN IN ONE DAY. GOOD THINGS. Things COULD be looking up. I'm feeling hopeful.

Sept 18

I'm trying to be positive, and then it all went to shit. I finally cried. I'm just tired of fighting the fight. Of hoping and praying and believing and having faith that things will get better. It turns out that job offer Tracy received was a *scam*. People love messing with other people's livelihoods. There is some element of fun in it for them. Karma.

I went to have coffee with Myriam. Something super weird happened. I get to the coffee shop and I saw a car parked with the license plate *"HVFAITH."* I cry-laughed. If THAT's not a sign! I hope it means *something*. Things WILL work out? I'm losing my faith and there is *literally* a sign there for me to see. I could've parked on the *other* side of the building, so many ways I could have NOT seen that, but the universe WANTED me to see it.

Later, by myself, I was thinking, I WANT to be here. I WANT to see where Tracy's and my life take us. I WANT to see the next phase of our lives together. I WANT to experience joy and *lightfulness*; I've never had that. Brief moments, glimpses but not big chunks of time, I've missed out on levity; I've always had a heavy heart, heavy brain, heavy insides…my whole life. I yearn for levity. I'm not so naïve to think there is a life *without* struggles, just periods of living freely. I'm so grateful for Tracy; I have my person in life, now I just need inner peace.

Sept 19

For the High Holidays, I have to talk to God in a certain way. On other days, I'm supposed to ask the universe for what I need. And at other times, I have to think positively because you get what you put out there. If you need something changed in your life, you have to pray and ask. The universe tells you to believe you have it already and say I

HAVE such and such already. Asking. Praying. Believing. Being positive. Having faith. Do this, do that. I don't know what I'm *supposed* to think, say or ask the universe for anymore. It's so much pressure to figure out what to think and put out there, to get what you want back. And yet how many people do NOT go through this ridiculous thought process and STILL get what they want?! AH!!

Sept 21

I spoke to Mom. Chana called my father, her grandfather. I said, He probably came out smelling like a rose where Levi was concerned, a picture-perfect parent.
He went on about how hard done by he is by his family, it's all about him. I asked her, Does he ever ask questions about *you*? No.
Mom said to me, His account of the way things *were* will be very skewed, and it's not up to *me* to straighten it out. She said to Chana, *You* know where *I* was all those years with the grandchildren. You know where *he* was (wasn't). If you believe *everything* he says, it *won't* be the whole truth. A lie is told so many times, it becomes the truth. The reality is far different than the story you imagined. He will spin the truth. Chana understood to take things with a grain of salt when talking with him.

Sept 27

Mom called: I wanted to tell you at this time I have no intention of going back to Israel, for *any* reason. There are many reasons, but I wanted you to know YOU are the *main* reason. I've been thinking about you. I think the issue is them finally accepting Tracy; 31 years is long enough, it's time they *did*.
I didn't realize we were *trying* to be *accepted* by the Israel family.
No, you weren't. This is my way of saying we aren't a perfect family, but there are certain courtesies. It's time for them to include you in *Simchas*(celebrations). I would never tell you to accept or not.
Uh, that's an interesting take on things. I reminded her of the letter they sent me. According to *them*, I got cancer because I married out of my

faith. They have apparently led a *sin-free* life, but ME, I'M the bad Jew here.

I don't even know what to say. Not to trivialize anything, but you came through this thing *Hashem* gave you. It brought out strength in you I didn't know anybody had. You paid a price, but you are an incredible person, even after all that happened to you. Regarding your father, what's painful is all the time *I* put into this family and it made *no* difference. She mentioned she had never heard such anger and rage in his voice.

I know what you mean; I've been on the receiving end of that. I warned you he'd be that way, but you had to hear it for *yourself.*

Yes, I did. I wouldn't have believed the extent of his anger. I don't believe this family will *ever* sit down together. I thought maybe you'd want to just *meet* the nieces and nephews.

Nope, it's not going to happen.

I hope I didn't upset you with all this.

No, I'm *glad* we can talk about all these things openly.

Oct 1

I bawled all the way to work and sobbed all the way home. I'm STILL crying. Nothing pans out for us. Why pretend like something will? It won't. God wants us to feel desperate. He wants us to beg and plead. I refuse to barter. Either he *wants* to help or he *doesn't.*

Tracy comes home and seeing me clearly upset he asks, Are you going to make it?

I shrugged. What's the point? We'll be living out of a shoebox pretty quick here.

He shows me our bank account on his phone – a balance of $4400.

What?! How?! He just smiled.

Oct 3

It's not about wasting your whole life learning things and collecting memories only to get an illness or die. It's about making the time you ARE here, doing the things you love, being productive, contributing ,and trying to make a difference. It's about living your life and not being fearful of what's to come. To be *optimistic* about life and not live in the fear of it. Huh. That was deep. I've lived in *fear* of death, of failure, of not *ever* fulfilling my goals and dreams. I need to continue on the path of MAKING my life happen the way I want it, and when the end of my life comes, I'll *know* I lived it the way I wanted. Having the love of my life beside me – I'm blessed. We've always had each other – us against the world. That to me is *everything*.

While preparing dinner, Tracy played "Lady in Red," and we danced, cheek to cheek. It's THOSE moments in life that make it *all* worth it. No one was watching. No one saw or knew. No one witnessed our love – it was just us, the way it's always been, having a beautiful moment. And it's in those beautiful MOMENTS that I'm talking about.

Lesson of the day: It's in those precious moments that we can drive the fear further and further away.

Oct 6

This world is a harsh place. Some make it, some don't. It's a messed-up planet. We each hope to feel happiness, be valued and loved. And when we *don't* experience those things, *that's* when we question *why* we are here. It's not the *successful* people asking those questions, it's the *lost* people; the people who have been burned by the wildly unpredictable flames of life. It's the people who have been tested over and over and over that question it. What's the end game here? I've impacted no one. No one would be destroyed by me not being here. Well, Mom would, but I don't think my purpose in life is to be around for Mom. Tracy? I love that man, but he could *still* have children...without me. I think feeling depressed and overwhelmed is a sign that your *realness* is bubbling over. Your fears and heartaches are screaming to be heard, and come to the surface. All the feelings that get stuffed down because we still have to function can't stay down anymore. And it comes out. It pours out. The flood gates break open and now you have to deal with *every* thought and feeling you have.

Oct 14

I reach out, and almost always no one reaches back. People have lost the ability to reciprocate. People...man, it's *my big* test in life. There would be no reason on the planet to stay in Calgary if we had the chance to leave.

At 50, it's hard not to take a hard look around. All I see is Tracy. I'm not perfect, but I AM a good friend. I am fiercely loyal, but when you don't get that same courtesy back, what is left in a relationship? The world is full of narcissists. You are of no value to someone unless they can *benefit* from you. Reciprocation. Common courtesies. Integrity. Character. These words and actions do not exist in today's world. Much like how the millennials have no clue what a rotary phone is, people these days have no concept of kindness, give-and-take, value and ethics. Understanding, supporting, and being compassionate *isn't* part of friendship either. People can't handle truth and honesty, even when they *say* they want it...it's a bit fucked up. People say what others WANT to hear. You tell the truth and it's held against you. If I were to die today, I'd stipulate no funeral or memorial service. There'll just be two-faced people standing there telling stories of how much I meant to them. I didn't. And they know it. If I *did* mean something, they'd *show* me **in life**, *not in death*. People suddenly realize what a person means to them when they are *gone*. People suck.

I just had such a clear vision of, and heard the sound of, his feet: Dudie running down the hall to the room to get fed. Clear as day. It made me smile. Even in *death* he's breaking me out of a funk.

We were watching a baby commercial. Tracy declares, We would've had *beautiful* children.

Oct 17

We were watching *A Million Little Things* (*AMLT*). It's about suicide. One friend said to the other, "*It wasn't ONE thing he killed himself over – it's a million little things.*" Yes, things build up, and then you snap.

521

You're overwhelmed and you feel like you just can't take one millisecond more of it.

Here's another thing: most girlfriends are truly overrated. There's no *unbreakable* "sisterhood" that exists. People are people, and if you find a *person* you connect with and knows you down to your gritty, imperfect soul, gender is *irrelevant*. Most of my "girlfriends" have let me down more than my husband has. I don't have that *one* person. Every *close* girlfriend I have has someone *else* who ranks higher than I do. I may be *one of* their good friends, but not THE one. Yes, Toby and Myriam *are* good girlfriends of mine, but sometimes I can still feel second-rate. It may or may not be true on *their* end, but it can feel that way to *me* at times.

Tracy IS my person, my highest-ranking one of them all. I can recall *many* interviews with Jennifer Aniston where she talks about her close-knit circle of girlfriends. I never had that. It has to be *even* numbers of girls when you get together. Groups in odd numbers never work. Someone is ALWAYS left out, and that person is usually me. Three girls together is the worst. I've never had luck in those gaggles. And the same person, who *excludes* me in group settings, is the sweetest and most giving, kind, and open person when it's *one on one*. It's very confusing when someone treats you one way in a group setting and *another* when you're alone. I automatically feel angst and discomfort knowing I'll be in a group setting. It's worrisome and exhausting. Even when I have my own get-togethers, I gravitate toward the *one* person I can hang with. I just never feel like *I'm* that ONE person others seek out to feel comfortable with. I guess I don't instil comfort in others.

Oct 19
Mom asked me how things turned out with trying to connect with friends.
I reached out to a half-dozen people and *none* of them reached back.
I'M busy too, but when no one makes the effort...No one is THAT busy.
I don't care who you are. Give me a break. I'm more comfortable

keeping to myself – it's an *effort* to reach out and try to be with people. And getting ignored reminds me WHY I don't bother with them in the first place. I've lost track of all the people I gave second, third, *tenth* chances to when their instinct was always to screw me over THEN apologize. Then do it again. At what point do you say, It's enough? They seem so genuine and heartfelt when they are pleading with you, and then they do it again. What does that say about *my* instincts? What does that say about *them*? What does that say about a person who couldn't give a crap about you and your feelings but then manipulates you into letting them do it to you all over again. Do we need THEIR friendship/love SO badly? Do we not feel worthy of having someone in our life who WILL treat us with respect? Are we not worthy of receiving what we give? No responsibility or accountability on their part – they say, I will do what I want because I KNOW you'll forgive me – again. They don't need to learn to do better or give better or be better. Where's the incentive for them to grow when they get what they want in the end anyway? We enable. We are "allowing" them to treat us this way because in part, we are going along with the bad behavior, then rewarding it. Is there treatment or rehab for narcissism? There are a few people I'd love to sign up for it.

And just then – a mirror broke, the *second* one in a few weeks. What do you suppose that means, Mom?

That you broke a mirror, and now you have to clean it up.

I laughed. Good one.

As Jewish people, we don't believe in or are affected by superstitions.

THAT is good to know.

A broken mirror is just a broken mirror. How could you be superstitious when you lived with a *black* cat?!

Exactly. I'm not. And Dudie walked under a ladder once. Friday the 13th, it's usually a *good* day for us.

Okay, so I don't have to worry about all the EXTRA bad luck we will have.

Oct 23

We were watching *AMLT*. A girl says to a guy, *"There was a study done on people who* survived *jumping off the Brooklyn Bridge. The very next second, they regretted it. It's not that they don't want to live; it's that they don't want to live* like this.*"* Then one of the characters was apologizing to her husband and friend: *"I'm sorry. I didn't know it was so bad. I didn't see." "Don't be sorry. I didn't* let *you see."*

YOINK! I feel so exposed when we watch that show. It oddly mirrors the way I feel. Things I've never spoken to anyone about. And when I reached out to friends and never heard back, they could've all been saying afterward, I wish I'd seen. I wish she had reached out...Oh wait, she *did*.

I woke up at 2:30 a.m. worrying about money. Then I changed my thinking. WE ARE GOING TO GET AN ABUNDANCE OF FINAN-CIAL WEALTH. I fell back asleep.

Oct 28

It was Dudie's birthday two days ago. I miss that little guy terribly.
So, I have my friends, as available as they are. Mostly, I have Tracy. He IS my best friend. I'm still smarting a little from the fact nobody made *any* grand gestures at my 50th. Jim was thoughtful; he always is. I remember *Tracy's* 50th and he was *spoiled. He's* loved. We've gone over the top for others, pitched in and helped out. I guess I'm grateful people even bothered to show up. That will have to be enough. I'M a loyal friend. I'M supportive. I'M empathetic. I drop what I'm doing to be there for others. I'm all the things no one is for me. That isn't being conceited either. I've had 40 years to evaluate how people *are* in my life – and how they are *not*. My assessment is accurate. It's easier for people *not* to bother. And they don't. It's too hard.

Lesson of the day: Relationships take energy and effort. And that *is* life in a nutshell!

<u>Oct 30</u>

I think my father would be tickled pink to know we've struggled even *more* since our last conversation. Here's some irony, my horoscope: *If you were to win the lottery tonight and wake up incredibly wealthy tomorrow morning, you would still be the same person. Some of your issues would no longer be issues because now they could be solved with your newfound wealth. But there would be other issues – deeper issues – that would not go away so easily. So even if something terrific happens, these will still be things you'll need to resolve. Work on that now and you'll be ready for the good fortune that is headed your way. It may not be a lottery win, but it will be something you'll cherish.*

Yes, I agree; emotional issues *don't* go away, but when the financial ones do, it leaves breathing room to work on the rest. I just need the opportunity. I have to start liking myself better before anything else in my life can change. Damn, that's so stupid and cheesy, but true.

I like Tracy's horoscope: *You will see that there is hope surrounding you and light on the horizon. You are in the right place. You are on the right path. And soon, you will see why.*

<u>Nov 4</u>

I had no choice. I HAD to have my surgeries. I was bleeding to death. Fibroids, cysts, endometriosis...there was no relief unless I had it all removed. And as it stands, there is probably *still* endometriosis in me – hence, part of the *constant* pain. So, I didn't get to have kids, I got to have the worst periods of my life, have everything removed, still be in pain, gain weight, vision going, feet going, hernias remain – and WTF do I have to show for ANY of it? Deep in debt, physical changes already happened/occurring/still to come, dark thoughts, thinking I'll never be enough for Tracy...How does one with cope with all this? Do they? Is there any reason to prolong my misery? Let's be realistic – my life has gone downhill since the day I was born. Tracy's a light in the dark, but he's not living the life I'm sure he imagined for himself. He didn't sign up for a life with LOTS of baggage, craziness, dysfunctionality and *this* "family." I'm not talking the d-word – *divorce*. I don't have a better life outside of him. I mean the OTHER d-word – *death*. Tracy will find love and kids.

My tombstone should read: It was never easy.
Or, Suffer quietly.
Or, No one can hear your cries from down there.
Or, You are truly invisible now – outta sight, outta mind.
Or, If only we could remember who she was.
Or, If only she'd have asked for help.

Or maybe my tombstone should read MY message to the world:
If only someone had cared enough.
If only the people she considered to be friends felt the same way.
Here lies the most loyal person on the planet – too bad she never got it back.
Don't bother, she's dead now.
She's sure you *meant* to bother.
Here lies a person who was NEVER too busy for a friend in need.
Here lies a person who was *burnt* and *backstabbed* by so many people; it's a wonder she died of *other* causes.

So, Universe, if you're listening at all – my *preference* is to live a long, HEALTHY, PROSPEROUS, fulfilling, dare I say happy life, with the love of my life. *That's* my preference. As it stands, you've given me nothing but tears and heartache. I don't think it's asking too much to give me some goodness, since I've put up with all the shit YOU'VE dealt me! How about we switch it up for shits and giggles? Are you SO invested in keeping me down, or is there some wiggle room here?

Because suffering is a silent affliction, no one knows *outwardly* what you are going through, and you feel more alone than ever. It's our choice not to talk about it, but what makes us **stay** silent? Shame? Stigma? Fear of not being believed or helped? Reaching out becomes paralyzing and prevents us from opening up or seeking the real help we so desperately crave. So, we stay silent. Unfortunately pretending you're okay is easier than sharing your innermost feelings. This needs to change.

Nov 8

I was getting ready for work and thinking, Okay, it's a *new* day. What GOOD things will come today? Then like a lightning bolt, another thought occurred to me. Maybe we couldn't have kids or find success in careers and work *because we have nothing to offer the world!* Maybe we have something to offer *each other* because *that's all we've got!* People succeed in business and in all sorts of areas. We seem to fail miserably, well, at everything. Maybe the world gave up on us *because we have nothing to contribute?* All these years we thought we *did* and tried and tried and tried and helped people. To what end? In all likeliness, we've given up on ourselves, too. Years and years and years of getting beat down will do that. We claw and fight back. Again, to what end? People crap on us, dismiss us, ignore us, use us up, and take advantage of us. And we are *not* jaded; we *still* help, usually to our detriment. So why does the universe not reward perseverance? 50 years, 54 for Tracy; when does the testing stop and the goodness begin? We've given people a thousand chances; when do we get OUR chance? The universe gave us Galaxy Securities so people could take and take from us while we kept giving, lost everything and were never given the chance to make a real difference? It's like we've been dismissed. We're just too dense to realize it. Everyone was born with *one* type of brain, and then God gave me *mine*. To think differently than everybody else, and not necessarily in a *better* way. It's kind of a lonely place to be. Boy, there is so much to learn in this life. Okay, brain, let's take a break.

I went to the new menopause specialist. The waiting room was full of pregnant women. I thought it was a *menopause* clinic: nope. How fun. I checked my horoscope while I listened to babies crying: *You need to banish fear from your mind and take a hopeful, optimistic approach to getting something you want.*

The doctor asks, Why are you here? as she poured over my forms and read my medical history.

I *don't* feel like myself.

She looked over my cancer history – Wow, you've had A LOT of chest X-rays and radiation! A lot. Wow. Your body has been through a lot, lots of stress. If you don't get *sleep*, nothing else is going to work. And Imovane is the *worst!* There is currently a Canadian alert on it. It is linked to memory loss and Alzheimer's! We need to get you *off* those ASAP!

I've been on them at least *20 years*.

Oh wow, that's *no* good. Start taking half a pill, then a whole one every *other* night, and by the third week none.

You absolutely need hormones, from the second you had surgery you needed estrogen. While you don't need progesterone, you have no uterus, it can help with sleep.

She was shocked I haven't had a mammogram yet. It blows my mind! So, first things first; we need to book you for a mammogram and re-evaluate your hormones. Omega-3 is SO important – it staves off Alzheimer's, improves brain function, and improves mood.

We went through some other supplements I need to be taking. We booked a follow-up visit for January 2019. I left there thinking, There IS a reason why I don't feel like myself! I could improve my mood? I could be in a *better state of mind*? THIS IS HUGE!! I'm NOT crazy.

Nov 10

I started the supplements, hormones, and took half a sleeping pill. Well, I survived the night, I woke up a few times but fell back asleep. When I got out of bed and looked at myself, I looked *well rested*. I don't remember the last time I saw that in myself. Or felt it. Tracy saw it too. Okay, so I could *finally* be on the *right* path to feeling like myself? All the crazy talk and bad feelings are hopefully a thing of the *past*?

Horoscope: When you think optimistically, that powerful energy can open doors for you, draw resources and allies to your side, and make you fitter for success. When you think negatively, it is kind of like starving yourself or denying yourself of life-sustaining water. If you have thought negatively about a certain goal in your life, Virgo, you need to turn it around. Make positive thinking an ingredient of your venture, and you'll have the fuel you need to move forward

Lesson of the day: Positive thinking. Positive thinking. Positive thinking. Positive thinking.

Nov 14

I went for my *first* mammogram! It was *not* fun. Apparently, it DOES count that my paternal grandmother had breast cancer and died from it. The technician noticed my port scar. We needed to note it in case the scar tissue showed up. We talked about how I was in fact doing the HRT **backward**. Estrogen GEL you put on your **SKIN**, progesterone you take **ORALLY**: I was doing the exact *opposite*. So, who knows how much, *if any*, hormones were getting into my system in the *past FOUR years*? No one told me any differently. That could *definitely* explain a thing or two. After, she explained breast density is categorized by A, B, C, and D. A being least dense, D being most. I'm a D. So, they need to send me for an ultrasound to get a better, deeper picture.

Nov 17

I woke up at 5:00 a.m. and talked to the universe for an hour. I put it out there we need help. I got up to an email from my manager saying I'm doing wonderful work, thank you, and great job! I was thinking, I'm *proud* of the work I do. Later in the day Tracy then showed me an email from one of the jobs we applied to. He has an interview November 26. Okay. Okay. This is positive stuff. We popped champagne.

Nov 19

Tracy and I were up all night – throwing up and with diarrhea. I thought for a second to stay home but I went to work, Tracy didn't. I had the chills and body aches since yesterday as well. Man, what *did* we eat?

Nov 28

So, we both had food poisoning. We've been in bed for a week and a half. You feel invincible, until you don't. You eat whatever, and do whatever, and then you get sick and think you'll *never* bounce back. I mean, I was depressed before; now I'm just praying I get back to where I was before this sickness. Today would've been my day off and I would have gone to see a doctor but I can't afford antibiotics. Tracy's pay is *gone*. We have no money for *two weeks*. I bit the bullet anyway and went to see Dr. West – I have bacterial and lung infections. He said it's GOOD my glands DO hurt; when they DON'T it's a problem, as *you know* all too well. Cough. Sinuses. My ears hurt. He checked it all. I'm on antibiotics for four days. Mom paid.

Dec 10

Mom called: I don't know how to talk to you about this. There's something I have to say and I hope it comes out okay. Your oldest nephew is engaged. I told Maria she *needs* to send you and Tracy an invitation.

Please don't give her our address. I have to think about whether I even *want* an invitation sent to me.

I just think you guys could start out with a conversation, or a text, or something; 30 years is long enough to not include you two in Simchas.

You think this is about Tracy *not* being Jewish?

Isn't it? You disconnected from family when you married Tracy.

WHAT? You think us not "connecting" with the Israel family is about TRACY? I could be an **unmarried** woman or have **married a Jew** and I would STILL not have a relationship with anyone out there! It's HARDLY about THAT!

She was quiet.

I continued, I'm so proud of Tracy, of being married to him; I could care less what any of them thought or think of him! He is a million times a better human than either of *them* could have ever hoped to have been. They, as Jewish men, did far *worse* than ANYTHING Tracy has EVER done as a non-Jew.

She interjected. I want to go to my grave with my family *speaking* to each other. Is that so bad? You could speak to Maria and just open the lines of communication.

And you want us to talk, to have a conversation? We'll talk about what, the weather? No. If I talk to her, it'll be about the TRUTH.

You mean your book, right? What's the benefit of that? Levi is dead. He's not around. What is your goal in writing the book and *destroying* lives? The children are innocent in all this.

My goal? The benefit? The benefit is it's **THE TRUTH**! My goal is maybe *I* don't want to take this to *MY* grave without the truth being told.

Oh wow, I never thought of that.

I'm STILL protecting THEM, 40 years later, and I'm *still* staying silent. *Everyone* has, to make it easier for THEM! And I'M the bad guy. *I* was the victim and *I'm* the one being outcast. THEY did this to the "family." THEY chose their actions, NOT ME. I didn't do *this*. THEY created this fractured family, *not me*. I'm taking the heat for it, but I *didn't* do this. THEY did. THEY created this reality. It's like they couldn't see the wreckage they left in their wake. Your sons are monsters; I'd even say they are evil. They ruined my life.

They *ruined* your life? They weren't religious when it happened.

So what?! What difference does THAT make? It's so irrelevant! OMG! You're stuck.

No, I'm NOT "stuck"! I've done what I've needed to my entire life. And I HAVE dealt with it. Their moving away gave me the opportunity to deal with it without them being around. Yes, I think about it from time to time and I'll always have reminders of what they did, but I assure you, I've moved on with my life. There is no being stuck about it with me. My book is far from coming out, but I will still continue to write because it's therapeutic and because I need to do that for **ME**. Because it is my truth, and it WILL come out. I've waited a very long time to get real about my life.

Well, I guess we wait and will cross that bridge when it happens, and deal with the aftermath.

Well, it's just the truth, *this* family's reality. This sickness in the family is our legacy. Unless we change it.

What advice would you give me as the mother in this family?

You know, people don't always get what they want. I would rather have *different* siblings. But I can't. I will not have a relationship with them for *you* or for *them*. I will continue do what is best for ME.

Do you still blame me for what happened? I feel like you do.

Nope, not at all. We've already established you guys could have done a better job at protecting me.

Well, back to my original statement – I'll tell Maria I've left it with you. She's just looking for the truth.

Tell her to be careful what she wishes for.

Mom called back a bit later and said, You are a strong and balanced woman. You speak with incredible clarity.

Yes, I do.

Dec 17

Mom calls: I'm all about peacekeeping now. Are you sure you don't want your *father* in your life?

You do what you need to in YOUR life, and I'll deal with MINE. Your "peacekeeping" efforts are all directed at how *I* can do things differently. He is poisonous and I don't need him in my life for *the sake of it. Not even for you*. I've reconciled with it. I'm good with my decision and where I'm at with it. When he calls me a liar and wants to believe I can commit fraud…he was so out of line. It's despicable he thinks I could be THAT person. So ya, I feel pretty good about keeping him OUT of my life.

Dec 27

I woke up at 8:00 a.m.! I slept eight and a half hours SOLID! What the shit!! Awesome sauce!

Dec 28

Maybe God isolated us from "friends" so, when we *are* gone, ties have *already* been severed, no one will miss us. What did *Tracy* ever do? Marry ME? Was that the same fate for Mom? She married the wrong guy and had a shitty-ass family? If something good IS coming our way, why has it taken so long to reveal itself? Is giving us SOMETHING to hope for just too much? God, if you can't tell us *what* we are doing here and *why* you are keeping us here, then screw it! I'm NOT looking for the meaning of life; I'm looking for a flicker of light that things *will be* okay, that things will and could get better. A flicker. Maybe the dog has bad separation anxiety because, on some level, she *knows* we may not be around.

I was looking at my horoscope for a glimmer of *something*. The last line was: *Good things are coming your way.* Tracy says thing *are* going to get significantly better for us.

I fully and completely and utterly understand there are people WAY worse off than us. I get it. But if you spend your whole life *comparing* yourself to others who are less fortunate, you'll *always* come up smelling like roses.

Dec 30

I had a sweet-ass purging session of the boxes in our crawl space today. I threw out *three* garbage bags full of old pictures, cards, and paraphernalia from "no longer in my life friends and family." It felt pretty damn *great* to say, Yup, I'm 1000% done with those! Like taking a good, long-overdue shit! You feel a million times better, lighter and freer! To read all those messages declaring their love and admiration for me. *Friends forever. You're the best person I know.* Blah, blah, blah. They were just words.

Horoscope: *When something upsetting or challenging happens to us, our friends and family members may say something like "everything happens for a reason," in an effort to make us feel better. But sometimes, when you experi-*

ence something upsetting or challenging, there doesn't seem to be a good reason for it. That's when you might wind up cursing your fate or feeling singled
out for punishment by the universe. That may be how you are feeling now, but
there really is a good – and auspicious – reason for what's happening. Hang in
there.

I like that one. Pretty spot on for how I've been feeling lately.
Auspicious – favorable, promising, encouraging. Works for me.

Dec 31

This has been a hurdle-some year; we've been tested over and over and
over. While I'm trying to *still* have a shred of faith, and believing there
is an ounce of hope to cling to, I'm beyond thrilled to say buh-bye to
2018!

Having said that, I'm using all my *positive energy* to make 2019 a better
year, full of laughter, ease, success, clarity, and healing. We still have
dreams and goals we want to make happen for ourselves. So, I guess I
still have some hope left in me. I have to believe there is more to life
than the past 50 years.

Last year is in the past, I'm looking *forward* now. So, see ya, 2018, I'm
not sad to see you go. In the genius words of Ariana Grande, "Thank
you, next."

2019

Jan 1

I'm purging papers again when suddenly I see a handwritten letter from *Kyle*. I almost threw up. Tracy had just walked into room. What's wrong?

I told him.

Oh. You should *burn* it, *all* of it.

I will! Great idea! And I DID, in our fireplace! Now THAT was cathartic! I was reading my autograph book from childhood; I had everyone sign it. In 1978, 16-year-old Levi wrote: *"To Sari, one day I hope you will look back on your childhood and remember the fun we had."* Wow. I can still hear those words dripping with sarcasm. I remember even at the time I had just looked at him, like, Are you serious?

Tracy is getting $500 *less* on his pay, again. God, Universe, I don't know what kind of lesson you're trying to teach us here but you *will* push us too far. Apparently, we are given what we *can* handle. What happens when we CAN'T handle it? Do we get an *Oops, sorry about that?* I used to panic and be fearful of money and our situation and Tracy would say, Things will be okay. There was comfort in hearing that. NOW, he's nowhere near a place to say, *It'll be alright.* I don't believe he believes that anymore. How do we keep believing things *will* get bet better? Nothing improves, not for a lack of trying. What happens now? If we've all but given up and the universe has *no intention* of answering our prayers, where do we go from here? What is left to try? So, I started thinking about that license plate I saw at the coffee shop that day: "HVFAITH." That was September, it's January now. Have faith in WHAT? We have tried to believe. We've done everything we can do to move *forward* with our lives in a *positive* manner, *still* believing *something* will manifest to make our lives better. But nothing happens. Is God's will to *keep* us where we are? Is *that* his grand plan?

Horoscope: *Something is shifting. Something is changing for the better. You can sense this, even if you haven't yet seen any concrete signs that validate what you are feeling. But that does not mean that everything is going to suddenly fall into place. It does not mean that there won't be an uphill battle or two to deal with. There may be, but the challenges you face won't be nearly as difficult as they have been. Things are getting better. Use that to motivate you to the happy ending you have been envisioning.*

I cried. Is THAT my sign? False hope? I couldn't bear that. I checked another site: *You're having difficulty dealing with it all. Take it easy. You don't need to struggle all the time to be accepted in the world. Lighten up!*

Ya, right.

Feb 7
I was researching alternatives to Imovane since it is linked to Alzheimer's. Then I read that *suicidal thoughts* were an after-effect of using it. THAT could explain a WHOLE big-ass lot! I wonder if my mind *wouldn't* be taking me to those unbelievably dark places if I WEREN'T on it? Good grief. I've got to get the hell off them ASAP! It's hard though, I NEED sleep. I WILL try again. This is no joke.

I also researched menopause and vision. THAT IS the cause of my blurry vision and watery eyes. As a result of the change in hormones, it affects sight as well. Good ol' menopause, another feather in its cap. It's too bad all the doctors I've asked about it *didn't* know that. Gotta be my own advocate.

I asked Tracy, Sincerely, we've been through so much together; we *wouldn't* throw in the towel at *this* point, right?
Oh God no. We are doing just fine.
Love him.

Feb 25

I left the house for work about 15 minutes *later* than usual, but I was in *such a good mood*, it didn't matter. I was about to merge onto my exit when I hit black ice. I could feel the left side wheels locking. I swerved to the right, spinning toward oncoming traffic. All I could see were bright headlights in front of me. I did a 360. As I straightened out, the passenger side of my Jeep collided with the driver side of another vehicle and we smashed together. It felt like a million years passed in those moments. Time stood still and I couldn't imagine how this was going to turn out. It felt like it was going to be catastrophic. As our vehicles came to a stop, I sat there clutching the steering wheel. Am I alive? Did that just happen? When we got out of our vehicles, the other driver and I realized we knew each other; Tracy worked with her husband at the software company. We moved to a side road to exchange info.

I was crying. I was shaking, and I was in shock. We agreed that we'd both fill out police reports today and call our insurance companies. Thank God it *wasn't* worse; it was rush hour on a majorly busy road. I called Tracy, then work.

I finally got home and it was *beginning* to sink in. All the aches and pains were settling in as well. I couldn't get the image of me spinning out of control out of my head. A million things *could've* gone horribly wrong. I'm sooo grateful the accident *wasn't* worse.

I called Mom.

You were protected. *Hashem* made it so you were hurt the *least* amount. Tracy came home and he hugs me and says, It's okay, it's okay.

Lesson of the day: A near-death experience reminds you to *cherish* life. If my life *had* ended, I would never have had the chance to be *heard*. Haranguing in my brain was the thought: My book hasn't come out yet! It *has to* come out *before* I leave this earth; otherwise, there's no *evidence* I existed. I have a lot of shit I want to get off my chest before I die. I could've gone to my grave *without* telling my story. It motivated me. The fire was lit! Today began the *finishing* of my book!

Feb 28

After having some time to think about the accident, I'm still at a loss regarding what other meaning it has. *Why* did this happen? What is the *purpose* of it? There *has to* be another *reason*. Well, Mom has had some time to think about it too and she called me to declare, You're given *preferential* treatment from *Hashem*; it gives me goose bumps to think about it! It could be you've come through *other* tests very well, maybe you did what you needed to in a *good way*, and He rewarded you with you not getting injured. It's mind-boggling, dear. It's *not* the way things *usually* go. I've got goose bumps again. You keep *walking away* from death. Think about it. You've been getting these messages for a *long* time. *Hashem* is applauding you from the side lines. It's nothing short of a miracle!

Perhaps. I need to think on this more.

Mar18

Okay, so I'M not a religious woman like Mom, but she *does* give me food for thought in trying to determine WHY I have survived so many near-death experiences. I seem to talk to God a lot. I don't know if that's Mom's influence or not. So many times, in my life, I've questioned why God made things happen the way they have. Why I've struggled the way I have. Why so often I've felt like no one is listening and I don't get to have my dreams fulfilled. Am I trying to blame God for MY afflictions? Am I responsible for the path my life has taken? Is this my life's destiny, or "God's will" as it were, and I need to accept it? Why is it so much easier and clearer to see what others need to do in *their* lives, but it can't be seen for our own? Why can't we see?

Upon more reflection, these are a few things I DO know about myself:
I don't allow people to bully me anymore– I DO stand up for myself, and let that inner voice come thrusting out from my gut.
I've come to realize all those years we were busy with friends, it prevented me from working on *myself*. I was far too busy tending to

them, to think of myself. Now that we have unloaded many of them, I have been able to do the work.

I have zero tolerance for toxic people in my life.

I am stronger than I ever realized I was.

My suicidal thoughts – it's not that I wanted to die; I just wanted the overwhelming pain, anguish, dilemmas, and obstacles to stop.

Being in group settings is still a challenge for me, and continues to be my Achilles' heel. Sure, I step out of my comfort zone and speak to people and initiate conversations, but in the end it's *not* in my makeup; I feel I'll *always* be that painfully shy girl. Because I am! It doesn't feel natural to me. I put on my *social mask*. That mask still fails me – I'm a terrible actress. I wear my heart on my sleeve. It's so difficult for me to be someone I'm not.

If I perceive a lack of interest on someone's part, I don't and won't share. I don't blab for the sake of it. I'm not a big sharer when I'm around acquaintances – small talk is painful. I feel fake. Even when I'm around people I DO know – I share when and if it suits the conversation. Most people just talk to fill awkward space; I talk when I have *something* to say. I mirror others; if *they* share, *I* share. If they seem interested, I'll show interest. If they ignore, I don't have time for them either. *Ignoring* me is the *quickest* way to get me to shut down and tune out. Being ignored, that's still a tough one; it goes to my core. Being left out...makes me reactive, angry, and I feel invisible. When there is *no* eye contact made toward *me* in a group setting, and the conversation is solely directed toward *one* person, it drives me batshit crazy. That's why one-on-one works best for me. I get *lost* in a group setting, trying to fit in and be heard. I'll say something, and I won't be heard, but then someone will say the *exact* same thing, verbatim, and everyone hears THEM.

I understand that some people thrive on being the centre of attention. The outgoing person *trumps* the quiet ones. An introvert will never draw attention to themselves. They just quietly remove themselves and disappear. I've left parties and get-togethers, walked out, hidden, because the situation was unbearably uncomfortable. I know for a fact these fun-loving people are *happier* being quieter. But they feel they have to be switched "on" all the time. I guess the outgoing people have THEIR role to play too. If EVERYONE was outgoing, no one would be listening. I'm a listener. I can't change who I am, and I don't really want to, in this regard. I want so *desperately* to evolve and *not* sweat the things that truly *don't* matter. I DON'T care what people think of me, I *never* have, but I care when I'm in a group setting where I can potentially look like an idiot, like sitting or standing alone and feeling insecure about it. I care when I feel humiliated and singled out. But in the end, that's MY beef, no one else's. When I'm having a conversation with someone, all I can think of, Are they looking at my wrinkles? They must have noticed I've gained a few pounds. I haven't done my roots yet, are they checking *that* out? My issues are anchored deep within me. I don't think they see *me*. I think I keep getting put in these situations because I need to keep working on it. If I had it *mastered* it, I *wouldn't* be fretting about it. I still need to do the work. Evolve. Evolve. Evolve.

My new mission: Be in a group setting and be okay with myself, no matter what happens. Ya. I can do this!

Horoscope: *You may have to make a fuss today to make your voice heard. This is not your usual way of doing things, but your feelings could be ignored if you don't take a stand and speak up. There may be others in your midst who are naturally boisterous, and as it's been said, the squeaky wheel gets the grease. Form your thoughts thoroughly before you speak up, and you can have a powerful impact. If you demand a chance to say what's on your mind, you will be heard.*

Apr 4
EPIC FAIL! I was in a group setting – it was like circling the ninth circle of hell. At no point is it easy for me. It is both physically and emotionally challenging. I even left the party, and no one noticed (in chatting with the hosts the next day, they *hadn't* realized we ducked out

early). I'll keep working on that one, even though I already know the outcome each time. I guess I feel I have nothing worthwhile to contribute and I'm boring them to tears with my mundane life. I sense they'd rather be talking to *anyone* else.

We went to our *usual* place for our anniversary. It was a wonderful, few hours, reminiscing and talking about the future. We have $36 to our name, but we are *choosing* to remain positive. Something WILL come to us in the form of a debt-free existence; I believe it with all my heart. I don't know *where* this belief comes from. I just feel it in my bones.

Our relationship has endured the scrutiny of naysayers and doubters, and the fact we are still together 32 years later is miraculous! To come from such different backgrounds and upbringings – it goes to show we can overcome anything, together. Our bond has only strengthened through our hardships. I never could have imagined finding a life partner whom I still *like* to this day. We beat the odds.

I was discussing the *point* of writing this book with Mom, again. It comes down to *this* – I'm writing this book for *me*. I'm unapologetic for that. I'm not doing it to make it okay for everyone else; I'm making it okay for *me*. I finally gave MYSELF *permission* to tell my story. My life *isn't* defined by my childhood; my story is *more* than that. Neither am I defined by having cancer. My life is a *culmination* of events – THAT'S who I am, the WHOLE ball of wax. I am *NOT* my abuse, my cancer, my accidents, my shyness...I AM *ALL* OF IT. I am *proud* to tell my story, I am *proud* of my achievements, and I am *proud* of myself. The simplest answer is: because I CAN, because I have something to say. I've had way too many close calls in my life to take for granted that I have all the time in the world to say what I need to. The time for speaking up is NOW.

May 6

I was at work today, and I ran into a customer who I often stop to chat with. He kept insisting *something* was *different* about me today. No, it's not your hair or makeup...he kept eyeing me up and down, trying to figure it out. *Whatever* it is, keep it up! Later, when I had a chance to reflect on it, I realized *what* he couldn't put his finger on. I was *content*. Maybe the writing, the therapy of journaling and selecting pieces for my memoir, has improved my overall mood. Maybe the fog is lifting from ceasing to take my sleeping pills. I cut my dose in half for the past six months. That's a far cry from the *seven per night* I was taking years ago. It's now been nine days since I've taken ANY! After roughly 22 years on them, nine days ago I said, *Enough!* Is it possible all the meltdowns and dark feelings are behind me? I barely had any sleep last night and yet I feel *good*. If this *lighter* state is *any* indication that I need to stay off them...I WILL!

June 6

Our sweet Fluffball had to be put down today. He's been "off" for about a week, but not eating for two days. It all happened so fast. I think he had a seizure. He was just sitting on my nightstand when he all of a sudden keeled over and was shaking uncontrollably. The look of terror in his eyes. I wasn't ready for him to leave our lives. Our 14-year-old baby. Tracy and I were both with him to the end. After *the* injection, there was no slumping like the others, and I didn't gasp like all the other times. He just looked like he was sleeping, so peacefully. I hope he found his brother, Dudie, and they are frolicking together. It's the first time *in my life* I don't have a cat.

June 7

No time to grieve – our house goes into pre-foreclosure today. It's been a few days of scrambling trying to pay for Fluffy's vet bill and finding money to save our home. I just feel sick. I've been awake since 12:30 a.m. Tracy assured me it's all going to work out.

Jim has been staying with us. He has some things to work out too. Even though we three musketeers are going through a turbulent time, it's nice we all have each other. I think we always will. There IS comfort in that. Jim's a masterful storyteller. He delves deep into long tales, one story blending into the next. He has wickedly dry and colorful analogies. And boy, does he have a way with words.

June 17
Tracy got paid *all* his contract work money, and just like that – we are back on track. The house is *completely* paid up to date! Clean slate! We get to keep our home! It's hard to trust the good when it happens.

July 20
We picked up our new eight-week-old kittens from Duchess, Alberta. We chose two out of about 30! Duchess is a long-haired black cat; Domino is a short-haired black-and-white beauty. Sisters. Coca looks at us like, Was that necessary? I'm in love! It'll be different having girls. Uh oh, we gotta pay for two spays. Yikes. Tracy hasn't been working full hours. It's getting scary again. Tracy and I have both been applying for other jobs.

August 27
We went to the pub with friends for my birthday, and I also got a job interview! We have money in the bank, and we pick up our brand-new truck in a week. We were leasing and had to get a new one. Everything just got transferred over. And maybe we'll both get new jobs. I'm so grateful.

Sept 10
Tracy and I both got our rejection calls this week. We had such high hopes, but not meant to be. I had coffee with Myriam – that always makes things better.

Oct 28
Jim moved out after several months with us. We will miss him.

Contemplating existentialism. Why do I exist? What is the meaning of my life in this messed-up world? What would make me happy? Money? If we had it, I wouldn't feel so stressed and could focus on *other* important aspects. What would fulfill me? Can't I just write full-time and not worry about paying bills? I feel like we need to do more normal things. I feel lost. I feel like I'm going in circles. Psychological weight can be as heavy as anything physical.

Nov 14
I asked Mom if she still has her house guest? Yes, your brother is still here. She thought I'd be upset Kyle's there, but I'm glad he's there to **help** *her*. Period. Although when she told me he was going to be there, it suddenly felt like Toronto was a bit too close for comfort.

Nov 28
Tracy got laid off. We can't lose our home. I feel sick. Mom said, Nothing small ever happens to you – it's always big stuff, but you handle it with strength and resilience. I guess that's what she sees. I hope she's right. It feels like we're running out of both.

Dec 5
We ARE those people, who other people talk about at holiday time who need help. Why can't WE bounce back? I've prayed so hard. Am I being heard? Am I being drowned out by the people who need it more? I went to the deepest and darkest places again. It's the worst feeling. Those moments where you feel you're succumbing to the abyss and then, in an instant, you kinda snap out of it. It's the biggest relief, those few seconds on the other side of the darkness.

I texted the CEO of my company for a raise.

Dec 10
If we are not meant to keep our stuff, we're not meant to. If the universe has decided it won't allow anyone to help us, so be it. If we weren't meant to be contributors in this society, so be it. If owning a

home, paying our bills and living a low-key life isn't in the cards for us, nothing we can do about it. We've been working against the forces that are trying to prevent us from having a normal life and maybe now I just realized – we have to relent. The forces are trying to undermine our efforts and trying to keep good people down. Is this world inherently bad, making the good ones suffer? Appears that way. The good ones with morals and values get continuously dumped on, while the shady ones get more money and power. That's this world we live in. Good vs. evil. Morality vs. underhandedness. The world is teaching its occupants that bad overrules. No wonder desperate people do unimaginable things. They are being forced to go to the dark side because they've learned that being good gets you nowhere. The universe gets a kick out of seeing how far they can push a person. What IS their breaking point? How bad does it have to get before a person does something wildly desperate? Everyone's saturation point is different.

When will I reach MY breaking point? What will I do when I reach it? Am I already there? Does a person just have to GET to that point and then the universe throws them a bone? Get to the brink and something good finally happens? My life has been like that – a pendulum where it goes to extreme heights on both ends. Just as you reach the height on the *positive* swing, and you're suspended for a second and feel the delight, there is no surprise in knowing it WILL swing back the other way, and the shit is about to hit. For a split second, before it goes back the other way again, you have hope, contentment, and peace. We are just waiting for it to swing back to the *good* side. We seem to be stuck midair on the bad. New title of my book: *Living Life on One Side of the Pendulum.*

2020

Jan 3
Can THIS be our year? Please. I don't have the energy. Give me the strength to stick it out.

Tracy's horoscope: *You have been coming ever closer to the light at the end of a long, dark tunnel. But because you have developed a rather hopeless and cynical outlook along the way, you may believe that light to be an oncoming train. Have faith and hope anyway. Keep proceeding, keep your chin up as best you can, and you should find very soon that something has shifted. Your life is about to become what you have been dreaming of.*

I needed to read that today. It sounds like things could be improving. Deep breath.

Jan 29
I saw Dr. West. I've had this itch since October 29. An itch means the c-word for me. Not panicking. Tracy got a job! A GOOD one! He'll be working for a security company that is based out of Vancouver. He is the only technician in Alberta, which means a lot of work and no empty holes in his work week, like his last job.

Feb 3
Saw the specialist. He was *very* thorough. Asked a million questions. He spent over an hour with me. He's sending me for ultrasounds, X-rays, and bloodwork. The pain of the hernias is taking away from the irritation of the itch.
Dr. West's office just called – to let me know about my CT date – June 26!

Feb 15

Anxious. Fatigued. Emotional. I have NOT let myself go to the c-place and consider what that would mean for Tracy and me. I just can't go there. I've never been able to stop my thoughts and feelings from boiling to the surface. I've BEEN there and the thought of going there again...I just can't. I'm actually waiting for more info before I give in to those thoughts. I don't feel confident I will get the answers I need, and I believe on Tuesday that I will leave disheartened and in limbo. Again. I'm not being pessimistic, just being a realist. Where my health is concerned, answers in a timely manner have never been my friend. I really don't know what I'll do if I don't get any answers. I'm not even praying for "no cancer." I'm praying for ***answers***. I will deal with *whatever* it is; I just want answers. I think it's worse knowing your body, knowing something isn't right, and getting no answers. That's worse. For me.

Today has been the toughest one yet. I've been fine until now. Now that Tuesday is "answer" day...I feel...uneasy. I will find no comfort in saying, I KNEW there'd be no answers. It will *not* be a good "I told you so" moment. Then I'll start thinking the itch and everything else was in my head. Yet I KNOW it's not. Man. Just like last time.

Feb 18

Felt like throwing up this morning. Will I GET results? Will I leave his office with no answers?
The specialist said, Your ultrasound was clear. Your X-rays were clear. Your bloodwork was clear.
I looked at him with a very blank, frustrated look. I find no comfort in that.
I know. I'll advocate for you. I'm not leaving you. We'll figure this out.
I spoke to a hematologist and he expedited your CT. It'll be in two weeks.
Oh my God, thank you! I do have to say, though, I didn't think I was going to get answers today. I had full-blown cancer and the tests still didn't reveal anything. I don't have much faith in these tests.

I understand that. With your history, I get it.

Feb 25
Tracy told me we need to go to the hospital. His mom is in Emergency. Don't panic. She was having trouble breathing. We got ready super quick and went. She looked okay. They did X-rays and blood. The doc said there is an elevated enzyme in her heart. They are doing more bloodwork. Her blood pressure is dangerously high. The doc came in with the results. She had a heart attack, but it looks more like heart *failure*. They are keeping her overnight.

I kinda feel dead inside. No emotion. No breakdown over my health or Tracy's mom's health. Nothing. Soooo not like me. I am SO emotional, yet I'm not reacting to any of it.

Mar 11
It's a banner day! Harvey Weinstein is sentenced to 23 years in jail. Maybe that will give the ones who haven't spoken out yet the courage to voice their story. If big powerhouses can come crashing down, there *is* hope. Sounds like he still doesn't see he did anything wrong. That is the sad, decrepit truth of it. Those people simply don't, and won't, see the error of their ways. He has whatever "life" he has left, to think about it, in prison. Or not. At least he's off the streets. He can no longer harm anyone! THAT is justice.

Mar 14
Had my CT scan. Here we go...
Yesterday I won $50 on the lotto. Tracy found $40. And he got a credit card. Wha? Is our luck turning for the better? One can only hope.

There is this viral pandemic afoot now. They say it could last a *year*. Huh. Life as we know it has changed.

Mar 23

Results day. I'm glad I'm going alone. There's probably nothing to report. It's in my head. So what if I've been itchy since October. Apparently, it means nothing. I used to say I know my own body. Maybe I don't. I did know it a few times, and I was right. Clearly, this time, I don't know a thing. Feeling pretty shitty. Avril Lavigne's "Keep Holding On" comes on. Funny how music can change your attitude. Powerful.

The specialist said, So the good news is the CT was clear. But I still don't know what you have. We talked about the kidneys, consistently showing cysts. He's referring me to hematologist and kidney specialist. I reiterated how I had lymphoma for *years and years* before anything was confirmed. Not until I got the lump in my neck was anything done about it. That's why I'm sending you to the hematologist. Maybe they could do a PET scan. I understand your history with this and that's why you're concerned. You should know once you're cured of Hodgkin's, the chances of getting it again are slim. If it were an allergy, you'd have a rash. And you wouldn't be itchy ALL the time. You'd get a break.

He said if I'm experiencing any other symptoms to come back and see him. He checked my lymph nodes. I can feel them, but they are small and nothing to be concerned about. He went back to 2007 to look at the test results for the kidney cysts. I said, I'd rather check into it than suddenly drop dead from it. That's why I'm sending you to the kidney specialist.

Back to square one.

Mar 31

I can hardly wait for Tracy's benefits to kick in, in April. My hip was out of its socket yesterday while working. Excruciating pain. Could barely walk. Then the itch. So, my hip, worrying about cancer/kidney disease or other, oh ya, and this pandemic we are in. My brain is bursting. They say it will get a lot worse before it gets better.

Mom is quite nervous and uneasy about this pandemic. It's so difficult for her to be isolated when she requires the help and support of others with her Parkinson's.

Today is the first time I could barely dress myself. I burst out crying. Goddamn hip! Scared me. And now I have to go to work. I was going to make a chiro appt even *without* benefits. They are closed due to COVID. Man.

This imposed distancing has afforded me the time to finish my book, and I find so much comfort in writing. Besides Tracy, it's my saving grace.

Apr 11
Music makes me happy. I'm listening to Nickelback, as always. Their lyrics speak to me. No other singer or group does that for me. I don't know what it is. They get it. They are truth-speakers. I listened to them all day. My happy place.

Feeling very fortunate that Tracy and I are both working (outside the home) and are healthy. I do worry about my immune system, but my merchandising work is deemed "essential." And Tracy can't install security systems from home, so we take every precaution possible to stay safe. Coca and the kittens are loving how much time we are both spending at home.

We paid all our bills and still have money LEFT. Wha?
Celebrated 33 years with the love of my life last week. I can't complain.

May 8
I was at the liquor store, then went to my truck. A minute later a woman crashed into the nail salon next door with her car. Demolished the place next door, and about 50 cases of booze against the wall in the liquor store smashed to the floor. I had *just* been standing there. It was all surreal, but not until I went back in and saw the mess in the liquor

store, did I realize I could've been hurt, and this could've turned out *way* differently. I stayed and filled out a police report since I saw the whole thing happen. No one was hurt. She's lucky the nail salon next door was closed due to COVID because people could have died.

Lesson of the day: You don't need close calls to remind you of what's important in life.

June 5
I watched *Cake* last night. Wow. Chronic pain. Thoughts of suicide. Just want the pain to go away. Check.

Jennifer Aniston really had the pain part down pat. The breathing, the pangs, seeing no end in sight to the nightmare. Feeling like she had to say the pain is REAL to her physical therapist. Boy, did THAT hit home. She has the surgery scars to PROVE she went through something and STILL needed to say that. I had no evidence of anything wrong with me and spent YEARS in pain. What a movie.

July 10
I never felt like my struggles mattered. Why would anyone care what I have been through? They are MY struggles, and they just don't mean anything to anyone but me. I've never felt like I had anything worthwhile to say. I'm the quiet one. The wallflower. The one who listens to everyone else. For me to be front and center...

When the book comes out, people WILL read about my struggles. And hopefully the preconceptions of what people think of me will change. I don't need my battles to matter; I just need them to resonate with others so THEY don't feel as alone as I did.

I think once I am heard, more healing will begin.

Also, I've questioned the existence of EVERYBODY in my life, at one point or another. Not a great feeling. When you give and get nothing back, it does make you question whether you are crazy for continuing to reach out. People don't realize how ostracized a person can feel when people are too "busy" to respond to your texts. No one is ever THAT busy. I give what I expect back. Questioning your key relationships is scary. It IS better to be alone than chase people. I'll forever stand by that statement.

Tracy is out of town all next week for work. It'll be me and my thoughts. *That's* a dangerous combo.

It would be nice for someone to reach out *without* me sitting desperately waiting for a lifeline. The waiting can be excruciating. I send out texts. I reach out. ALL the time. People take *hours* before they bother responding. What if they knew it could be too late? What if their pittance of a reply just came too late? No matter what is happening in my life, I answer people's texts. I always answer. I could be knee-deep in...an episode and I STILL answer. The difference that makes ALL the difference. To know someone is interested in answering you, cares enough to do such a simple task. A task. That's what it comes down to. It's a chore. You reach out and it feels like a chore for them to get back to you. Boy, some people NEED that wake-up call. People reach out because...they NEED to. It's a need. A lifeline. Is anyone out there? Does anyone care? Is everyone so wrapped up in their own shit that the mere effort to simply ANSWER is just too great? Perhaps. It's a real thing. Humans. Selfish. The *simple "task" of answering* – could be the difference between life and death. Literally. Why do we need others? Life is simpler without them. The energy I expend on wondering if people care about me is exhausting. I'm tired. That hole I want to go live in is looking better and better.

It's like the world is pulling the rug out from underneath me. There is no salvation for me. No one is going to save me. I have to save myself. I've spent my life saving everyone else. Huh. Dark thoughts. What the fuck is going on?

I WAS on the *other side* of all this. I'll be 52. When does this end? Can someone, anyone, just reach out to me right now? I need a sign. A *big* one. I'm *begging* for a sign.

Oh my God. Leslie just texted. Are you okay?

Holy shit. Holy shit. Someone just asked me if I'm okay. Holy shit.

Play it cool. You're doing great, Sari. You didn't text her to unload. Yup, it's all good, I told her.

Geez. I suck. I blather on. Then pretend. I'm pretending. I hate people who pretend. I'm a hypocrite. The worst kind.

Nickelback's "What Are You Waiting For?" just came on. Man. Perfect timing. Snapped me right out of it.

Tracy woke up from his nap. None the wiser to what's going on inside my crazy head.

July 19

Just thought of this. FriENDship. In my experience, that's what it means. Almost everyone is in my life for a time, then it *ends*. Not always a bad thing, but inevitable. They swear they love me and would do ANYTHING for me, until they don't. My use has worn out. They TELL me what I want to hear at the time, but they're not SHOWING me how important I am to them. That's the loyalty part. I'm there for ALL of it – good, bad, ugly, and the beautiful stuff. Count me in! But people leave because they...I dunno, suddenly realize I'm too good to be true. I am. I'm loyal to a fault. God, I hate clichés. Until death, I'm a forever friend. Others just don't feel the same. But I guess they were never true friends to begin with. Just ENDs. And as I get older, I become more okay with it because I'm over helping them figure out. It's too late for them in MY life. It's shit THEY have to figure out. I know my capacity. I know what I'm willing to give. They don't. You will piss people off when you do what's best for YOU, when you leave that bullshit behind. If I'm cutting people off it's because they gave me the means to sever our ties. Real people, the ones truest to themselves, have the fewest close ties. Again, I'm okay with that. The alternative is toxic. I endured betrayals from people who pretended to care about me. Every time I've let my guard down, I've been burnt. When I've let people in, they'd use my vulnerability against me. I've realized I haven't "lost friends"; I've just discovered who the real ones are. It's tiring giving everything to everyone I'm close to. I wind up with nothing in the end. Well, not entirely true. I'm walking away with the knowledge they were incapable of giving more than they had. And it wasn't enough for me. Real friends tend to reveal themselves in times of trouble and triumph.

Lesson of the day: I'm more than okay with the few people I have in my life because I don't have to guess where I stand with them.

Aug 11
Watching *SWAT*. A colleague wants to kill himself. Close to home? Ya. Also made me realize it's been quite a while since I have felt *that* dire. I haven't been in a dark place for some time. I've been singing and dancing and bouncing around the past few days. Yes, all my various pains and the itch still exist, but when you feel like dancing, you gotta go with it! The world is going to hell in a handbasket and I have a big question mark over my health, but I feel better than I have in a long time. Go figure.

Before the virus, everyone was "winning," except us. All was right with the world, but *we* were sinking. Now, *we* are so fortunate to still have jobs and be healthy. I'm feeling GREAT. It's SO bizarre! Life is in chaos, and my health IS up in the air, and people are sick and dying, and I feel better than I have in years!! Mentally, anyways. WTF?! It's very confusing to me, but I'm embracing it because I've had too many yucky YEARS to *not* acknowledge this good feeling. For as long as it lasts, I will feel – lighter.

I FEEL LIGHTER!

It's a conundrum. For certain. I've been analyzing it to death because these feelings are SO foreign to me. It's such a strange time and I have bouts of panic over it, but mostly I feel okay. There is so much to feel afraid about – and I'm not. I'm not an optimistic person. I think I've been snatched and replaced by an alternative me.

"What if today WAS your last day?" (Nickelback lyric). I feel, somehow, I can leave this earth – with peace.
I've achieved…LIGHTNESS, in my heart and my head.

I never gave up.

HOPE IS POWER

HOPE is an exceptionally *powerful* thing; it can make <u>ALL</u> the difference in a person's mind and well-being. It can change the most debilitating mindset into an illuminating outlook. It's a colossal force to be reckoned with. In AN *instant*, hope can shift your mentality from desperation to calm, from angst to ease, from feeling dire to a sense there's a <u>*chance*</u> at something. Hope infiltrates your negative thought patterns and ignites them into optimism and inner peace. The <u>*possibility*</u> of being able to crawl out from under a massive boulder to feel lighter and brighter is *electric*! To go from feeling grave to optimistic *in one single moment* is transforming. It's the difference between merely going through the motions to actually feeling like you're DOING *something* constructive! To anticipate a *positive* outcome as opposed to dread and despair, your brain being filled with thoughts of helplessness and worst-case scenarios. I don't know the science behind the biological and chemical shift that happens in the body and brain, but there IS most definitely a feeling that pours over your ENTIRE being – *when there is hope*. It's undeniable. It's an energy that is unstoppable. You can't help but transform; there's an automatic, involuntary shift in your mind! It's empowering. A mere glimpse into "what could be" *radically* changes your entire demeanor and thought process. By being mindful, we can flip that switch to hope. Music did that for me; listening to a great song gave me strength to be more optimistic, in an instant. You get to choose your mindset. So, choose!

Hope is the universe's way of telling you it's listening.
It's the light in the dark.

What an exceptionally powerful thing.

MY FINAL THOUGHTS

SUCK IT UP. GET OVER IT. I hate those expressions. It's like saying, Quit being such a baby! It completely *invalidates* how someone is feeling and what they are experiencing. We're dealt life events, some good and some bad. We have the *power* to choose – we can stay stuck or we can work through it. Staying stuck keeps us trapped in the past and prevents us from moving forward. We can allow that truth to hold us back (like I did) so we don't fulfill our ambitions and keep us in a place of UNgrowth and fear, with no room for personal development., Or we can put on our best coping hats and forge ahead! Life is *both* enjoyable and unpleasant, but sometimes we feel we are supposed to *only* have wonderful experiences. It's not realistic.

Bad experiences *are* good too. It makes us who we are. To deny yourself *negative* experiences is to deny yourself growth. HOW we *deal* with those bad experiences is the determining factor in the degree of our *"moving on-ness."* ONE bad experience can make people bitter, jaded, or resentful; and letting it fester can impact *every* aspect of their lives. *Embrace* the bad experience and *move through it, not past it*, but in a *productive* manner. Moving *through* it is *coping* with it. Moving *past* it is *denying* it happened.

The darkness always follows the light. But the light follows the darkness too. We know the bad seems to draw to us like a powerful magnet, but so can the good. Forgiveness goes with resentment. Growth with stagnation. We embrace and revel in all the *good* things that come our way – with no questions asked – but we *have to accept* the bad things too. It's the great irony of this universe.

By not being aware that these past bad experiences *are* affecting our *present* lives, it keeps us dormant and not moving forward. Being *aware* of it is the first step in creating a life beyond the negativity and misery. And these aren't huge steps or adjustments; just *acknowledging* the experience makes it have *less* of a grip on you. Allowing a memory to take on a life of its own will strangle you. We need to lessen that grip. Don't allow the past to prevent your future.

How we deal with our disappointments and surface-y problems will pave the way for when we need to deal with our *larger* issues. Problems NEVER go away until you *deal* with them! Fact. Don't be fooled into thinking they'll go away if you *ignore* them – they will *always* still be there *and* pile up. You have to FACE the pain in order to heal. When we start dealing with our issues head on, it becomes a habit so when bad things happen, you *have* the tools to dismantle the issue until it's doesn't feel so huge anymore. Feel the pain of it, do the work, then let it go. You DON'T have to "suck it up"' or "get over it" – there is *no* time limit. Everyone moves through pain and difficulties at different paces. Remember this, no matter how many people say they are there for you, you *still* have to go through it *alone*. You have to get to the other side – on your own. Having supportive people around you *helps*, no question, but ultimately you have to feel it all; *no one* can do the work *for* you.

People admire those who have *overcome* hardships. Positivity is contagious, but so is negativity; people feed off both. People *don't* want to be around negative people. People are drawn to and want to be around, perhaps learn from and mimic the behavior, of optimistic people. It's a conscious effort to react to situations differently than you have before, in a *healthier* manner. Easier said than done, *yes*, but *awareness* is the first step in making the process a bit more painless. If I had stockpiled *all* my issues, remained bitter about my friendships, jaded about my abuse, cancer and accidents, imagine where I'd be *now*? I dealt with things as they came, in the *best way* I knew how. And I KNOW, I *was better* for it. I always had an awareness of needing to change my thoughts, to help myself when I *knew* no one else could do it *for* me. You'd think positive thinking alone would be the path to inner peace and serenity, but it's not. Despair and turmoil are as strong as factors – it's difficult to break through the riffraff and realize your destructive thoughts serve no purpose. It's hard to heal and move forward when you bombard yourself with constant, non-constructive beliefs.

Embrace your uniqueness. We may feel like outcasts, have feelings of not belonging *anywhere*, have identity crises and wish we were more like someone else, but *you are you* no matter how much you try to run away from it or try to change it. I've struggled with wanting to be ANYONE else but myself. I hated my name growing up because it was *too* different. For a year of my life when I was a teenager, I *insisted* people call me by my *middle* name, Tania; it was more common. I love my name now and the fact that few share it with me. While at times I have felt cursed for having an overactive, analytical brain, I accept it now. I see now that overthinking things (to death!) has made me a good planner, an effective problem solver, and has given me the propensity for great attention to detail (it sounds like a résumé). So, for all the things I *used to* rip myself down for and agonize over, I've now *embraced. I don't want to be like everyone else*. If we were all the same, how ridiculous would this world be? I sure don't want to be a cookie cutter image of *anyone* else. I'm my own person. Period.

I am a work-in-progress. I'm *still* trying to figure life out, but I plan on being the *best* version of myself. Recovery is a never ending process. My pledge is to keep speaking and standing up for myself and projecting my voice for all to hear – I *will* continue to tell my truth. Until my last breath, I will seek the light, and seek lightness, and avoid the dismal corners of my mind. Your traumas are not the end of your story. Going THROUGH them is just the beginning! Don't waste another moment not telling your story, and not being who you REALLY are; it takes far *less* energy. We *don't* know what the future holds for any of us and how much time we have to *be* ourselves – *everything* <u>*can*</u> change in a split second.

Suffering quietly is no longer an option.

-----------/////------------

I stopped dreaming; I thought dreams didn't come true for someone like me.
I never believed I'd live to see the other side.
I had given up and lost hope so many times, I'd lost count.

One of my saving graces was listening to the music of Nickelback.
Their words spoke to me and somehow gave me, and continue to give me, hope and healing.

What an amazing gift.

For those of you who have heard their song, "What Are You Waiting For?" you understand where I'm coming from. If these lyrics are new to you, I hope they give you food-for-thought and inspire you.

Thank you, Nickelback, from the bottom of my soul.

---------//////---------

"What Are You Waiting For?"
By Nickelback

What are you waiting for?

Are you waiting on a lightning strike?
Are you waiting for the perfect night?
Are you waiting 'til the time is right?
What are you waiting for?
Don't you wanna learn to deal with fear?
Don't you wanna take the wheel and steer?
Don't you wait another minute here
What are you waiting for?

You gotta go and reach for the top
Believe in every dream that you got
You're only living once so tell me
What are you, what are you waiting for?
You know you gotta give it your all
And don't you be afraid if you fall
You only living once so tell me
What are you, what are you waiting for?

Are you waiting for the right excuse?
Are you waiting for a sign to choose?
While you're waiting it's the time you lose
What are you waiting for?
Don't you wanna spread your wings and fly?
Don't you wanna really live your life?
Don't you wanna love before you die?
What are you waiting for?

Tell me what you're waiting for
Show me what you're aiming for
What you gonna save it for?
So what you really waiting for?

Everybody's gonna make mistakes
But everybody's got a choice to make
Everybody needs a leap of faith
When are you taking yours?
What are you waiting for?

What are you waiting for?

ACKNOWLEDGEMENTS

To my husband Tracy: Without your fierce support, love, and encouragement, I would not have had the courage to publish my memoir. I'm grateful for your selfless and limitless ability to have my back, especially when I was unbearably raw and vulnerable. You'll never quite understand what a gift you have been, and continue to be, to me. You're my anchor, refuge and soft place to land. You are the person I was *always* meant to be with, to stand beside me, holding my hand, on this wild ride. You are an amazing human being, who can still make me laugh like no other. I am so glad I walked into *that* bar.

Mom, I thank you for your wisdom, your bottomless barrel of advice and your unwavering, unconditional love. I love you tons and bushels.

Heather Andrews, my publishing coach, thank you. We spoke the same language and that made this overwhelming undertaking flow smoothly. You championed for me and encouraged me every step of the way. Your graciousness, guidance, and mentorship, made our collaboration an unforgettable experience.

Thank you, Heather Sangster, my editor, for your invaluable insights. When I gave you my memoir to edit, I was terrified to be so vulnerable, and you never judged me, ever. You were determined to make *my* voice loud and clear, and you did just that.

Thank you, Nickelback for your generosity in allowing me to use your lyrics to, "What Are You Waiting For?" in my memoir.

To all the other essential contributors who helped make this book a reality: Robin Albright for your amazing graphics and input. Trevor Baker and Carlos Santos - you have my deepest gratitude.

To those few who remained loyal to Tracy and me, who gave me the strength and fortitude I needed to tell my story, who believed in me and encouraged me to write, I wholeheartedly thank you.

Thank you Dr. Erin Oksol for your extensive knowledge of the sensitive subject matter of trauma, and delivering an insightful expert opinion.

Thank you to my distributor, LeeAnn Lessard of Lachesis Publishing for your recommendations and bringing my book to multiple platforms.

I'd also like to acknowledge those of you who *do not* share in my telling of my long-overdue story. Without you, I never would have fought so hard to break through and find my voice, and be heard.

little.
warriors

Little Warriors is a national, charitable organization focused on the awareness, prevention and treatment of child sexual abuse. We also advocate on behalf of and with child sexual abuse survivors.

Little Warriors offers a free workshop called Prevent It! to educate adults across Canada on how to help prevent and respond to child sexual abuse. The workshop is offered in-person, online and live via Zoom.

The Little Warriors Be Brave Ranch, located east of Edmonton Alberta, is a specialized, intensive, trauma-informed, evidence-based treatment centre solely focused on helping children from across Canada who have been sexually abused, as well as their families. The program is for girls and boys from 8-12 years old, and girls between the ages of 13 and 16, and is a one-year combined onsite and outpatient program designed with significant input from many leading academic and clinical experts who specialize in child sexual abuse and trauma.

The Little Warriors Be Brave Bridge is a comprehensive online program that connects specialized counselors and coaches with children, teens, and parents impacted by child sexual abuse, who might not otherwise receive timely mental health support. The program offers similar evidence-based, specialized trauma treatment that's provided at the Be Brave Ranch, as we have taken the insights used at the Ranch and embedded them into the Be Brave Bridge online program. All of the information provided has been carefully researched and offers the most effective interventions and strategies.

For more information visit **www.littlewarriors.ca**.

NSVRC (National Sexual Violence Resource Centre) offers a wide range of resources on sexual violence including statistics, research, position statements, curricula, prevention initiatives, and program information. With these resources, NSVRC assists coalitions, advocates, and others interested in understanding and eliminating sexual violence. Please call the National Sexual Assault Hotline – 1.800.656.HOPE (4673) – to be connected with a trained staff member from a sexual assault service provider in your area.

The Lifeline provides 24/7, free, and confidential support for people in distress, prevention and crisis resources for you or your loved ones, and best practices for professionals.

NATIONAL
SUICIDE
PREVENTION
LIFELINE
1-800-273-TALK (8255)
suicidepreventionlifeline.org

Endorsements

"Having known Sari for one year shy of her entire life, I can say that the words in this book are without a doubt honest. Sari gives herself to every page. Her book reads of courage, strength, and resilience. Sari is a true spirit that always finds a way to shine. Thank you from the bottom of my heart, my friend, for sharing your story with such courage and grace."

~ Toby-Lynn Herscovitch

"This story is about all of our families. It is filled to the brim with all of the standard kinship messiness of dysfunction, betrayals, secrets, and love. But at its core, it is the story of victory.

Sari Knock's brave, authentic voice has emerged from near hopelessness. In this book, we are privileged to witness the first hand, scribed account of a shy, anxious teen growing into a brave and bold woman. We experience Sari's growth and identity formation infinitely compounded by soul wrenching events. How Sari ever arrived at this place, voice strong, confidence unwavering, is rather unfathomable.

"Suffer Quietly" provides proof that even a hair's breadth of belief in oneself (and the unwavering love and support of a good partner), can help us transform and triumph over trauma. This book is a gift. Sari is a treasure."

~Kerry White-Tucker

"The candour and generosity that Sari offers her readers renders this book an important work for all people in our society. Sari has written an honest and powerful narrative that enables us to see the way that child sexual assault lies hidden in plain sight; a fact that we should no longer ignore."

~ Myriam Derosa

About the Author

Ironically, self-described wallflower Sari Knock has written a memoir about finding her voice and being heard. While her first project was a well-received comedic play produced locally, her memoir, *Suffer Quietly*, is anything but funny. Sari offers a raw and candid deep dive into her thoughts and feelings, as she shares her story through her journal entries spanning 40 years. Her desire to break through stigmas and open up conversations surrounding taboo subjects is remarkable and refreshing. Sari ultimately shows us that while we can't avoid pain and hardships, we can move past them into a place of hope and purpose.

When she's not busy analyzing life to death, Sari is feasting on her husband's gourmet meals, and thriving in the company of her endlessly energetic menagerie of pets. To satisfy their satirical sense of humor, Sari and her husband binge-watch *Brooklyn Nine-Nine, Mom* and *2 Broke Girls*.